To Empower as Jesus Did: Acquiring Spiritual Power Through Apprenticeship

To Empower as Jesus Did: Acquiring Spiritual Power Through Apprenticeship

AARON MILAVEC

Toronto Studies in Theology
Volume 9

The Edwin Mellen Press
New York and Toronto

Library of Congress Cataloging in Publication Data

Milavec, Aaron, 1938-
   To empower as Jesus did.

   (Toronto studies in theology ; v. 8)
   Includes index.
   1. Theology, Practical. I. Title. II. Series.
BV4.M54   253   82-6466
ISBN 0-88946-966-0 (hard) AACR2
ISBN 0-88946 967-9 (soft)

Toronto Studies in Theology ISBN 0-88946-975-X

Copyright © 1982, The Edwin Mellen Press
All rights reserved. For more information write:

   The Edwin Mellen Press
   P.O. Box 450
   Lewiston, New York   14092

Printed in the United States of America

In gratitude to those mentors who have shaped, redeemed, and enriched my life:

* my parents, who conveyed to me an instinctual experience of their God;

* Michael Stimac, who heralded, during my adolescence, the zeal and discipline of my God;

* Herman Waetjen, who first blessed and broke open the Gospels so that I was nourished by my Father's wisdom;

* Matthias Gehatia, who imparted to me his Jewish spirit so that I might feed upon the tenakh as well;

* Michael Polanyi, who built for me an intellectual home in which my scientific demand for precision lived comfortably with my religious romanticism;

* Linda Milavec, my wife, who healed my lonely heart and thereby enabled me to live, teach, and write for others;

* Marie Morgan, who taught me to untie knotty subordinations so that I might write this book clearly and forcefully.

For these and the untold others who, in their turn, shaped the greatness of my mentors, I praise and thank the Lord.

Contents

Preface by Herbert Richardson ix

I. Introduction: How a Religious Heritage Is Transmitted 1

II. How the Cinderella Mentality Obscures Apprenticeship 15

    A. Case I: Failure to cast out a demon 18
    B. Case II: The making of a priest 24
    C. Case III: Speaking in tongues among Pentecostals 31

III. How the Atonement Theory Trivializes Apprenticeship 41

    A. The medieval origins of Anselm's atonement theory 43
    B. The atonement theory at odds with Matthew's Gospel 47
    C. The atonement theory at odds with Paul 57
    D. The Thomistic correction of Anselm's doctrine 64

IV. How English Translations Conceal Apprenticeship . 79

    A. Jesus as the master apprenticing his disciples 83
    B. Jesus as prophet vs. Jesus as master 91
    C. Jesus addressed as "sir/lord" (*kyrios*) . . . 96

V. Jesus' Practice in Apprenticing His Disciples . 105

    A. Jesus' calling of disciples 107
    B. The financing of disciples 114
    C. The place and posture of apprenticing 120
    D. The content and goal of apprenticing 124
    E. The highest estimate of Jesus' apprenticing . 134

VI. The Transmission of Jesus' Power After His Death 149

    A. How Paul received and passed on Jesus' power 150
    B. The power of the catechumenate in the early centuries 163
    C. The contemporary quest for spiritual power . 170

VII. The Human Dynamics Undergirding a Christian Formation 177

	A. How one's particular upbringing fashions one's habitual religious experience	179
	B. How a child first learns to perceive God	183
	C. How adult apprenticeships enable one to transcend one's upbringing	188
	D. How personal faith functions throughout a Christian apprenticeship	193
	E. How divine initiative functions throughout a Christian apprenticeship	198
VIII.	How Fresh Discoveries of God Transform Mature Commitments	213
	A. The importance of making fresh discoveries of God	214
	B. Examining classical instances of prophetic discovery	220
	C. How fresh discoveries of God are to be authenticated	226
IX.	Recovering the Power of the Scriptures in Today's Church	241
	A. The origins of the Gospels in the practice of apprenticing	242
	B. Authority and free initiative in the interpretation of the Scriptures	245
	C. The use of the Scriptures as the Christian classics which both conserve the past and evoke prophetic experience	249
	D. The limitations of scholarly exegesis and of fundamentalism	253
	E. A tentative program for renewing the church using the Scriptures	257
X.	Prayer, Sacraments, and the Messianic Hope in Today's World	267
	A. The thrust of private prayer: Sympathy with God	267
	B. The thrust of public rites: Acting with God	274
	C. The thrust of messianic hope: Thy kingdom come	283
XI.	Jesus as the One Fashioned and Apprenticed by God	291
	A. How the Logos fashioned the organic identity of the Messiah	294
	B. How the Logos apprenticed the spiritual identity of the Messiah	307
Index		339

Abbreviations and Translations

DS = Denzinger and Schoenmetzer, eds., <u>Enchiridion symbolorum</u> (Rome: Herder, 1965). The older section numbers are used.

ST = <u>Summa Theologica</u> of St. Thomas Aquinas, tr. by Fathers of the English Dominican Province (3 vols.; London: Burns & Oates, 1947).

TDNT = <u>Theological Dictionary of the New Testament</u>, ed. by Gerhard Kittel (10 vols.; Grand Rapids: Wm. B. Eerdmans, 1964).

Biblical references are cited from <u>The Jerusalem Bible</u> (London: Darton, Longman & Todd, 1966).

Rabbinic materials were newly translated from the original sources, thanks to the labors of an Israeli scholar and personal friend.

Acknowledgment

In addition to those mentioned in my dedication, I acknowledge the gracious assistance of my colleagues at Sacred Heart School of Theology for their personal support, critical reading, and patient proofreading of my manuscript. Any errors remaining in this book are my responsibility and do not reflect upon the care and workmanship of the Edwin Mellen Press.

Preface

There are two kinds of adventurers: the first goes to strange places to experience novelties; the second remains at home to discover hidden depths in the familiar. Imagine, for instance, that you had been born and grew up in Chartres or Cahokia -- so that the ancient cathedral or those amazing Indian mounds were your everyday neighbors. You realized that people came from everywhere to visit your home town, but you never quite appreciated why. One day, for a lark, you decided to join a group of tourists who were tailing a professional guide. For the first time, you experienced something of the awe and mystery that visitors knew. Filled with wonder, you asked yourself,"Have I been living here, surrounded by these marvelous monuments of the human spirit, and never noticed them?"

Aaron Milavec's book is not an adventure of the going-far-away type. It is an adventure of the suddenly-I-can-see type. Milavec doesn't take us into unfamiliar aspects of Christianity; he guides us into our own hometown experiences and opens our eyes to their marvels. In this book, for example, Milavec describes the experience of growing up in a Christian home -- he invites us to marvel at the divinely ordained mechanisms which enable the infant to progressively and successfully reproduce the full range of human and religious experiences of his/her parents. Then, in simple and clear lines, Milavec shows how the awakening of hero worship in the adolescent years ushers in a second expansive period of imitative learning. Now the young person fashions his/her religious identity by taking on the settled judgments and habits of achievement of his/her self-chosen mentor(s). Finally, this book describes the religious experience of adults -- a period characterized by the conservative intensification of the past. Yet, even for an adult, religious rites, the use of the bible, and personal prayer are all humanly and divinely calculated to prepare one for those novel insights and prophetic impulses that periodically alter and mature one's personal and religious identity. In the end, I came to reflect upon and understand my own religious journey -- from my mother's knee to the professor's chair -- as emerging from the peculiar series of inspiring mentors and moments that have marked my life. I now saw that God had indeed fashioned my inmost religious convictions, not despite of or alongside of, but precisely <u>within</u> a religious journey that was and will continue to be historically and sociologically conditioned.

When I first read Aaron Milavec's manuscript a year ago, it allowed me to meet the person of Jesus afresh. New Testament texts and Christological doctrines that I had been teaching for years appeared under a new light. Why had I never seen them in this way before? I was like the citizen of Chartres or Cahokia, living in the midst of wonders, but still needing a guide to help me experience them vividly.

In <u>Christus Victor</u>, Gustav Aulen, the Swedish theologian, describes three approaches to Christology: the moral, the legal, and the dramatic. According to Aulen, the moral approach presents Christ's life and death as our example; the legal, as substitutionary expiation for our sins; and the dramatic, as God's war against Satan for the liberation of humankind. But, after reading this book, I discovered that Aulen's classifications all assume that the Christian's relation to Jesus is that of a spectator: Jesus acted, we look on. Jesus healed the blind man on the road to Jerico. We applaud him. Jesus died as a martyr for God's cause and for our salvation. We thank him. He rose. We worship him. Yet, in all this, we are spectators -- Jesus did it and we applaud his achievement.

Milavec shows that there is no power that Jesus exercises that he does not train his disciples to assimilate and exercise as their own. The marvel of Jesus Christ is not that he does what we are unable to do; the marvel is that the unable are enabled. Under his direction, the disciple comes to act on his own: to herald God's cause, to heal the infirm, and to dispel evil spirits. The power of Jesus is in his empowering. The would-be spectator becomes an apprentice and a doer. Jesus leads us to stand with him and share his achievement. He does not ask us to put him on a pedestal.

In brief, this book is a guide book. It gives us the insight to perceive how, when, and why each of us were enabled to assimilate for ourselves something of the power of Jesus. It makes understandable how, when and why many of us have become trapped in a spectator Christianity.

Preface

I confess that I grew up in Cahokia. I grew up passing those magnificent Indian mounds (native cathedrals!) on my way to school, to skating, and to the store. They were so present that I barely noticed them. Then a guide took me to see them. He prepared me to be affected by their hidden depths. From that time onward, I have always felt their presence, their speaking to me, their intrusion into the dreams and activities of my life.

Perhaps the key to this book is Milavec's own training under the direction of Michael Polanyi. Surely, Polanyi's philosophy offers a valuable alternative to those distancing epistemologies that have us examining and probing at givens while studiously remaining unaffected by them. I do not want to overlook the importance of Polanyi to Milavec's own intellectual pilgrimage. Yet, there is a theological brilliance and courage in Milavec's book which goes far beyond what Polanyi has said. So I want to thank the book's author rather than the author's mentor. I think that you will want to, too.

Herbert Richardson

I

Introduction: How a Religious Heritage Is Transmitted

When an engine is running smoothly, there is no need for knowing automechanics. One can even have an entirely misleading automechanics. A friend of mine, for instance, once told me that he figured that the gasoline he put into his car was changed into electricity. The electricity, in its turn, ran the motor, the headlights, the radio. This mistaken notion of automechanics never interfered with the running of my friend's car. Whenever he wanted to improve his engine's performance or to repair it in the event of a malfunction, he always turned his car over to a qualified mechanic. Needless to say, if my friend were ever forced to try to fix his own car, his tinkering under the hood would be doomed to create more harm than good.

The situation within the major denominations of Christianity has an affinity to the situation I describe above. For many generations the Christian tradition has been operating smoothly. The adherents of the churches were routinely cured of the brokenness due to their recognized sins, and the blessings of God were manifestly felt. Of late, however, the Christian tradition has been sputtering and backfiring. There has been a recognizable loss of power. Lay persons, by and large, have looked to the clergy for the necessary know-how for fixing things up. The clergy, meanwhile, have spent hours of hard labor tinkering under the hood. Unfortunately, however, even "the mechanics of the church" were quite unprepared for the unfamiliar malfunctions that the Christian tradition is now suffering.

A major indication of a malfunction within Christianity is the number of persons who find that they no longer have any need for the church. A few weeks ago, for instance, a bewildered farmer told me of his concern for his two sons. After they had returned from Vietnam, they categorically refused to have any association with Christianity. Even on the occasion of the marriage of their younger brother, this father lamented, they refused to enter the church. This father cannot understand why his two older sons are so changed. Some time earlier, I met a mother who was shocked to discover that her daughter and son-in-law had left the church and joined the Ba'hai religion. The daughter explained to her mother that the Ba'hai faith had effectively purified her from the evils of this age in a way that Christianity had never been able to do. Such instances are no longer the rare exception. They occur with alarming frequency. Parents are no longer assured that when their children leave home they will retain the Christianity that they had been taught to cherish.

In the last ten years, the major denominations have all lost more members than they have gained. Meanwhile, those who are regular church-goers often have no perceptible Christian identity which distinguishes them from the nonchurched. Secular interests and secular values dominate both groups.

Ministers of religion, meanwhile, have tried to analyze the sputtering and backfiring of Christianity. Based upon their analysis, they have tried to retune the engine. In most cases, however, they are guided by incomplete and misleading notions of the "automechanics" of Christianity. By dint of tinkering with the liturgy or of fashioning better social outreach programs, they had hoped to bring things back to normal. Some of the tinkering helped; some of it did just as much harm.

The seminaries might be blamed. In fairness, however, it must be remembered that seminary programs were designed when things were running smoothly and routine maintenance sufficed. Ministers and priests were well-equipped to take care of minor repairs. The present order of breakdown within the operation and the transmission of Christianity, however, has exceeded everything that their "automechanics" was designed to tackle. No amount of tinkering based upon an inadequate "automechanics" can hope to effect the needed repairs. No amount of sincerity and zeal can suffice when it is linked to an inadequate "automechanics."

The purpose of this book is to provide an "automechanics" that is adequate to the present level of breakdown within the church. To accomplish this task, my intent is to critically examine the process whereby Jesus transmitted his own personal powers to his disciples and how they, in their turn, went on to do the same for others. In

Introduction: How a Religious Heritage Is Transmitted   3

the end, my book intends to offer a framework whereby theologians, pastors, catechists, and concerned parents might gain a solid understanding of how the various elements of religion (prayer, rites, Scriptures) function to empower (or, alternatively, malfunction or disempower).

The germinal ideas for the preparation of this book are derived from the epistemology and sociology of human knowing as explicated by Michael Polanyi.[1] Up to this time, Polanyi's thought has had its greatest impact among philosophers of science. None the less, a few theologians have fruitfully applied segments of Michael Polanyi's thought to issues in fundamental theology. John Apczynski's <u>Doers of the Word</u>, Avery Dulles' <u>The Survival of Dogma</u>, and Thomas F. Torrance's <u>Theological Science</u> provide noteworthy illustrations of these efforts.[2] This present book endeavors to further enlarge the application of Polanyi's thought to the issues confronting fundamental and pastoral theology.

Michael Polanyi (d.1976) was principally interested in providing a comprehensive description of the scientific pursuit of truth. In this endeavor, Polanyi provided incidental parallels between the scientific and religious quest for truth, but he did not offer any sustained, systematic description of the Christian enterprise. In the course of this book, I have endeavored to extend Polanyi's thought in this direction.

Polanyi's genius lies in his careful analysis of the key roles provided by systematic apprenticeships and the dynamics of discovery within the scientific enterprise. The first process insures that apprentices assimilate for themselves the settled instincts and performative skills which characterize the living masters of the tradition. The second process insures that such apprenticeships do not deteriorate into a benevolent brainwashing but that new masters dedicate their energies to revealing as-yet-undisclosed manifestations of those realities which they serve. The first process insures the faithful handing down of the tradition; the second process insures that the tradition itself is being periodically renewed. The first process requires the personal self-giving (faith) of the apprentice to a tradition which he/she regards as authoritative. The second process requires that the masters of the tradition give themselves over to lines of inquiry in the confident expectation (faith) that their trained instincts will securely guide them into an extended series of fresh and relevant contacts with those realities that they seek.

The task that I have set for myself in this book is to spell out how the two key processes, systematic apprenticeships and the dynamics of discovery, form the backbone for a corrected understanding of Christianity. In so doing, I intend to provide a new working model so that Christians might again appreciate the human dynamics whereby Jesus Christ transmitted his own personal powers to his disciples and they, in their turn, transmitted and transmuted what they had received for future generations.

The ten chapters following may be divided into three phases: preparation, exposition, application. Within the preparatory phase (Chapters II to VI), I spell out the major obstacles through which I had to pass before I could take seriously the human dynamics undergirding spiritual power in today's church. Chapters II to IV reexamine the dogmatic and biblical notions which conceal or misrepresent the human dynamics within Jesus' transmission of power. Chapters V and VI reconstruct the human interactions employed by Jesus and his successors as they apprenticed disciples to effectively reproduce their personal powers. Within the exposition phase (Chapters VII and VIII), I spell out the dynamics of the generalized apprenticeship model which forms the backbone of any and every effective transmission of a religious heritage. In this section I give special attention to how divine initiative is implicated within and presupposes the human dynamics undergirding the passing on of the powers of Jesus. Within the application phase (Chapters IX to XI), I elaborate theological and pastoral ramifications of the generalized apprenticeship model presented.

By way of introducing the preparatory phase of my book, I want to rapidly present three musings which are designed to unsettle existing assumptions and prepare for the more studied analysis to come. My three musings are titled as follows:

  A. Even God depends upon human apprenticeships
  B. The forgotten truth: parents do communicate their religious experience
  C. The implications of Suzuki's discovery regarding musical talent

Introduction: How a Religious Heritage Is Transmitted

A. <u>Even God Depends Upon Human Apprenticeships</u>

In the preface of <u>On Christian Doctrine</u>, Augustine endeavors to justify the human training which exists in the Christian enterprise over and against those who want to insist that God alone should be their teacher. Augustine bases his argumentation on the fact that divine providence clearly intends that every domain of culture be transmitted by human interactions. These human interactions first take place in the parent-child relationship and then later in the master-disciple (teacher-student) relationship. For Augustine it was manifestly clear that Christianity played no exception to the general rule which divine providence decreed. As for those who pretend that they have no human masters and are inspired exclusively by God, Augustine asks them to reflect as to whether their introduction to the true God and their present ability to read the text of Scriptures does not largely derive from human teachers. Following upon this, he directs toward them the rather biting question as to why, since they acknowledge only the Holy Spirit, they do themselves presume to teach others rather than to send them to the selfsame teacher whereby they claim to have been infallibly taught.

Following upon Augustine's suggestions, I have been moved to sense the acute vulnerability that greets the transmission of any religious tradition, especially in its beginnings. Consider, for a moment, the situation of Abraham. Here was a man who broke from the paganism of his father on the basis of his own prophetic discoveries of the living God, YHWH. Yet, the God who Abraham discovered and to whom he dedicated his entire existence was to have no future for Isaac, his son, unless Abraham could systematically bring his son to assimilate his religious experience. If a thorough assimilation did not take place, Abraham could surmise that, following his death, Isaac would be gradually lured to hear the voices of the well-established pagan gods that Abraham had formerly reputiated. Abraham himself was well aware that the pagan rituals and practices surrounding his father's home had the effect of enabling all who were in it to hear the voices of the pagen gods therein. Abraham had presumably heard these voices in his youth prior to the time when the voice of YHWH broke through and impelled him to leave his father's home. Moreover, Abraham had Isaac at an advanced age and had no assurance that he would be able to supervise Isaac's formation until such time when his son demonstrated maturity and stability.

History assures us that Abraham succeeded in his task. Isaac did sympathetically hear the voice of YHWH, and he did entrust his entire existence to the God whom his father loved. In truth, however, Abraham might have failed. Despite his father's efforts, Isaac might have felt abandoned and isolated within his father's religious commitments and chosen to supplement the guidance of YHWH with one or the other socially established deities. He did not; yet, he could have and would have, had the apprenticeship of his father been defective or half-hearted. One can even imagine that YHWH appeared to numerous other pagans prior to Abraham but that they failed to decisively alter their own commitments or to effectively communicate their religious experience to their children. In such cases, it is natural that history would quietly pass them over and not even know of their existence.

The situation of Jesus was no less tenuous. No matter how supremely valid Jesus' fresh vision of God's cause might have been, if this vision was not communicated to his disciples, then it would remain exclusively his and be irretrievably lost to civilization the moment that he departed. No matter how supremely powerful Jesus' redemptive divinity might have been, if this power was in no way assimilated by his disciples, then they would remain existentially unchanged and the world would slip back into the same morass that it knew prior to the advent of Jesus. As such, the career of Jesus, the beloved Son of God, would be remembered as a brief "Camelot" which came unexpectedly and disappeared just as suddenly. This would leave the kingdom of heaven just as remote from human affairs as it has previously been.

History assures us that this gloomy prospect did not materialize. The disciples of Jesus did assimilate his spirit/Spirit, and they did go on to accomplish in their ministries those feats which Jesus exhibited in his own.

The failure and betrayal of one disciple, Judas, remains a sobering memorial to the possible failure of any and every religious apprenticeship. There is no reason to imagine, therefore, that the status of Jesus before God gives him any automatic or guaranteed success when it comes to passing on the divine charisms that animated his entire existence. If such is the case with Jesus, it is ludicrous to naively make believe that the passing on of the Christian charism in today's churches is somehow guaranteed because it is "in God's hands."

Even God depends upon adequate apprenticeships. <u>Where the human dynamics for the growth and the transmission of a religious tradition are wanting, even God</u>

Introduction: How a Religious Heritage Is Transmitted   7

is doomed to be continually starting over from scratch. The appearance of God within historical occasions is one thing, the recognition and passing on of momentous religious commitments is quite another. The former is largely secured by virtue of God's initiative; the latter largely rests upon human efforts.

In the end, therefore, Augustine was quite right in insisting upon the necessity of undergoing a systematic training under the direction of those who are steeped in the Christian tradition. Those who want to bypass the church and to seek God alone are foolhardy. They are like persons unskilled in cooking who want to put aside all written and oral guidance and to experimentally reconstruct the art of cooking from scratch. Such disregard for the existing traditions of cooking (French, Italian, etc.) dooms their free initiatives to insignificant results. Rather, they would be wise to master a tradition first and then to commit their energies to pioneering achievements. The same thing holds true, with an even greater force, when it comes to seeking God.

B.   The Forgotten Truth: Parents do Communicate Their Religious Experience

Most Christians have been raised to regard their religious experience as private and incommunicable in nature. Parents of their persuasion are convinced that they can only expose their children to the external trappings of their religion; God alone must be counted upon to shape the private experience of their children directly. Such a position does not bear close examination.

In the first place, children in every religious tradition grow up perceiving the "gods of their ancestors," and foreign gods do not appear "real" to them. Even the child of Christian parents who had been baptized would manifest no special interest in Jesus if that child were orphaned and raised by Moslem or agnostic parents.

In the second place, deaf-mutes in Christian families report that they knew nothing of "God" until such time as they learned about him/her in their sign-language training.[3] There is nothing innate or intuitive that allows someone cut off from culture to find the God of that culture. If children were indeed entirely left to their own resources in religious matters, they would be prone to create something akin to "the Lord of the Flies" rather than any Christian sanctuary.

In the third and last place, if parents did entirely believe that their religious experience was incommunicable, then they should logically leave everything to God and forget even the trappings of religion.[4] Of what use are religious institutions with their particular histories and rites if God indeed is entirely charged with the interior religious formation of each new individual? Furthermore, if religious experience were as incommunicable as some suggest, then each individual would be incapable of profiting from the religious experience of others and communal prayer would degenerate into a multiplicity of private idolatries. How could anyone, for instance, announce that he/she has had a "born-again experience" if no one could communicate to any other person anything of the substance of this experience?

The actual practice of every religious tradition demonstrates that parents and pastors do effectively pass on their religious experience. My own upbringing within my father's house demonstrates this to me. My father never consciously set out to communicate his religious sensibilities. If he had been told that he was to share his experience of God, he would have pleaded his incapability. Yet, truth to tell, if he had been told that he had to train his child to reproduce his language skills, his problem-solving techniques, his strengths of character, he also would have pleaded his incapability. None the less, my father did masterfully communicate to me his linguistic skills for I did end up using the same English idioms that he used to express himself. The same holds true for his strengths of character, his prejudices, his commitments, and even his experience of "God." The imitative powers of a child are not to be underestimated; they allow the child to progressively intuit and assimilate the meanings and the feelings exhibited by his/her parents and guardians.

How is it that Christians have forgotten this truth? For the most part, this is because we, as adults, cannot reenter the lost world of childhood. The adult cannot any longer experience the fright that takes place when his/her mother "disappears" out of sight and of hearing. The adult cannot any longer remember when his/her father's words were only a string of "adult chirping" that has only some vague emotional overtones but no more intelligible content than the song of birds. Similiarly, the adult cannot any longer enter the world in which God at no time and at no place makes his/her presence

Introduction: How a Religious Heritage Is Transmitted

felt.[5] This point was driven home to me on the occasion when I asked a child of six to write her name for me on a greeting card. I watched in silence during the long intervals in which the child was laboring to remember the letters in her imagination such that she might painstakingly transcribe them on the card. Upon printing an "E," she frowned, recognized it as backwards, awkwardly erased it, and reprinted it correctly, i.e., as her parents and guardians taught her to do it. During this time, I could have easily written my own name thirty times. Just the other day, I wrote my name on a check while at the same time explaining to the grocery clerk how I had noticed the dramatic rise in the cost of peanut butter. What a tremendous feat this is! Yet, I take it for granted. By virtue of my past training I can no longer feel the conscious straining and deliberate practicing that went to make up the marvelous feat that I habitually and effortlessly perform. It takes the dogged efforts of the little girl to remind me that the grace that I now exhibit have very humble beginnings. While I cannot reenter this lost world, I can, none the less, persuade myself that I was once in her skin. And this applies with equal force respecting my experience of God. My parents and guardians not only taught me to trace the letters "G," "O," "D," they also taught me to experience their God at particular times and in particular places. Conscious straining and deliberate repetition accompanied my initial efforts. In time, however, by virtue of their training, I could not help but take their God into account. By this time, their God had become my God. As an adult, it is quite easy for me to forget this. I need only to watch the little children who sometimes escape their parents in church and wander down the aisles to remind me that my own response to this particular sacred rite at this particular time is a marvelous feat that has very humble beginnings.

C. The Implications of Suzuki's Discovery Regarding Musical Talent

While my book was in its final stages, a friend introduced me to the startling discovery that Shinichi Suzuki had made in the field of musical talent. In essence, Suzuki has discovered that musical talent is not inherited; it is acquired within the milieu in which one grows up. On the basis of this discovery, Suzuki has originated special training programs which take children who are tone deaf and marvelously develop for them a musical talent.

In explaining his discovery, Suzuki is fond of making reference to the training of a nightingale:

> I had always thought that a nightingale's incomparable song was instinctive and inherited. But it is not so. Nightingales to be used as pets are taken as fledglings from the nests of wild birds in the spring. As soon as they lose their fear and accept food, a "master bird" is borrowed that daily sings its lovely song, and the infant bird listens for a period of about a month. In this way the little wild bird is trained by the master bird . . . . Whether the wild bird will develop good or bad singing quality is indeed decided in the first month by the voice and tone of its teacher. It is not a matter of being born a good or a bad singer.[6]

Suzuki uses this story by way of explaining to parents how it is that their children have learned to be tone deaf.

> Just as nightingales are not born tone-deaf, neither are human infants. On the contrary, a baby absorbs perfectly any out-of-tune pitch of its mother's lullabies. It has a marvelous ear.[7]

Recognizing that being tone deaf is as much an achieved skill as being perfectly pitched, Suzuki works with parents in such a way that they can cultivate musical talent for their children.

On the basis of his discovery, Suzuki has endeavored to revolutionize the very mentality of teachers of music. As things now stand, parents send their children to a teacher of music hoping to discover whether their child has any musical talent or not. Most teachers, meanwhile, imagine that musicianship requires an innate gift which cannot be merited or assimilated through personal efforts. To endeavor to train someone who doesn't have "the basic gift" is doomed to frustration in just the same way as endeavoring to teach a clumsy person acrobatics. Suzuki strongly disagrees. Even children who cannot hear tonal differences and who sing on a monotone

Introduction: How a Religious Heritage Is Transmitted

("droners") have been progressively led to perceive and execute complex musical pieces to which they were formerly "deaf."

The discovery of Suzuki has a distinct parallel to my own. Within Christian circles it is popularly imagined that the gift of faith cannot be merited or acquired. Accordingly, Christians habitually regard those who are atheists in their midst as those who, for some inscrutable reason, God has not given the will to believe. In effect, such persons are tone deaf to God and cannot profit from religious rites or sermons. Yet, in every case of atheism that I have encountered, I have either found that their "deafness" to God was part of their early training or that the "God" once believed and cherished was later rejected as being either infantile or smothering. Moreover, I find that children who do believe in God invariably find his/her presence in and only in those events in which their parents habitually and instinctively find him/her. Thus I myself was trained to find God principally within the sacred rituals enacted within my church. Meanwhile, I was immune from perceiving divine initiative within the political events or the social movements of the day. Had my Christianity been fashioned by Quaker parents, God would have appeared quite different to me. One's early training, consequently, greatly determines how one will subsequently "hear" God -- if, indeed, one has been trained to "hear" God at all.

The task of this book is to consider seriously the implications of regarding one's religious awareness of God as a learned skill. Needless to say, such a perspective will require new sensitivities in affirming the reality of God and in acknowledging his/her insertion within history. My investigations in this area will endeavor to provide a truer perspective and a more faithful guide for those who, like myself, are gravely concerned with the present transmission of spiritual power within the church.

Footnotes for Chapter I

[1] Michael Polanyi's (1891-1976) formal training was in medicine and chemistry; he held doctorates in both fields from the University of Budapest. His distinguished record as a physical chemist at the Kaiser Wilhelm Institute included 218 publications. In 1933, Polanyi took up a post at Victoria University, Manchester, and gave increasing attention to the philosophy and sociology of science. His qualified judgments in this arena have been widely publicized.

Polanyi's most significant writings are Science, Faith, and Society: The Riddell Memorial Lectures of 1945 (Chicago: The University of Chicago Press, 1966); Personal Knowledge: The Gifford lectures of 1951-52 (New York: Harper and Row, 1964); The Study of Man: The Lindsay Memorial Lectures of 1958 (Chicago: The University of Chicago Press, 1965); The Tacit Dimension: The Terry Lectures of 1962 (Garden City, Doubleday, 1967); Meaning: a series of lectures given at the Univeristy of Texas and the university of Chicago in 1969 (Chicago: The University of Chicago Press, 1975). For a complete listing of Polanyi's publications from 1935-1968, see T.A. Langford and W.H. Poteat, eds., Intellect and Hope (Durham, N.C.: Duke University Press, 1968), pp. 432-436.

[2] Additional works that have used Michael Polanyi's thought to address issues in fundamental theology are the following: Robert N. Bellah, "Christianity and Symbolic Realism," Journal for the Scientific Study of Religion 9 (1970) 86-96; Robert J. Brownhill, "Michael Polanyi and the Problem of Person Knowledge," Journal of Religion 48 (1968) 115-123; Avery Dulles, "Revelation and Discovery," Theology and Discovery, ed. by William J. Kelley (Milwaukee: Marquette University, 1980) 1-29; Richard Gelwick, "Discovery and Theology," Scottish Journal of Theology 28 (1975) 301-322; Jerry H. Gill, The Possibility of Religious Knowledge (Grand Rapids: William B. Eerdmans, 1971) & "The Tacit Structure of Religious Knowing," International Philosophical Quarterly 9 (1969) 533-559; Thomas A. Langford, "Michael Polany and the Task of Theory," Journal of Religion 46 (1966) 45-55; Carl Michalson, The Rationality of Faith (N.Y.: Charles Scribner's Sons, 1963); Thomas F. Torrence, ed., Belief in Science and in Christian Life (Edinburg: The Handsel Press, 1980).

[3] Harlan Lane, The Wild Boy of Aveyron (N.Y.: Bantam Books, 1976), pp. 27-28, 60-61, 99-100. Eighteenth-century philosophers were persuaded that one of the

Introduction: How a Religious Heritage Is Transmitted   13

characteristics that distinguished humans from primates was the human's innate idea of God. The discovery of children living in the woods without the benefit of training promised to provide evidence for such innate ideas. No such evidence was forthcoming. Werner Herzog dramatizes this in his film, "The Enigma of Kasper Hauser."

4 Horace Bushnell, in Christian Nurture (New Haven: Yale University, 1916), offers a classical treatise on how and why the religious experience of children is to be nurtured. Bushnell opposed those who saw nothing of the work of God in a person's life prior to the day that the "saving grace" brought them to a consciousness of their sins followed by the experience of God's forgiveness.

5 Even those Christians who subsequently become confirmed atheists do not thereby reenter the lost world of their childhood for they have to take into account their "past religious experiences" which they now regard as "eruptions of the subconscious" or as "wishful projections and fantasies." Just as it takes many years to develop the tacit skills to habitually discern God's presence; so, too, it takes many years of intellectual effort to retrain these tacit skills. It is not unusual, therefore, that former Christians are sometimes "betrayed by their past" into experiencing "childish religious feelings" when they reenter a place and/or situation that had a role in their former Christian upbringing.

6 Shinichi Suzuki, Nurtured by Love (N.Y. Exposition Press, 1977), pp. 18-19.

7 Ibid., p. 20.

II

How the Cinderella Mentality Obscures Apprenticeship

The Synoptic Gospels testify that Jesus did transfer power to his disciples:

> He [Jesus] called the Twelve together and gave them power and authority over all devils and to cure diseases, and he sent them out to proclaim the kingdom of God and to heal (Luke 9:1-2 and parallels).

This testimony is important because it specifies that the disciples did receive the power to achieve in their own ministry those feats which Jesus exemplified in his. This text calls into question any Christianity which would advocate that "disciples" are to be spectators who merely watch their master and applaud his greatness. This text also questions any presentation of Jesus which would exaggerate his divinity so as to make it inconceivable that a disciple could function like his master. In brief, this text leaves little doubt that a disciple of Jesus ought to expect to assimilate the personal performance skills which characterize his/her master. Thus, Jesus says:

> The disciple is not superior to his [her] master . . . . It is enough that he [she] should grow to be like his [her] master . . . (Matt 10:24-25).

For the moment it is not necessary to specify precisely what the exact nature of the proclamation and the healing power which Jesus and his disciples shared. This chapter intends to focus on the <u>process</u> -- how Jesus communicated his personal powers -- and to leave the specification of these powers fluid and open-ended.

My own religious upbringing was dominated by what might be called the Cinderella mentality. By this I mean that the processes of human transformation advocated by the church fell into line with the mood and the thought patterns surrounding Cinderella's transformation. As such, those narratives in which Jesus empowers his disciples always appeared to be effortless and instantaneous acts on Jesus' part. I was taught that the disciples contributed nothing to this transfer of power save for their willingness to be passive recipients. They were thus as powerless to contribute to their own self-transformation as was Cinderella. When the disciples were sent out in pairs to preach and to heal, their success was to be accounted for only in terms of the awesome hidden power of Jesus that backed up their human words and deeds. Discipleship had left their own personal powers substantially unaltered. By themselves, they could do nothing of what Jesus commissioned them to do. The moment that Jesus would withdraw his hidden power, they would immediately fall from grace just as did Cinderella when the clock struck twelve. It stood to reason that someone who was powerless to participate in their own self-transformation would be likewise powerless to perpetuate their new identity at the moment that hidden power was withdrawn from them.

The mood surrounding Cinderella's transformation was enacted by my own parents relative to my own Christian formation. On the first Saturday following my birth, my parents dutifully took me to their parish church and presented me to the parish priest for baptism. They firmly believed that the sacrament would work some great and mysterious transformation that they themselves were entirely incapable of effecting. They stood by helplessly and nervously as the priest conducted the awesome rite. By virtue of what they had been taught, they were made to feel incapable of sharing with their own child the grace and the holiness that they themselves possessed. They were convinced that they could and would take care of my secular growth in grace and wisdom but that the religious domain must be carefully entrusted to God and his/her priests and religious. After my baptism was completed, they felt a sigh of relief: my soul had been purified -- their child was now a son of God and had received the gift of the Christian faith. They could then wait for five years and then dutifully hand me over to the religious Sisters who would marvelously manage my religious transformation from that point forward.

The same mood generally surrounds the Protestant minister who gives him/herself to the preaching of the Gospel. In numerous conversations with Protestant clergy, I have heard them explain how they have been called to preach the Word of God in season and out of season. By virtue of their calling, they are required to prepare their sermons prayerfully. At the same time they firmly insist that the fruit of their preaching is left entirely in the hands of God. God alone moves the hearts of the listeners as he/she sees fit. During the preaching, the minister knows not who is being touched by grace. He/she is entirely unprepared to say that this theme will evoke such and such a conversion while another theme will effect another. The minister's task is only to sow the seed; God alone designs the fruit which it will bear. At the time of the altar call or in the private conversations following the service, the minister may glimpse how the Spirit of God has worked in this or that listener. The minister has only to thank God for this and to pray that the Spirit will continually use his/her sermons as the occasion for healing and transforming his/her congregation. Now it is the minister's turn to feel like the Cinderella who can gather the pumpkin from the garden and the rat from the trap but who is entirely powerless to determine when or how the godmother will use these humble offerings for her purposes.

In Pentecostal circles, the Cinderella mentality similarly prevails. Speaking in tongues, being slain in the Spirit, being healed miraculously -- all these are identified as the direct works of God. No person can directly promote these gifts in themselves or in others. God gives appropriate gifts to those whom he/she chooses. A Christian can only passively abandon him/herself to divine power which comes directly from on high.

For over thirty years my Christian existence was dominated by the Cinderella mentality. As in the case with other habits of thought, the Cinderella mentality tacitly and tenaciously gripped my knowing powers. Being tacit, the Cinderella mentality informed my most trusted perceptions and habitual judgments without being directly noticed. Being tenacious, the Cinderella mentality resisted any exterior coercion or any interior willingness directed toward change. As with any ingrained habit, the Cinderella mentality militated even against imagining attractive alternatives. With time, patience, and suffering, however, I have gradually undergone an intellectual conversion from the Cinderella mentality to the apprenticeship mentality. As a result of my conversion, the apprenticeship mentality now appears to me to offer a vastly more satisfying account of how spiritual power is transmitted. Conversely, the Cinderella mentality which I left behind now appears to exaggerate and to profoundly misconstrue the intimate harmony between spirit and flesh and between the Spirit of God and the human spirit informed by God.

Within this present chapter, I intend to explore three test cases which, when carefully examined, will stretch the Cinderella mentality to its limits. It was by sympathetically and imaginatively entering into cases such as this that I originally found my settled habits of mind stretched to the breaking point. Thus, with each test case the apprenticeship mentality will be offered as a tenable and potentially attractive alternative.

The three test cases to be examined are as follows:

A. The disciples' failure to cast out a demon
B. The ordination of a priest by a bishop
C. Contemporary glossolalia among Pentecostals

A.   Case I: Failure to Cast Out a Demon

The Synoptic Gospels testify that Jesus gave his disciples power over demonic disturbances but they do not explicitly delineate <u>how</u> this power was given. The texts do not speak of an "effortless" and "instantaneous" transfer of power. Many Christians have taken the silence of the Gospels on this point and filled it in with the Cinderella mentality. The fact remains, however, that none of the Gospels spell out the process for transferring spiritual power.

Matthew's Gospel offers the following account:

> He [Jesus] summoned his twelve disciples and <u>gave</u> them authority over unclean spirits with power to cast them out and to cure all kinds of diseases and sicknesses (Matt 10:1).

The Greek word for "gave" is a form of the verb <u>didomi</u>. This verb appears fifty-six times in Matthew's Gospel. The ordinariness of the word suggests something of the ordinariness in which the transfer of power is depicted. There is no hint of ritual. There is no suggestion that Jesus felt power leaving him or that the disciples felt power entering them. The same verb, <u>didomi</u>, appears a few lines thereafter -- this time with the disciples as the active agents:

> Proclaim that the kingdom of heaven is close at hand. Cure the sick, raise the dead, cleanse the lepers, cast out devils. You received without charge, <u>give</u> without charge (Matt 10:7-8).

Not only do the Synoptic Gospels describe the transfer of power in ordinary terms and without fanfare, they also fail to call up the sort of questions which the Cinderella mentality would invariably suggest. Imagine, for instance, how appropriate it would have been for Matthew to emphasize the bewilderment of the disciples if, in fact, he himself had shared the Cinderella mentality:

> And then the twelve disciples said to Jesus, "We feel your power vibrating within our bones. Our hearts are indeed glad. It remains for you to tell us how we are to release this power. Must we use special words? If so, tell us which? Must we use special rites of exorcism? And what is the proper way to release our power for the healing of diseases?"

Needless to say, the Synoptic Gospels never give the slightest hint that Jesus first gave his disciples power and, secondly, taught them the proper words and gestures with which to safely release "the unfamiliar power" which they had received.

The silence of the Gospels on this point suggests that the disciples intuitively knew the scope and intent of the power that Jesus had given them. This familiarity, however, ordinarily results when a master has progressively enlarged his/her disciples' personal powers such that the diciples' own practice indicates their nature. Thus, for example, a student cellist can sight-read a piece of music and know intuitively whether his/her performance skills can execute it or not. In parallel fashion, a medical student can discern in any given instance whether his/her personal skills are advanced sufficiently to diagnose and treat a presenting illness. It would appear, therefore, that the disciples knew the scope and the intent of the power that Jesus had given them because this power had become <u>theirs</u> in the same sense as when medical students and student cellists come to assimilate the particular powers of their respective masters.

At this point three clues are evident: (1) the ordinariness of the verb <u>didomi</u>, (2) no hint that the transfer of power was "astonishing," effortless," or "instantaneous," and (3) the absence of any instructions related to the scope and the release mechanism for the powers received. These clues, taken by themselves, would suggest that <u>didomi</u> envisioned a systematic and strenuous apprenticeship. The fact that the recipients of Jesus' power are habitually designated as "disciples" and that he himself is honored as their "master" lends further weight to this suggestion.

On the other hand, large segments of the Christian tradition have so heightened the healing powers of Jesus' disciples that they appear utterly "miraculous." And, as popular theology would have it, only God can perform miracles. Thus, it becomes functionally impossible to imagine that Jesus used a systematic apprenticeship so as to impart his personal powers to his disciples.

The Synoptic Gospels do not raise the question as to (a) whether the disciple's powers are heightened performance skills harmonized with God's Spirit or (b) whether they are divine skills which utterly surpass the zenith of human functioning. This question is ours and not theirs. We can gain clues, however, as to how they might respond to "our" issue by probing the narrative in which the Evangelists depict the disciples as failing to cast out a demonic disturbance from a young boy (Matt 17:14-20 and parallels). In effect, this is the only Gospel narrative which depicts the disciples in a concrete healing situation in which failure is the outcome. The very existence of this narrative in the Synoptics presumes that their success stories were passed over in silence.

Matthew's narrative opens with Jesus and three disciples coming down out of the mountain of transfiguration to find a crowd surrounding his remaining disciples. The father of the boy who is demonically disturbed approaches Jesus and goes down on his knees saying:

> Lord, take pity on my son; he is a lunatic and in a wretched state; he is always falling into fire or into the water. I took him to your disciples and they were unable to cure him (Matt 17:15-17).

Jesus is hardly pleased. He not only fails to commend the faith of this father, but he criticizes him severely:[1]

> Faithless and perverse generation! How much longer must I be with you? How much longer must I put up with you? (Matt 17:17)

Then Jesus does quickly what his disciples failed to do. Later, in private, the disciples ask, "Why were we unable to cast it out?" (Matt 17:19)

This question is revealing. It presupposes that the disciples attempted this case because they judged themselves quite capable of handling it. It also presupposes that their confidence born of prior successes had been unexpectedly shattered.

Assume, for the moment, that the disciples operated out of the Cinderella mentality. Then they would be deeply conscious that it was not their power but the "borrowed" power of Jesus which made for all their past successes. In the face of this failure, consequently, a vigorous complaint might be a more appropriate response:

> Why did you allow us to make fools of ourselves? You could have told us that you were taking our power away or that you hadn't given us enough power to succeed in this particular case. Why didn't you inform us? Why did you set things up so that we would fail?

But no such complaint is raised. Jesus is not directly implicated. Their question is: "Why were we unable to cast it out [whereas you evidently were able]?"

Jesus responds to the disciples' question by admonishing them for their "little faith" (Matt 17:20 only). What can such an admonition mean in this case? Did Jesus want them to have more faith in him and, consequently, to reserve such difficult cases for himself? There is nothing in Jesus' instructions to his disciples to support this. Could Jesus then be admonishing them for their insufficient faith in God? It is difficult to know what more faith in God might mean for the disciples confronted with a demonic disturbance. Today, many Christians would suggest that faith in God means to pray with the confidence that he/she will do what is necessary. For Jesus, however, this can hardly be his meaning. There is not a single instance of Jesus praying to the Father when faced with demoniacs. Furthermore, Jesus has admonished his disciples not to multiply their prayers (Matt 6:7) nor to pray in public (Matt 6:5). Jesus' admonition, therefore, is not directed toward their faith in God nor their faith in Jesus.

Faith in whom, then? One can discover this only by examining the sarcastic hyperbole which follows upon Jesus' admonition:

> I tell you solemnly, if your faith were the size of a mustard seed, you could say to this mountain, "move from here to there," and it would move; nothing would be impossible to you (Matt 17:20).

Note that Jesus emphasizes that it is <u>they</u> who are to move mountains. On the other hand, "moving mountains" appears to be something that God alone might accomplish. Jesus' words, thus, appear as a baffling contradiction.

This contradiction disappears the moment that one comes to recover the lost Jewish sense of "moving mountains." I myself stumbled across this sense while reading in the rabbinic literature of Rabbi Akiba's determination to master Torah even though he began at the late age of forty years:

> To what can this [Rabbi Akiba's determination] be compared? To a stonecutter who was quarrying stones from mountains. One day he took his pick in his hand, went out and sat on the mountain, and chipped away small stones. When people came and asked him what he was doing, he told them, "I mean to uproot the mountain and cast it into the Jordan."
>
> They said to him, "You cannot possibly uproot the whole mountain."
>
> Nevertheless, he continued chipping away until it became the size of a large boulder. He inserted himself beneath it, unloosened it, uprooted it, and cast it into the Jordan, saying, "Here is not your place but there."[2]

I suggest that Jesus' admonition to his disciples embraces a parallel usage of "moving mountains." Jesus' metaphor emphasizes the strength of a verbal command as accomplishing the seemingly impossible task. This appears fitting within the original context since exorcism traditionally required addressing demonic disturbances with a firm voice. In both cases, however, strenuous human energies are applied to a seemingly impossible task. There is not the slightest hint that those setting out to move mountains are to be humble, to step aside, and to plead that God would accomplish "the impossible deed" for them and instead of them. No. Those who have great <u>faith in themselves</u> can do it!

All the clues offered within Matthew's narrative fall into a superb harmony when viewed within the apprenticeship mentality. Jesus exhibits the power to dispel demonic disturbances.[3] His disciples entrust themselves to him with the expectation of gaining for themselves the expertise which he exemplifies. Any master who would cultivate dependency for its own sake would reduce his disciples to servile dependents. Not even Jesus acts out of a servile reliance upon God's direct intervention. Above all, the Gospels never present Jesus as advocating a self-abasement which stands helpless in the face of evil while piously offering prayers to heaven. Such may be the learned conduct of many Christians, but they did not learn such conduct from Jesus and his primitive disciples. Disciples are constrained to follow the example of their master in everything. Jesus took action in the face of demonic disturbances; his disciples, in the instance presented, took action also. Their failure only shows up the fact that they did not act with sufficient firmness and insight. Jesus' admonition is quite like that of the master musician who chides his pupils because they failed to perform a difficult score which he judged to be quite within their capabilities. In sum, it is their "little faith" that dooms them to failure.

Anyone habituated to the Cinderella mentality will necessarily find a certain repugnance at imagining Jesus exhorting his disciples to increased determination and self-confidence. The Cinderella mentality intimates that the disciples never contribute anything substantial to the great work of God. Under this rubric, the disciple can only be blamed for not cultivating sufficient dependency or for letting their own activity get in the way of God's power. Within the apprenticeship mentality, an entirely different focus is achieved. God does not use his/her power to supplant or to complete what is wanting in the disciples; rather, the disciples' personal powers accomplish the great feat in virtue of their being stretched and transformed within their apprenticeship. To submit to an apprenticeship under the direction of Jesus means to have one's personal energies in harmony with the Spirit of God.

In this scheme of things, prayer figures into the training of a disciple by way of discerning God's cause and aligning his/her energies thereto. Prayer never substitutes for action. Above all, prayer is never a stepping aside with the expectation that God wants to handle things alone. Far from it. Prayer, in the apprenticeship mentality, can only result in a greater urgency and vigor in acting. It is as though the Father had decided not to move ahead unless his sons and daughters are there with him. Only such a father could prize patient nurturing and strenuous efforts over and against the option of doing it all alone. Jesus, understandably, has made this same option his how own when it comes to sharing his mission with his disciples.

B.   Case II: The Making of a Priest

Within my own Catholic upbringing, there was no more emphatic factor for enforcing the Cinderella mentality than the theology and practice of priestly ordination. My teachers explained to me that the ordination of a priest by a bishop effected the same transformation as when Jesus originally ordained his disciples. My teachers further explained that the sacramental powers which Jesus possessed by virtue of his office as "high priest" have been faithfully transmitted to each successive generation through the rite of ordination. The Baltimore Catechism, which was then the universally-accepted guide for belief, stated it thusly:

> The priests and bishops of today have received their supernatural powers from an unbroken chain or ordination ceremonies going back to the apostles, who received them from Christ himself.[4]

The practice of priestly ordination made it appear as though the rite operated "instantaneously" and "effortlessly" in transforming the candidate. Prior to the rite, the candidate would have many occasions to practice the various sacramental rituals; yet, not even the candidate's closest family and friends would dream of asking him to act as their priest. Any rite performed by a candidate prior to his ordination would be regarded as no more efficacious than the child who plays priest for his/her companions. Following the imposition of hands by the bishop, however, these same persons would gladly seek out his blessing and rejoice to be present at his "first Mass."

Following the lessons of the Baltimore Catechism, there could be no doubt that the ordination rite (in and by itself) was regarded as effecting the entire transformation of an ordinary person into a priest:

> Q: What are the effects of ordination to the priesthood?
> A: The effects of ordination to the priesthood are: first, an increase of sanctifying grace [i.e., holiness]; second, sacramental grace, through which the priest has God's constant help in his sacred ministry; third, a character, lasting forever, which is a special sharing in the priesthood of Christ and which gives the priest special supernatural powers.
> Q: What are the chief supernatural powers of the priest?
> A: The chief supernatural powers of the priest are: to change bread and wine into the body and blood of Christ in the Holy Sacrifice of the Mass [i.e., the Lord's Supper], and to forgive sins in the Sacrament of Penance.[5]

When the rhetoric of ordination was placed within the context of the larger Catholic practice, however, it was well recognized that ordination did not suffice. Any young man who aspired to be a priest had to first leave home and submit himself to an arduous seminary training during four to eight years prior to ordination. With this in mind, even the explanatory notes of the Catechism state that the bishop ordains only that "man who, after a sufficient period of preparation and trial, gives signs that he has been called by God to the priesthood."[6] Such "signs" are manifestly visible. They include not only a sound character and holiness of life but the demonstrated aptitude to minister as a priest.

In truth, therefore, the rite of ordination presupposes a prior, prolonged apprenticeship. And it is during this time of apprenticeship that the personal powers of a young man are nurtured and enhanced so as to reproduce those of his masters who are already proven ministers of God. Any one who has had the opportunity to follow the development of a young man through his many years of seminary formation would be keenly aware of this fact. During these years, anyone who did not respond to the seminary formation and demonstrate an increasing proficiency in priestly skills was dismissed as lacking the requisite "signs" of a call by God. In the end, only those who manifest a priestly character and demonstrate ministerial skills are presented to the bishop for ordination.

The personal performance skills of the priest-to-be remain substantially unaltered during the time of the ordination rite. The Baltimore Catechism is misleading in so far as it localizes within the two-hour rite effects which took years to realize. But, even beyond this, growth in holiness (sanctifying grace) and growth in ministerial skills (sacramental grace) are ongoing processes which will embrace the remaining years of a priest's life as well.

What, then, does the ordination rite effect? It dramatically alters the status of the candidate vis-a-vis the people who will henceforth accept him as their priest. Through the ordination rite, the bishop can, by virtue of his already confirmed position among his people, publically elevate a given person to act as his "double" in performing priestly ministry. Through the laying on of hands, the bishop effectively declares: "Anyone who welcomes you welcomes me; and those who welcome me welcome the one who sent me" (Matt 10:40).

The ordination of a priest can be paralleled with the certification of a medical doctor. The brief act of receiving state certification implies a previous period of intensive apprenticeship and demanding testing. During this period, not even the members of the candidate's family would presume to seek him/her out for any significant medical attention. Once certified, however, all this is altered. The candidate's "character" is entirely transformed vis-a-vis the public. Practicing doctors will now recommend patients to him/her and will collaborate in diagnosing or treating difficult cases. The rite of priestly ordination is richer in form and different in intent than the certification of a medical doctor; yet, the sobering parallel remains: (a) both presume a prior, prolonged apprenticeship and (b) both effect a "character" or role transformation vis-a-vis the public whom they serve.

The upshot of what I am suggesting here is that the theology of ordination represented by the Baltimore Catechism fails to take into account the efficacy of the apprenticeship which precedes ordination. Instead of acknowledging that the Spirit of God was manifest throughout the formation period and that the ordination ceremony witnesses to the charism that has been already received, an exaggerated and misleading emphasis is given to the rite in isolation.

Recently Roman Catholic theologians have given more careful attention to how their understanding of ordination has changed over the centuries. Bernard Cooke, for example, has conducted a detailed study of ordination in which he concludes that the essence of ordination was originally that of an initiation ceremony. In part, he states:

> If one tries to recapture the understanding that the early Christian centuries had of ordination, it seems to have been that of a man being incorporated into an "order" (an "official level") of the community and beginning to share the responsiblities and powers proper to that order. For quite some time there was little notion that ordination gave the ordinand a new physical power to cause such sacramental effects as Eucharistic changing of bread and wine.[7]

An examination of the biblical texts depicting "ordination" does not so easily vindicate the Cinderella mentality as is commonly thought. Since these texts are often actually read during the ceremony of ordination, they are often misinterpreted in terms of the defective sense of ordination in which they are situated. It will serve our investigation, therefore, to give close attention to some of the biblical texts in question and to demonstrate how little support they give to the Cinderella mentality.

Before examining actual texts, a clear distinction must be made between the ritual of touching and the ritual of leaning one's hands (wherein the weight of one's body is clearly intended). In the first category are Jesus touching the little children (Luke 18:15) and Jesus touching someone about to be healed (e.g., Luke 8:54). In the second category are Moses leaning his hands upon Joshua (Num 27:23) and the apostles leaning their hands upon the Seven (Acts 6:6). Careful analysis of the Greek/Hebrew vocabulary and the intent of these to rites demonstrates that they are not to be confused.[8] The first is characterisitic of blessing and of healing; the second is characteristic of "ordaining" someone to act as one's double.

Beginning with the Synoptic Gospels, it is significant that Jesus is never depicted as ordaining his disciples. This is especially remarkable in so far as the Pharisaic masters of Jesus' day seemingly employed the rite of the leaning of hands by way of "ordaining" their mature disciples to represent them in the public arena. If Jesus had employed this rite, it would hardly have been omitted from the Synoptic accounts because it would have formed the basis for the then-present usage of the church. Thus, the very practice of the rite by the primitive disciples intensifies the "silence" of the Synoptic writers regarding any ordination by Jesus.

Faced with this silence, most scholars are willing to conclude that Jesus most certainly did not lean hands upon his disciples. In fact, when one examines the issue more closely, considerations emerge which explain <u>why Jesus could not ordain anyone</u>. To ordain meant to acknowledge someone as one's double before a given community. The Synoptics make it clear that Jesus sent his disciples out to act as his double, i.e., to proclaim the Kingdom, to heal, and to exercise in his name: "Anyone who welcomes you welcomes me" (Matt 10:40). What is wanting, however, is a given community which already recognizes Jesus and would, consequently, recognize those whom he ordained. Lacking this, <u>a private ordination makes no sense</u>. For the moment it sufficed that Jesus alone recognized his disciples as acting in his name.

Within this understanding, the familiar rite of the leaning of hands would be readily introduced the moment that the Twelve were surrounded by a supportive community and it came time to publically designate their doubles. The public nature of ordination thus accounts for why Jesus could not ordain and for why his own disciples later could and would do so. In this regard it should be remarked that the Cinderella mentality of ordination can make no sense out of the "silence" of the Gospels save to assume that Jesus did use the same ordination rite that his disciples perpetuated after him. <u>It is hardly plausible, however, that the Evangelists would have remained silent if they had known of a single rite that entirely empowered the disciples with Jesus' priestly character in a few brief moments</u>.

Both the Old and New Testament present a remarkable agreement as to the nature of the rite or "ordination". Examine, for instance, the conduct of Moses when he appointed Joshua as his double:

>Moses said to YHWH, "May YHWH . . . appoint a leader for this community, to be at their head in all they do . . . ."
>YHWH answered Moses, "Take Joshua,

> son of Nun, a man in whom the spirit [Spirit] dwells. Lay [lean] your hands upon him. Bring him before Eleazar the priest and the whole community, to give him your orders in their presence and to give him a share of your authority, so that the whole community of the sons of Israel may obey him . . . ."
> Moses did as YHWH had ordered. He took him and brought him before Eleazar the priest and the whole community, laid [leaned] his hands upon him and gave him his orders . . . (Num 27:15-23).

An examination of this text reveals the following: (1) Moses does the ordaining and not the priest, Eleazar, since Joshua is being raised to the status of Moses' double (which has no priestly functions). (2) Joshua is presented as having the necessary spirit/Spirit prior to the leaning of hands; hence, the ritual cannot imply that it confers the spirit/Spirit. (3) The narrative clearly specifies the public character of the rite. After the rite those who recognize the leadership of Moses are constrained to obey Joshua, his new double. A purely private ordination would be self-defeating and senseless.

Now, with this instance in mind, examine the parallel instance of the use of the leaning of hands in the Acts of the Apostles:

> The Hellenists made a complaint against the Hebrews . . . . So the Twelve called a full meeting of the disciples and addressed them, "It is not right for us to neglect the word of God so as to give out food [literally, to serve tables/table fellowships?]; you, brothers, must select from among yourselves seven men of good reputation, filled with the Spirit and with wisdom; we will hand over this duty to them . . . ."
> The whole assembly approved of this proposal and elected Stephen, a man full of faith and of the Holy Spirit, together with Philip, Prochorus, Nicanor, Timon, Parmenas, and Nicholaus . . . . They presented them to the apostles, who prayed and laid [leaned] their hands upon them (Acts 6:1-6).

This ordination has the same defining characteristics as in the previous illustration from the Old Testament: (1) The Twelve ordain the Seven to act as their doubles; any priests who might be present (as suggested by Acts 6:7) would definitely not lay hands upon the candidates. (2) The Seven are already established as possessing the necessary Spirit and wisdom prior to the rite. (3) The leaning of hands functions principally as a public rite whereby the Twelve alter the identity of the Seven vis-a-vis the whole assembly (which already acknowledges the authority of the Twelve).

Not only do these two instances demonstrate a parallel understanding of the leaning of hands which span the Old and New Testaments, but they demonstrate that "ordination" did not originally relate to priestly powers. The priesthood of the Old Testament was a hereditary office, and the New Testament priesthood was not yet explicitly defined in Acts. Thus, neither Old or New Testament envisioned or knew of any rite of priestly ordination. When the church of the late second century did begin to associate "priestly" and "cultic" functions with their chief ministers, it was entirely natural to regard the established rite of ordination as embracing these functions as well. Ministerial ordination was thus prior to and larger than what has come to be embraced by "priestly ordination."

There are some isolated texts in Acts in which the rite of the leaning of hands is used without any "ordination" being effected. An instance of this is Peter and Paul leaning hands upon the Samaritans (Acts 8:17). The Samaritans, it will be remembered, were commonly regarded as "heretical." The apostles, in this case, seemingly employ the leaning of hands to indicate that the Samaritan community founded by Philip has the same spirit/Spirit as themselves. The rite is thus associated with the receiving of the Holy Spirit. Catholic circles commonly associate this text with the Sacrament of Confirmation, and Pentecostals sometimes associate the leaning of hands with their baptism of the Spirit. Both of these understandings are very late in origin and there is no way to confirm or deny that current Pentecostal or Catholic experience is even remotely congruent with what Luke-Acts intended. In any case, an informed Christian needs to be aware that the early church extended the gesture of the leaning of hands into an associated meaning which did not imply ordination.

The upshot of this whole discussion is that the perception of ordination defined by the Baltimore Catechism is seriously misleading. On the one hand, the Catechism

How the Cinderella Mentality Obscures Apprenticeship 31

focuses into the brief moments of ordination what was properly achieved during a prior seminary apprenticeship. On the other hand, the very texts of the Old and New Testament which are sometimes thought to support the Cinderella mentality of ordination do, in fact, offer disconfirming evidence. A careful attention to Catholic practice and to the biblical texts leaves one with the conviction that ordination does effectively create an altered identity for the candidate vis-a-vis the community. For this there can be no doubt; Joshua did act as Moses' double in the eyes of the Israelites and the newly-ordained priests is received in his ministry by the same people who accredit the bishop ordaining him. Once the exaggerations of the Cinderella mentality are brushed aside, a Roman Catholic ought to be satisfied that the Spirit of God again becomes visible within the operation of their seminaries.

C.   Case III: Speaking in Tongues Among Pentecostals

The third test case to be considered pertains to the phenomenon of speaking in tongues (glossalalia). For a long period, glossolalia has been unknown by most Christians because its practice was isolated among the various Pentecostal churches (e.g., the Assembly of God, the Pentecostal Holiness Church). In the last few decades, however, speaking in tongues has been widely practiced by prayer groups composed of Christians from the mainline denominations. In most instances, such Christians refer to themselves as "Charismatics" and regard their speaking in tongues as a form of prayer which is entirely under the direction of the Holy Spirit.

The theology and the practice of glossolalia is generally presented by Charismatics so as to emphasis that it is a work of God which is entirely beyond the limits of human ingenuity. Only on rare occasions have I met Charismatics who considered their glossolalia as only a passing phase in which they are moving toward the art of praying fluently and courageously in a public setting. In most cases, Charismatics regard the spontaneous sounds which they utter to be ancient or foreign languages which the Spirit of God miraculously gives to them in their moments of prayer. Out of this climate, a large number of confirmation narratives, such as the following have been generated:

> Dr. T.J. McCrossan of Minneapolis tells the story of nine U.S. Marines who, one Saturday night, entered a small Pentecostal church in Seattle, Washington, drawn by the music, and then listened in growing amazement as an American woman whom they knew arose and gave a message in tongues. All nine of the Marines were Filipinos, all nine recognized an obscure Filipino dialect and agreed on the sense of what they'd heard. The woman, they knew, could not naturally speak Filipino at all, much less this strange dialect from a region rarely visited by Westerners.[9]

Some Charismatics regard their glossolalia as incidental to their personal justification or sanctification. Others, however, regard glossolalia as a decisive confirmation of the Holy Spirit attesting to their personal sanctification. Those in this latter class are prone to claim that glossolalia is not only beyond the limits of human ingenuity but beyond the limits of demonic powers as well:

> No one speaks in tongues until after he [she] is born again and the Holy Spirit is permanently within. Devils <u>cannot</u> speak in tongues. Thus, when one speaks in tongues one can never speak devilish or wrong things. Devils can possess people to prophesy, but devils can never speak in tongues. Those who teach that devils can inspire one to speak in tongues have been misled.[10]

Faced with such impressive claims, most of those who are Charismatics or sympathetic with Charismatics necessarily operate out of the Cinderella mentality. Even the slightest hint in the direction of suggesting that glossolalia is a learned phenomenon must be firmly rebuffed by most Charismatics. The careful studies made in this direction, therefore, are quietly ignored or branded as "demonically inspired" and as "doubting the power of the Holy Spirit." Yet, I believe such studies cannot be easily dismissed if Charismatics are to arrive at a balanced assessment of the role which both human and divine initiative have in the speaking of tongues.

How the Cinderella Mentality Obscures Apprenticeship 33

An initial clue that human initiative does have a role to play in the production of glossolalia can be glimpsed from the encouragement and the coaching operative within Charismatic circles. As a specific instance of this, the Charismatic Community of Notre Dame conducts programs which allow new members to be successfully oriented towards speaking in tongues. These "Life in the Spirit Seminars" are conducted by persons who both practice and prize glossolalia. Among the guidelines given to the directors of the seminars, one finds the following suggestions respecting the overcoming of resistance and the place of encouragement:

> Yielding to tongues is an important first step [toward being baptized in the Spirit], and it is worth putting effort into encouraging a person to yield to tongues, even to run the risk of being labelled "imbalanced" . . . .
>
> Often people can be helped to yield to tongues rather easily . . . . After praying with a person to be baptized in the Spirit, the team member [guide] should lean over or kneel down and ask the person if he [she] would like to pray in tongues. When he [she] says yes, he [the team member] should encourage him [her] to speak out, making sounds that are not English . . . . He should then pray with him [her] again. When the person begins to speak in tongues, he should encourage him [her] . . . .
>
> Tongues come when a person is baptized in the Holy Spirit . . . . After you ask to be baptized in the Holy Spirit and ask for the gift of tongues, then yield to it. Begin by speaking out, if necessary by just making meaningless sounds. The Holy Spirit will form them.[11]

In other Charismatic groups, overt coaching is almost entirely absent. When the respected leaders of a group model speaking in tongues, this, in itself, suffices for allowing enthusiastic adherents in the group to come to glossolalia quite by themselves. I myself have participated in prayer groups in which everyone present surrounded and touched someone asking for prayers. Then each one broke out in verbal prayer, in glossolalia, or in silent prayer -- all at the same time. In such a setting, I have observed that newcomers begin with silent prayer, graduate to glossolalia, and finally arrive at giving clear voice to their prayers. In practice, the mature members of the community easily alternated between the various prayer styles during the five to ten minute period in which someone was being prayed over.

Intensive research has been compiled relative to the conditions which promote or discourage praying in tongues. Dr. Kildahl, for example, conducted a ten-year study which was funded jointly by the American Lutheran Church and the National Institute of Mental Health.[12] Dr. Kildahl concluded in his study that glossolalia is a learned phenomenon which characteristically shows up under given conditions. The more significant conditions noted by Dr. Kildahl are the following: (a) a magnetic and trusting relationship with a leader who prizes his/her own gift of tongues, (b) a feeling of personal distress or crisis, (c) a knowledge of the theological rationale for glossolalia, (d) a supporting and encouraging group of fellow believers.

Dr. Kildahl's study found that glossolalia does not appear in prayer groups or churches where no special efforts are made to encourage the phenomenon. Among those churches in which the gift is encouraged, however, not all find themselves able to pray in tongues. Why is this? The typical answer that Dr. Kildahl received from the Charismatics themselves was as follows:

> I believe that it has to do with the person him[her]self . . . . [To receive the gift] there must be travail in prayer and worship, with much repenting . . . .

> I believe that it depends upon whether the person is open to God and willing to accept what God wants of him [her] . . . .[13]

By careful observation, however, Dr. Kildahl discovered that there are other factors which the Charismatics never mentioned. For instance, Dr. Kildahl discovered that all those who had the gift of tongues had developed "deeply trusting and submissive relations to the authority figures who introduced them to the practice of glossolalia."[14] In fact, so much was this the case that numerous instances were discovered of persons who were zealous tongue-speakers until such time that they had a falling out with the authority figure that introduced them to the art.[15] The persons themselves were not consciously aware of why they lost their gift. Only by extensive interviewing with a trusted counsellor were the full circumstances revealed.

The most telling evidence for the learned nature of glossolalia came from the remarkable linguistic similarities which characterize a master and his/her disciples. Dr. Kildahl found that an exhibitionistic master produced exhibitionistic disciples while a reserved master produced reserved disciples.

> A linguist engaged in glossolalia research found that prominent visiting speakers affected whole groups of glossolalists. Although no two tongue-speakers sound exactly alike, if the prominent leader spoke in a kind of Old Testament Hebraic style, those who were taught by him also spoke in this manner. If the leader of the group evidenced Spanish diction and mannerisms, his followers also developed that style. It is not uncommon for linguists to be able to tell which prominent itinerant glossolalist has introduced a congregation to tongue-speaking. Relatively few men and women travel the tongue-speaking circuit. The glossolalic styles of Bennett, Bredesen, Christenson, du Plessis, Mjorud, and Stone are distinctive enough to be identifiable by observant linguists.[16]

The research of Dr. Kildahl does not prove that the Holy Spirit is not instrumental in the production of glossolalia. Such negative conclusions cannot be demonstrated. However, Dr. Kildahl has shown that those facts which surround every form of imitative learning are involved when select persons come to speak in tongues. The entire production of tongue-speaking cannot, therefore, be attributed to the Holy Spirit; due account must be taken of human initiatives as well.[17]

In some communities, the productions of glossolalists are understood to be coded messages of the Holy Spirit. When this is the case, the community invariably honors certain of its members as being inspired to decode the messages of the Spirit. As explained by a Charismatic . . .

> Glossolalia is not complete without there also being someone who can

> interpret the tongues. This is very definitely a gift of God. The interpretations that I have heard are wonderful. God will use this gift when God wishes to give a direct message to the people, and there will always be someone in the congregation who will be given the interpretation by God . . . .[18]

At first glance, I submit that it does appear unusual that the Holy Spirit has to use a two-step operation in order to deliver messages. Upon close observation, however, Dr. Kildahl has found that two or more divergent interpretations will sometimes be offered as the inspired meaning of the same utterance in tongues.[19] This can be only partially justified by Charismatics who explain that some inspired interpreters decode very accurately while others paraphrase loosely. In one instance, for example, an African Pentecostal recited the Lord's Prayer in his native dialect. Another Pentecostal immediately interpreted this as a message from the Holy Spirit announcing the approaching second coming of Christ. This "inspired inerpretation" was accepted by all present.[20] In this instance, it is clear that no one save the speaker understood the verbal intent of the utterance. The others simply assumed that the offered interpretation was indeed the correct one. It would appear, therefore, that some or all of the inspired interpretations have little to do with the content of the utterance that they were supposed to decode. Given the very nature of glossolalia, not even the inspired interpreter in the above example could detect that his intuitive, Spirit-directed translation had missed the verbal intent of the African speaker.

Some glossolalists go so far as to claim that their utterances cannot be their own since they are speaking unknown or extinct languages that they have never studied. I myself know of a Charismatic who explained how he had recorded a segment of tongue-speaking at a prayer meeting and discovered later that by playing the tape backwards it came out in perfect English. I find that it is pastorally unwise to try to refute such claims. In actuality, such claims function more as an invitation to share some of the more personal changes that a person has experienced due to his or her Charismatic associations. By sympathetically listening to such persons, I have usually found that I can enable Charismatics to discover some abiding personal changes in their lives which better serve to recommend the presence of the Holy Spirit in their group than feats of language.

In still other cases, a Charismatic may be looking for a chance to check out practices within his group which hint of misplaced zeal or covert exploitation. By telling such a person that not a single instance of recorded glossolalia has proved to be a known foreign language, one would only turn such a person away and deny him/her the opportunity to get feedback from a Christian outside of the immediate group to which he/she belongs.

Every religious group has the potential of doing irreparable harm under the guise of being led by the Holy Spirit. Charismatics are no exception to this rule.[21] By embracing Charismatics as Christian seekers like oneself, one can help them regain a truer estimate of their worth and safeguard them against abusive forms of religion which sometimes emerge. On the other hand, Charismatics can also perform a service for Christians who are seeking God through alternate institutional forms.

Conclusion

Looking backward, I would like to summarize the main points of my inquiry. Three test cases were examined. In each instance, the Cinderella mentality was strained by a close inspection of the particulars of the case. The apprenticeship mentality was then offered as providing greater honesty and increased intellectual satisfaction in accounting for the givens. Thus, when it is imagined that Jesus progressively enlarged the personal powers of his disciples, then it makes sense that the disciples knew intuitively how to deploy their powers and that Jesus could rightly chide them in the case of their failure. In parallel fashion, when it is remembered that a candidate for ordination has submitted to a prolonged specialized apprenticeship, then it makes sense that his/her bishop would acknowledge the candidate's priestly skills as comparable to his/her own and properly entrust the people assembled at the ordination rite to accept the candidate's ministry as they now accept the bishop's. So, too, it would come as no surprise that the biblical texts pertaining to the leaning of hands assure us that the candidates were fit and Spirit-filled prior to the rite. Finally, when it is recognized that those who ecstatically speak in tongues can progressively lead those who entrust themselves to them to embrace the selfsame skill, then it makes sense that the linguistic character of the disciples' glossolalia replicates the productions of their self-chosen master(s).

The continued use of the Cinderella mentality does not imply any pious fraud or inadvertent dishonesty.

Moreover, it must be remembered that <u>no matter how elliptical and misleading the Cinderella mentality might appear, one can be assured that it was always supplemented by correct practice</u>. In effect, therefore, the thrust of this chapter has been to find an apprenticeship program oprating alive and well but unnoticed in each instance in which instantaneous divine intervention was appealed to. Thus, the exaggerations of the Baltimore Catechism appear to function in practice only as long as there is an effective seminary training behind each priestly candidate. To let the quality of seminary formation deteriorate and to rely upon the transformation power of the rite alone would prove disasterous. In the same vein, if Charismatic leaders restricted their glossolalia to their private prayer and declined to encourage it as a sign of the Spirit so as to give God the complete responsibility for evoking it within their communities, then they would find that the existing glossolalia would slowly die out. Then the Spirit would most probably demonstrate to those leaders that it is unlawful to test God (Matt 4:7) and that they ought to resume to model glossolalia and to eagerly encourage everyone to pray for the gift.

If the Cinderella mentality is to be discarded, it must be because one is moved to adopt a truer and more responsible version of how human and devine initiative are interdependent. The young man who surrenders his belief in love potions and undertakes the hazardous responsibility of wooing a woman for his wife does not necessarily find that his new model insures success when his old model failed. So it is with those who bring the apprenticeship model to their Christian endeavors. The challenge at first appears greater and more arduous. Yet, they have the confidence that their energies are firmly established in the reality which God created. Once one has realized holiness in these terms, any appeal to magical forms of religion only appears as a senseless distraction. Truth, be it known, has more appeal than magic.

Footnotes for Chapter II

[1] This is not the only instance in which Jesus shows strong irritation when he is appealed to for assistance. Jesus, for example, rebukes his disciples when they wake him up during the storm: "Why are you so frightened, you men of little faith?" (Matt 8:26). The meaning of Jesus' rebuke will appear from the forthcoming analysis within this chapter. In parallel fashion, when Peter walks out to meet Jesus on the heavy sea, begins to sink, and appeals to Jesus, he also is rebuked: "Man of little faith, why did you doubt?" (Matt 14:31). Jesus'

rebuke makes it clear that Peter had been doing well and that Jesus had expected him to continue to do so. For an analysis of how Matthew develops the theme of discipleship in these two narratives, see Heinz Joachim Held, "Matthew as Interpreter of the Miracle Stores," <u>Tradition and Interpretation in Mathew</u>, ed. by Guenther Bornkamm et al. (Philadelphia: Westminster, 1963), pp. 200-211.

[2] <u>Abot de Rabbi Nathan</u> 6:2 (20b).

[3] William Blatty's novel, <u>The Exorcist</u>, and the film based upon his book can only serve to distort (a) the nature of present day exorcisms and (b) the nature of the demonic disturbances which Jesus and his disciples encountered. Interested readers consult Juan B. Cortes, S.J. and Florence M. Gatti, "Exorcising 'The Exorcist'," <u>Human Behavior</u> 3, 5 (May, 1974) 16-23.

[4] Confraternity of Christian Doctrine, <u>Baltimore Catechism No. 3</u>, with notes and study helps of Rev. Francis J. Connell (N.Y.: Benzinger Brothers, Inc., 1952), p. 262.

[5] <u>Ibid.</u>, qq. 454-455, p. 260.

[6] <u>Ibid.</u>, q. 452a, p. XI.

[7] Bernard Cooke, <u>Ministry to Word and Sacraments</u> (Philadelphia: Fortress, 1976), p. 642, also pp. 197-214. The theological and historical conclusions reached by Cooke are confirmed by the careful studies of Edward Schillebeeckx: "The Catholic Understanding of Office in the Church," <u>Theological Studies</u> 30 (1969) 567-587, and <u>Ministry</u> (N.Y., Crossroad, 1981), esp. pp. 38-65.

[8] David Daube, <u>The New Testament and Rabbinic Judaism</u> (London: The Athlone Press, 1956), pp. 224-246.

[9] John L. Sherrill, <u>They Speak With Other Tongues</u> (Old Tappan, N.J.: Spire Books, 1964), p. 96. Sherrill has uncritically gathered together well over a hundred such amazing stores.

[10] Victor Paul Wierwille, <u>Receiving the Holy Spirit Today</u> (New Knoxville, Ohio: American Christian Press, 1972), pp. 47-48. Sherrill shares this same judgment in his book, <u>supra</u>, p. 79ff.

[11] <u>The Life in the Spirit Seminars Team Manual</u> (Notre Dame, Ind.: Charismatic Renewal Services, 1973), pp. 147, 148-49, 150-51.

[12] John P. Kildahl, The Psychology of Speaking in Tongues (N.Y.: Harper & Row, 1972).

[13] Ibid., p. 7.

[14] Ibid., p. 50.

[15] Ibid., p. 79.

[16] Ibid., p. 53. Felicitas D. Goodman, Speaking in Tongues (Chicago: The University of Chicago Press, 1972), offers a linguistic analysis of the glossolalia in three diverse cultural settings: Apostolic congregations in Mexico City, Maya Indians in the Yucatan, and Charismatics in Hammond, Indiana.

[17] Over the last twenty years, the mainline churches have created study commissions which have drawn conclusions which parallel those of Dr. Kildahl. Such study commission reports have been collected by Kilian McDonnell in three volumes, Presence, Power, Praise (Collegeville: The Liturgical Press, 1980). Throughout these reports, one finds statements such as the following: (a) "Tongue-speaking . . . is not a distinctive Christian practice"; (b) "Because of exegetical problems it is not easy to identify the current phenomena with the Corinthian practice"(I:399, 136); (c) "Even with the 'extraordinary' gifts like speaking in tongues and healing, a certain aptitude can often be pinted out" (I:176, 540); (d) "Tongues-speaking frequently is induced . . ." (I:87, 142).

[18] Kildahl, The Psychology of Speaking in Tongues, p. 8.

[19] Ibid., p. 63.

[20] Ibid., p. 63.

[21] Two excellent studies showing some of the potential and actual dangers within Catholic Pentecostalism are P.J. Kerkhofs, ed., "The Catholic Pentecostal Movement: Creative or Divisive Enthusiasm," Pro Mundi Vita Bulletin 60 (May, 1976) 1-36 and Kilian McDonnell, Catholic Pentecostalism: Problems in Evaluation (Pecos, New Mexico: Dove Publications, 1970).

III

How the Atonement Theory Trivializes Apprenticeship

From my earliest years, my teachers focused upon the sufferings and the death of Jesus as the all-embracing means of human salvation. In every classroom there was a crucifix. During Lent, we went to the church each Friday. There we soberly reflected upon the great sufferings which Jesus experienced as depicted by the fourteen Stations of the Cross. Even the rosary which we recited each morning in May began and ended with the crucifix attached at the head of the beads.

My teachers explained that Jesus was the unique God-man and alone capable of effecting salvation. <u>No other person, no matter how holy, could contribute anything substantial to the atoning death of Jesus</u>. Our personal sufferings and even the heroic excesses of sufferings known to the martyrs were all understood as "deserved suffering" (due to our sinful condition) or as "corrective suffering" (by which God wished to discipline those whom he/she loved). Jesus <u>alone</u> was the sinless one. Jesus <u>alone</u> did not deserve to suffer and needed no corrective suffering. His willingness to suffer, therefore, was "on our behalf." He died the excruciating death that was coming to us by virtue of the gravity of our sins. He applied to us the merits of his death so that all who associate with him through faith and baptism have their sins forgiven.

Some form of this atonement theory of redemption has penetrated every major denominational form of Christianity existing today. The net result has been the trivialization of the redemptive efficacy of Jesus' apprenticing his disciples:

(a) Jesus' own active ministry, into which he painstakingly initiated his disciples, is obscured as the locus of redemption. The image of the willing victim on the cross tends to entirely efface the Messiah apprenticing disciples to serve God's cause and the teacher transforming culture with truth-power.

(b) As far as salvation is concerned, Jesus is entirely differentiated from his disciples. The atonement theory forces us to imagine that Jesus is supremely alone and supremely efficacious as the "cause" of human redemption. No disciple can contribute anything essential. The disciples are reduced to being the beneficiaries and the heralds of Jesus' dying on the cross.

(c) Redemption is imagined as a once-and-for-all-time completed affair. The graces merited by Christ only need be applied to historical persons in the courses of time. The saints, the martyrs, the prophets who strenuously brought the Spirit of Jesus to bear upon the sinful structures of each age of the church are not to be recognized as contributing anything to redemption that they had not entirely received from the cross of Christ.

In order to safeguard the redemptive efficacy of Jesus' apprenticing his disciples, I propose to relativize the value and importance of the atonement theory within the Christian tradition. I shall do this, firstly, by showing that the atonement theory has late origins within the pastoral and theological climate of the medieval church. Secondly, I shall examine the texts of Matthew's Gospel which are commonly cited in support of the atonement theory. Not only will these texts be shown to offer no substantial support to a medieval atonement theory, but Matthew's own understanding of the tragic end of Jesus will emerge as an orthodox alternative to the medieval understanding. Thirdly, I shall examine some key texts in the letters of Paul and demonstrate how they can be understood, in their contexts, to offer little support for an atonement theory of redemption. Finally, I will sketch out how Thomas Aquinas incorporated Anselm's atonement theory and how he supplemented and corrected it by using the theological traditions stemming from the Fathers of the Church. My chapter divisions will read as follows:

    A.   The medieval origins of Anselm's atonement theory
    B.   The atonement theory at odds with Matthew's Gospel
    C.   The atonement theory at odds with Paul
    D.   The Thomistic correction of Anselm's doctrine

A.   The Medieval Origins of Anselm's Atonement Theory

For the Jewish followers of Jesus, the cross was unquestionably a hideous instrument of Roman torture. No disciple of Jesus would have fashioned a crucifix as a fitting remembrance of Jesus. In fact it took a solid thousand years before Christians would introduce the cross as a decisive symbol into the sanctuary of their churches. The Christians of the eleventh century had never witnessed a crucifixion. Yet, since their liturgy had gradually become a mime of the passion and death of Jesus, it was fitting that artistic presentations of Jesus hanging on the cross should form the backdrop for the main altar. The Eucharist had obviously shifted its emphasis a long way from the time when it was fellowship meal anticipating eating and drinking with Jesus in the Kingdom of God.

The Gospels and the letter of Paul gave various meanings to the death of Jesus, but none of these meanings coincided with what Christians today commonly regard as the atoning death of Jesus. It is only our recent Christian conditioning that allows us to page through the Scriptures and to find our atonement theories amply supported throughout. The Fathers of the Church, who first interpreted the Scriptures, found therein no uniform interpretation of the death of Jesus. Their interest was principally focused upon the redemptive efficacy of the incarnation. Jesus was principally upheld as the Teacher of Truth, the enfleshed Logos. In the early medieval period, however, Anselm, the Archbishop of Canterbury, was moved by pastoral and theological necessities to bring forward a rationally compelling and juridically contemporary system for establishing the decisive importance of Jesus. The atonement theory, as it now comes down to us, was thus born.

Anselm's theory was ingenious. He discerned the pastoral hazards of imagining (as did some of the Fathers) that a ransom had to be paid to the devil for the release of souls in his servitude. Instead, Anselm used the then-existing terms of jurisprudence and demonstrated that the sins of Adam's children had disrupted the divine order intended by God. The honor of God, therefore, required that either the guilty be punished (by death) or restitution be made. Nothing was owed the devil.

Even the simplest peasant could appreciate Anselm's theme of justice and order. When a peasant commits a crime, no king or lord could hope to uphold justice if they were to simply forgive the offense. Such easy forgiveness would invite disrespect for local regulations and would invite offended parties to seek vengeance privately. Justice was, therefore, required of magistrates and, with the greater force, of the Divine Magistrate.

Adams' sin, Anselm argued, introduces a special complication. A peasant can make restitution for a crime committed against a fellow peasant; yet, a peasant's crime against the king is of another order. Due account must be taken for the nobility of the personage offended. In Adam's case, absolute obedience was owed to his Creator. What might otherwise be a slight offense among equals (i.e., the unlawful eating) becomes an act of treason before the Almighty God. And, in the case of treason, no restitution can be made by a peasant, so justice requires that his/her life be forfeited so as to discourage this outrageous crime in others. Furthermore, since a man implicates his whole family in such a crime, all his sons and daughters must also be accounted as participating in the selfsame subversive inclinations.

From within this predicament, Anselm made his decisive appeal to the importance of Jesus. Being fully human, Jesus is fully linked with the treasonous race of Adam. As true God, however, Jesus is juridically an equal with the King of the Universe and can make restitution for any crime. Anselm assumed that the Son was suitably disposed by the Father himself to make restitution for the tyranny of Adam's race. It remained only to determine what suitable restitution was to be made.

Would Jesus' whole life of loyalty to God suffice as a restitution for worldwide treason? "No," said Anselm, "for every rational creature owes this obedience to God."[1] Something not strictly required must be done. But what? Then Anselm went on to show that Jesus' personal sinlessness freed him from the death penalty. Thus, if Jesus should freely suffer and die "for God's honor," this would constitute such an infinite act of loyalty that infinite merit would be his due. Yet, in so far as Jesus bears an organic oneness with the treasonous ones, he might freely transfer to them the merits due to his own deed. And so it was done.

Anselm compresses the compelling juridical sense of his atonement theory into a single parable which runs as follows:

> For suppose that there is a king, and that the whole population of one of his

cities -- with the sole exception of one man, who nonetheless belongs to their race -- has sinned against him, so that none of them can escape condemnation to death. But suppose too that the one innocent man is in such favor with the king that he is able -- and so kindly disposed toward the guilty that he is willing -- to reconcile all who believe in his plan by some service, sure to please the king greatly, which he will perform on a day set by the king's decision. And since all who need to be reconciled cannot meet on that day, the king grants absolution from every past fault, because of the greatness of this service, to everyone who either before or after that day confesses his readiness to seek pardon through the deed done that day, and to ratify the agreement then made. And if they happen to sin again after this pardon, he is ready to grant them pardon again because of the efficacy of this agreement, if they are willing to make due satisfaction and then amend their conduct.[2]

The compelling impact of Anselm's theory was so great that it made its way into the standard manuals of teaching and of preaching everywhere. The fact remains, however, that prior to the thirteenth century, no such single-minded perspective on the death of Jesus was accepted within Christendom.

Some form of this atonement theory of redemption has penetrated into nearly every denominational form of Christianity existing today. The sermons and the catechisms of the Protestant Reformers embraced this doctrine of redemption. Meanwhile, the Catholic counter-reformation codified its own variation of this doctrine at the Council of Trent. Each denomination has its own preferred formulations, to be sure, yet in each the same basic rationale for redemption persists. Note, for example, how each of the following three denominational catechisms describes redemption/election in terms of Jesus' atoning death:

(1)   Q: What is meant by Redemption?
       A: By the Redemption is meant that Jesus Christ, as the Redeemer of

(2)   Q:
(3)   Q:

the whole human race, offered his sufferings and death to God as a fitting sacrifice in satisfaction for the sins of men [women], and regained for them the right to be children of God and heirs of heaven.

(2) Q: What is your only comfort, in life and in death?
A: That I belong -- body and soul, in life and in death -- not to myself but to my faithful Savior, Jesus Christ, who at the cost of his own blood has fully paid for all my sins and has completely freed me from the dominion of the devil . . . .

(3) Q: What do we confess and acknowledge regarding election?
A: That [the] same eternal God and Father . . . appointed him [Jesus Christ] to be our head, our brother, our pastor, and the great bishop of our souls. But since the opposition between the justice of God and our sins was such . . . , it behooved the Son of God to descend unto us and take himself a body of our body . . . . Further, it behooved the Messiah and Redeemer to be true God and true man, because he was able to undergo the punishment of our transgressions and to present himself in the presence of his Father's judgment, as in our stead, to suffer for our transgression and disobedience and by death to overcome him that was the author of death . . . .[3]

These catechisms informed the religious sentiments and guided the theological judgments of Christians everywhere. It was only with the advent of modern biblical exegesis that some Christians for the first time were able to perceive that the New Testament writers had religious sentiments and theological judgments of their own which did not neatly harmonize with the catechisms of a later era.

B. The Atonement Theory at Odds with Matthew's Gospel

When one takes up and examines the Gospel of Matthew (or any other Gospel, for that matter), it is immediately apparent how few texts can be construed as supporting the atonement theory. If such a doctrine were indeed so important and so decisive for understanding Jesus, one must inquire why it receives so scant attention within the Gospels themselves.

Matthew's Gospel offers three texts (Matt 1:21, 20:28, 26:28) which have been widely acclaimed as specifying Matthew's adherence to the atonement theory. In this section, each of these texts will be carefully examined in the context of Matthew's overall presentation of Jesus. As a result of this investigation, not only will Anselm's doctrine begin to fade from Matthew's texts, but Matthew's own orthodox alternative will begin to shine through. Our ears will then again hear Matthew's message without being blocked by the thundering roar of the cumulative voices speaking for Anselm.

The first text habitually claimed to support an atonement theory is found on the lips of the angel who brings a divine message to Joseph in his dreams:

> The angel of the Lord appeared to him in a dream and said, "Joseph son of David, do not be afraid to take Mary home as your wife . . . . She will give birth to a son and you must name him Jesus, because he is the one who is to save his people from their sins" (1:20-21).

The act of naming of a child frequently has the force of assigning a person's lifelong destiny. In itself, "Jesus" is a common Hebrew name (Jesus = <u>Iesous</u> in Greek = <u>Yehoshua</u> in Hebrew = Joshua). The name means "YHWH saves." The angel deliberately explains that "Jesus" is a fitting name "because he is the one who is to save his people from their sins" (1:21).

As seen through Anselm's eyes, the very naming of Jesus makes it clear that he is "the one who is to save his people" through his atoning death. "From their sins" refers to the religious nature of Jesus' salvation which merits forgiveness for the cumulative human rebellion against God from Adam onward.

As seen through Matthew's eyes, however, some account must be made of the following clues: (1) Matthew's entire Gospel makes not the slightest mention of Adam or of Adam's sin. (2) Matthew does not either state or imply that the saving work of Jesus is to be accomplished on the cross. (3) Matthew uses the verb "to save" (<u>sozein</u>) sixteen times. Not a single instance is linked with Jesus dying on the cross.

Special care must be taken in examining the words whereby the chief priests, the scribes, and the elders mock Jesus while he is dying: "He <u>has saved</u> others; he <u>cannot save</u> himself" (27:42). Their mocking implies (a) that Jesus has saved others from the destructive consequences of their sins and (b) that Jesus, none the less, is powerless to save himself from the penalty which he is now suffering as a heretical prophet and enemy of true religion. Through a subtle innuendo, Matthew may be suggesting that the very terms in which the judges of Jesus mock him serve also <u>to accredit him</u>: "He saved others." If so, the very tense of the verb indicates that the saving activity has already been accomplished. Matthew's text does not say, "He claims he <u>will save</u> others [at his death]; he cannot even now save himself." At what point, then, does Matthew regard the saving activity to have taken place?

When one examines the detailed interest which Matthew devotes to the public ministry of Jesus, there can be little doubt that Matthew regards the whole space of this ministry as fulfilling his destiny "to save his people." Matthew presents John the Baptizer as warning the people of the "retribution that is coming" (3:8) and as inviting them to undertake a soul-searching baptism of conversion. After John's arrest, Jesus undertakes to extend this passionate cry of the Bapitzer to the lakeside towns of Galilee (4:12-17). From that time onward, Matthew presents Jesus as the one who pleads God's cause to "the lost sheep of the House of Israel" (10:6, 15:24). Those troubled with demonic hinderances are cured. The blind see; the deaf hear. Yet, Jesus can do little to cure the blindness and deafness of the scribes and Pharisees who were popularly recognized as the divinely appointed guides and healers of the people. In contrast, Jesus makes inroads even among the hardened social outcasts: the tax collectors and the prostitutes. The irony is that such as these become "salt of the earth" and "light of the world" (5:13) -- they make "their way into the kingdom of God before you [the priests and elders]" (21:31).

How the Atonement Theory Trivializes Apprenticeship 49

Matthew clearly regards Jesus' pastoral ferment as spelling out his God-given destiny "to save his people from their sins" (1:21). Our first text, therefore, offers no support for Anselm. How Matthew regards the tragic end of Jesus will appear shortly.

The second text, the one much used to support Anselm, reads as follows:

> You know that among the pagans the rulers lord it over them, and their great men make their authority felt. This is not to happen among you. No; anyone who wants to be great among you must be your servant, and anyone who wants to be first among you must be your slave, just as the Son of Man came not to be served but to serve and to give his life as a ransom for many (20:25-28).

The key word in this text is "ransom" (<u>lytron</u>). This word only appears once in Matthew and only two other times in the New Testament: Mark 10:45 and 1 Tim 2:6. A "ransom" designates that service or payment which effects the release of a prisoner-of-war or someone sold into slavery to pay outstanding debts (TDNT IV:340). Both prisoners-of-war and debt-slavery were common in Matthew's era. In one of the Gospel parables, explicit reference is made to the debtor who "had no means of paying, so his master gave orders that he should be sold, together with his wife and children and all his possessions, to meet the debt" (18:25). In the text under examination, however, it remains to be determined <u>in what</u> the ransom consists, <u>to whom</u> and <u>for whom</u> it is given.

The text specifies that "the Son of Man came . . . to give his life." When read through Anselm's eyes, this is interpreted to mean that "Jesus came to die." His death may then be understood as a ransom in so far as his brothers and sisters are released from the eternal death that was their due.

The expression "to give his life (<u>psychen</u>)" does not necessarily refer to Jesus' death. Matthew designates the actual death of Jesus by the expression "yielded up his spirit (<u>pneuma</u>)" (27:50). John's Gospel exhibits the stronger expression "to lay down his life (<u>psychen</u>) for the sheep" (John 10:11 & 15); yet, from its context, the expression refers to holding one's ground against wolves at the risk of one's life.

When the expression "to give his life" is examined in its particular context, a definite parallelism is implied:

> . . . just as the Son of Man came not to be served but to serve and [just as the Son of Man came] to give his life as a ransom for many (20:28).

Jesus' immediate concern here is to defuse the rivalry among his disciples. To effect this, Jesus points to his own example: (1) the dedicated service which he offers his disciples in apprenticing them and in making them great in the kingdom of heaven and (2) the giving of his life-energies (psyche) in winning the blind and deaf hearts of many back to the true service of YHWH. This latter self-giving may be construed as "a ransom" in precisely the same way as Philo, writing in the same period, could say, "Every wise man is a ransom (lytron) [i.e., a means of deliverance] for the bad" (TDNT IV:340 n.9). At best, Matthew's text might be stretched to say that he envisions the death of Jesus as the extreme of his servitude; but, even in this case, Matthew's emphasis would fall solidly upon the heroic service which carries the tangible value of effecting the ransom of the lost sheep of the House of Israel.

The juxtaposition of dedicated service and death is amply illustrated by the parable of the wicked tenants (21:33-43). "When vintage time drew near he [the landowner] sent his servants to the tenants to collect his produce" (21:34). While the servants are endeavoring to collect the produce, they are seized by the tenants and abused. Some are even killed. But the produce still remains to be collected and returned to the landowner. Thus, the landowner sends out "a larger number" (21:36) of servants. They suffer the same fate. At this point, the landowner sends his son with a new assurance: "They will respect my son" (21:37). The same fate befalls him. In the end, the landowner is moved to "bring those wretches [the tenants] to a wretched end and lease the vineyard to other tenants who will deliver the produce to him when the season arrives" (21:39).

Biblical scholars such as Joachim Jeremias persuasively demonstrate that this parable has been retained and modified by Matthew because it so vividly specifies the mission and the fate of Jesus.[4] In fact, this parable almost becomes an allegory. The vineyard suggests the House of Israel which YHWH planted and loved (Isa 5). The servants are sent to collect the harvest -- a theme which Jesus himself used to describe the task awaiting his disciples (9:37). The two separate missions suggest the earlier and the later prophets -- with "stoning" (21:35) being the traditional fate of those servants of YHWH (23;37; 2 Chron 24:21; Heb 11:37). "The son" who is also "the heir" can be easily identified with Jesus.

When examined quite attentively, Matthew's parable has little to recommend it to someone fixed upon Anselm's doctrine:

In the first place, "the son" has a mission which is indistinguishable from that of the earlier servant-prophets. This harmonizes well with Matthew's presentation of Jesus' prophetic activity (which Chapter IV will spell out), but it hardly favors Anselm's depiction of the unique mission of the Son of God.

In the second place, the suffering and the death of YHWH's servants (including his son) are not assigned any particular value whatsoever. Their deaths are ugly and violent. Their mission was not to die but to bring the harvest of righteous deeds to YHWH.

In the third place, one must be struck by the great forbearance of the landowner. Unlike the God of Anselm who disinherits Adam and all his children on the basis of a single act of treason, the landowner seems more bent upon yet persuading the tenants to act justly toward him. In fact, the sending of his son in the third round is motivated by the conviction that they will come around: "They will respect my son [even though they did not know how to respect my servants]" (21:37). The drama of redemption is herein spelled out in the patient and progressive "sendings" by the landowner. Anselm could only deplore the softheaded forbearance and the misguided justice of the landowner in the face of repeated acts of treason.

In the fourth place, Matthew's parable decidedly presents the <u>failure</u> of redemption. The servants are killed; the tenants never come around. Far from being redeemed, the excessive crimes of the tenants move the landowner to anger so that "he will bring those wretches to a wretched end" (21:41). How remote this is from Anselm's assurance that the merits of Jesus' death can even suffice to pardon his murderers.

Finally, in the fifth place, the climax of Matthew's parable is directed toward a reversal of leadership: (a) "the stone rejected by the builders . . . became the keystone" (21:42) and (b) "the kingdom of God will be taken from you [chief priests and scribes] and given to a people who will produce its fruit" (21:43). These phrases would be manifestly apparent to someone in Matthew's community as alluding (a) to how Jesus, who was rejected by the divinely authorized religious establishment of Israel, was ultimately exalted by God and (b) to how God's cause will be given into the charge of Jesus' disciples. Anselm's parable of redemption knows nothing of this revolutionary transformation in Israel's leadership.

In sum, therefore, the character of Matthew's parable clearly indicates that it could not have originated with anyone who held Anselm's assessment of Jesus' death. Only by glossing over the five points of discontinuity mentioned above could such a parable even be upheld by a community guided by Anselm's doctrine.

Matthew's parable may even be extended so as to provide a possible meaning for how the death of God's servants can function as "a ransom for many." Let me explain. The parable depicts a corrupt religious establishment. Under such circumstances, the just are penalized and harassed while those who go along with their leaders are rendered "twice as fit for hell" (23:15). God endeavors to redeem this situation by inspiring his/her prophets to win back the hearts of the corrupt. The corrupt religious leaders, meanwhile, sanction the use of naked power so as to silence these "protestors". Their propaganda also justifies this violence by showing that the servants of God are "false prophets" and the "enemies of religion." Jesus enters this milieu. His ministry is also obstructed by the religious leaders "who shut up the kingdom of heaven in men's [women's] faces, neither going in yourselves nor allowing others to go in who want to" (23:13). He, too, is defamed and liquidated. The death of these innocent ones cries out to heaven for vindication (23:35-36). In time, God is moved by these cries and destroys the corrupt. Leadership is turned over to the just, and the true prophets/servants of God are finally recognized for who they were. They failed at the task that God had given them; yet, their blood moved God to liberate his/her people from the corrupt religious establishment and to vindicate the saints.[5] By extending the use of "ransom," the blood of the prophets may be understood as serving as the ransom which liberates the just remnant. In this sense Matthew may understand Jesus "to give his life as a ransom for many" (20:28).

Even should Matthew allow this extended meaning for "ransom" based upon his parable, he would still allow little support for an atonement theory. The parable makes it clear that the servants of God are not using their

How the Atonement Theory Trivializes Apprenticeship 53

deaths to substitute for the deserved death of "the sinners" or that their deaths effect the forgiveness of sins. Thus, any ransom theory derived from Matthew must necessarily differ from Anselm's theory.

The third text used to support the atonement theory is found in Jesus' blessing over the cup at the Last Supper:

> Then he took a cup, and when he had returned thanks he gave it to them [his disciples]. "Drink all of you from this," he said, "for this is my blood, the blood of the covenant which is to be poured out for many for the forgiveness of sins. From now on, I tell you, I shall not drink wine until the day I drink the new wine with you in the kingdom of my Father" (26:28-29).

As seen from Anselm's perspective, Jesus here testifies that he looks forward to the shedding of his blood so as to make the restitution necessary for the forgiveness of sins.

From Matthew's text, however, the blood is clearly to be identified as "the blood of the covenant." It is not "the blood of atonement" nor even the "the blood of martyrs."

This is the only occurrence of the word "covenant" (diatheke) in Matthew's Gospel. Standing by itself, it has no apparent sense or integrated meaning within the rest of the Gospel. It is only in the Letter to the Hebrews that one finds any consistent, extended association of Jesus' blood with a covenant. Seventeen out of the total of thirty-three occurrences of "covenant" in the New Testament are found in this letter. It is possible, consequently, that the theology of the letter to the Hebrews can provide an insight into this isolated (and, perhaps, borrowed) expression in Matthew's Gospel.

The key text in Hebrews is the following:

> Even the earlier covenant needed something to be killed in order to take effect, and [this explains] why, after Moses had announced all the commandments of the Law [Torah] to the people, he took the calves' blood, the goat's blood, and some water, and with these he sprinkled the book [of the Torah] itself and all the people . . . saying

> as he did so: "This is the blood of the covenant that God has laid down for you."
>
> After that, he sprinkled the tent and all the liturgical vessels with blood in the same way. In fact, according to the Law [Torah] almost everything has to be purified with blood; and if there is no shedding of blood, there is no remission [of sin] (Heb 9: 19-23).

It is important here to note that Hebrews does not present Jesus as a sacrifice killed as a sin-offering. In the Jewish tradition, no human being could be killed as a sacrifice;[6] only specified animals could function in this way.

The Letter to the Hebrews envisions Jesus' death only by way of obtaining the necessary blood with which to establish a new covenant which was to replace the old covenant of Moses. If blood was necesary for consecrating those persons and things which were bound to God in the old covenant; then, the Letter to the Hebrews argues, the blood of Jesus must have been poured out to consecrate the new covenant. In the former case, it sufficed that the blood was sprinkled as a sign that it would "restore the holiness of their outward lives" (Heb 9:13). Now, however, the sacramental "blood" of Jesus is drunk as a sign that it "can purify our inner self from dead actions" (Heb 9:14).

This brief examination of Hebrews gives some clues as to what Jesus' blessing over the cup might have originally meant. The fact remains, however, that Matthew's Gospel does not support the theology of Hebrews outside of this one isolated text. Quite to the contrary, one might suppose that Matthew would have opposed the theology of Hebrews on at least three points: (1) Matthew resists the notion that Jesus has consecrated a "new covenant" and insists, rather, that Jesus has brought to light the authentic sense of the one covenant made with Moses (5:17-19). (2) The forgiveness of sins was practiced in Matthew's community without any appeal to the blood of Jesus. Seemingly Matthew's preferred appeal is to the example of Jesus (9:2), to the instructions of Jesus (18:21-35), and to the prayer style of Jesus (6:12-15). Each of these appeals implies that the very doing of the Torah of Jesus brings with it the forgiveness of sins prior to and independent of the death of Jesus. (3) Hebrews maintains that "although he was Son, he learnt to obey through suffering" (Heb 5:8) -- suffering being the mode of discipline that every father extends to the son whom he loves (Heb 12:5-13). Nowhere does Matthew present suffering in this light. Such "suffering" has little in common with the violent shedding of blood which cries out to heaven for vindication.

In sum, the more that one relies upon Hebrews to make sense of the blessing over the cup, the more one becomes convinced that Matthew himself does not support the theology found within Hebrews. I am led to conjecture, therefore, that Matthew has embraced this blessing over the cup as having an established place within the Jesus-tradition. It is even possible that this blessing is habitually used within the communal meals of Jesus' disciples. Therein <u>the sharing of the cup is understood as consecrating those who drink it to serve God's cause in the way which Jesus showed them</u>. Being consecrated to follow Jesus, one's sins are forgiven -- forgotten - wiped clean from the memory. Meanwhile, in another community setting, the blessing over the cup may have sparked a rich set of theological reflections. Out of such reflections, the Letter to the Hebrews was constructed. Matthew, however, most probably knew nothing of them.

In review, three texts have been examined. Each of them represented what, at first glance, would seem to be support for the atonement theory of Anselm. Upon closer inspection, however, when the texts were examined within the larger context of Matthew's Gospel, the alternative meaning intended by Matthew appeared. At times Matthew's meanings contradicted Anselm's; at other times, they were complementary. In no instance, however, was there complete congruence between Matthew's intent and Anselm's interpretation.

Lacking any single supporting text, appeals are sometimes made to the fact that the largest narrative segment in each of the Synoptic Gospels is the so-called "Passion Narrative." This seemingly points to the enormous importance which the primitive church placed upon the death of Jesus. Close examination of the Passion Narrative, however, shows it to be relatively disinterested in the passion as such for it focuses on the conduct of Jesus prior to and during the time of his interrogations. Thus, I would judge that the primitive church placed great importance upon vindicating Jesus by describing the course of his interrogations. In Matthew's account, for instance, one finds important indicators of Jesus's innocence: (a) Judas returns the silver coins confessing, "I have betrayed innocent blood" (27:4); (b) the wife of Pilate sends to her husband the message, "Have nothing to do with that just man" (27:19); (c) Pilate washes his hands attesting, "I am

innocent of this man's blood" (27:24). Meanwhile, the
distorted justice and the mocking cruelty of the chief
priests and scribes is heightened. Only a few brief verses
are given over to describing the crucifixion itself. Each
of these verses are factual and restrained. Nothing
suggests that this is the focal moment of the entire
narrative. The text, at this point, remains curiously
silent about the redemption of the world, the atonement for
sins, the reopening of the gates of heaven. These "events"
figured strongly in the religious imagination of Anselm and
his followers; but, in sober truth, the Synoptics do not
immediately evoke or support such imaginings.

The closer the one examines the events surrounding
the death of Jesus, the more disconcerting do the clues
become. According to Anselm, Jesus' death on the cross is
the brightest moment within the whole salvation history.
Matthew, however, considers it the darkest: "From the
sixth hour there was darkness over all the land until the
ninth hour" (27:45).

I know not what sense Anselm could make of Jesus
heart-rendering cry from the cross: "My God, my God, why
have you deserted me?" (27:46) This cry seems appropriate
in the mouth of "the beloved son" who had hoped to succeed
in the mission of his Father. It makes little sense in the
mouth of Anselm's Jesus who is supposed to appreciate his
present sufferings as the glorious moment in which the sins
of the whole world are being atoned for. Should not such a
Jesus cry out: "My God, my God, what a terrible price do I
pay for the sins of the world!"

At the moment of Jesus' death, my Baltimore
Catechism presented a sketch of the gates of heaven as
being thrown open after having been securely locked
following the sin of our first parents. This correctly
presents Anselm's imagination. For Matthew, however, the
moment of Jesus' death is marked by the rending of the veil
of the Temple (27:51). Most scholars have interpreted
Matthew's symbolism as suggesting that the crime of the
priests is so grievous that God abandons the holy of holies
-- tearing through the Temple veil as he leaves. Such an
interpretation fails to take into account that the
community of Jesus' disciples had the practice of meeting
daily in the Temple for prayer and for training by the
Apostles (Acts 2:46, 3:1, 5:42). To correctly interpret
Matthew's image, one has to be aware of the modes of
expressing grief then current among the Jewish people.
When a father of Jesus' day would hear of the death of a
son, he would invariably rend his garment by grabbing it at
the neck and tearing it from top to bottom.[7] This is
precisely the gesture suggested by the particulars of

Matthew's text: "the veil of the Temple was torn in two from top to bottom" (27:51). In truth, God is Spirit. Symbolically, however, the presence of God within the holy of holies was rendered secure from prying eyes by the veil which surrounded that place. As such, the veil conceals the "nakedness" of God. It is this "garment" which the grief-striken Father of Jesus tears from top to bottom when he hears the final death-cry of his beloved son. Even for the Father, therefore, the death of Jesus is bitter tragedy and heartfelt grief. Matthew's God provides not the slightest hint that the torturous death of the Innocent One has some inherent redeeming value.[8] With even greater force, therefore, Matthew's God would never suspect that the death of the Innocent One is the long-awaited redeeming moment around which the whole of history revolves.

C. The Atonement Theory at Odds with Paul

If Matthew provides surprisingly few texts which have been construed to support an atonement theory, this lack is surely corrected by Paul's letters which provide nearly a hundred such texts. Up until the turn of this century, all of these texts were interpreted through Anselm's eyes and gave tremendous weight to the various interpretations of Anselm's doctrine. Today, however, this situation no longer persists. Numerous Pauline scholars have endeavored to demonstrate before their colleagues that most or all of Paul's references to Jesus' efficacious death not only do not support Anselm but offer alternative understandings quite at variance with an atonement theory. In this section, I cannot hope to review all of the Pauline texts involved. By examining some few key texts and themes, however, the diligent reader will be able to capture something of the changing mood within Pauline scholarship.

Unlike the Gospels, Paul does make explicit reference to Adam's role in contaminating the human race with sin:

> Sin entered the world through one man, and through sin death, and thus death has spread through the whole human race because everyone has sinned . . . .
> Adam prefigured the One to come . . . .
> If it is certain that death reigned

> over everyone as the consequence of one man's fall, it is even more certain that one man, Jesus Christ, will cause everyone to reign in life who receives the free gift that he does not deserve, of being made righteous (Rom 5:12-17).

As seen through Anselm's eyes, this text assigns the same juridic universality to both Adam's sin and Jesus' obedient death on the cross.

The actual text of Paul, however, does not imply a <u>juridic</u> universality to Adam's fall. Rather, Paul begins with the empirical observation that "death" reigns universally because it is apparent that "everyone has sinned." Paul then pushes this empirical observation backward in time so as to point up the tremendous influence that Adam's fall has had upon his children. If this establishes the contagious influence of "death'; then, Paul argues, "it is even more certain that one man, Jesus Christ, <u>will</u> cause <u>everyone</u> to reign in life" (Rom 5:17). The future tense here points to the expected force and scope of Jesus' influence <u>in the future</u>. At the moment, Paul can perceive how the righteousness of Jesus has spread within the scattered Christian communities of the Empire. "All persons" (Rom. 5:18b), however, have not yet fallen under the influence of Jesus. But if "death" has proved itself so marvelously influential, how much more "life." Just give it time!

So understood, Paul's text suggests nothing of the juridic mentality which is necessary to understand how the sin of Adam is applied to his children and how the merits of Jesus are applied to those "reborn" into his family. The Adam speculation of Paul may have inspired Anselm, but one can hardly conclude that Anselm has caught the original perspective of Paul.

Another set of difficulties arise when it comes to the interpretation of Paul's sacrificial language. Two typical texts are the following:

> Christ, our passover, has been sacrificed; let us celebrate the feast, then, by getting rid of all the old yeast of evil and wickedness, having only the unleavened bread of sincerity and truth (1 Cor 5:7-8).

> For anyone who is in Christ, there is a new creation; the old creation has gone . . . . In other words, God in

> Christ was reconciling the world to himself [herself], not holding men's [women's] faults against them . . . . For our sake God made the sinless one into sin [i.e., a sin offering], so that in him we might become the goodness of God (2 Cor 5:17-21).

Texts such as these make it quite clear that Paul finds it entirely natural to describe Jesus as "the pascal lamb" or as "a sin offering." When such terms are interpreted within the atonement mentality, the Jewish perspective is entirely hidden under inappropriate notions: (a) that the sacrifices of the Old Testament prefigure Christ's sacrifice on the cross and (b) that the efficacy of sacrifices lies within "vicarious suffering." Such notions are quite foreign to Paul's Jewish mentality.[9]

In the first text (1 Cor 5:7-8), Christ is called the passover lamb. Within a Jewish understanding, the passover lamb prepares for the exodus and has no relationship to a sin offering. This is clear from what Paul suggests are the consequences of Jesus having been sacrificed: (a) "getting rid of all the old yeast of evil and wickedness" and (b) eating "only the unleavened bread of sincerity and truth" (1 Cor 5:8). Herein Paul takes the external preparations for the passover celebration and assigns them an associated life-giving disposition based upon the character of Jesus Christ, "our passover" (1 Cor 5:7). Paul then continues this theme by presenting Christ as the one who leads his diciples to make their exodus from the company of sinners (1 Cor 5:9-13).

In the second text (2 Cor 5:17-21), the theme is God's work. "It is all God's work" (2 Cor 5:18): (a) the new creation, (b) reconciling the world and forgiving sins, (c) making the sinless one into a sin offering. Some English translations persist in overlooking the fact that the Hebrew word for "sin" and "sin offering" is precisely the same. God does not make the sinless one into "sin," but into a "sin offering." When Paul suggests that God makes Jesus into a sin offering, there is not suggestion of human sacrifice. Nor does Paul suggest a vicarious suffering which atones for sin. Rather, Paul embraces the common Jewish notion that the entire rite of the Temple sin offering effects a reconciliation. Thus, it follows that the entire work of Christ is to be regarded as functioning as a sin offering. And God is using the entire work of Christ "so that in him we might become [one with] the goodness of God" (2 Cor 5:21).

That Paul does not envision the shedding of blood when speaking of Christ as a sin offering can be further attested by Paul's characterization of the Christian life as a "holy sacrifice":

> Think of God's mercies, my brothers, and worship him, I beg you, in a way that is worthy of thinking beings, by offering your living bodies (<u>somata</u>) as a holy sacrifice, truly pleasing to God. Do not model yourself on the behavior of the world around you, but let your behavior change, modelled by your new mind (Rom 12:1-2).

In another place, Paul regards his own ministry of the Word as a "sacrificial service" (Rom 15:15). Obviously no shedding of blood is implied in these instances. Rather, Paul is making use of the <u>spiritualization</u> of sacrifice which had already begun with the prophets.[10] Such spiritualization meant a distrust of ceremonial action and a renewed emphasis upon following God's way with deeds of loving kindness and justice. Thus, Paul frequently calls the Christian community to remember that it is "God's Temple" (1 Cor 3:16-17, 6:19; 2 Cor 6:16) which mediates God's holy presence in the world. By way of summary, I offer the conclusion reached by Robert Daly, S.J., in his investigation, <u>The Origins of the Christian Doctrine of Sacrifice</u>:

> For the New Testament church, Christian sacrifice was not a cultic but rather an ethical idea, an idea that could include prayer and worship in the formal sense, but was not constituted by them. It was centered not in a formal act of cultic or external ceremonial worship but rather in the everyday practical life of Christian virtue, in the apostolic and charitable work of being a good Christian, of being "for others" as Christ was "for us." It was a totally free and loving response, carried out on the practical level of human existence, to Christ's act of self-giving love.[11]

There are still other texts in Paul which specifically present Jesus as <u>dying for our sake</u>. Such texts do not make reference to sacrifice and cannot be associated with the texts discussed above. A typical text in this new category would be the following:

> It is not easy to die even for a good man -- though of course for someone really worthy, a man might be prepared to die -- but what proves that God loves us is that Christ dies for us while we were still sinners. Having died to make us righteous, is it likely that he would now fail to save us from God's anger? (Rom 5: 7-9).

What does Paul mean when he states that Christ "died to make us righteous?" To this Anselm's doctrine of vicarious atonement provides a simple and ready answer.

Paul himself, however, in his letter to the Galatians spells out the meaning of Christ's death in quite a different manner. The setting for Paul's letter is the disturbing practice of some well-meaning Christians who have reintroduced the Torah of Moses by way of supplementing the Way of Jesus. Paul will have none of this. In contrast to Matthew's Gospel, it is strictly an either/or situation: "faith in Christ" or "fidelity to the Torah" (Gal 2:16).[12] Paul clinches his position by declaring: "If the Torah can justify us, there is no point in the death of Jesus" (Gal 2:21).

How does Paul envision the death of Jesus as doing away with the Torah? He argues in this fashion: (1) The Torah makes an absolute claim upon all Jews and all Gentile converts in so far as it represents YHWH's guidance to his chosen people: "Cursed be everyone who does not perservere in observing everything prescribed in the book of the Torah" (Gal 3:10 = Deut 27:26). (2) Jesus, however, did not rely upon the Torah but acted with the liberty which Abraham knew prior to the giving of the Torah: "He put his faith in God, and this faith was considered as justifying him" (Gal 3:6 = Gen 15:6). (3) By so doing, Jesus was condemned by those who upheld the absolute claim of the Torah. He died cursed and excommunicated. God, however, stepped in and reversed this curse by undoing the death sentence; God raised him to life. This intervention establishes that God now favors the Way of Jesus and overturns those who suppose that the Torah of Moses was to be binding forever.

With Jesus approved, the Gentiles can follow Jesus' way of righteousness without becoming Jews. With Jesus approved, even Jews can follow Jesus' way of righteousness without regard for the Torah of their ancestors. Thus Paul can say:

> Christ redeemed us from the curse of the Torah by being cursed for our sake, since scripture says: <u>Cursed be everyone who is hanged on a tree</u>. This was done so that in Christ Jesus the blessing of Abraham might include the pagans, and so that through faith we might receive the promised spirit (Gal 3:13-14).

Paul is quite realistic here. If Jesus pioneered a new way of righteousness and it was found heretical according to divinely-given standards, then all the disciples of Jesus fall under the same condemnation which Jesus received. Only if God takes a decisive stand for Jesus by undoing his death sentence can Jesus be definitively favored over and against the Torah of Moses.

Paul envisions two elements in the death-resurrection of Jesus which Anselm entirely overlooks: (1) It is not sufficient that Jesus suffer an undeserved death, as Anselm claimed. The death of Jesus can be efficacious for overturning the Torah if and only if Jesus is judged as an enemy of God <u>according to the Torah</u>. Consequently, if Jesus had been condemned to death only under civil law, then the resurrection would only have overturned the civil law which judged him and leave the Torah of Moses untouched in its binding power. (2) It is not sufficient that the resurrection be depicted as Jesus coming back to life by his own divine power. For Paul such a resurrection would amount to a self-vindication and leave the question of Jesus' position with respect to the Father forever unanswered. Yet, in Paul's perspective, Jesus has no natural immortality. His death means extinction, and the curse on his life means eternal extinction, i.e, no resurrection on the last day. For a Jewish thinker, "resurrection" can only mean that God has created Jesus anew from his fond remembrance of him. Moreover, the unexpected and premature resurrection of Jesus can only mean that he is to have the first place in the world to come, i.e., in the new creation established after the universal resurrection of the just. Resurrection, consequently, functions for Paul as vindication of the person of Jesus and establishes his Way as the righteousness of God's future kingdom on earth.[13]

Jesus' death does imply a certain "vicarious significance" but not of the kind that Anselm envisioned. Just as the pioneer in a new enterprise can be said to bear a burden of anguish and risk that his/her followers do not suffer; so, too, Jesus can be called the pioneer of the new salvation. According to Paul's logic, Jesus tested the new righteousness unto the death of the cross so that all who follow him might walk in security. Wolfhart Pannenberg expresses this in apt terms:

> Jesus dies the death that all [especially all his disciples] have incurred, the death of a blasphemer. In this sense he dies for us, for our sins [against the Torah]. Of course, this does not mean that we no longer have to die. But it does not mean that no one else has to die in the complete rejection in which Jesus died. Jesus' death meant his exclusion from community with the God whose coming kingdom he proclaimed. He dies as one expelled, expelled by the entire weight of the divine law [the Torah of Moses], excluded from the nearness of the God in whose nearness he had known himself to be in a unique way the messenger of the imminent Kingdom of God. No one else must die this death of eternal damnation, to the extent that he has community with Jesus. Whoever is bound up with Jesus no longer dies alone . . . . divorced from community with God and his future salvation.[14]

In sum, Paul understands "faith in Jesus Christ" to mean following his footsteps in the security that YHWH will not use the Torah against Jesus' disciples at the final judgment. "Faith in Jesus Christ" further means that Jews and Gentiles are on an equal footing when it comes to embracing holiness and living in expectation of the blessing of YHWH's future kingdom.

Bringing this section to a close, it can be surmised from the few examples given that Pauline scholarship has indeed uncovered patterns of thought which are quite divergent from Anselm's doctrine. The alternative explanations offered in this section only represent a very partial selection of those voices which are contending to break Paul free of the long-established grip of atonement theories.[15] Many living scholars, needless to say, continue to read most or all of Paul's letters as unambiguously sustaining Anselm's doctrine or some variation thereof. For our purposes here, it suffices to consider some viable alternatives so as to enable the reader to conclude that Anselm was not the definitive interpreter of Pauline thought.

D.   The Thomistic Correction of Anselm's Doctrine

The atonement theory of Anselm, Archbishop of Canterbury, spread from England to the Continent and took root among the theologians of the famous University at Paris. Here the atonement theory was disputed and modified. As a result many versions of the atonement theory were upheld simultaneously by the various theological scholars of the day. Of paramount importance was the opinion formulated by Thomas Aquinas (d. 1274), the Dominican friar whose synthesis, The Summa Theologica, became the most widely accepted presentation of Catholic doctrine in later centuries. The formulations of Thomas are very instructive because they indicate how the Fathers of the Church (esp. Augustine) were used to correct the imbalance and excesses of Anselm. Unfortunately the corrective measures of Thomas seldom made their way into the sermons and catechisms of later centuries. Even the Catholic Baltimore Catechism preferred the simplicity of Anselm over the nuanced sophistication of Thomas. My purpose in this section, therefore, will be to sketch out how Thomas corrected Anselm using the traditions from the Fathers. Such corrective measures would seemingly be imperative for using Anselm today.

When Thomas attempted to integrate Augustine (d. 430) and Anselm (d. 1109), he was faced with two divergent theologies that had been fashioned out of vastly different cultural and pastoral settings. Augustine was a convert who painfully came to Christianity by way of securing his lifelong quest for Truth. Augustine rightly hailed Jesus as the Great Persuader who exposed the foolishness of idolatry and the vanity of the philosophers. In contrast, Anselm was raised by a Christian family living in a nominally Christian world order held together by the bonds of personal fealty. In the absence of contending sects promising divine salvation, Jesus could hardly any longer appear as the Divine Persuader, and the passionate quest for Truth could hardly provoke the experience of salvation tasted by Augustine in his day. In Anselm's world it made much more sense to talk of Jesus as the peasant-lord who undertook a heroic service so as to vindicate the honor of his Father (the Lord of All) and to atone for the high treason of Adam's race. It was Thomas Aquinas who tried to keep a foot firmly planted in both of these worlds and to knit together the wisdom of the past with the fresh vigor of his contemporaries. This was no simple task, as will soon become apparent.

For the Fathers of the Church, the entrance of Divine Wisdom (the Logos) into human form was the central event of God's redemption. Thomas embraced this perspective by offering no less than ten reasons why the incarnation can be viewed as the fitting mode of redemption. The first nine reasons are attributed to Augustine and center around the incarnation as fittingly bringing divine Truth <u>to the human level</u> so that deluded and prideful humans might return <u>to the divine level</u>. For the tenth reason, Thomas gives an Anselmian twist to an Augustinian text:

> [In the tenth place, the incarnation was fitting] in order to free men [women] from the thraldom of sin, which, as Augustine says, <u>ought to be done in such a way that the devil should be overcome by the justice of the man, Jesus Christ</u>, and this was done by Christ satisfying for us. Now a mere man could not have satisfied for the whole human race, and God was not bound to satisfy; hence, it behoves Jesus Christ to be both God and man (ST III, 1, 2, co).

Augustine's emphasis is upon a redemption in which the Just One overcomes the devil. The interpretation attached to the quote from Augustine, however, equates redemption with satisfaction. In fact, Thomas merely paraphrases Anselm's argument as to why the one making satisfaction must be both God and human:

> The person who is to make this satisfaction must be both perfect God and perfect man [i.e., entirely human], because none but God can make it, and none but true man owes it. Thus, while it is necessary to find a God-Man in whom the integrity of both natures is preserved, it is no less necessary for these two complete natures to meet in one person . . . .[16]

Upon close analysis, therefore, Thomas seems to be providing some room for an eventual legitimation of

Anselm's redemptive theory by suggesting that his paraphrase of Anselm captures the intent of Augustine's text. Indeed <u>it does not</u>. Yet, it must be supposed that Thomas thought it would pass inspection.

In discussing the public life of Jesus, Thomas follows Augustine closely. Anselm has nothing to contribute here. In effect, however, the thrust of Thomas' exposition demonstrates the importance many Fathers placed upon the public ministry of Jesus quite independent of his passion and death. Consider, for instance, the reasons which Thomas adduces for justifying Jesus' preference for personal associations over and against the solitary life:

> Christ's manner of life had to be in keeping with the end of his incarnation . . . . Now he came into the world:
> * first, that he might publish the truth; thus he says himself: <u>For this was I born, and for this I came into the world, that I should give testimony to the truth</u> (John 18:37) . . . .
> * secondly, he came in order to free men [women] from sin; according to 1 Tim 1:15: <u>Christ Jesus came into this world to save sinners</u>. And hence, as Chrysostom says, <u>although Christ might, while staying in one place, have drawn all men [women] to himself, to hear his preaching; yet he did not do so, thus giving us the example to go about and seek those who perish, like the shepherd in his search of the lost sheep and the physician in his attendance on the sick</u>.
> * thirdly, he came that by him <u>we might have access to God</u> (Rom 5:2), as it is written. And thus it was fitting that he should give men [women] confidence in approaching him by associating familiarly with them (ST III, 40, 1, co).

In this response, <u>Thomas gives first priority to the power of truth as specifying the purpose of the incarnation</u>. This is the positive thrust of God's plan of salvation. The negative follows in the second place: "to free men [women] from sin." Here Thomas appeals to Chrysostom who situates the liberation from sin as the character of Jesus public ministry. If Thomas were to follow Anselm alone, freedom from sin and access to God would have to be affected only on Calvary, for Anselm does not recognize Jesus' public ministry as the locus of human redemption. In this case, therefore, Thomas appeals entirely to the <u>pastoral theory</u> of justification of the Fathers and entirely remains silent respecting Anselm's <u>juridic theory</u>.

When Thomas goes on to consider the power of Christ's teaching ministry, the theology of the Fathers again prevails. Thus, Thomas finds it entirely natural to speak of the "the efficacy of his persuasion" and "the force of his righteousness" (ST III, 42, 1, ad 2). The Divine Persuader here emerges as compellingly attractive in his deeds and in his words. Thus, it is the very presence of the Master that creates God's salvation. It is not strange, therefore, that Thomas later identifies the chief miracles of Christ to be those wherein "he tames the minds of thousands of men [women]" (ST III, 44, 3, ad 1).

When Thomas turns his attention to Jesus' disciples, he gives great weight to the historical fact that it was they, and not Jesus, who converted the Gentiles. The persuasive power of disciples serves to recommend the truth-power of the Master. Thus, Thomas concludes:

> It is the sign, not of lesser, but of greater power to do something by means of others [i.e., disciples] rather than by oneself. And thus the divine [persuasive] power of Christ was specially shown in this: that he bestowed on the teaching of his disciples such a power that they converted the Gentiles . . . (ST III, 42, 2, ad 2).

Lest it be thought that the disciples of Jesus are puppets mouthing a doctrine that they do not comprehend, Thomas contrasts the crowds with the disciples. Jesus addressed the crowds "employing parables in teaching them spiritual mysteries which they were unable or unworthy to grasp;" yet, for his disciples, "our Lord expounded the open and unveiled truth" (ST III, 42, 3, co). As for Jesus' method with his disciples, Thomas explains that Jesus was not content with mere written doctrines or memory lessons:

> The more excellent the teacher, the more excellent should be his manner of

teaching. Consequently it was fitting
that Christ, as the most excellent of
teachers, should adopt that manner of
teaching whereby his doctrine is
imprinted on the hearts of his hearers;
wherefore it is written that <u>he was
teaching them as one having power</u> (Matt
7:29). And so it was that among the
Gentiles, Pythagoras and Socrates, who
were teachers of great excellence, were
unwilling to write anything for
writings are ordained, as to an end,
unto the imprinting of doctrine in the
hearts of the hearers (ST III, 42, 4,
co).

From this it is clear that Thomas regards Jesus as having powerfully apprenticed his disciples for their truth-mission to the Gentiles. In fact, in one place, Thomas goes so far as to say that extraordinary powers were given to Jesus "not only that he might work miracles, but also that he might communicate this grace to others [i.e., his disciples] "(ST III, 13, 2, ad 3). In this place, it should again be remembered that Thomas regarded all the miracles of Jesus as directed toward "the bestowal of righteousness and the infusion of wisdom"(ST III, 44, 3, ad 1).

As Thomas moves on to consider the passion and death of Jesus, the various conflicting speculations of the Fathers are entirely bypassed, and Anselm's doctrine holds the field uncontested. Statements such as the following are numerous and typical:

That man [humanity] should be
delivered by Christ's passion was in
keeping with both his mercy and his
justice. With his justice, because by
his passion Christ made satisfaction
for the sin of the human race; and so
man [humanity] was set free by Christ's
justice: and with his mercy, for since
man [humanity] of himself could not
satisfy for the sin of all human nature
. . . , God gave him his Son to satisfy
for him . . . (ST III, 46, 1, ad 3).

At one point, Thomas considerably weakens the juridic necessity of Anselm's doctrine by allowing that God could have pardoned sin without any satisfaction whatsoever (ST III, 46, 2, ad 3). This contention runs directly contrary to Anselm's ironclad argument that God could not forgive without betraying the requirements of justice. With a remarkable <u>tour de force</u>, Thomas sidesteps Anselm by making an astute distinction between the justice of the magistrate and the justice of a private individual. In the first case, the magistrate must secure retribution for crimes or else the offended parties will be moved to seek retribution on their own. In the case of private individuals, however, they may forgive personal offenses against themselves without disrupting the public order and without acting unjustly. To do so is even to act "mercifully" (ST III, 46, 2, ad 3). Thus, for example, the owner may pardon someone who has stolen his/her cow but the civil magistrate may not. The magistrate must seek a just retribution on behalf of the owner. Thomas, at this point, reminds Anselm that the Lord is the owner of the Garden and the "owner" of the people who committed treason against him/her. Thus, God does not have to seek a just retribution on behalf of another party. He/she may accordingly forgive the offense of Adam. But, Thomas notes, he/she preferred not to do so lest Adam should have thought that an offense against God is only a small affair. God's plan of redemption, moreover, promised to exalt human beings far beyond anything which Adam enjoyed.

As a direct consequence of this departure from Anselm's norms, Thomas presents the passion as <u>a more fitting mode</u> of redeeming humanity than the granting of an outright pardon:

> In the first place, man[woman] knows thereby how much God loves him [her], and is thereby stirred to love him[her] in return . . . .
>
> Secondly, because thereby he [Jesus Christ] set us an example of obedience, humility, constancy, justice . . . .
>
> Thirdly, because Christ by his passion . . . merited justifying grace for him[self] and the glory of bliss . . . .
>
> Fourthly, because by this man [woman] is all the more bound to refrain from sin . . . .
>
> Fifthly, because it redounded to man's [humanity's] dignity, that as man [humanity] was overcome and deceived by the devil, so also it should be a man [person] that should overthrow the devil . . . (ST III, 46, 3).

It can be seen here that once Anselm's juridic necessity is undercut, Thomas supplies pastoral reasons for explaining the fittingness of the passion. To be sure, these are the same pastoral reasons which weighed so heavily with the Fathers. Even in the fifth reason, Thomas mitigates the standard of "juridic necessity" proposed by Anselm and allows that "the dignity" of the guilty party is preserved when such a one can make restitution for the crime committed.

Thomas drops this pastoral orientation as soon as he considers the redeeming efficacy of Christ's passion. Instead of saying that the passion demonstrates God's love and moves us to love God in return, etc., Thomas settles for Anselm's doctrine of merits. Typical conclusions are as follows:

> Consequently Christ by his passion merited salvation, not only for himself, but likewise for all his members [i.e., his followers] (ST III 48, 1).

> And therefore Christ's passion was not only a sufficient but a superabundant atonement for the sins of the human race . . . (ST III, 48, 2).

> Now Christ made satisfaction, not by giving money or anything of that sort, but by bestowing what was of greatest price -- himself -- for us (ST III, 48, 4).

In each of these conclusions, efficacy is entirely attributed to the vicarious atonement whereby Christ merits forgiveness for the sins of Adam's race. There is not the slightest hint in all of these responses that Thomas had formerly concluded that "from the beginning of his conception Christ merited out eternal salvation . . ." (ST III 48, 1, ad 2). All of the efficacy formerly attributed to the truth-power of Jesus' public ministry is likewise overlooked. There can be no doubt that the logic and the mood of Anselm seemingly overcome all former considerations in this section of the <u>Summa</u>.

In retrospect, I conclude that Thomas embraces the wisdom of the Fathers so as to correct the imbalance in Anselm's doctrine, but that he achieves no satisfactory integration. At best, I would judge that Thomas endeavors to supplement the perspective of one with the other but that their incompatibility remains. Thus, at one point Thomas assigns the incarnation supreme efficacy in freeing us from sin and meriting our sanctification; whereas, at another point, the passion is so described. The incarnation, which is directed toward persuading the world of Truth, is spoken of principally in terms of interpersonal, pastoral efficacy. The passion, on the other hand, is spoken of principally in terms of a juridic efficacy.

Thomas' logic insures that one perspective demands the other and thereby attains a tenuous integration of incompatibles. Here is the force of his logic: (1) Jesus' passion, taken by itself, can effect a universal juridic redemption. This, however, does not concretely alter the personal orientation of a single sinner or produce a single saint (save Jesus). As a consequence, the juridic redemption of the cross demands the pastoral redemption effected by the public ministry of Jesus and his disciples. (2) Jesus' public ministry, along with that of his disciples, can be expected to effect a universal pastoral redemption. The brokenness of individuals and societies can thus be healed and the reign of God's blessedness can prevail. Yet, there are certain juridic obstacles resulting from the cumulative sin of Adam's race which no amount of truth-power can overturn. As a consequence, the pastoral redemption inaugerated by Jesus demands the juridic atonement for sin effected by his passion and death on the cross (ST III, 48, 1, ad 2).

In sum, Thomas did attain a certain tenuous integration of the pastoral emphasis of the Fathers with the juridic emphasis of the atonement theory. The unsatisfactory nature of this integration is attested by the easy way in which the compelling simplicity of Anselm's doctrine has time and time again slipped free of any regard for the wisdom of the Fathers. The catechism responses cited at the beginning of this chapter indicate typical instances of the one-sided preference for juridic redemption which Thomas endeavored, already in the thirteenth century, to correct. In contrast, it is heartening to find instances in which contemporary catechisms are correcting and modifying the atonement theories of the past. I illustrate this with two questions from the <u>American Catechism</u>:

> Q: Why do Christians see the death of Jesus as redemptive?
> A: Christians claim that the death of Jesus is redemptive not directly because of the suffering involved, but because they see it as the ultimate possible act of creative love . . . .

> Q: In what sense . . . is the crucifixion seen as the will of the Father?
> A: The Christian teaching is that God wills the personal fulfillment of all men [women], that he takes the part of the poor and the oppressed and wills the liberation of [hu]mankind from the network of sin that destroys men [women] by oppression, fear, hatred, disgust, greed. Therefore it is properly described as the will of the Father that Jesus should confront and radically challenge the network of sin in human society even though this polarized all the forces of sin against him to destroy him.[17]

Conclusion

This chapter began by exploring the original pastoral genius of Archbishop Anselm in formulating an understanding of salvation that harmonized with and safeguarded the standards of justice and mercy prevailing in his day. Then, attention was turned to the texts of Matthew's Gospel and the letters of Paul. In each of these cases, texts normally read through Anselm's eyes were broken loose from the Anselmian mystique and were perceived to have decisively different alternative meanings when carefully examined within their original contexts. Finally, the corrective measures of Thomas Aquinas were considered by way of emphasizing that even the medieval theologians were hesitant to accept a one-sided canonization of the Anselmian doctrine.

Following upon this critical examination of Anselm's emphasis upon the atoning death of Jesus, the way is now cleared for a renewed biblical estimation of the redemptive ministries of Jesus and of his disciples. This undertaking will be developed and enlarged in the forthcoming chapters.

Over and beyond this, the present chapter constitutes a specific case study which illustrates how different cultural epochs are led by the Spirit of God to evolve new heartfelt meanings to replace the old. This inspired transmutation of meanings implies that the selfsame Scriptural text evokes different meanings to different generations. From the perspective of a longitudinal historical study, therefore, every text of Scripture appears as a fluid, living Word which, in each age, is still pregnant with as yet unforseen guidance and wisdom for unborn future generations.

The gradual displacement of meanings is a source of blessed renewal for a living religious tradition. At each point when the original intent of the Scriptures no longer carried any felt meanings or wise guidance, new meanings emerged which displaced and revivified what was in danger of being lost. Take Matthew's understanding of Jesus' death as an instance. Matthew's parable, it will be remembered, presents the murder of Jesus as the "last straw" which breaks the patient forbearance of the Father. In anger now, the Father "will bring those wretches to a wretched end and lease the vineyard to other tenants" (Matt 21:40). Matthew's community may have recognized this threat to have been carried out in the terrible years in which Jerusalem was surrounded and destroyed by the Roman army in 70 A.D. Yet, even after the deaths of nearly all the priests and Pharisees, the disciples of Jesus did not historically take over the vineyard (i.e., the religious leadership of Israel). In fact, it was the disciples of Yohanan ben Zakkai who cleverly escaped Jerusalem during the seige and resettled at Yavneh (Javne) that took charge of the vineyard. The rabbinic Judaism stemming from Yavneh continued to be fruitful independent of and antagonistic to the Jesus movement. The intent of Matthew's parable was thus unfulfilled; the leadership never did pass to the disciples of Jesus. The pressure of history called for an alternative parable depicting Jesus' tragic end.

Paul, in his zeal for the Gentile mission, supplied such an alternative. For Paul, the condemnation of Jesus demonstrated the inadequacy of the Torah for guiding Jews toward righteousness. The Torah, after all, excommunicated him whom God raised as the Just One. Yet, even this understanding of Paul was culturally-bound. Once Christianity had entirely broken clear of the Torah of Moses (a break that Matthew could never embrace), the clear logic of Jesus' death as liberating all from the curse of the Torah was no longer understood.

The initiative of the Greek and Latin Fathers then prevailed. These men lived in a world which was gradually being socially transformed by the truth-power of the Jewish messiah. Athanasius depicted Jesus as entering into a life and death combat with evil.[18] At the end of the match, Jesus is done in but the power of evil is considerably exhausted and presents a weaker opponent for his disciples. Augustine, in his turn, depicted the devil as tempting Jesus, becoming frustrated, and killing his body because he could not touch his soul.[19] Yet, this was a divine plot to lure the devil into overstepping his proper rights (by killing the innocent). God, consequently, is now free to take from the devil those persons whom the devil had claimed as his own. Rufinus, after Augustine, depicted Jesus as the bait which the Father let down into the world to lure the devil-shark.[20] He took it. And the Father pulls the devil out of the world and butchers him. And so the various imaginative narratives ran on and on -- each of them depicting in its own way the pastoral struggle of Jesus with the demonic structures present within Roman civilization.

But even this milieu passed. Christianity marvelously succeeded. Then the door was open for Anselm to seize the day with an understanding of Jesus' death which corrected the demonic emphasis of the Fathers and which fortified the importance of justice and fealty in the medieval world.

Each age of Christianity, consequently, had to modify what it believed so as to insure that it continued to profess that the tragic end of Jesus had served a transcendent purpose. This gradual displacement of meanings may be lamented in so far as it necessarily entailed the growing old and the passing away of religious perceptions that were tried and true. On the other hand, the death of past meanings was the necessary side effect of the emergence of new meanings which the living God inspired within the hearts of those who were in danger of being stifled by a routinized and regimented adherence to the past demands of God. The mere preservation of the past may suffice for a historical society, but only a series of heartfelt transmutations can preserve the vitality of a religious tradition for those who hunger and thirst for righteousness of God within an altered cultural milieu.

Once this is realized, I do believe that the Christians of the present era will not be overly hesitant to explicitly investigate the deficiencies of the atonement theories of their youth and to courageously seek new ways to correctly honor the tragic end of Jesus without trivializing the redemptive efficacy of Jesus' disciples. Matthew, Paul, and the Fathers have already provided some tested alternatives for how this might be done. It is indeed possible that Christians today will find within the storehouses of the forgotten past their own solutions to the crippling effects of a long-standing and unchallenged atonement theory.

Footnotes for Chapter III

¹ Anselm *Cur Deus homo* 2.11.

² *Ibid.* 2.16.

³ The citations here come from the following sources: (1) *Baltimore Catechism No. 3* [Roman Catholic] (N.Y.: Benzinger Brothers, Inc., 1952), q. 90. This catechism was designed for Catholic immigrants to the United States. Its replies were based on the Council of Trent (1563). (2) *The Heidelberg Catechism: 1563-1963* [blends Lutheranism with Calvinism] (Philadelphia: United Church Press, 1962), q. 1. (3) *The Scots Confession: 1560* [Presbyterian], rendered into modern English by James Bulloch (Edinburgh: The St. Andrew Press, 1960), Ch. 8.

⁴ Joachim Jeremias, *The Parables of Jesus* (N.Y.: Charles Scribner's Sons, 1972), pp. 70-76.

⁵ Sam K. Williams, in *Jesus' Death as Saving Event: The Background and Origin of a Concept* (Missoula: Scholars Press, 1975), makes a strong case for showing that the traditions derived from the suffering of the Maccabean martyrs provided the ground for perceiving the suffering of Jesus in the same categories. Edward Schillebeeckx, in *Jesus: An Experiment in Christology* (N.Y.: Seabury, 1979), pp. 273-319, traces the Hebraic traditions relative to the sufferings of the righteous (Ps 18, Ps 143, Isa 53, etc.) and finds therein a long tradition wherein the righteous draw down upon themselves the afflictions of the wicked. Schillebeeckx shows that the Evangelists draw upon these traditions by way of accounting for the tragic end of Jesus. In effect, therefore, Jesus' death is interpreted as participating in the pattern of suffering that the holy saints and prophets exemplified.

⁶ Lev 18:21, 20:2-5; Deut 12:31, 18:10; Ezek 16:20, 20:31; Jer 7:31, 19:5. Roland de Vaux, in *Ancient Israel* (N.Y.: McGraw-Hill, 1961), pp. 441-446, argues that human sacrifice was never practiced in the name of YHWH and that those instances of human sacrifices that can be found within the history of Israel are attached to the names of foreign gods.

⁷ The rending of one's garment as an expression of intense grief is found in Gen 27:34 and Job 1:20. This rending (*keriyah*) later becomes a standard feature of public mourning. See b. Moᶜed Qatan 25a and *Semahot* 48a where one reads: "One only rends as far down as the region

of the navel." Accordingly, when Matthew presents the divine rending "from top to bottom" (27:51), he might be expressing the intensity of this grief which surpasses that of mortal persons lamenting the death of a parent, a spouse, or a child.

⁸ Biblical scholars have offered a highly diversified set of explanations as to the soteriological efficacy of Jesus' death. See D. Hutton, <u>The Resurrection of the Holy Ones: A Study of the Theology of the Matthean Passion Narrative</u> (Unpublished Harvard Ph.D. dissertation, 1970), for an interpretation of Matthew's soteriology which strongly parallels my own. Donald Senior, in "The Death of Jesus and the Resurrection of the Holy Ones." <u>Catholic Biblical Quarterly</u> 38 (1976) 312-329, offers an overview of current biblical scholarship respecting this issue. A corresponding survey article respecting the position of contemporary systematic theologians is offered by Donald G. Bloesch, "Soteriology in Contemporary Christian Thought," <u>Interpretation</u> 35 (1981) 132-144.

⁹ For an accurate exposition of the Jewish notions of "sin" and "atonement," see Robert J. Daly, <u>The Origins of the Christian Doctrine of Sacrifice</u> (Philadelphia: Fortress, 1978), esp. pp. 25-35. Daly suggests that the Greek Septuagint failed to correctly translate Lev 17:11 and thereby became "a primary source for those exaggerated theories of penal substitution which many Christians have erroneously thought to be expressive of the central teaching of Christian sacrificial soteriology" (p. 35). Consult A. Buechler, <u>Studies in Sin and Atonement in the Rabbinic Literature of the First Century</u> (N.Y.: Ktav, 1967), pp. 416-425, for a detailed description of how the confession of sins to the priest introduced a pastoral ministry within the heart of every sin/guilt offering in the Temple.

¹⁰ Robert J. Daly, <u>The Origins of the Christian Doctrine of Sacrifice</u> (Philadelphia: Fortress, 1978), pp. 6-8, 136-140. Daly describes the three phases of the progressive spiritualization of sacrifice which began with the prophets and culminated in the intertestamental period. See also Francis M. Young, <u>The Use of Sacrificial Ideas in Greek Christian Writers from the New Testament to John Chrysostom</u> (Cambridge: The Philadelphia Patristic Foundation, 1979). Dr. Young has provided a highly readable and pastoral exposition of her conclusions in another volume, <u>Sacrifice and The Death of Christ</u> (Philadelphia: Westminster, 1975).

¹¹ <u>Ibid</u>., p. 140.

[12] Here and elsewhere, I prefer to render nomos as "Torah" rather than "Law," since the latter translation tends to encourage the wide-spread myth that Jewish religion was "legalistic" and "bound to the literal meaning" at the time of Jesus. I will justify this position in the following chapter.

[13] The primitive understanding of Jesus' resurrection as marking his divine vindication has become widely accepted in the theological literature of the last two decades. See, e.g., the pivotal essay of Ulrich Wilkens, "The Understanding of Revelation Within the History of Primitive Christianity," Revelation as History, ed. by Wolfhart Pannenberg (N.Y.: Macmillan, 1967), pp. 55-122.

[14] Wolfhart Pannenberg, Jesus -- God and Man (Philadelphia: Westminter, 1968), p. 263. For an extended discussion of the vicarious efficacy of the cross as perceived by Paul and his interpreters, see pp. 245-280.

[15] E.P. Sanders, in Paul and Palestinian Judaism (Philadelphia: Fortress, 1977), chapter I, endeavors to review the present situation in Pauline scholarship. Sanders then goes on to spell out the nature of religious atonement, see esp. pp. 84-150, 183-198, 463-470. Many other excellent treatments of Paul's theology are available which support the thesis that Anselm failed to capture the original intention of Paul. Interested readers might consult Morna D. Hooker, A Preface to Paul (N.Y.: Oxford University Press, 1980), esp. p. 41; Herman Ridderos, Paul: An Outline of His Theology (Grand Rapids; Wm. B. Eerdmans, 1975), esp. pp. 186-197; Edward Schillebeeckx, Christ (N.Y.: Seabury, 1980), pp. 112-222, 477-514, 694-730; Robin Scroggs, The Last Adam (Philadelphia: Fortress, 1966).

[16] Anselm, Cur Deus homo 1.7.

[17] Monika Hellwig, a professor of theology at Notre Dame, contributed this section to An American Catechism, originally published as Chicago Studies 12 (1973) 293.

[18] Athanasius De incarnatione 2.24 and 27.

[19] Augustine De libero aritrio 3.10.31

[20] Rufinus Commentarius in symbolum apostolorum 16.

IV

How English Translations Conceal Apprenticeship

The last two chapters were calculated to cultivate "new ears" for hearing the New Testament message. It is no small accomplishment to break the hold of the Cinderella mentality and to momentarily hear for the first time that Jesus did expect his disciples to have succeeded in driving out the demon (Matt 17:14-20). It is no small accomplishment to break the hold of one's lifelong atonement mentality and to perceive Jesus' tragic end along the lines of the parable of the wicked tenants (Matt 21:33-43).

This chapter hopes to extend this accomplishment by showing how the systematic biases of Christian scholars translating Greek Scriptures into English have unwittingly misled their readers. Every translator is quite aware that at every point there is a certain amount of slippage between the original Greek idioms and the English phrases which approximate them. Someone who has no competence in biblical Greek cannot expect to distinguish where the rendering is "tight" or when it is "loose." Furthermore, it is not unthinkable that even a whole school of translators can systematically misinterpret given Greek idioms because of a shared dogmatic upbringing that they embrace.

With this in mind, the task of this chapter will be to explore some problematic Greek expressions which have a critical bearing upon apprenticeship. Before doing so, however, I want to consider briefly the frailty of language and the scope of the difficulties encountered by biblical translators today.

Only two persons who have identical language histories could expect to communicate with complete congruence. Since, in practice, this is never the case, there is always some degree of slippage between what a speaker intended and what a listener understood. In most cases, this slippage goes entirely unnoticed. After all, the speaker feels the correctness of his/her words. The listener, meanwhile, feels the correctness of his/her interpretation of the verbal clues which the speaker offered. The difficulty here is that the mood and the intent of the speaker never find themselves situated within the horizon of the listener in precisely the same posture in which they exist in the horizon of the speaker.

Every speaker, it must be remembered, can only offer clues in the form of sounds and gestures. The listener must use his/her own skills in decoding the clues offered. Every listener, consequently, projects meanings gathered from his/her personal history onto clues which have been fashioned by the other's personal history.[1] It is indeed a marvel that people trained in widely different sectors of the same language community can maintain a modestly reliable facility in sustaining effective communication.

When two persons are informed by two semi-isolated branches of the same language community, the occasions for misunderstanding are greatly increased. I found this to be the case when I lived in Oxford, England, for four months. I discovered that the British have a sizeable group of idioms which I invariably had to translate if they were to make sense. I remember that a student once asked me, "What are you reading this term?" I instinctively thought he referred to the book under my arm. It took me quite a while to realize he wanted to know "what courses I was taking that Michaelmas term."

The communication gap is even more pronounced when I read the English classics which go back two or three centuries. The older classics, meanwhile, are only marginally intelligible. Consider, for instance, this segment of Chaucer (d. 1400):

> Ye knowe eek, that in forme of speche is chaunge
> With-inne a thousand yeer, and wordes tho
> That hadden prys, now wonder nyce and straunge
> Us thinketh hum; and yet they spake hem so,
> And spedde as wel in love as men now do.

Chaucer's daily speech has been so transformed within the commerce of the years that his English has to be translated into our own twentieth-century idiom. The segment above thus becomes:

> And then you know, the forms of language change
> Within a thousand years, and long ago

How English Translations Conceal Apprenticeship 81

> Words had a value that will now seem strange
> Or even quaint, and yet they spoke them so
> And fared as well in love, for aught I know.[2]

The scholars who translate Chaucer's daily speech into their own daily speech are aware of the difficulties and the adventure which threatens their enterprise. Listen, for example, to what Neville Coghill says of his work at translating Chaucer:

> One of the most famous lines in the Prologue, which anyone might think could be perfectly translated by simply modernizing the spelling, must in fact be rewritten to convey its full meaning, even at the risk of being accused of a wanton and pedantic destruction of a beautiful and familiar music.
>
> He was a verray parfit gentil knight
>
> Now 'verray' does not mean 'very,' but 'true'; nor does 'gentil' mean 'gentle' in our ordinary sense of the word. It includes that meaning but also, and more importantly, carries the sense of high breeding and good birth. Consequently it would be seriously misleading to render the line
>
> He was a very perfect gentle knight
>
> for the meaning -- as near as one can get to it in a single line -- is
>
> He was a true, a perfect gentle-knight.[3]

From these explanatory notes, I would judge that the translator's final choice has little chance of conveying Chaucer's original meaning if one's linguistic history associates "gentle" with "kind" and "courteous" but not at all with "high breeding." An alternative translation would be:

> He was a model, upper-class knight.

Every translator knows that he/she has made a choice. He/she can sense where he/she has rendered the meaning tightly and where there is slippage. <u>The reader, meanwhile, who depends solely on the translation, can detect nothing of this</u>. The translation appears to be rendering reliably and uniformly the intentionality of the original author.

The reader of Chaucer encounters the slippage due to the time-bound alterations within English usage and culture. If the translator encounters difficulties here, imagine the scope of the difficulties when it comes to translating Matthew's Gospel. To begin with, Matthew's Greek is three times as old as Chaucer's English. This means that even contemporary Greeks encounter grave difficulties when it comes to interpreting their ancient ancestoral language. As things stand, it is a monumental task to translate the New Testament into contemporary Greek idioms. The task is even more monumental when an American attempts to translate biblical Greek into English -- a language with a distinctly different syntax and idiomatic construction. With this very difficulty in mind, every English translator might preface his/her work with a sober caution that models itself after the words penned by Ben Sira's grandson at the opening of the Book of Ecclesiasticus:

> You are therefore asked to read this book with good will and attention and to show indulgence in those places where, notwithstanding our efforts at interpretation, we may seem to have failed to give an adequate rendering of this or that expression; the fact is that you cannot find an equivalent for things originally written in Hebrew when you come to translate them into another language; what is more, you will find on examination that the Torah itself, the Prophets and the other books differ considerably in translation from what appears in the original text (Sir preface:15-26).

As if these difficulties were not enough, I must also call attention to the fact that the risks of translating Matthew's Gospel are also intensified by the impossibility of a living dialogue with Matthew. When I speak to another person, the give-and-take of the exchange alerts me to the moments when a misunderstanding occurs. With Matthew, however, there is no feedback. The scholarly translator endeavors, over many years, to stretch his/her horizon of understanding so as to embrace the thoughts, the customs, the values of Matthew's community. Even when the translator is systematically mistaken, Matthew remains silent. The whole community of biblical translators can be systematically deluded into projecting the same misunderstanding onto the same Greek text and, still, Matthew remains silent. Only by virtue of living translators discussing and disagreeing with each other can any collective advance be made. Slowly and laboriously, the collective horizon is pushed back. Meanwhile, each scholar is firmly locked in the twentieth century. No one can miraculously slip back in time and take on a first-century upbringing. Even if one could do this, such a miracle would end one's career as a translator: one would be locked in the first century and find the twentieth entirely incomprehensible. A translator must remain rooted within his/her contemporary culture and, at the same time, systematically stretch his/her powers of understanding so as to be informed by a culture which has been largely lost in the past. A translator, therefore, is akin to a person who is a citizen of two highly-diverse cultures.

Having thus suggested some of the grave difficulties encountered by biblical translators today, I can now explore some problematic Greek expressions which have a bearing upon the evidence for apprenticeship in the New Testament. Special stress will be placed upon those expressions wherein English translations have systematically concealed those Greek expressions which imply an apprenticeship mentality. The forthcoming material will be divided as follows:

A. Jesus as the master apprenticing his disciples
B. Jesus as prophet vs. Jesus as master
C. Jesus addressed as "sir/lord"

A. <u>Jesus as the Master Appenticing His Disciples</u>

The four Evangelists display significant differences in their presentations of Jesus; yet, they all agree that Jesus was received by his contemporaries as a master apprenticing disciples. The Greek designation for Jesus was <u>didaskalos</u> (master), and his principal activity was <u>didaskein</u> (to apprentice). Within the horizon of understanding shared by Jesus' contemporaries, a <u>didaskalos</u> embraced one of the most exalted professions -- that of artfully guiding a <u>mathetes</u> (disciple) into perceiving and doing God's cause rightly.

Within our contemporary horizon of understanding, one finds no functional equivalent to the <u>didaskalos</u>. In the East, the Hindu guru is a didaskalos; but, for most of us, even the ways of a guru are stange and misunderstood.

When English translations of the New Testament render didaskalos as "teacher" and didaskein as "to teach," they mislead us into imagining some association with our own experience of teachers and teaching. In this vane, Pasolini's film on St. Matthew's Gospel represents Jesus as walking about delivering the Sermon on the Mount to sympathetic bystanders. Jesus is made to appear as a teacher without a classroom -- only a step removed from the street corner preachers still found today. Such images are grossly misleading. They do more to misrepresent Jesus, the didaskalos, than to represent him.

On the other hand, there may be a few of my readers who have been so fortunate as to know a teacher who became for them a didaskalos. Such a teacher would be recognized by the profound impact that he/she had upon their personal life-orientation. They can remember their admiration for such a person. And they can remember the sympathetic interest and expert guidance which such a teacher exerted upon their values and skills. For such a relationship, they have a permanent sense of gratitude and they can hardly imagine how miserable their lives might have been had they never met. Such an experience is indeed much closer to what the Gospels intend by didaskalos than the average teacher-pupil relationship in even our best schools.

Careful studies of secular Greek literature reveal that didaskein specified the systematic acquisition of a performance skill under the direction of an accomplished master (didaskalos). Hunting, writing, and singing afford appropriate examples of skills transmitted under the term didaskein in the first century. It is especially important to note that didaskein was never employed when the mere transmission of information was implied. Didaskein always signified what the master does by way of progressively enhancing the personal skills of his apprentice:

> Thus, didaskein is the word used more especially for when the impartation of practical or theoretical knowledge when there is continued activity with a view to gradual, systematic and therefore all the more fundamental assimilation (TDNT III:135).

Based upon this, the character of Jesus' association with his disciples is to be rightly associated with that of an accomplished artist with his/her understudies or with that of a medical specialist training interns. It would be

How English Translations Conceal Apprenticeship 85

entirely misleading to imagine that Jesus is presented as a didaskalos simply on the basis of his giving divine information which his disciples passively accept and remember.

With this in mind, therefore, I prefer to render didaskalos and didaskein as "master" and "to apprentice" so as to better catch the intent of the Gospels. "Master" is to be associated with the one who has mastery over the performance skills which are being transmitted and not taken to suggest the master-slave relationship. All the texts which I cite from the New Testament will accordingly be modified to follow this determination.

Within the New Testament, the ninty-seven occurrences of didaskein never once designate what skill is being transmitted. The silence of the New Testament on this point would have caused confusion for any Greek-speaking individual who was not familiar with Jewish culture. For a Greek-speaking Jew, however, the referent would be absolutely clear. Guided by both the Hebraic and Aramaic usage, the Jew would know that the Hebrew or Aramaic word for "appenticing" could be applied to carpentry, weaving, etc.; but, when this word had no referent whatsoever, it could only refer to that apprenticing which consumed the whole life and purpose of every Jew -- that of assimilating the ways of YHWH.

YHWH had blessed other peoples and made them great; to Israel alone, however, did YHWH share his own Torah. And "torah" in this context refers to the wisdom and know-how which a father passes on to his children. And it is in this sense that Jews considered YHWH as their Father -- for YHWH gives life to every living creature and not just to Jews. And it is in this sense that Israel is YHWH's beloved son whom he called out of Egypt and trains in the desert as Moses explained:

> Remember how YHWH your God led you for forty years in the wilderness . . . .
> He humbled you, he made you feel hunger, he fed you with manna . . . to make you understand that man [woman] does not live on bread alone but that man [woman] lives on everything that comes from the mouth of YHWH . . . .
> Learn from this that YHWH your God was training you as a man trains his child . . . , and so follow his ways [Torah] and reverence him (Deut 8:2-6).

The Jew, consequently, felt that his whole lifelong learning was directed toward assimilating the holy ways by which YHWH himself was the Holy One.

In the perspective of the prophets, Israel had an international mission to save the world. Torah, therefore, was not to be the private preserve of Israel which Jews enjoyed for themselves. Quite to the contrary, the righteousness of Israel was to be "light" and "hope" for those nations who were blinded and imprisoned by the false torah of their deceiving gods:

> I, YHWH, have called you to serve the cause of right; I have taken you by the hand and formed you; I have appointed you as a covenant of the people and light of the nations [i.e., the Gentiles], to open the eyes of the blind, to free captives from prison, and those who live in darkness from the dungeon. My name is YHWH, I will not yield my glory to another, nor my honor to idols (Isa 42:5-7).

In this same spirit, another prophet interpreted the dispersion of Jews among the nations as the privileged moment wherein the Gentiles, attracted by the righteous of YHWH's people, might later be moved to return to Jerusalem to seek YHWH:

> And many peoples and great nations will come to seek YHWH Sabaoth in Jerusalem . . . . In those days, ten men of nations of every language will take a Jew by the sleeve and say, "We want to go with you [to Jerusalem], since we have learnt [from your life] that God is with you" (Zech 8:22-23).

It is with this same mood and with this same expectation that the Gospel of Matthew represents Jesus as preoccupied with Torah:

> Do not imagine that I have come to abolish the Torah or the Prophets. I have come not to abolish but to complete [i.e., not to disregard but to effectively implement] them. I tell you solemnly, till heaven and earth disappear, not one dot, not one little stroke, shall disappear from the Torah

until its purpose is achieved (Matt 5:17-18).

And what is the purpose of the Torah, according to Jesus? One finds the answer to this at the end of Jesus' exposition on the Torah: "You must therefore be perfect just as your heavenly Father is perfect" (Matt 5:48). This implies that the disciple must assimilate the attitudes and standards of excellence whereby his/her Father is the Holy One. Jesus' own exposition of Torah in Matthew 5 illustrates, by offering some concrete instances, how the popular understanding works <u>to abolish</u> the Torah; whereas, the disciple, by following Jesus, learns <u>to complete</u> the intended purpose of Torah.

When Jesus' task is understood in these terms, it appears quite normal for Jesus to go one step further and recognize his disciples as "the light of the world" (Matt 5:14). Resonating with the message of Isaiah cited above, Jesus fully anticipates that the ways of YHWH which his diciples follow will bring all persons to again recognize that the God of Israel is the Holy One. The universal mission of Israel is thus to be accomplished by the small band of Jesus' disciples:

> Your light must shine in the sight of men [women], so that, seeing your good works, they may give the praise to your Father in heaven (Matt 5:14).

Paul, in his letter to the Romans, indicates that he too is keenly aware of the call to holiness and the universal mission which is incumbent upon Jews in virtue of their intimacy with YHWH's Torah. Paul, however, represents the disastrous consequences of the failure of his people to live Torah -- namely, the ugliness of their ways causes the Gentiles to curse them and to curse the God who created them in his/her image:

> If you call yourself a Jew, if you really trust in the Torah and are proud of your God . . . , if you are convinced that you can guide the blind and be a beacon [a light] to those in the dark, if you can teach the ignorant and apprentice the unlearned because your Torah embodies all knowledge and truth, then why not apprentice yourselves as well as the others? You preach against stealing, yet you steal; you forbid adultery, yet you commit adultery; you despise idols, yet you

> rob their temples. By boasting of the
> Torah and then disobeying it, you bring
> God into contempt. As scripture says:
> <u>It is your fault that the name of God
> is blasphemed among the pagans</u> [the
> nations] (Rom 2:17-24).

Paul, consequently, has the highest regard for the Torah of Moses and the universal mission of Israel. He follows Jesus, however, in saying that "it is not listening to the Torah but keeping it that will make people holy in the sight of God" (Rom 2:13). Paul can leave aside Torah only because he is convinced that the following of Jesus gives the Torah its intended result (Rom 3:31). Jesus has "the spirit of holiness" (Rom 1:4), and Paul contends that he embodies this same spirit/Spirit by virtue of his following Jesus.[4] Finally, as was explained in the last chapter, the resurrection of Jesus gives God's seal of approval to his "new spiritual way" (Rom 7:6) and overturns the Torah which condemned Jesus to death.

It is unfortunate Christians have mistakenly equated the Torah of Moses with hypocritical piety and empty conformity. Such an equation is fostered by the practice of translating <u>nomos</u> in the new Testament as "Law." Here again, our contemporary horizon of understanding associated "law" with legal codes and juridical penalties. Americans have little sense that their laws embrace a transcendent wisdom and a practical guidance which insures their blessedness within the American "spirit." This being absent, the English Bibles can only disguise and misrepresent the Torah of <u>our</u> forebears.

With this in mind, I intend to consistently render <u>nomos</u> as "Torah." I am supported in this by the studies of W.D. Davies which show that "Torah" in the Hebrew Old Testament was consistently translated as <u>nomos</u> in the Septuagint[5] (the authoritative Greek translation of the Old Testament done in the third century B.C.E.). On this basis, Davies argues that Paul and the Evangelists would have naturally chosen <u>nomos</u> to convey what they experientially knew as "Torah" within their Jewish tradition and upbringing.

A further difficulty that Christians encounter is the identificaton of the Torah with "the ten commandments." It is with good reason, therefore, that the rabbinic literature emphasizes that Moses was being apprenticed by YHWH during forty days and forty nights in the mountain.[6] When Moses came down the mountain, he carried two tablets. On these tablets were inscribed ten practical directives which caught some of the implications of the Torah which Moses had received. Such directives can no sooner embrace the whole of the Torah then can the practical rules which a father gives his son exhaust the wisdom assimilated in a father-son relationsip. Practical directives express the father's torah, but they by no means exhaust it. The same holds for the tablets of Moses. These tablets could be broken and even lost. What could not be destroyed or lost, however, was the Torah of YHWH written within the very heart of Moses. It was out of the depths of this interiorized Torah that Moses could formulate not only the ten directives of the tablets but scores of other directives pertaining to the guidance which YHWH intended for his people. The book of Deuteronomy, for example, takes twenty-three chapters to record the guidance which Moses received from YHWH (Deut 5-28).

On the mountain Moses had been transformed by his encounter with YHWH; he was now living Torah. And it was now his task to infuse his spirit/Spirit into the people so that they too might be also transformed. Thus he says to the people:

> You shall love YHWH your God with all your heart, with all your soul, with all your strength. Let these words [Deut 5-28] I urge on you today be written on your heart. You shall repeat them to your children and say them over to them whether at rest in your house or walking abroad, at your lying down or at your rising . . . (Deut 6:4-7).

The chain of tranmission begins. YHWH apprentices a single person. Moses apprentices the adults. The adults, in their turn, apprentice their children. Just before Moses died, Deuteronomy notes that he "committed this Torah to writing" (Deut 31:9) and commissioned the priests and elders to continue his practice of apprenticing the people (Deut 31:9-27).[7]

With time the leaders and priests of Israel were corrupted; they failed to circumcise the hearts of the people as Moses had done (Deut 10:16). They no longer made it evident that "the Torah is your life" (Deut 32:47). Then, according to the rabbinic literature, the prophets became the masters of Torah for the people. And the rabbinic masters, in their turn, were the disciples to the prophets.

This is the setting, then, in which Jesus appeared as <u>didaskalos</u> to the inhabitants of Galilee. As master of Torah, Jesus is experienced as passionately consumed with the wisdom that the Father has revealed to him. He is one possessed by the spirit of holiness. His disciples hope to assimilate his spirit/Spirit and, thereby, become perfect just as their heavenly Father is perfect (Matt 5:48).

In order to appreciate the frequency with which certain words are used to designate Jesus and his disciples, I have prepared the following table. The numbers in braces indicate the number of instances in which persons other than Jesus or his disciples are designated by the term in question.

	Matt	Mark	Luke	Acts	John
<u>didaskalos</u> (master)	11[0]	12[0]	16[2]	00[1]	06[1]
<u>didaskein</u> (to apprentice)	11[3]	15[2]	15[2]	1[15]	08[2]
<u>prophetes</u> (prophet)	3[36]	2[05]	4[27]	0[30]	4[10]
<u>mathetes</u> (disciple)	72[2]	43[2]	34[4]	29[1]	48[5]
<u>apostolos</u> (apostle)	01[0]	01[0]	06[0]	30[0]	01[0]

This table reveals that each of the Gospels practically reserves <u>didaskalos</u> for Jesus. Other persons so designated are Nicodemus (John 3:10), John the Baptizer (Luke 3:12), and those with whom the boy Jesus discusses the Torah in the Temple (Luke 2:46). The book of Acts no longer sees fit to designate Jesus as <u>didaskalos</u>. This is undoubtedly due to the fact that the resurrected one can no longer function as <u>didaskalos</u> for the living. As would be expected the disciples are now the ones who are apprenticing after the manner of Jesus.

Within the Synoptic Gospels, <u>didaskalos</u> is the single most frequently used verb to designate the activity of Jesus. The disciples frequently address Jesus as "master" but never as "prophet." The table reveals that the Gospels have a comparatively low interest in Jesus' prophetic activity. I will consider this in more detail in the upcoming section.

The disciples are not the only ones who recognize Jesus as <u>didaskalos</u>. The servants of Jairus, the synagogue official, say to him, "Your daughter is dead: why put the master to any further trouble?" (Mark 5:35) Another unnamed man breaks up Jesus' discussion with some scribes saying, "Master, I have brought my son to you . . ." (Mark 9:17). Even the Pharisees who oppose Jesus on the ground of the training they received from their own masters seemingly do not hesitate to call Jesus "your master" (Matt 9:11, 17:24) when challenging his disciples. In sum, both the common people and the Pharisees join with the disciples in designating Jesus as fitting the role model of what they know as <u>didaskalos</u>.

The intimate companions who move about with Jesus are accordingly recognized as fitting the role model of "disciples." The Synoptic Gospels use this designation habitually for them. A disciple (<u>mathetes</u>) refers to a person who is being apprenticed by a master. Just as Jesus is understood to be a master of Torah, it is understood that his associates are disciples being trained in Torah (and not in some other craft). On a few occasions, outsiders are designated as "disciples." In Matthew's Gospel, for instance, one finds reference to "the disciples of John" (Matt 9:14) and "the disciples of the Pharisees" (Matt 22:16). John's Gospel makes reference to "the disciples of Moses" (John 9:29), and Acts makes a probable reference to the disciples of Paul (Acts 9:25). "Disciple" is always a relationship term presupposing a known "master."

B. <u>Jesus as Prophet vs. Jesus as Master</u>

During the time of Jesus, a Jew would instinctively distinguish the activity of a prophet from the activity of a master (<u>didaskalos</u>). The prophetic role is that of preaching/telling/announcing while the master's role is that of apprenticing. The prophet addresses anyone for whom his message is relevant. The master focuses attention only on his/her disciples. A prophet stands in a prominent place and shouts his/her message in a strong voice for he/she wants to attract and address a crowd. A master sits in a quiet place, usually in a home or a synagogue, and quietly speaks to his/her disciples who sit on the ground around him/her. A prophet generally seeks to inform his/her listeners of YHWH's judgment on some current issue. A master seeks to progressively alter his/her disciples' habits of perception and standards of judgment so that they duplicate his/her own. Once a prophet has delivered his/her message to one group of hearers, he/she immediately goes from there to seek yet another group. The master, in contrast, requires that his/her disciples live with him/her.

The Greek text of the New Testament takes great pains to consistently distinguish apprenticing from the prophetic activities of preaching/telling/announcing. In our English translations, however, this distinctiveness is often blurred or distorted. Let me consider two instances which illustrate this. Both citations are taken from the Jerusalem Bible:

> He [Jesus] went around the whole of Galilee teaching in their synagogues, proclaiming the Good News of the kingdom and curing all kinds of diseases . . . (Matt 4:23 = 9:35 = 11:1).

> They [the Twelve] preached every day both in the Temple and in private homes, and their proclamation of the Good News of Christ Jesus was never interrupted (Acts 5:32).

In the first text, the Greek original associates the verb didaskein (here rendered as "teaching") with the synagogue and kerussein (here rendered as "proclaiming") with the Good News. Didaskein is a typical synagogue activity and presupposes that Jesus was accompanied by his disciples from synagogue to synagogue. Kerussein is not a normal synagogue activity. It is correctly associated with "the Good News" that marks a prophet addressing crowds in the streets or in an open plaza. In the English text, these distinct activities are blurred.

The second English text is even more remote from the Greek intent. The translator has used the single word "preached" to render two distinct verbs in the Greek text: didaskontes kai euaggelizomenoi (literally: "apprenticing and heralding-good-news"). No English reader could even guess from the translation the verb didaskein even appeared in the Greek. In this regard, the King James Version is more accurate:

> And daily in the temple, and in every home, they ceased not to teach and preach Jesus Christ (Acts 5:42).

The New American Bible also distinguishes two activities:

> Day after day, both in the temple and at home, they never stopped teaching and proclaiming the good news and Jesus the Messiah (Acts 5:42).

A Palestinian Jew would know that "in the temple" referred to the courtyards of the Temple. In these courtyards apprenticing (cf. Acts 5:12) and the heralding of news (cf.

Acts 3:11ff) were commonly practiced. The heralding of news could take place in a private home; but most likely the text here refers to the private homes wherein the community broke bread and wherein only apprenticing would be appropriate (Acts 2:42). Once again, the average Christian reader today hardly has a sufficient horizon of understanding to make such distinctions.

In order to better understand how the Gospels carefully distinguish between Jesus' functioning as master or as prophet, I intend to rapidly trace through the Gospel of Matthew those clues which the Evangelist offers his readers.

In the beginning, Matthew presents Jesus as a solitary individual coming from Nazareth to seek John the Baptizer at the Jordan. After John's imprisonment, Jesus is depicted as moving out of the wilderness into the towns of Galilee and heralding therein the prophetic message which he received from John. Matthew drives this home by placing the same words in the mouth of Jesus which he formerly assigned to John:

> Repent, for the kingdom of heaven is
> close at hand (Matt 4:17 = 3:2).

Matthew uses two verbs, <u>kerussein kai legein</u> (to broadcast and to say), to describe Jesus' activity -- the same two verbs used for John's activity in the desert (Matt 3:1-2). The activity of Jesus in this period is thus entirely prophetic.

An entirely new phase opens up when Jesus chooses four fishermen to follow him (Matt 4:18-22). Those chosen are almost immediately identified as "disciples," and Jesus' activity now embraces "apprenticing in their synagogues" (Matt 4:23) in addition to his normal prophetic activity.

The Sermon on the Mount follows: This summary of Jesus' discourses is intended primarily for the formation of the attitudes and conduct of his disciples. The beginning makes this quite clear:

> Seeing the crowds, he [Jesus] went
> up the hill [mountain]. There he sat
> down and was joined by his disciples.
> Then he began to speak [lit.: And
> opening his mouth he instructed them
> saying] . . . [Matt 5:1-2].

Matthew portrays Jesus as deliberately escaping the crowds so as to give his attention to his disciples. When Jesus later comes down from the mountain, the crowds are seemingly still there waiting for him (Matt 8:1). While on the mountain, Jesus sits down. This very gesture of a master indicates his readiness to begin their formal training. The disciples, accordingly, immediately approached him and sat around him. Perhaps, as was the custom, other interested persons took their places behind the disciples, for Matthew ends his collection of Jesus' training sessions saying:

> Jesus had now finished what he wanted to say, and his teaching [didache, a derivative of didaskein] made a deep impression on the people . . . (Matt 7:28).

Matthew presents ten healing narratives following Jesus' descent from the mountain. These narratives are effectively sandwiched between Jesus' formal training session with his disciples and his sending them out alone to announce the kingdom and to heal. One must surmise that these healing narratives represent a practical demonstration on the part of Jesus of what the disciples will shortly do on their own. Jesus is not unique in combining private instruction with practical demonstrations. The disciples of the Pharisees were also aware that a large part of their training consisted in attentively observing how their master responded to the needs and issues of the persons who came to him.

The disciples are sent out in pairs, for the witness of two persons is trustworthy. They are heralds of the kingdom (Matt 10:7) -- a clear prophetic activity. They are also received into private homes (Matt 10:11-13) -- implying that there are persons who receive them as disciples and wish to gain a familiarity with the way of the master. Accordingly Jesus says:

> Anyone who welcomes you welcomes me . . . . Anyone who welcomes a prophet because he is a prophet will have a prophet's reward; and anyone who welcomes a holy man because he is a holy man will have a holy man's reward. If anyone gives so much as a cup of cold water to one of these little ones because he is a disciple . . . , he most certainly will not lose his reward (Matt 10:40-42).

Each disciple is thus a prophet in the street: a holy man-disciple in the private homes. They themselves do not yet apprentice disciples; <u>didaskein</u>, accordingly, is not used to characterize their activity.

In Matt 13 one finds a collection of the parables that Jesus used time and time again to illustrate his prophetic announcement of the forthcoming kingdom. Matthew presents Jesus as teaching from inside the boat. He is sitting. The people are standing on the shore. I cannot believe that Matthew presents this as a workable arrangement which Jesus actually used. Rather, Matthew seems to be representing how Jesus <u>sits</u> in the boat (the church) with his disciples while the crowds stand outside receiving only parables of the kingdom. A strong distinction is thus apparent. The disciples are being apprenticed in Torah. The people, however, perceive Jesus only in his prophetic activity of heralding the kingdom at hand. In the end, Jesus dismisses the multitude and "enters the house" (Matt 13:35) where he explains in a face to face dialogue the meaning of his public ministry to his disciples. In brief, he sits with them while the crowds stand outside. Anyone with a Jewish horizon of understanding would immediately make sense of such clues.

The people and the disciples are also juxtaposed in the two feeding narratives (Matt 14:15-21, 15:32-39). Feeding is a long-standing Jewish mode for representing how a master nourishes his disciples or how YHWH nourishes his/her people with Torah (e.g., Deut 8:3, Amos 8:11, Prov 9:5-6, 10:21).[8] In the feeding narratives, the sitting position of the multitudes indicates their readiness for apprenticing. At the same times Jesus is pressing his disciples to "give them something to eat" (Matt 14:16, also 15:32). They hesitate. So, Jesus blesses the loaves which the disciples have and gives it back to them so that they can give it to the expectant crowds. And so they do. As such, therefore, these feeding narratives enable Matthew to represent how the Christian communities of his day are fed from the Torah which the disciples received from Jesus. All are amazed that so many are fed from the nourishment that Jesus gave his disciples.

Later when Jesus moves with his disciples into Jerusalem, the people point to him as the prophet from Nazareth (Matt 21: 11). A prophetic activity follows: Jesus closes down the Temple of sacrifices and declares it to be a "house of prayer" -- the alternative designation for a synagogue. Accordingly, Jesus returns the following day apprenticing his disciples in the Temple courtyards (Matt 21:23). He is confronted there by the religious authorities of the Temple. By the end of the week, Jesus declares prophetic judgment against the religion of the scribes (the priestly masters) and the Pharisees. These judgments are explicitly addressed to "the people and his disciples" (Matt 23:1).

Then two chapters (Matt 24-25) are devoted to the collected guidance which Jesus gave his disciples alone regarding their conduct as the present epoch passes away and the new replaced it. Within this guidance, some parables of the kingdom are found. These are significantly different from the former kingdom parables addressed to the people (Matt 13). The former merely heralded the assurance that God's cause would inevitably be accomplished; the latter offer specific guidance as to the suddenness and the terms of God's final judgment. The former announce what is coming to pass; the latter orient those who are facing the future.

In conclusion, therefore, by giving attention to the linguistic clues, one quickly discovers that Matthew was quite consistent in differentiating Jesus-prophet from Jesus-master. English translations coupled with our contemporary horizon of understanding tend to hopelessly blur what Matthew (and the other Evangelists) wished to differentiate.

C.   Jesus Addressed as "Sir/Lord"

The most frequent and the most controversial designation for Jesus in the Greek New Testament is kyrios (sir/lord). The following table allows one to contrast the number of instances in which kyrios and didaskalos are used to designate Jesus. Here again the numbers in braces designate how often persons other than Jesus are so designated.

	Matt	Mark	Luke	Acts	John
didaskalos (master)	11[0]	12[0]	16[2]	00[1]	06[1]
kyrios (sir/lord)	28[55]	06[15]	39[68]	46[67]	48[5]

The controversial nature of kyrios derives from the fact that it represents the proper designation for someone who exercises control without indicating precisely the nature or the extent of the control exercised. Thus, the disciples of Jesus frequently address Jesus as kyrie (the

How English Translations Conceal Apprenticeship   97

vocative form of kyrios). They do not explain, however, why kyrie is an appropriate designation for Jesus and how it differs from didaskale (the vocative form of didaskalos).

Given the silence of the Gospels on this issue, two extreme positions have developed. The first extreme assumes that the disciples of Jesus recognized his metaphysical divinity. They accordingly addressed him as kyrie in the same sense that YHWH was addressed as kyrie. Kyrios thus implies that Jesus is the Lord of the Universe and the Lord of History -- co-equal and co-eternal with the Father. The second extreme assumes that the disciples related to Jesus principally as their master (didaskalos). They accordingly addressed him as kyrie to acknowledge that he had charge of their training in Torah. Every disciple would appropriately use kyrios to designate his/her personal master.

The translators of the Greek New Testament have been strong supporters of the first position. Accordingly, they have consistently rendered kyrios as "Lord" when Jesus or YHWH were so designated. When kyrios was applied to other persons, however, they took the liberty to render this in correspondingly weaker terms: "lord," "sir," "master."

This inconsistency is perfectly defensible from the view-point of dogmatic and confessional theology. From the view-point of accurately rendering the Greek texts, however, this practice necessarily obscures the original intent of the Greek authors. The Greek New Testament does not employ selective capitalization. The Evangelists found no embarrassment at using the same word to designate the master of house-dogs and the master of the universe. Thus, in illustration:

> Even house-dogs can eat the scraps that fall from their master's [kyrion] table (Matt 15:27).
> You must worship the Lord [kyrion] your God, and serve him alone (Matt 4:10).

The Greek word here is precisely the same; yet one could never guess this from reading the English translations.

The Greek-speaking Jew had to determine, in each instance, what the speaker meant by using kyrios. In some instances kyrios was used for the Lord of the Universe. The custom had developed to avoid pronouncing the proper name of God, "YHWH," and to substitute an appropriate term in its place. Thus, while the Hebrew Old Testament normally uses "YHWH your God" (e.g., Deut 6:13), the

Evangelists instinctively wrote "the Lord your God" when citing such a text in their Gospels (e.g., Matt 4:10 above). Greek-speaking Jews immediately knew by this that kyrios was a stand-in for "YHWH."

Outside of familiar biblical texts, the impact of kyrios had to be surmised from the context. In the Gospels, for instance, kyrie is used by the Jews to address Pilate (Matt 27:63), by the seemingly-obedient son to address his father in Jesus' parable (Matt 21:31), by Mary of Magdala addressing the gardner (John 20:15). Furthermore, the Evangelists have Jesus himself using kyrios to designate the one who exercised control over the vineyard (Mark 12:9), over an ass (Luke 19:33), over the business of harvesting (Matt 9:38), over the business of the sabbath (Mark 2:28). In each of these instances, one readily picks up the force of the term kyrios by relating the person to the enterprise over which he/she has control.

This still leaves unresolved the sense in which kyrios applies to Jesus. Careful linguistic studies provide helpful clues here. They show, for instance, that kyrie is the proper equivalent for the Hebrew/Aramaic terms, rabi/raboni, whereby the disciples of the Pharisees addressed their personal masters. It furthermore is known that rabi had a range of applications in the first century which parallel that of kyrie in Greek.

> The one called rabi is recognized thereby to be higher in rank than the speaker: the prince by the people, the master by the slave, the master craftsman by his associates, the robber captain by his accomplices. Rabi can also be used on occasion for the prophet Elijah, the Messiah, and God. Above all, it was a custom for a pupil [disciple] to address his teacher [master] thus (TDNT VI:961, also III:1093).

It follows from this that Greek-speaking Jews who had a high regard for masters of Torah and who esteemed Jesus as such a master would find it entirely natural to regard kyrie as the most appropriate term of respect in the mouths of his disciples. Within the Gospels, consequently, kyrios applies to Jesus in the very sense in which it applies to every other master of Torah.

But did not the disciples of Jesus regard him as more than simply the one who directed their progress in holiness? Yes. The disciples did, after a certain point, regard Jesus as the Messiah and the Son of Man (who would judge all persons on the last day). When Jesus is addressed by his disciples as <u>kyrie</u>, however, they are acknowledging him as first and foremost as their master (<u>didaskalos</u>).

But did not the disciples regard Jesus as equal to God and use <u>kyrios</u> for him in the very sense in which they used it for YHWH? No. The disciples of Jesus did not and could not regard their master as equal to God. Such a thought would be entirely unthinkable within the Jewish horizon of understanding. Already, for centuries, the Jewish mentality had been shaped by the persistent struggle to assert the absolute oneness of YHWH and to prohibit any created image from standing in for YHWH. <u>Jesus, therefore, by no stretch of the imagination could be envisioned as equal to or as the created image of YHWH.</u>

Liberal Protestant scholarship has been wrestling with the rediscovery of the Jewish horizon of understanding pervading the Gospels for over four generations. Fundamentalists, meanwhile, have absolutized their own notions of Jesus and have insisted that the Evangelists must think like them or be excluded from the church. Consequently, Fundamentalists accept biblical scholarship only when it supports their confessional theology. Catholics, meanwhile, have in the last two decades been quite receptive to historical studies which show that an authentic development of belief necessarily exists from the New Testament times to the present.

For our purposes here, I would like to offer two instances in which Catholic scholarship has wrestled with the proper Jewish regard for Jesus in the Gospels. The first is a study undertaken by the highly-esteemed Raymond Brown, S.S. In 1965, Brown carefully examined all the relevant New Testament texts pertaining to the "divinity" of Jesus. In his published essay, "Does the New Testament Call Jesus God?" he concluded as follows:

> Jesus is never called God in the Synoptic Gospels, and a passage like Mark 10:18 would seem to preclude the possibility that Jesus used the title himself. Even the fourth Gospel never portrays Jesus as saying specifically that he is God . . . . This negative conclusion is substantiated by the fact that Paul does not use the title in any epistle written before 58 [C.E.].9

The second instance is a footnote in the Jerusalem Bible which was translated by the Dominican Biblical School in

Jerusalem (1955-1961). In an attempt to explain the sense in which Jesus is acknowledged as "Son of God" in the New Testament, the footnote says:

> The biblical title 'Son of God' does not necessarily mean natural sonship but may imply a sonship which is merely adoptive, i.e., which as a result of God's deliberate choice sets up a very intimate relationship between God and his creature. In this sense the title is given to angels (Job 1:6), to the chosen people (Exod 4:22; Wis 18:13), to individual Israelites (Deut 14:1; Hos 2:1; cf. Matt 5:9, 45 etc.), to their leaders (Ps 82:6). Where therefore it is attributed to the royal Messiah (1 Chr 17:13; Ps 2:7, 89:26) it does not necessarily imply that he is more than man; nor need we suppose that it has any deeper significance when used by Satan (Matt 4:3, 6) or by the possessed (Mark 3:11, 5:7; Luke 4:41) . . . .

Having endeavored to sketch out the proper Jewish horizon of understanding for "Son of God," the footnote concludes;

> During the lifetime of Christ, it is true, his disciples had no clear conception of his divinity . . . . But it is equally true that Jesus expressed with his own lips, and with as much clarity as his audience could support, his own consciousness of being Son of the Father in the fullest sense.[10]

Based upon such scholarship, I conclude that the use of kyrios for Jesus in the Gospels points directly to the master-disciple relationship. The current practice of translators to render kyrios as "Lord" when it pertains to Jesus or YHWH and as "lord/sir/master" when it refers to other persons positively obscures the 167 occasions when Jesus is so designated. Within the remainder of this book, I shall accordingly adopt the practice of uniformly rendering kyrios as "lord/sir" whenever it appears in the biblical text. In so doing I will thereby return to the practice of the Evangelists in which the reader had to decide the force of the term from the context in which it is used. But even more importantly, I intend to have my readers remember that "lord/sir" is the most common form of addresses for disciples speaking to their master.

The above discussion considered the usage of kyrios as it appear in the Synoptics. Outside of the Synoptics, there are instances in which Jesus is designated kyrios when there is no thought of the master-disciple relationship nor of metaphysical divinity. Peter's oration to the Jews on Pentecost offers an instance of this:

> For this reason the whole House of Israel can be certain that God has made this Jesus whom you crucified both lord (kyrion) and Christ (christon) (Acts 2:36).

Here kyrios is used to designate who Jesus becomes by virtue of his resurrection. In association with christos, this term probably designates the effective leadership and power that Jesus will exercise during the forthcoming messianic era. When this text is read in connection with Peter's sermon to Cornelius, kyrios could also be taken to imply that Jesus will judge the living and dead on the last day (Acts 10:42). Ths use of kyrios by Peter cannot specify Jesus' earthly function as Master of Torah since the term clearly intends to specify that function to which Jesus has been appointed after the resurrection. In like fashion, kyrios could not refer to the metaphysical divinity of Jesus for the reasons already given above as well as a pressing additional reason: Peter would be implying that Jesus was made divine only after the resurrection.[11] From this instance one can judge the problems that face the translators. Perhaps their most honest solution at this moment is to render every instance of kyrios as "lord/master" and, as in the case with the original Greek reader text, to force the reader, in each instance, to decide upon the scope of the term.

Conclusion

This chapter began with the sober realization that an English reader of the New Testament can be entirely oblivious of the slippage supplied by translators. The remainder of the chapter endeavored to stretch the reader's horizon of understanding so as to recover some of the sensibilities which guided the original Evangelists in their writing. The highlights of the chapter were as follows:

> (a) that Jesus is habitually recognized by his contemporaries as a didaskalos (master) whose characteristic activity is didaskein (to apprentice) his disciples. The English language and contemporary Western culture have no

personages who perform the task of apprenticing in Torah as was characteristic of the masters of Jesus' day;
(b) that the Greek Gospels habitually offer clues so as to differentiate Jesus as master from Jesus as prophet;
(c) that English translations positively obscure the wide range of applications which are proper to <u>kyrios</u> (lord/sir) in the Greek text. Guided by dogmatic considerations foreign to the Evangelists, <u>kyrios</u> has been rendered as "Lord" only when referring to Jesus and YHWH. Such a rendering positively obscures the appropriateness with which any disciple would acknowledge his/her master by addressing him/her as <u>kyrie</u>.

Building upon this, the task of the upcoming chapter will be greatly facilitated. Once the vocabulary of the Gospels allows the true character of Jesus as master of Torah to appear, then it is quite simple to seek and find an abundance of clues relative to Jesus' practice in transmitting his spiritual power to his understudies. To this our attention will now turn.

Footnotes for Chapter IV

[1] For an enlarged description of the formation of tacit skills requisite for linguistic self-expression, see Michael Polanyi, "Articulation," **Personal Knowledge** (N.Y.: Harper & Row, 1964), pp. 69-131.

[2] Geoffrey Chaucer, **The Canterbury Tales**, tr. into modern English by Neville Coghill (Baltimore: Penguin Books, 1952), pp. 21-22.

[3] <u>Ibid</u>, p. 23.

[4] The Pauline notion of "salvation by faith alone" has often been mistakenly interpreted. When faith and works are contrasted, Paul is distinguishing the two great ways of salvation: (1) following the Torah of God delivered to Moses and worked out by the Pharisees; (2) following the Torah of God revealed in the deeds/sayings of Jesus. According to Paul, those who are attached to the works/deeds of the Mosaic Torah are putting their trust in the very system that condemned Jesus, the Righteous One. Christians, for their part, put their trust in God and follow the ways of the Righteous One whom God raised and vindicated. Jesus Christ, therefore, presents the new pattern of righteousness whereby both Jews and Gentiles are called to sons and daughters of God. Accordingly,

"salvation by faith" does not mean a heralding of Jesus as Lord with an indifference toward ethical conduct nor a purely juridical transfer of Jesus' merits to sinners. Throughout Paul's letter, he exhorts, admonishes, reminds those who have faith that it is incumbent upon them to follow the rule of life that Paul delivered to them (e.g., 1 Cor 11:1, Phil 2:12, Gal 2: 17-19). This understanding will be further defined in Chapter VII.

For a promising study in which a Lutheran scholar distinguishes between the intent of Paul and the intent of Luther interpreting Paul, see Joerg Rothermundt, "The Meaning of Justification," Lutheran World, Supplement to No. 1 (1965), esp. pp. 26-45. For a proper understanding of Paul against the rabbinic background in which all parties agreed that God alone justifies sinners and brings them to salvation, see E.P. Sanders, Paul and Palestinian Judaism (Philadelphia: Fortress, 1977), esp. pp. 84-150, 217-223, 449-469, 479-480, 496-97; and Edward Schillebeeckx, Christ (N.Y.: Seabury, 1980), esp. pp. 86-159.

[5] W.D. Davies, The Setting of the Sermon on the Mount (Cambridge: University Press, 1966), pp. 128-129.

[6] According to the rabbis, Moses was apprenticed by God during the forty days, and Moses reviewed what God had taught him during the forty nights (Exod. Rabbah 47:8). Not only did Moses learn God's written Torah but his oral Torah as well, including all the various interpretations that future masters of Torah would devise (Exod. Rabbah 47:1).

[7] I am following here the simplified chain of transmission suggested by the sources. The actual situation was much more complex. See, for example, Ellis Rivkin, The Shaping of Jewish History (N.Y.: Charles Scribner's Sons, 1971), for a well-written and controversial protrayal of how the Hebrew Scriptures themselves both disguise and reveal a complex chain of transmission.
For the most part, scholars agree that Moses himself did not set down in writing the Torah (as Deut 31:9 suggests) but that it was later done by others "in his name."

[8] Augustine analyzes John's account of the feeding narrative by noting that the five loaves represent the five books of Moses. The "small boy" (John 6:9) represents the people of Israel who are burdened carrying the loaves while, ironically, they hunger to be fed from them. Jesus enters into this arena as the one who knows how to bless and to break open the Torah such that God's

people are again nourished. "In the breaking they were multipled . . . . For those five books of Moses, when they are expounded, what a multitude of books have they made . . ." (Augustine <u>Tractatus in Joannis evangelium</u> 24.5).

[9] Raymond Brown, <u>Jesus God and Man</u> (Milwaukee: Bruce, 1967), p. 30. This was first published in <u>Theological Studies</u> 26 (1965) 545-573.

[10] <u>The Jerusalem Bible</u> (London: Darton, Longman & Todd, 1966), Part II, p. 19, n. 4c. Cf. also <u>TDNT</u> VIII: 357-397.

[11] Once Christianity moved into Gentile circles, <u>kyrios</u> was already applied to a large class of persons, both historical and mythological, and implied divine functions and/or a divine nature. See, e.g., 1 Cor 8:5. Within this milieu, the followers of Jesus rightly claimed Jesus as the pre-eminent <u>kyrios</u> "through whom all things come and through whom we exist" (1 Cor 8:6). Christian scholars are attempting to reconstruct the growth in the horizon of understanding that characterized the Jesus movement as it moved out of orthodox Jewish circles (which even in Jesus' day, were always slightly Hellenized). A representative essay is that of Francis Young, "A Cloud of Witnesses," <u>The Myth of God Incarnate</u>, ed. by John Hick (Philadelphia: Westminster, 1977), pp. 13-47.

V

Jesus' Practice in Apprenticing His Disciples

The foregoing chapters were designed to correct three major hearing disorders -- the Cinderella mentality, the atonement theory, and faulty English translations. One should now be prepared to hear the Evangelists with fresh ears.

The present chapter will focus upon Jesus' practice in apprenticing his disciples. For greater clarity, I have chosen to limit myself to the clues offered by Matthew's Gospel. For amplification and contrast, I will occasionally make reference to the practice of the Pharisaic masters in apprenticing their disciples in this same period. Throughout I shall endeavor to discern in what sense Jesus might be said to be a unique master of Torah in his own day. My considerations will fall into five sections:

        A.   Jesus' calling of disciples
        B.   The financing of discipleship
        C.   The place and posture of apprenticing
        D.   The content and goal of apprenticing
        E.   The highest estimate of Jesus' apprenticing

Before beginning the first segment, I want to spell out three difficulties which any reconstruction of the practices of Jesus and/or of the Pharisaic masters must take into account:

(1)   Neither Jesus nor any of the Pharisees left private journals nor did any of their disciples use notebooks to record their sessions with their master. None the less, a well-trained disciple could be relied upon to accurately and faithfully present the deepest concerns and patterns of judgment that were exhibited by his master. To accomplish this, the disciple did not act as a modern press reporter

who observes and probes his subject. Nor did the disciple give himself to memorizing faithfully and repeating meticulously the collected discourses of his master.[1] No. The disciple entered much more intimately into his subject than this. He roomed and roamed with him. He learned his moods, his passions, his sorrows. He learned "how he unlaced his sandals and how he laced them up again."[2] Out of this experience, the disciple later spoke of his master as his long-time companion and his "father" -- the one who shaped his life. In fact, the disciple was undoubtedly always disappointed as to how little of what he knew he could convey in words.

(2)   The written documents that do come down to us were never composed by way of creating a neutral historical record. The writers were always concerned disciples, who must be expected to promote their master(s) and to acknowledge their readers. They promoted their master(s) by sometimes attributing to them judgments which they did not directly make but which inevitably followed from the force of wisdom that was passed on.[3] They acknowledged their readers by selecting material which had some current interest and by expressing it in the idiom of their readers.[4] The Gospel of Matthew (70-80 C.E.), the Mishnah (200 C.E.), the Tosefta (250 C.E.), the Palestinian Talmud (400-450 C.E.), and the Babylonian Talmud (500-600 C.E.) must all be respected, therefore, as being shaped by authentic remembrance, on the one hand, and by pastoral recognition of the prevailing situation, on the other. In point of fact, even the most demanding of press reporters prepares the front page articles with the selfsame factors influencing what he/she writes. To write is to attempt to communicate; to communicate effectively is to meet one's readers' horizon of understanding.[5]

(3)   The upheaval of the wars of 66-73 C.E. and the destruction of the Temple had a marked influence on all groups concerned. Both Pharisees and Christians had to adjust their practices and expectations to take into account the slaughter of the priests and the cessation of all Temple activity. Meanwhile, the diversity of movements within Judaism (e.g., the Sadducees, the Zealots, the Essenes) was decisively upset leaving only the Pharisees and the Christians to represent the other extinct movements in their own terms. Matthew's Gospel, therefore, projects back into the time of Jesus the comparatively simplified state of affairs which prevailed in Matthew's era: namely, the Pharisees are everywhere influential and Jesus is seemingly contending with them at every turn. Historical studies would indicate that, during the time of Jesus, the Pharisees had little following in Galilee and certainly had

no political power save for a few seats in the Sanhedrin. In view of Matthew's actual situation and in view of the growing conflict with the Pharisees in his own day, it is not surprising that Jesus' conflict with the Pharisees is considerably heightened.[6]

When these three observations are taken into account, it is obvious that every saying or activity attributed to Jesus or to a Pharisaic master has been shaped by multiple factors: (a) the authentic remembrances of the original disciples, (b) pastoral recognition of the prevailing situation of the readers, and (c) the momentous historical events that transpired since the death of the master. It would be very cumbersome to stop and try to sort out these individual factors each time one makes reference to a Gospel or rabbinic test. In practice, therefore, I intend to take my texts at their face value. In those cases where I suspect that the situation prevailing within Matthew's community has modified his presentation of Jesus' practice of apprenticing disciples, I will draw this to my reader's attention. The same holds true when I make use of rabbinic texts. With this understanding, I can now proceed to examine the clues Matthew offers relative to Jesus' practice in training disciples.

A. <u>Jesus' Calling of Disciples</u>

As explained in the last chapter, Matthew initially presents Jesus as functioning exclusively as a prophet whose message exactly follows that of John the Baptizer. Then, in the course of this activity, Matthew presents Jesus as approaching two pair of fishermen and inviting them to follow him (Matt 4:19, 4:22). This stark account will be repeated later when Jesus approaches Matthew with the same invitation: "follow me" (9.9). In these moments, Matthew undoubtedly intends that his readers recognize Jesus to be taking on a new identity -- that of a master (<u>didaskalos</u>) whose energies are directed toward apprenticing disciples (<u>mathetes</u>).

It is quite natural for an English reader of the Gospel to inquire whether "follow me" can indeed carry the weight of an invitation to an apprenticeship. Careful linguistic studies demonstrate that this is precisely the

Jewish idiom which carries that understanding (TDNT I:213). The Gospel itself presents the fishermen as "leaving their nets" (i.e. their present career) and begins to refer to them as "disciples." These clues confirm the linguistic studies.

Jesus' act of calling disciples has profound implications that are commonly overlooked. It established that Jesus' personal vocation before YHWH and before Israel is of the kind that can and ought to be shared. As such, this distinguishes Jesus from the prophets of old who attached their divine calling exclusively to themselves and did not presume that they could initiate another into it. The prophets sometimes had distinguished servants, but these servants were always understood to have gained their charismatic gifts independently of their superiors (TDNT IV:427ff).

Jesus' act of associating disciples with himself also establishes a certain identity between Jesus and Pharisaic masters. The Pharisees represented a lay movement which grew out of the discontent with the secularization and the corruption introduced by the priestly administrators of Judaism. Members of this group were united in establishing the importance of a heartfelt love of YHWH as central to Judaism and not the Temple sacrifices advocated by the priests. They were also united in promoting the religious renewal of the laity through the establishment of synagogues. The synagogues served as local centers for promoting the skills necessary to read and to apply the Torah to their daily lives. The Pharisees supplemented the written Torah with the oral Torah which they believed was passed down from Moses, through Joshua, the elders, and the prophets, and finally delivered to the Pharisaic masters. In the synagogues, the resident masters not only taught basic reading and interpretation of the Scriptures but they taught the art and practice of holiness which they, in their turn, had received from their master before them.[7] A tradition of holiness and of service was thus sustained and passed down by virtue of each master thoroughly apprenticing a few disciples.

The Gospels are silent regarding the age of the disciples whom Jesus called. In practice, they could be as young as twelve and as old as forty. Peter is already married and has a home of his own (8:14). Unlike James and John, who work for their father, Peter is seemingly co-partner with his brother in their own fishing enterprise. It would be expected therefore that Peter is more than twenty years old. On the other hand, since Jesus frequently refers to his disciples as "these little ones"

(10:42, 18:6, 10, 14) and as "children" (18:5) or "infants" (11:25), one must presume that most of his disciples were under sixteen. Even if these terms are meant metaphorically, they might have some basis in fact also. Moreover, if it is to be supposed that John the disciple is the same person as John the Evangelist, then one has to assume that John joined Jesus at a very tender age in order to have sufficient vigor to write a Gospel some fifty or sixty years later. Since this presupposition cannot be established, however, it offers no additional evidence as to the age of the disciples surrounding Jesus.[8]

The Gospels are also silent regarding the literacy of the fisherman who joined Jesus. There were no public schools in this era, and the sons of fishermen were required to help their fathers from their earliest years. Some fathers, of course, might have taught their sons to read and to write, and other young boys might have had the opportunity to be educated in a local synagogue. But of this we can say nothing definite. It can only be presumed that Jesus took them where they were and brought them forward from that point.

The Pharisaic masters customarily required that their disciples be able to read the text of the Scriptures before undertaking to train them in its proper interpretation. From Matthew's account of Jesus' exposition of the Torah (5:20-48), there is no indication that Jesus is working from printed scrolls. On the contrary, since he repeats the phrase, "you have heard that it was said to our ancestors" (5:21, 27, 31, 33, 38, 43), he may be relying entirely upon the Torah which they <u>heard</u> at home and in the synagogue. This, in itself, however does not preclude that the fishermen knew how to read the Torah for themselves or that, at some later point, Jesus himself taught them to do so.

Since two of the disciples, Matthew and John, are credited with having written their respective Gospels in Greek, this suggests that some of the disciples were bilingual. On the basis of extensive studies of this period, Martin Hengel has shown that the Greek language and the Greek culture had made extensive inroads in many Palestinian cities. On the basis of this, Martin Hengel concludes:

> We have to count on the possibility that even in Jewish Palestine, individuals grew up bilingual and thus stood on the boundary of two cultures. This problem arises not only with

> Jerusalem, but also with Galilee, which had for a long time had special links with the Phoenician cities [near its borders]; we may ask whether some of the immediate circle of Jesus' disciples were not themselves bilingual. At any rate, two of the twelve, Andrew and Philip, had Greek names (Mark 3:18), and Simon Cephas-Peter, Andrew's brother, later undertook extensive missionary journeys among the Jewish Diaspora of the West, which spoke only Greek.[9]

Whatever may have been the age and background of the disciples, one can be quite sure that Jesus was quite familiar with the fishermen whom he singled out to share his vocation. A master who would surround himself either with simpletons who piously accept everything or with stubborn types who systematically reduce everything to their own entrenched categories would eventually be entirely discredited by his disciples. In this perspective, one can sense that <u>Jesus' choice of collaborators was one of the most critical of his career</u>.

A master must discern who is capable of entering into his/her vocation and turn down those who are deficient. Matthew's Gospel accordingly retains hints that Jesus turned away many who sought him for their apprenticeship (8:18-20). At one point, it appears that Jesus had initially accepted someone as a disciple and then discovered that this disciple wanted to return home and remain there until his father died (8:21). Matthew does not make clear, in this instance, whether the father was vitally dependent upon his son or whether, on the contrary, the son was dependent upon his father (for his approval, for his inheritance, etc.). In any case, Jesus responded: "Follow me, and leave the dead to bury their dead" (8:22). This strong advice leaves no doubt that the would-be disciple must choose life in the ways of YHWH when family ties have a deadening influence. Matthew does not indicate whether the disciple followed Jesus' advice. The presumption would be that he did.

In this era, the pursuit of an apprenticeship normally involved breaking off one's family life and one's former occupations. An apprenticeship in Torah required that the disciples came to live with their master. Accordingly, Matthew depicts the fishermen as leaving their parents and their nets and moving everywhere with Jesus. Jesus, from his side, regards his disciples as his true family and, accordingly, refuses to neglect them even when his own blood relatives make demands upon him (12:46-50).

It is noteworthy that Matthew's Gospel offers not a single word to disparage married life, the raising of children, the pursuit of a productive occupation. Not even Matthew's leaving aside his professions of tax collecting is used as an occasion to disparage what was a popularly despised source of livelihood. In effect, only when wealth or family positively obstruct serving God's cause are they disparaged (6:24, 10:37-39). As for married life, it can simply be assumed that Peter slept with his wife when Jesus stayed at his home (8:14-17). Discipleship had nothing to do with vows of virginity or with a puritanical anti-sexuality. It must be remembered that Jesus himself discouraged even the standard ascetical practices of his day when they served no functional purpose other than "to win men's [women's] admiration" (6:1-4, 16-18; 9:10-15). The Pharisaic masters, in parallel fashion, considered it difficult for a married man to undergo an apprenticeship; yet, following an apprenticeship, marriage was strongly advised. There is no reason to doubt that Jesus would have had parallel advice for his disciples and may have taken a wife himself if it hadn't been for his prophetic mission to herald the Kingdom in all the towns of Israel (4:23, 9:35, 10:23). Being on the move naturally prohibits family life. Moreover, Jesus manifested an extraordinary high regard for women and never disparaged associating with women as did some of the rabbinic masters.

Matthew records that Jesus said, "Follow me and I will make you fishers of men [women]10" (4:19), when he first invited Peter and Andrew. I would suggest that Jesus did indeed say this as an expression of the vision that he offered his first two disciples. In themselves, all beginnings are very important. It strikes me quite natural that Peter would have very vivid memories of his first deciding to apprentice himself to Jesus and undoubtedly told the story of his calling many times. Moreover, Peter did later distinguish himself as one who effectively lured many into the Way of Jesus and thereby fulfilled Jesus' initial high estimate of what Peter might become.

Within the rabbinic sources, one finds parallel accounts which present the vocational beginnings of exceptional disciples. The beginnings of Eliezer (c. 50 C.E.) have been recorded with exceptionally rich detail:

> What was the beginning of Rabbi Eliezer ben Hyrcanus? He was twenty-two years old and had not yet

> studied Torah. One day he resolved, "I will go and study Torah under Rabban Yohanan ben Zakkai."
>
> His father, Hyrcanus, [interrupting his resolve] said to him, "You are not even to taste any food before you have plowed the entire field."
>
> [As a result] he [Eliezer] rose early the next morning and plowed the entire field. Then [without even tasting any food] he departed for Jerusalem.

The narrative, up to this point, suggests that Eliezer is a late starter and that his father is not enthusiastic about his resolve. A second account of Eliezer's beginnings gives his age as twenty-eight and has his father say, "Get married and have sons, and take them to the academy [to study Torah] . . . ." Three weeks later, however, the prophet Elijah appears to Eliezer saying, "Go up to Ben Zakkai in Jerusalem." Then, both versions continue as follows:

> As he was walking along the road, he saw a stone. He picked it up and put it in his mouth [for he was very hungry]. (Some say it was actually a piece of cattle dung.) He continued on his way and spent the night in an inn.
>
> [In the morning] he went and sat in front of Rabban Yohanan ben Zakkai in Jerusalem [listening to his Torah]. Meanwhile a bad stench rose from his mouth . . . .
>
> (Thereupon) Rabban Yohanan said to him, "Just as this bad stench spreads from your mouth, so too shall your future fame spread due to your mastery of Torah".[11]

This amusing incident set in the highly-charged initial moments of meeting serves to allow the master, Yohanan, to express the promise which he detected in Eliezer. This onetime farmer went on to become his most renowned disciple and thereby fulfilled Yohanan's initial high estimate of him.

Christian scholars have generally endeavored to establish some "fundamental difference" between Jesus' manner of gathering disciples and the manner of the Pharisaic masters such as Yohanan. Dr. K.H. Rengstorf, the renowned scholar who prepared the study of discipleship for the Theological Dictionary of the New Testament, sets forth two such "fundamental differences": (1) The disciples of the Pharisees are admonished to seek out their own master, while Jesus, as a rule, takes the initiative himself. (2) The disciples of the Pharisees are led to attach themselves to their self-chosen masters because they are drawn by their "knowledge and method"; the disciples of Jesus, meanwhile, are attracted by his person and, in an act of faith, sumbit themselves "to be stamped and fashioned by him" (TDNT IV:444, 447, 449).

In his discussion of Jesus' initiative, Rengstorf overlooks the consequences following from Jesus' self-presentation as a prophet: namely, no one can guess that he intends to be a master also. As a consequence, Jesus must take the initiative at first. Once four disciples surround him, then he will be recognized as a master, and other candidates will take the initiative to come to him. Matthew even offers a specific instance of this (8:19-20). In the case of Yohanan, his reputation as a master is already established within the Jerusalem academy and it is only natural that potential disciples should seek him out. Within this perspective, what Rengstorf specifies as a "fundamental difference" becomes only "incidental."

Rengstorf's second "fundamental difference" stems from a dual misrepresentation. On the one hand, Rengstorf imagines that Pharisaic discipleship is knowledge-oriented whereas Jesus' disciples are person-oriented. On the other hand, Rengstorf imagines that the word of Jesus is accredited "by the will [to believe]" and not by intellectual persuasion (TDNT IV:449). In both cases, I find that Rengstorf tries to distiguish an either-or situation where, in fact, a both-and situation exists. Thus, Jesus' disciples are concerned to know God's standards of excellence as they are understood and lived by Jesus. To accomplish this, Jesus demands an intellectual assimilation of the intent of his parables, of his disputes with the Pharisees, of his interpretation of Torah. On the other hand, Pharisaic discipleship is also person-oriented. Eliezer's attachment to Yohanan ben Zakkai is based on the faith that his self-chosen master embraces the right perception, the right thinking, and the right doing of the Torah. A contemporary Jewish scholar who studied Yohanan ben Zakkai (c. 1-80 C.E.) expressed the character of Eliezer's attachment to Yohanan as follows:

> [Pharisaic] disciples were not merely students who came to a master to learn facts or holy traditions. They came to study the master as much as what he said. "Torah" was revealed in traditions handed on orally as in writing. Just as one studied what was written, so he had to imitate what was not written but living in the master himself. A living Torah, his every gesture must have some basis in the ancient traditions. The disciples lived with the master because daily life, like classroom discourse, was a school for Torah.[12]

As seen from this perspective, I must conclude that Rengstorf suffers from an overly rigid and misleading characterization of the Pharisaic masters. There are differences, to be sure, in the standards of holiness which distinguish individual masters. I, myself, however, find no "fundamental differences" which distinguish Jesus' manner of gathering disciples from that of the Pharisaic masters.

B. The Financing of Discipleship

From the moment that the fishermen left their nets in order to follow Jesus, their master assumed the responsibility for providing them with the necessities for living. Matthew does not give any explicit attention to this issue; he simply quietly assumes that Jesus had sufficient funds to provide for 'his family' (12:50). Jesus himself is identified by his neighbors as "the carpenter's son" (13:55), but there is no hint that Jesus continued his trade or that his father had a large patrimony which covered the expenses of his circle. Furthermore, since Jesus is never accused of neglecting to provide suitably for his disciples, one can be certain that they were reasonably well-fed and well-clothed. In fact, since Jesus was accused of being "a glutton and a drunkard"

(11:19), it must be assumed that both he and his disciples did, with some regularity, enjoy substantially above-average meals.

How did Jesus finance his roving academy?

Among the Pharisees, there was the tradition that demanded that the masters among them be self-supporting. The Pharisees, it will be remembered, constituted a lay movement that had no political power and no access to public funds. Consequently, once a disciple finished his apprenticeship, he normally returned to the trade of his youth. As an example of this, we know that Yohanan ben Zakkai studied under Hillel in Jerusalem. After Hillel's death, Yohanan settled in Arav, Galilee, for the next eighteen years (c. 20-40 C.E.). During this period . . .

> Yohanan entered some kind of business. We do not know exactly what he did, merely that he was in a trade. All the rabbis of this time supported themselves either in business, farming, crafts, or as common laborers. The rabbinate was not a paid profession but a lifelong calling. The rabbi may have exerted great influnce, but that did not result in much economic benefit. It was forbidden to "use the Torah as a spade to dig with." Teaching [in the synagogue] was not compensated, nor was presiding in court [i.e., settling disputed cases among the populace]. Each rabbi provided for himself as best as he could. A few were well-to-do, but most were not. Those who were rich were unable to support many others, though they did maintain students [disciples].[13]

Jesus was trained as a carpenter, but there is no indication that he ever continued his trade following his momentous baptism in the Jordan. On the other hand, Jesus did not receive any monies from his disciples. This is clearly implied when Jesus sends out his disciples with the instruction: "You received without charge, give without charge" (10:8). This is further supported by Jesus' directive to the rich young man whom he invited to become a disciple: "Go and sell everything you own and give the money to the poor, and you will have treasure in heaven; then come follow me" (19:21). Jesus, in effect, would have received no monies even should a rich man have joined him. The Talmud offers strong support for this practice:

> Teach others your understanding of Torah for free. Take no compensation whatever for her [Torah], since the Omnipotent gave her [Torah] to you gratitiously. And it is forbidden to make compensation for [telling another] the words of Torah. If you take compensation for [telling another] the words of the Torah, it is considered as though you had destroyed the whole world. Do not plead, "I have no money to live on [and I am thereby constrained to take compensation]." For [remember that] all money is his [the Lord's], as it is written: "The Silver is mine and the gold is mine! These are the words of the Lord of Hosts" [Hag 2:8], [and he will provide for you].[14]

This understanding clearly parallels that of Matthew's Gospel.

If both Jesus and his disciples received nothing for their sharing of Torah, it still remains to be shown how Jesus financed his enterprise. For this, Matthew provides a small clue in an unsuspected place:

> And many were there, watching [the crucifixion] from a distance, the same women who had followed Jesus from Galilee and looked after him. Among them were Mary of Magdala, Mary the mother of James and Joseph, and the mother of the Zebedee's sons (27:55-56).

It is unclear here whether "looking after him" embraces the paying of Jesus' expenses. Luke's Gospel has a parallel text which names Mary of Magdala, Susanna, and others as those "who provided for them [Jesus and the Twelve] out of their own resources" (Luke 8:3). By using Luke to clarify what Matthew leaves vague, it thus becomes apparent that a group of women financed Jesus' academy (and may even have traveled with Jesus while doing so).

One of the women whom Matthew names might have been extremely rich. Mary of Magdala is traditionally identified as the unnamed woman who "came to him with an alabaster jar of the most expensive ointment and poured it on his head as he was at table" (26:7).[15] "The disciples were indignant" because "this could be sold at a high price and the money given to the poor" (26:8-9). This signals not only the extreme wealth of the woman but it also shows that the disciples had instinctively come to regard the care of the poor as an important religious obligation. It is significant here that the disciples do not make any reference to any debts of Jesus or any material want that they themselves might have.

The second Mary is the mother of Jesus. Matthew refers to her as "the mother of James and Joseph," the same designation which he used earlier (13:55). It is not clear why Matthew deliberately avoids relating Mary to her son unless, of course, he wishes to heighten Jesus' resolve only to recognize his disciples as "my mother and my brothers" (12:48). For whatever reason, Matthew continues this pattern for the remainder of the Gospel by writing simply "Mary Magdala and the other Mary" (27:61, 28:1). If our identification is correct, it can hardly be supposed that Jesus' mother was independently wealthy; but, as was most probably the case, she was herself provided for by others.

The third-named woman, the mother of Zebedee's sons, shows up earlier in the Gospel as pressing Jesus to advance the status of her sons (20:20-23). As a benefactor of Jesus, she would certainly have ground for making such a request. Zebedee, meanwhile, was presented as mending his nets in his own boat (4:21). Presumably this represents at least a moderate affluence since ownership of a fishing vessel insured a steady catch out in the deep Galilean waters.

In addition to relying upon the resources of some sympathetic women, Jesus is also aware that there are sympathetic persons everywhere who would provide for his disciples. Thus he tells them:

> Whatever town or village you go into, ask for someone trustworthy and stay with him until you leave. As you enter his house, salute it, and if the house deserves it, let your peace descend upon it . . . (10:11-13).

This instruction would seemingly represent Jesus' own practice in moving about. Within contemporary America, such a mode of living could hardly hope to succeed. If one was to wander around the San Francisco bay area in the mid-60s, however, it would work well. I myself have had the opportunity to hitch hike in North Africa and know that the people there were positively anxious to have me stay with them in their homes. In the time of Jesus, as in North Africa today, the people felt a sacred trust to provide for the needs of travelers.

The Old Testament is filled with instances of hospitality being acted out. Most noteworthy is the account of the widow who willingly shared her last meal with the traveler, Elijah, during a period of general famine (1 Kgs 17:7-16). Deuteronomy offers the generalized recognition that YHWH "loves the stranger and gives him [her] food and clothing" (Deut 9:18). The Talmud develops this passion of YHWH for hospitality to travelers in the following manner:

> When the great calamity befell Job, he addressed the Holy One, blessed be He, saying, "Lord of the Universe! Did I not feed the hungry and give drink to the thirsty . . .? And did I not clothe the naked . . .?"
>
> The Holy One, blessed be He, answered him, "For all that, Job, you have not attained to one half the standard [of hospitality] displayed by Abraham. You waited in your house for guests to come to you. To him who was accustomed to eat wheaten bread you gave wheaten bread, to him who was accustomed to eat meat you gave meat, and to him who was accustomed to drink wine you gave wine. Abraham, however, did not act so. He went abroad [literally, "in the world"], and when he met wayfarers he brought them to his home. Even to him who was unaccustomed to eat wheaten bread he gave wheaten bread, to him who was unaccustomed to eat meat he gave meat, and to him who was unaccustomed to drink wine he gave wine. Not only that; he even went and built large inns along the roadways and placed in them a supply of food and drink, so that whoever entered ate and drank and blessed Heaven. Therefore he was granted happiness . . . .[16]

Jesus' Practice in Apprenticing His Disciples   119

If one carefully reads Jesus' parable of the last judgment (25:31-46), one finds the same theme born out in so far as blessings and punishments are determined on the basis of one's hospitality to the disciples of the king.

In addition to the religious cultivation of hospitality, Jesus and his disciples could also trust that their dedication to Torah would insure that they would be received as honored guests. There is a tradition stemming from the master, Jose (d. 160 B.C.E.), to this effect:

> Jose ben Joezer said: Let your house be a meeting-house for the wise. What is meant by this? It teaches that a man's house should be available to the wise, their disciples, and the disciples of their disciples; in the same manner that a man might say to his fellow, "I will wait for you at such and such a place."[17]

The last line implies that one's home would be so familiar to those occupied with Torah that they would naturally specify it as that well-known haunt where they can easily find one another. In sum, therefore, Jesus' expectation of finding food and lodging for himself and his disciples undoubtedly met with great success in the particular cultural milieu in which he lived.

Matthew provides further hints to the effect that Jesus himself had a home in Capernaum which served as his home base between his prophetic wanders:

> According to the distinctively Matthean tradition of 4:13, "he took up residence in Capernaum." This as 9:1 indicates, becomes "his own city," and the edited verses of 9:10, 28; 13:1, 36 and 17:25 show that he had a dwelling there . . . . In 9:10 "tax collectors and sinners" join him "in his house" in order to recline at table and share a meal with him; the clause, "they were reclining with Jesus . . ." points to him as the host. Later in 9:28, he is followed "into his house" by two blind men whose sight he restores. Jesus leaves "his house" in 13:1 in order to speak to the masses by the sea; he re-enters "his house" in order to impart special teaching to his

disciples alone. Jesus' reprimand of Simon Peter's all to quick responses to the tax collectors in 17:24f occurs privately after having gone "into his house."[18]

If this is the case, it is entirely conceivable that Jesus continued his trade as a carpenter while in residence. If not this, one must assume that the women who supported him provided for his wants and for the needs of his disciples and guests as well.

C.   The Place and the Posture of Apprenticing

The Gospel of Matthew makes it clear that Jesus apprenticed his disciples in the towns and open spaces surrounding the Sea of Galilee. While general summary statements depict Jesus as moving through "the whole of Galilee" (4:23), the furthest specified town which Jesus visited was Nazareth, which lies twenty-four miles from the Sea. Only with the final trip to Jerusalem (20:17ff), does Matthew depict Jesus as taking his circle of disciples beyond these familiar boundaries.

Since Galilee was culturally diversified, it comes as no surprise that Jesus there encounters non-Jews: a Roman centurion (8:5), the Gadarenes who raise pigs (8:30), a Canaanite woman (15:22). By and large, however, Matthew presents Jesus as preoccupied with Jews and with Jewish concerns. This is very forcefully shown when Jesus instructs his disciples before sending them out on their own:

> Do not turn your steps to pagan territory, and do not enter any Samaritan town; go rather to the lost sheep of the House of Israel . . . (10:6).

> I tell you solemnly, you will not have gone the round of the towns of Israel before the Son of Man comes [to make the final judgement] (10:23).

In accord with this, Matthew presents Jesus as gravitating toward the local synagogue upon entering a town (12:9, 13:54). Thus, by implication, Jesus bypasses the Gentile sector of town in order to reach the heart of the Jewish sector. The synagogue represents the natural place for apprenticing (4:23). The local synagogue need not have been a building set apart. In many instances it was a spacious private home or an outside courtyard set aside for instruction, prayer, and apprenticing.[19] The very movement of Jesus with his disciples toward the local synagogue would have been a natural signal that a master was preparing to begin a session. Interested persons would know that such sessions would be open to them and would follow behind.

Within the synagogue itself, the master signaled his readiness to begin by sitting down. Matthew clearly retains this procedure when he introduces the Sermon on the Mount:

> Seeing the crowds he went up into the mountain. And when he sat down, his disciples approached him, and, opening his mouth, he apprenticed them . . . (5:1-2 literally translated).

Here it can be seen that the disciples pick up on Jesus' cue and form a circle, sitting around him. Interested persons would take their places behind the disciples.

The rabbinic literature presents innumerable instances of the practices of sitting while apprenticing. The following illustration emphasizes this:

> Once Rabban Yohanan ben Zakkai was riding on an ass when going on a journey. Rabbi [i.e., the future rabbi] Eleazer ben Arakh was driving the ass from behind.
>
> Rabbi Eleazar said to him, "Master, teach me a chapter of the <u>Work of the Chariot</u> [a book recording the visions of Ezekiel]."
>
> He responded, "Have I not explained to you that it is forbidden to teach the <u>Work of the Chariot</u> privately to one disciple, unless [of course] that disciple is wise and insightful?"

> Rabbi Eleazer then said to him, "Master, permit me to say before you something which you have taught me."
> He answered, "Say on!"
>
> Forthwith, Rabban Yohanan ben Zakkai dismounted from the ass, and wrapped himself up, and sat upon a stone beneath an olive tree.
>
> Said Rabbi Eleazar to him, "Master, why did you dismount from the ass?
>
> He answered, "Is it proper that I should ride upon an ass while you are expounding the Work of the Chariot, and the Divine Presence (Shekinah) is with us, and the ministering angels accompany us?"[20]

In this instance, the master, Yohanan, deliberately dismounts so as to sit on the earth while his disciple repeats to him a lesson which the master had formerly taught him. The narrative continues by describing how Eleazar's exposition brought fire and song from heaven -- visible symbols of YHWH and his/her angels.

In another place, the disciple sitting before his master is admonished to put himself in the original experience of Israel when "on the mountain, from the heart of the fire, YHWH spoke to you face to face" (Deut 5:4; 4:33, 36; 5:22, 24, 26; Exod 18:19, 24:17):

> Let him [your disciple] not sit in your presence on the couch or stool or bench. Instead let him sit before you on the ground. And, every single word which comes forth from the mouth, let him take in with awe, fear, dread, and trembling -- the way our fathers received [the Torah] from Mount Sinai: with awe, fear, dread, and trembling; so let him too take in every single word which comes forth from your mouth with awe and fear, dread and trembling.[21]

The transfiguration narrative in Matthew's Gospel suggests a certain parallel experience. Peter, James, and John are alone "on the mountain" (17:1) with Jesus. This mountain (oros) appears to be the familiar place, the pseudo-synagogue, in which Jesus apprentices his disciples (5:1, 28:16) and retires for prayer (14:23). On this occasion, Jesus is apprenticing his disciples. While the disciples are listening, Jesus is marvelously transformed in their eyes and Moses and Elijah appear "to them" (17:3). They listen to all three. Finally, a bright cloud overshadows the mountain, and a fourth voice is heard. For the Jewish mind, these clues harken back to an earlier mountain:

> The cloud covered the mountain, and the glory of YHWH settled on the mountain of Sinai; for six days the cloud covered it, and on the seventh day YHWH called to Moses from inside the cloud (Exod 24:16).

The disciples are left "overcome with fear" (17:6). No where in the Gospel does Matthew ever indicate the reaction of the disciples to their training sessions with Jesus. Perhaps here Matthew typifies what the sessions with Jesus were like upon the mountain -- like hearing Moses (the Torah) and Elijah (the escatological prophet) and YHWH (the Father) first hand. And YHWH says, "Listen to my son" -- again pointing to the fact that the entire experience takes place while Jesus is speaking.

In addition to emphasizing Jesus' apprenticing in synagogues, Matthew devotes over two chapters to the collected discourses of Jesus while apprenticing "in the Temple" (21:22ff). While on trial, Jesus makes it clear that "he sat apprenticing in the Temple day after day: (26:55, emphasis mine). This practice of Jesus was shared by the masters of the Pharisees:

> The academy [of Yohanan] did not have its own building, for the stairway leading to the Temple mount, on the westward side of the Offal Gate, was the place where Yohanan sat and lectured to his students [disciples]. The Temple area, like others in the classical world, was used as a place for public instruction . . . . Yohanan did not use the courts of the Temple. He sat in the shadow of the Temple, where he could see it [easily, since his eyes would be shaded].[22]

After Jesus' death, the disciples continued to meet "by common consent in the Portico of Solomon" (Acts 5:12-14). I would guess that this was Jesus' own practice which the disciples were now continuing in absence. This being the case, it would seem that Jesus had clearly intended to permanently move his academy to Jerusalem.

There was an extended period of up to thirty years in which the academy of Jesus operated within the Temple courts along side the academy of Yohanan, the academy of Gamaliel, the Temple scribes, etc. There were periods of harassment by the priests, to be sure, but there were also periods of peaceful coexistence. Paul's inquisition does not represent the stand of the Pharisees. His own master, Gamaliel, opposed his course of action (Acts 5:34-39). The Acts of the Apostles makes it quite clear that Paul was acting as a henchman for the high priest and not for the Pharisees at large (Acts 9:1, 21). After the destruction of the Temple, the Pharisees tried desperately to consolidate the shattered fragments of Judaism. In this period they became increasingly intolerant of diversity even within their own ranks. The situation was thus set for the total animosity between Pharisees and Christians as reflected in Matthew's Gospel. One must not allow this later situation, however, to cloud over the long-standing presence of the academy of Jesus within the Temple courts.

D. The Content and Goal of Apprenticing

It is very difficult to discuss the content of Jesus' apprenticing because each of us automatically assumes that our own particular church accurately presents us with that content. Thus, for example, those of us who have received Christianity as a set of doctrines to be believed, Jesus spontaneously appears as the one who divulges privileged information about God. For those of us who have received Christianity as a divinely-authorized moral code, Jesus spontaneously appears as the authoritative lawgiver. For those of us who have received Christianity as a peak experience in which God is felt and tasted, Jesus spontaneously appears as the one who carries away his disciples into experiencing the forgiveness of sins and God's grace for overcoming evil. In sum, each of us comes out of a particular Christian upbringing which tends to determine in advance the content of Jesus' apprenticing which one finds in the Gospel clues.

Furthermore, it is quite impossible to expect that any Gospel ever sufficed to present the content of Jesus' apprenticing. The content, as has been already suggested, embraces nothing less than the lived wisdom of Jesus. A disciple becomes a living re-presentation of his master. Accordingly, Matthew offered his listeners more than just narratives about Jesus, he exemplified in his own tangible existence those performance skills and habits of judgement which characterized the master. Today, however, we no longer have the presence of Matthew to illustrate the lived wisdom hinted at in his narratives. The narratives alone remain.

In the last three decades, Christian scholars have produced many fine reconstructions of the content of Jesus' teaching as perceived within the Jewish horizon of understanding.[23] It would be foolish for me to endeavor to summarize these studies or to arbitrate among them. For my purposes here it will suffice to extend the horizon of these studies by drawing out aspects which are frequently overlooked in specifying the content of Jesus apprenticing of his disciples.

Every significant historical movement endeavors to impart a new consciousness to its participants. The Jesus movement is no exception to this rule. The disciples must undergo a profound change if they are to correctly perceive God's cause and dedicate themselves within it as Jesus shows them. The master, therefore, must arrange the apprenticeship of his disciples so that they emerge with his own consciousness and performance skills. If one examines the Black Panthers, the Women's Movement, or the Grey Panthers, one will find that the participants have each moved through a conversion experience that imparts to them <u>a new personal identity</u>. It is by appreciating one or the other of these contemporary movements that one gains a correct posture for appreciating the impact of the master, Jesus, upon his disciples.

Jesus specifies the personal identity of his followers to be that of "salt of the earth" and "light of the world" (5:13). As salt, the disciples are to regard themselves as the indispensable agents whereby humanity is favored and/or preserved. If they "go flat," nothing can be done; they "can only be thrown out to be trampled underfoot" (5:13). As light, the disciples are brought face to face with the expectation of Isaiah -- that of bearing the light of Torah before the face of the nations:

> I, YHWH, have called you to serve the
> cause of right;
> I have taken you by the hand and formed
> you;
> I have appointed you as a covenant of
> the people and light of the
> nations, to open the eyes of the
> blind, to free captives from prison,
> and those who live in the darkness
> from the dungeon (Isa 42:6-8).

Frequently Jesus' ministry has been characterized as "the conversion of sinners." "Conversion" is here understood to designate the profound experience of forgiveness that the acknowledged sinner feels when he/she wholeheartedly repudiates the tenacious source of sin within the heart. Thus it happens that the drunkard thanks God that the desire for liquor has been checked. The adulterous husband cries tears of regret and anticipates an atoning fidelity to his anguished wife. The public official (such as Charles Colson) repents of his/her distorted loyalties to schemes of corruption and dedicates his/her future as a "servant of Jesus Christ." In contrast, the Jesus of the Gospels is surprisingly indifferent to the conversion of this or that public sinner to the standards of public morality. <u>Jesus is more intent upon transforming the very norms of public morality</u>. The Gospels contain not a single censure or call to conversion directed at public sinners. On the contrary, Jesus frequently censures the Pharisees, the scribes, the priests, i.e., those very persons whom the public sinners consider to be close to God. Jesus' contention is that these so-called "religious leaders" are precisely the blind guides "who shut up the kingdom of heaven in men's [women's] faces" (23:13).

As a consequence, the conversion which Jesus calls for is nothing less than a transformation of the <u>status quo</u> of religious self-understanding. It is conversion to a new possibility for living the Torah of one's Father. Morality is involved -- but only as the by-product of the orientation of one's moral consciousness. In this the Jesus movement again finds a fitting secular counterpart in the Women's Movement:

> From this new perspective [following conversion] nothing is left unchallenged. One day a woman realizes that something that she has held sacred -- her parents' ideal for her life, a favorite story from childhood or

> adolescence, a dream she has had about life -- is part of the vast social mythology which keeps women in the inner space and refuge of home and family.[24]

It must be supposed that the fishermen whom Jesus called already had a functional religious identity prior to their association with Jesus. During their apprenticeship, however, they willingly submitted even their most cherished notions of God's cause to be enlarged and transmuted so as to reproduce those of their master.

Within the Sermon on the Mount, Matthew collects and summarizes some of the training sessions that Jesus held with his disciples. In this collection Matthew has offered six case studies which indicate how Jesus trained his disciples to live out the Torah of Moses so a to be "salt" and "light." For our purposes here, I will consider only the sixth:

> You have learnt how it was said: <u>You must love your neighbor</u> and [so it would seem to follow that you must] hate your enemy. But I say this to you: love your enemies and pray for those who persecute you; in this way you will be sons of your Father in heaven, for he causes his sun to rise on bad men as well as good, and his rain to fall on honest and dishonest alike. For if you love those who love you, what right have you to claim any credit? Even the tax collectors do as much, do they not? And if you save your greetings for your brothers, are you doing anything exceptional? Even the pagans do as much, do they not? You must therefore be perfect as your heavenly Father is perfect (5:43-48).

In this case study, Jesus begins by citing the text which his disciples were accustomed to hear: "You must love your neighbor as yourself" (Lev 19:18). This would be a standard procedure for a master of Torah (TDNT III:139-142). Then, Jesus begins to unravel the meaning therein. In particular, Jesus opposes himself to those who would specify "neighbor" in such a narrow sense so as to exclude "those who persecute you." He brings forward two lines of argumentation: (1) He draws attention to the common observation that the Lord of the Universe distributes his/her blessings of sunshine and rain upon both friend and enemies. It immediately follows that anyone who would be a son/daughter of this Father must follow the same Torah. (2) Jesus then indicates that tax collectors and pagans, who know nothing of Torah, already practice the code of honorably looking out for their friends and benefactors. It immediately follows that anyone only practicing this code cannot be "the salt of the earth" and "the light of the world" because they are conformed to already existing standards. The disciple must exhibit higher standards: "You must therefore be perfect as your heavenly Father is perfect" (5:48).

When Jesus proposes that his disciples must learn to love their enemies (5:44), this does not imply an insipid "being nice to everyone." Nor does it imply cultivating timidity and habitually backing down in the face of confrontation. One has only to consult Jesus' lived Torah in order to make the correct sense of his verbal Torah. Jesus is the kind of lover who disturbs the prevailing order. He, accordingly, makes enemies.

> Do not suppose that I have come to bring peace to the earth: it is not peace I have come to bring, but a sword. For I have come to set a man against his father [i.e., to cut them off from each other], a daughter against her mother, a daughter-in-law against her mother-in-law. A man's [woman's] enemies will be those of his [her] own household (10:34-36).

The same experience of being cut off occurs today for those who have been profoundly changed by the Black Muslims, by a Women's consciousness-raising group, by two full weekends of est (Erhard Seminar Training). One's enemies are then found among the unconverted members of one's own household. When Jesus refers to "loving one's enemies," therefore, this must initially mean acting benevolently toward those blood relatives who oppose one's new calling. Jesus himself was opposed by his relatives (12:46-50, 13:53-58). The Pharisees, also became his "enemies" (12:1-45). No doubt Jesus used the events of his own life to make clear, to his disciples, the full intent of what he meant by "love your enemies." Matthew, it must be remembered, retains only the barest skeleton of the original training sessions in his Gospel.

The training sessions summarized by Matthew in the Sermon on the Mount clearly indicate that Jesus has no intention to feed his disciples with esoteric doctrines about God. The above case study, for instance, may be regarded as revealing that God does not play favorites -- he/she takes care of good and evil persons alike. This revelation, however, Jesus does not present as a doctrine for assent; rather, it is proposed for implementation. "You must therefore be perfect as your heavenly Father is perfect" (5:48). Jesus trains his disciples in a functional holiness which consists in harmonizing themselves with the attitudes and the standards of excellence exhibited by their Father. "In this way you will be sons [daughters] of your Father in heaven" (5:45).

In like fashion, Jesus gives not the slightest intimation that perfection lies in cultivating mystical experiences or in being overwhelmed by the Holy Spirit. There are experiences in Jesus' apprenticing, to be sure, but they are the experiences of how the Father's rain falls and of how the pagans take care of their own. And, as for the spirit that may overwhelm a person, it must be strictly tested by the deeds that it promotes:

> A man's [woman's] words flow out of what fills his [her] heart. A good man [woman] draws good things from his [her] store of goodness; a bad man [woman] draws bad things from his [her] store of badness (12:34-35, also 7:16-27).

As a consequence, Jesus never boasts of having received the Holy Spirit. He points to the fruit that his life bears and allows his supporters and his enemies to draw their own conclusion (e.g., 11:2-5, 12:22-28, 21:28-32).

The Sermon on the Mount is frequently interpreted as presenting Jesus as handing down divinely-revealed laws and obligations. At the same time, God is made to appear as the One who can impose any restrictions that he/she may want upon his/her creatures. The mentality is: "I must obey this or God will punish me." In so doing, Christianity is reduced to a set of servile obligations motivated by a spiritualized greed for rewards and fear of punishments. As such, one completely loses sight of the Jewish horizon of understanding wherein Torah is the wisdom lived by the Father and entrusted to his cherished children.

> This [wisdom] is expounded in historical terms, e.g., that Israel should plant the land as God planted the Garden of Eden, in ethical terms, that the

righteous should clothe the naked as
God clothed Adam, visit the sick as God
visited Abraham, comfort the sorrowful
as God comforted Isaac, and bury the
dead as God buried Moses (TDNT
I:212).

Not even God can be arbitrary. And there can be no religious obligation that God does not impose upon him/herself prior to offering it to those whom he/she nurtures in his/her likeness.

It is quite inconsistent for Christians to condemn the supposed legalism of Jewish religion and then turn around and impose a new legalism in the name of Jesus. It would have been unthinkable for Jesus to imagine that he was dispensing hard and fast rules -- rules that were to be followed blindly and which knew of no exception. Thus it is that Jesus is criticized time and time again for being too liberal in making exceptions (9:11, 14; 12:2, 10; 15:2; 17:24). And time and time again Jesus demonstrates that the wisdom of the Father necessitates knowing how to make exceptions when the circumstances warrant it.

The Pharisees were scandalized by Jesus' freedom in making exceptions to the requirements of Torah. YHWH had made a covenant with their forefathers. Infidelity to that covenant caused YHWH to momentarily abandon them. The Pharisees believed that once perfect fidelity to the terms of the covenant (the Mosaic Torah) was restored, YHWH would rescue and redeem his people with power and glory. If the future of the Jewish people depended upon fidelity to the Mosaic Torah, then the Pharisees rightly suspected that Jesus' conscientious freedom with regard to the Torah undermined respect for Torah.

Consider, for a moment, the test case that Matthew offers for our instruction in his twelfth chapter: Jesus and his disciples were out for a sabbath walk. "His disciples were hungry and began to pick ears of corn [wheat] and eat them" (Matt 12:1). Jesus had trained his disciples to honor the holiness of the sabbath as well as the more generalized rule: "What I [YHWH] want is mercy [deeds of loving kindness], not sacrifice" (Hos 6:6 = Matt 12:7, 9:13). Thus, the silence of Jesus implies that he honored the discretionary exception that his disciples were claiming for themselves. Note also that the disciples did not feel any compulsion to consult Jesus each time they acted; the disciples were quite well-trained at this point and were accustomed to acting responsibly on their own (following Matt 10). The Pharisees, however, are scandalized at the silence of Jesus and said to him:

"Look, your disciples are doing something that is forbidden on the sabbath" (Matt 12:2). The Pharisees undoubtedly believed that Jesus would halt his disciples on the grounds that the discomforts of hunger do not entitle one "to harvest grain" on the sabbath. If there was a case of a life and death need, the Pharisees would have allowed the exception, but Jesus' disciples are clearly not dying of hunger. Moreover, the Pharisees figured that Jesus, by his silence, might mislead his disciples and neglect their proper training in the Torah. At their best, therefore, the Pharisees are exercising both a legitimate concern and a fraternal correction. But, Jesus, to their chagrin, does not correct his disciples. He justifies them:

> Have you not read [1 Sam 21:4-7] what David did when he and his followers were hungry -- how he went into the house of God [the Temple] and how they ate the loaves of offering which neither he nor his followers were allowed to eat, but which were for the priests alone?
>
> Or again, have you not read in the Torah [Num 28:9-10] that on the sabbath day the temple priests break the sabbath without being blamed for it? (Matt 12:3-5)

Jesus' response reveals that he and his disciples held the Torah in high esteem. In fact, when carefully studied, Jesus notes that it is the Hebrew Scriptures themselves which demonstrate the art of making legitimate exceptions. Jesus tried to appeal to the Pharisees on common ground in order to win them over to his standards of judgment.

Now (as Matthew intimates) it is the Pharisees who are silenced. They neither approve nor refute Jesus. Do they then agree with him? Probably not. They would find it hard to compare what David and his men did while fleeing for their lives with what the disciples of Jesus did when suffering the discomforts of humber on a sabbath walk through the wheat fields. Furthermore, the priests do what they do by virtue of their office. Yet Jesus says:

> Now here [in the case of my disciples], I tell you, is something greater than [the case of] the Temple. And if you had understood the meaning of the words: <u>What I want is mercy</u>, <u>not</u>

sacrifice, you would not have condemned the blameless (Matt 12:6-7).

Only someone who was filled with the divine pathos, someone who had the supreme confidence that he knew his Father's heart in addition to knowing his word (Torah), could think and speak like this. Anyone who considered YHWH as distant and inscrutable would be very slow to make exceptions to the terms of the Mosaic covenant. Only someone who habitually felt a familiarity with YHWH could act with such freedom. The fact that Jesus addressed YHWH in prayer as "Father" (Matt 6:9, 11:25f, 26:42), or even as "Abba" (Aramaic: "Dad" = pater in Mark 14:36), further testifies to Jesus' sense of intimacy with YHWH.

What must astonish us even today is the further fact that Jesus trains his disciples to participate in the selfsame spirit/Spirit and horizon of understanding. Thus it is that, again and again, Jesus does not hesitate to speak to his disciples about "your Father" (5:16, 45, 48; 6:1, 4, 6, 8, 14, 15, 18a, 18b, 26, 32; 7:11, 21; etc.) and invites his disciples to pray in the inclusive term of "our Father" (6:9). Maybe this is why Jesus, for the most part, apprenticed his disciples "on the mountain" (5:1) -- such training would have evoked too much uneasiness and opposition "in their synagogues" (4:23, 9:35, 10:17, 12:9 13:54, 23:34).

Infants are bound by rigid rules: "Don't ever touch matches; don't ever cross the street alone." The child is punished or praised on the basis of strict conformity. With time, however, parents expect their children to enter into their own sensibilities and practical sense so that they know how to interpret the life-giving values which prompted the earlier rules. An adolescent who would continue in a childish conformity would be deemed "retarded." The very same thing holds with respect to the Torah of the Master of the Universe. A son/daughter of God must enter into the life-giving values of Torah or else be "retarded" within an infantile religion that stifles maturity. The ultimate irony is that Jesus who trains his disciples to grow out of infantalism is sometimes co-opted by contemporary priests/ministers and used to justify and enforce religious systems that foster conformity and blind acceptance (even for adults).

The Gospel retains numerous hints of the methods that Jesus employed while apprenticing his understudies. He is frequently depicted as taking his disciples aside, away from the crowds. Sometimes Jesus asks them questions so as to gauge their understanding (13:41, 14:14, 17:25).

At other times the disciples take the initiative by asking Jesus a question (13:10ff, 17:19, 18:1ff, 18:21ff, 19:10, 19:27ff). Sometimes they draw the attention of their master to matters which he may be overlooking (14:15; 15:12, 23; 24:1). The disciples are around when Jesus deals with opponents who challenge his Torah. They also observe carefully his practice in exorcizing and in healing and imaginatively rehearse how they themselves will act in parallel circumstances.

Jesus expects his disciples to take the initiative in acting. The detailed analysis in Chapter II demonstrated this. In another instance, the disciples alert Jesus regarding the hunger of the crowd. Jesus responds by urging them to "give them something to eat yourselves" (14:16). They hesitate. In the end, however, it is they who do indeed feed the crowd (14:19). At still other times Jesus criticizes the initiative of his disciples as, for example, when they prevented the children from fatiguing him (19:14) or when one of them tried to prevent his arrest (26:51). In due time, Jesus sends them out in pairs to do by themselves those things which they had learned in his presence (10:1ff).

During this missionary period and following his death, the disciples acted "in his name" (en to onomati). This technical expression occurs frequently relative to the initiatives of the disciples: they apprentice and speak "in the name of Jesus" (Acts 4:18, 5:28, 9:27, 29), they baptize (Matt 28:19; Acts 2:38, 8:16, 10:48, 19:5, 22:16), heal (Acts 3:6, 16; 4:7), and exorcise (Acts 19:13-16) in the same name. Contrary to a widespread misunderstanding, "there is in the New Testament no belief in the magically [or even supernaturally] potent names; in fact, there are no mysteriously dreadful words or names at all" (TDNT V:278). When a disciple acts "in the name of Jesus," this implies that he is acting out of the training that he received from Jesus. A disciple assimilates and lives into the personal vocation of his/her master. Later, following this apprenticeship, the disciple is authorized to re-present his/her master. And so it is that the disciples of Jesus account for themselves and for their deeds "in his name." Jesus, for his part, can accordingly say, "Anyone who receives your words and your deeds receives my words and my deeds" (10:40 expanded).

The upshot of this whole discussion is that Matthew offers abundant clues which present Jesus' practice in apprenticing his disciples and displays not the slightest embarassment in singularly honoring Jesus as a master (didaskalos).

> The Gospels make it clear point by
> point that the relation between Jesus
> and the disciples corresponds to that
> of Rabbinic pupils to their masters and
> that the crowd treated him with the
> respect accorded to the teachers
> [masters of Torah] (TDNT III:153).

Where, then, is the uniqueness of Jesus as a master? I have concluded that his uniqueness is not to be placed in his mode of calling disciples. Nor is there any substantial differences in the setting and the posture of Jesus apprenticing. His mode of financing his circle of disciples is unusual, but the Gospels themselves attest that it attracted no great attention and posed no serious problems. Jesus' pedagogical methods do not differ substantially from the methods employed by the other masters.

If one seeks to identify the substantial uniqueness of Jesus, it appears that this uniqueness shows up best within his very wisdom and effectiveness <u>as a master</u>. Employing the time-honored methods of his day, Jesus was the master who sensitively immersed himself in God's Torah with his disciples and, at the same time, exercised an urgent responsibility to attract all the lost sheep of the House of Israel back to its wisdom. Jesus' prophetic activity insured that he would never become just a local master attached to a fixed synagogue. He and his disciples were passionately committed to address and heal the brokenness of all the towns in Israel (esp. 10:23). After his death, this urgency was extended to embrace the apprenticing of Gentiles (28:19). Other masters endeavored to alter the personal identities of their disciples so that they would be "salt" and "light." None of them, however, stands out as having so effectively enhanced the powers of their disciples so that they were enabled to do just that: to be "the salt of the earth" and "the light of the nations." For, as the record of history entirely affirms, he provoked a decisive redetermination of the religious orientation of Western civilization.

This momentous result indicates that Jesus' sympathies were well-attuned to the deepest longings of his contemporaries -- longings, it must be added, that were ripe for realization. On this level alone, Jesus may appear as a clever opportunist. When one remembers, however, that it is the Spirit of God that fashions the hearts of God's people; then Jesus' success might be more aptly registered as his profound sympathy with the Lord of History. In this capacity, Jesus has been rightly honored as "servant of God" (e.g., Acts 3:13, 26; 4:27, 31) and as "Messiah" (e.g., Acts 2:31, 36; 3:18, 20). It is especially this latter designation that crowns Jesus ministry as Master of Torah. Our attention will accordingly now shift to examine how this is so and in what sense Jesus is unique as the Master of Righteousness who went on to become God's Messiah.

E. The Highest Estimate of Jesus' Apprenticing

When Jesus is identified as the expected Messiah, he is thereby honored as God's <u>anointed</u> (<u>christos</u> in Greek) who will bring to completion God's cause within universal human history. As such, no more exalted designation can be imagined whereby Jews might honor and embrace Jesus' apprenticing of Torah and his heralding of the Kingdom of Heaven. Gentiles will later rightfully honor Jesus as the incarnate Logos, but this horizon of understanding is foreign to Matthew's Gospel and will be appropriately taken up at a later point.

The following table allows one to contrast the frequency with which <u>christos</u> and <u>didaskalos</u> are used to refer to Jesus. The numbers in brackets refer to the number of instances in which the term in question is used to designate persons other than Jesus.

	Matt	Mark	Luke	Acts	John
<u>christos</u> (messiah)	14[3]	06[1]	12[0]	31[0]	15[6]
<u>didaskalos</u> (master)	11[0]	12[0]	16[2]	00[1]	06[1]

The statistics are somewhat deceptive in so far as each of the Synoptic Gospels has only one occasion in which the historical Jesus is expressly identified as the Messiah. This one occasion is Peter's response to Jesus' inquiry as to "who do you say I am?" (Mark 8:27-30, Matt 16:13-20, Luke 9:18-21).

Matthew narrates his Gospel in the consciousness that Jesus is the Messiah. Thus, he opens his Gospel with "a genealogy of Jesus Messiah" (1:1). The astrologers ask "where the Messiah was to be born" (2:4). Even before John the Baptizer makes inquiries of Jesus, Matthew, as narrator, tells his audience that "John in his prison had heard what the Messiah was doing" (11:2). Consequently, it is no surprise when Matthew's readers first learn that Peter confessed Jesus as the Messiah (16:16). Later in the Gospel Matthew has the members of the Sanhedrin mockingly call him "Messiah" (Matt 26:68). Pilate, in his turn, refers to "Jesus who is called Messiah" (27:17, 22). In sum, therefore, Matthew writes his Gospel for persons who already recognize Jesus as the Messiah. Within the drama of the Gospel itself, however, Jesus is not addressed supportively as the Messiah save in the single instance in which Peter does so.

Biblical scholars of the last century were almost all agreed that the contemporaries of Jesus expected a political Messiah in the image of a king like David who would crush the enemies of Israel. The fact that the insurrectionist, Bar Kochba, was designated as "the Messiah" by a large number of rabbis in 140 C.E. seemed to establish the political nature of the expected Messiah. Today, however, with a rediscovery of intertestimental literature and of the library of Qumran, scholars recognize that no simple and unified notion of the Messiah existed at the time of Jesus.[25] The community of Qumran, for instance, ardently expected two Messiahs: one, a descendent of David, to implement God's cause in the political sphere and the other, a descendent of Aaron, to restore holiness in the religious sphere.

In the face of diverse notions of "the Messiah to come," it appears as though the Gospels themselves must be consulted if one is to discover the messianic consciousness which prevailed among the disciples of Jesus. Yet, when one does this, one is struck by the fact that nowhere in the Gospel does one find any discussion of the Messiah or any attempt to correct mistaken notions. Jesus, himself, seemingly never discusses any messianic expectation other than that of the Kingdom of God. The strongest hint comes when John the Baptizer inquires whether Jesus is "the one who is to come" (11:3). The reply is given:

> Go back and tell John what you hear and see; the blind see again, and the lame walk, lepers are cleansed, and the deaf hear, and the dead are raised to life and the Good News is proclaimed to the poor . . . (11:4-5).

Against this background, it is evident that the Messiah is a doer. When Jesus is asked whether he is the one to come, he directs John's attention to his social impact and leaves it for John to decide for himself on the basis of the presenting evidence.

What is the nature of this evidence? Most of our contemporaries look at the evidence as pointing to medical cures. If such were the case, Jesus would be identified as the miraculous physician and not as the Messiah. But those within the Jewish horizon of understanding would not fall into this contemporary trap for the very terms in which Jesus' ministry is cast are none other than the very terms in which the prophets looked forward to the future righteousness in Israel. Thus, Isaiah writes:

> Courage! Do not be afraid. Look, your God is coming . . . . Then the eyes of the blind shall be opened, the ears of the deaf unsealed, then the lame shall leap like a deer and the tongue of the dumb sing for joy (Isa 35:5).

What does it mean for Matthew and for Isaiah to write of <u>blind eyes being opened</u>? One must examine the clues. Isaiah indicates (a) that the condition of blindness afflicts the whole people and not just isolated members (Isa 6:10), (b) that those who credit themselves with clear-sightedness are the very ones judged blind (Isa 42:20 & 43:8), and (c) that those who have been appointed as God's watchmen over the people are most culpably blind (Isa 56:10). In parallel fashion, Matthew presents Jesus as judging that all the Pharisees are quite blind even though they claim to see (15:14, 23:16, 17, 19, 24, 26). In each of these instances the Jewish usage of "blindness" appropriately expresses the helplessness and the lack of judgement which plagues those who are effectively out of harmony with the ways of YHWH.

A rabbinic commentary on "the Lord openeth the eyes of the blind" (Ps 146:8) runs as follows:

> Who are the blind? Men [women] of the present generation who go groping like blind men [women] in the Torah, saying "We wait for light, but behold obscurity, for brightness, but we walk in darkness. We grope for the wall like the blind" (Isa 59:9-10). All of them read, but do not know what they read. All of them study, but they do not know what they study. In the time-to-come, however, "the eyes of the blind shall be opened" (Isa 35:5).[26]

The curing of blindness, therefore, "is a favorite theme of escatological hope" (TDNT VI:281). And it is pecisely within this atmosphere that Matthew wishes to present the impact of Jesus as directed toward the removal of blindness (9:27-31, 12:22, 15:30, 20:29-34, 21:14). Matthew even cites Isa 6:9-10 to indicate the blindness of the people; yet, in contrast, he has Jesus say to his disciples:

> But fortunate are your eyes because they see, your ears because they hear! I tell you solemnly, many prophets and holy men longed to see what you see, and never saw it; to hear what you hear, and never heard it (13:16-17).

And this is the clue needed to understand Peter's identification of Jesus as the Messiah. Peter is not situated like the people at large. They experience Jesus' heralding of the Kingdom and immediately associate him with the expectations of one or the other prophet: "Some say he is John the Baptizer, some Elijah, and others Jeremiah or one of the prophets" (16:14). Peter, in contrast, has experienced Jesus within the intimacy of the master-discipline relationship. Within this relationship I would hazard to guess that Jesus has so attracted Peter and so transformed him that Peter is entirely convinced that Jesus will eventually attract and transform the hearts of all of Israel back to the Torah of their Father. Then the Kingdom will have come: the Torah of the Father will be done on earth as it is done in heaven (6:10).

The prophet heralds the future righteousness of Israel; the Messiah brings it to pass. Once the messianic era has arrived (and the expectations of the prophets fulfilled), it will be evident who has the one anointed by God to bring it about. <u>But the Kingdom has not arrived: the people are stumbling in their blindness. Yet, already Peter has seen the light and has touched and tasted the expectation of the prophets and has extrapolated the influence of his master into the future.</u> Thus Peter says to Jesus, "You are the Messiah, the son of the living God" (16:16).

To appreciate the experiential roots and the prophetic rashness of Peter's identification, one has to stop imagining that Peter is playing a guessing game or that he has been prompted by heavenly visions. No, Peter is not guessing. He has not received any privileged information from above. It suffices that he knows Jesus.

Meanwhile, Jesus knows that to be honored as "the Messiah" in advance and to effect the messianic age of righteousness are two quite different things. Jesus, consequently, acknowledges Peter as "a happy man" who has tasted that future which is known only to "my Father in heaven" (16:17). "Then he gave the disciples strict orders not to tell anyone that he was the Messiah" (16:20). In effect, Jesus judges that hailing him as Messiah would be rash and premature. The course of history will reveal the Messiah in due time. A premature identification of Jesus with "the Messiah" could only lead to vigorous denials on the part of the uninitiated and obstruct their conversion of heart toward the messianic holiness which Jesus presented. For the moment, it was imperative that master and disciples give their every energy to the preparing for the Kingdom and not enter into squabbles as to who will be the greatest in the Kingdom (18:1-4, 20:20-28).

It has frequently been suggested that Jesus must deliberately conceal his identity as the Messiah or else he will obstruct his enemies from playing their part in his atoning death. Such a horizon of understanding appears foreign to the Gospels. The previous chapter already concluded that Matthew offers little support for Anselm's doctrine of atonement. From what has already been discussed in this chapter, it is clear that Jesus' work as prophet and as master are the focus of Matthew's Gospel. As in the case of the parable, the owner of the vineyard sends his only son with the expectaton that he might finally bring the murderous tenants to their senses. It is unthinkable for a Father to send his son to a certain death. It is even more unthinkable to imagine that the Father would instruct his son to conceal his identity so as to be certain that his enemies will not spare him on account of who he is.

When the Messiah is again perceived in functional terms, there will no longer be any need for Christians to fuss and speculate regarding Jesus' self-consciousness as the "the Messiah." In point of fact, it will be recognized that <u>the only necessary and sufficient consciousness of the Messiah is a passionate preoccupation with living Torah and apprenticing Israel to do likewise</u>. Every great historical personage starts with only a burning zeal for the task which calls for accomplishment. Premonitions of future fame can only serve to obstruct the energies and to poison the motives of those who might have become great benefactors to their people. Jesus can be no exception here. He cannot persuade his disciples that "anyone who wants to become great among you must be your servant" (10:43) and then secretly ignore his own best advice.

In the end, therefore, the only appropriate advice that Jesus can give relative to the Messiah is to beware of pretenders:

> If anyone says to you then, "Look here is the Messiah" or "He is there," do not believe it; for false messiahs and false prophets will arise and produce great signs and portents, enough to deceive even the chosen, if that were possible. There; I have forewarned you (24:23-25).

In effect, Jesus warns his disciples that any megalomaniac can claim to be "the Messiah." Many such claimants will even be able to perform miracles. What specifically makes deception impossible is Jesus' principle that "you will be able to tell them by their fruits" (Matt 7:16). The Messiah must be the one who draws the hearts of Israel to Torah. Talk is cheap. Miracles are deceptive. The fruits of the Messiah must be tasted.

Jesus applies this selfsame principle by way of discerning disciples who are pretenders:

> It is not those who say to me, "sir/lord, sir/lord," who will enter the kingdom of heaven but the person who does the will of my Father in heaven. When the day [of judgement] comes many will say to me, "Sir/Lord, sir/lord, did we not prophesy in your name, cast out demons in your name, work many miracles in your name?" Then I shall tell them to their faces: "I have never known you; away from me you evil men!" (7:21-23).

Here Jesus indicates that those who honor him as their master, addressing him as _kyrie_, have no part in God's cause if they do not abide in his Torah. And even more strongly, Jesus indicates that those who prophesy and heal as he apprenticed them and yet do not abide by his Torah will be renounced as evil men. Thus, with this sober appraisal of worth, it is no wonder that Jesus has no taste for announcing himself as the Messiah (either before Israel or even privately before his God). True worth is to be measured by one's functioning:

> The man [woman] who keeps them [Torah and the prophets] and apprentices

> [others to keep] them will be
> considered great in the kingdom of
> heaven (Matt 5:19).

And by this rule the greatness of the authentic Messiah is also to be measured and weighed. Even if Jesus is destined to be the Messiah, he can be no exception to this rule.

In sum, I have endeavored to resituate Peter's affirmation of Jesus as the Messiah. Operating within a functional mentality, Peter's affirmation would necessarily be an extrapolation from the very fruits that Jesus' work as prophet and master have produced. Jesus accepts Peter's taste of the future but strictly binds him to silence. In the end, Jesus knows that claims are cheap, divisive and deceptive. In the end, even Jesus will be measured by the service he rendered in apprenticing the lost sheep of the House of Israel to reappropriate the wisdom of their Father in heaven. And in this, the disciple is like his master -- measured by the same rule.

Conclusion

When all is said and done, all of the exalted claims made for Jesus must stand or fall on the basis of Jesus' personal effectiveness as a master of Torah.[27] "You will be able to tell them by their fruits" (7:16, 20). Talk is cheap. Many would-be saviors of the world have claimed to be Sons of God. The disciples of these individuals wrote glowing reports. Their masters are reported to have worked such signs and wonders as to make the Jesus of the Gospels appear as third-rate.[28] Yet, their cults have passed and have not left the world purified, transformed, blessed. The single distinction that assures that the claims made for Jesus held up with the time was the slow and progressive expansion of the Jesus movement throughout the Roman world during the five hundred following the death of Jesus. Jesus precipitated a series of personal/social transformations that shattered and remolded the civilized world. History can never retract this magnanimous "YES" to Jesus and his enduring chain of disciples.

The measure of the greatness of any religious master lies in the depths of the blessed transformation that he/she effects within his/her disciples. In effect, there is no adequate way for a disciple to gauge the divine power of his/her master save by becoming a participant in that power through a systematic apprenticeship. The mature disciple knows the spiritual power of his/her master by personal participation. The beginning disciple, meanwhile, can only conjecture and romanticize. As the immature lover who is rapt in infatuation, this disciple only relishes and tastes his/her own projections upon the master. Any master who is surrounded with only infatuated adherents is doomed to a quick end. Infatuation dies easily. Even when infatuation is sustained by a rabid fanaticism, a movement so founded later deteriorates into an admiration society which is powerless to effect permanent and irreversible human transformation.

Since reality testing is the only secure measure of religious claims, Jesus necessarily takes the highest honors within Western civilization. Augustine himself used this appeal when he endeavored to draw his fellow Neoplatonists after him into the Jesus Movement following his own conversion (390 C.E.). I will cite Augustine at length since I find that it admirably demonstrates how every claim for the divinity of Jesus is intimately woven within the pastoral renewal effected by his disciples. The stature of a master is exalted or doomed by the effective stature of the chain of disciples who claim to share in his/her power. In this perspective, Augustine makes his appeal for Jesus out of the mouth of his former master, Plato:

> In Christian times there can be no doubt at all as to which religion is to be received and held fast, and as to where is the way that leads to truth and beatitude.
>
> Suppose Plato were alive and would not spurn a question I would put to him; or rather suppose one of his own disciples, who lived at the same time as he did, had addressed him thus:
>
>> You have persuaded me that truth is seen not with the bodily eyes but by the mind, and that any soul that cleaves to truth is thereby made happy and perfect. Nothing hinders the perception of truth more than a life devoted to lusts and the false images of sensible things . . . . [The speaker continues here to describe at length the salvific effects of progressively laying hold of truth.]

> Now, if some great and divine man should arise to persuade the people that such things were to be at least believed, if they could not grasp them with the mind, or that those who could grasp them should not allow themselves to be implicated in the depraved opinions of the multitude . . . , would you not judge that such a man is worthy of divine honors?

I [Augustine] believe that Plato's answer would be:

> That could not be done by [a human], unless the very virtue and wisdom of God delivered him from natural environment, illumined him from his cradle not by human teaching but by personal illumination, honored him with such grace, strengthened him with such firmness and exalted him with such majesty, that he should be able to despise all that wicked men [women] desire, to suffer all that they dread, to do all that they marvel at, and so, with the greatest love and authority, to convert the human race to so sound a faith. But it is needless to ask me about the honours that would be due to such a man. It is easy to calculate what honours are due to the wisdom of God. Being the bearer and instrument of the wisdom of God on behalf of the true salvation of the human race, such a man would have earned a place all his own, a place above all humanity.

Now this very thing has come to pass. It is celebrated in books and documents. From one particular region of the earth in which alone the one God was worshipped and where alone such a man could be born, chosen men were sent throughout the entire world, and by their virtues and words have kindled the fires of the divine love. Their sound teaching has been confirmed and they have left to posterity a world illumined.²⁹

Footnotes for Chapter V

¹ Birger Gerhardsson, in *Memory and Manuscript* (Lund, Sweden: C.W.K. Gleerup, 1961), has endeavored to establish the reliability of a disciple's memoirs on the basis of the large role given to memorization and systematic repetition in the training of a disciple. Gerhardsson's thesis has not been well received due to the evident variations that exist among the sayings attributed to Jesus within the separate Gospels. These variations also have their rabbinic counterparts.

² This is how Rabbi Leib, a Hasidic zaddik explained why he sought out his master. See Martin Buber, *Tales of Hasidim* (N.Y.: Schocken Books, 1970), p. 107.

³ The majority of living Christian scholars acknowledge that the Gospels can be reliable without providing a word for word dictation of what Jesus said. Edward Schillebeeckx, in *Jesus* (N.Y.: Seabury, 1979), argues that even those sayings that are put in the mouth of Jesus by the later church "may indeed reflect a basic posture adopted by the earthly Jesus, and thus may be 'true in substance,' even though the earthly Jesus had uttered never a word on the matter" (p. 87). For a larger treatment of this matter, see Schillebeckx, *op. cit.*, pp. 43-104 or Norman Perrin, *Rediscovering the Teaching of Jesus* (N.Y.: Harper & Row, 1967), pp. 15-53.
Jewish scholars have been slow to recognize form and redaction criticism. See S. David Sperling, "Judaism and Modern Biblical Research," *Biblical Studies*, ed. by Lawrence Boadt et al. (N.Y.: Paulist, 1980), pp. 19-44. By exception, a few Jewish scholars have systematically recognized that material attributed to a particular rabbi may have a later origin or even show editorial changes (where multiple sources exist). See especially Jacob Neusner, *Development of a Legend: Studies of the Traditions Concerning Yohanan be Zakkai* (Leiden: E.J. Brill, 1970), pp. 1-11, and his *The Rabbinic Traditions About the Pharisees Before 70* (Leiden: E.J. Brill, 1971), Part I, pp. 1-10.

⁴ The Pontifical Biblical Commission in its 1964 *Instruction on the Historicity of the Gospels* ("Sancta Mater Ecclesia," *Acta Apostolicae Sedes* 66 [1964] 712-718) explained that the disciples of Jesus "interpreted his words and deeds according to the needs of the listeners" (sec. 8). When these same disciples, or their successors, set their hand to writing the Gospels, the Commission

suggests that "they selected some things [from the apostolic tradition], reduced others to a synthesis, and [still] others they explicted as they kept in mind the situation of the churches" (sec. 9). In effect, this means that authentic remembrance and pastoral adaptation go hand in hand in creating the Gospel narratives. Most Christian scholars, even those who reject modern bibilical scholarship, would agree in principle to this judgement. Relative to specific texts, however, scholars widely differ as to what components are "authentic remembrances" and what are "pastoral adaptations/additions."

5 The reporting of news and the recording of history always presume a personal perspective. A native and a foreigner, for example, necessarily experience and report to their respective colleagues quite different perspectives. Strictly impersonal reporting is therefore both useless and unattainable. Hans-Georg Gadamer, in Truth and Method (N.Y.: Seabury, 1975), carefully traces how Western civilization came to understand that all history (as well as art and literature) presupposes a particular human horizon of understanding. Michael Polanyi has shown that this applies as well to the formulation and the acceptance of scientific theories.

6 In contrast, Luke's Gospel presents Jesus as frequently dining with the Pharisees (Luke 7:36, 11:37, 14:1). Luke removes Mark's suggestion that the Pharisees plotted with the Herodians to destroy Jesus. Compare Luke 6:11 with Mark 3:6 and Matt 12:14. Luke even presents some Pharisees as warning Jesus against a plot of Herod (Luke 13:31).

7 Martin Hengel, in Judaism and Hellenism (Philadelphia: Fortress, 1974), pp. 78-82, traces the critical role of the "Jewish house of learning" for both general education and Pharisaic holiness. For a very readable and provocative Jewish account, see Ellis Rivkin, The Shaping of Jewish History (N.Y.: Charles Scribner's Sons, 1971), pp. 44-87.

8 Both the internal and external evidence relative to the authorship of John's Gospel remains inconclusive. See, for example, Raymond E. Brown, The Gospel According to John: The Anchor Bible, Vol. 29 (Garden City: Doubleday, 1966), pp. LXXXVII-CII. Even if John the Apostle is identified as the author, one might presume that the book was penned many years after the death of John by a disciple writing under his authority and in his name. In sum, therefore, nothing conclusive can be established as to John's age when he was called by Jesus.

[9] Martin Hengel, Judaism and Hellenism, p. 105.

[10] In this and in other texts, the Greek term anthropos does not designate sexual exclusiveness; hence, I insert "women" in brackets so as to amend the misleading translation provided by the Jerusalem Bible. Anthropos refers to "a human person."

[11] Abot de Rabbi Nathan 6:3 (20b). The variant accounts with an analysis are presented by Jacob Neusner, Development of a Legend (Leiden: E.J. Brill, 1970), pp. 242-247.

[12] Jacob Neusner, A Life of Yohanan ben Zakkai (Leiden: E.J. Brill, 1970), p. 97.

[13] Ibid., p. 48.

[14] Derek Eres Zuta 4.58b. See also b. Nedarim 37b.

[15] Some scholars doubt the correctness of this identification. Even John's Gospel recasts the same narrative within the home of Lazarus where Mary the sister of Lazarus, does the anointing (John 12:1-11).

[16] Abot de Rabbi Nathan 7:1 (21a).

[17] Ibid. 6:1 (20b).

[18] Herman C. Waetjen, The Origin and Destiny of Humanness (Corte Madera: Amega Books, 1976), pp. 77-78.

[19] Asher Finkel, The Pharisees and the Teacher of Nazareth (Leiden: E.J. Brill, 1964), pp. 143-155.

[20] b. Hagiga 14b and parallel, Abot de Rabbi Nathan 6:2 (20b).

[21] Abot de Rabbi Nathan 6:2 (20b).

[22] Jacob Neusner, First Century Judaism in Crisis (Nashville: Abingdon, 1975), p. 79.

[23] E.g.: W.D. Davies, The Setting of the Sermon on the Mount (Cambridge: The University Press, 1966); Joachim Jeremias, New Testament Theology: The Proclamation of Jesus (N.Y. Charles Scribner's Sons, 1971); Norman Perrin, Rediscovering the Teaching of Jesus (N.Y.: Harper & Row, 1967).

24 Carol Christ and Marilyn Collins, "Shattering the Idols of Men: Theology from the Perspective of Women's Experience," Reflection (Yale Divinity School) 69, 4 (March, 1972) 12.

25 Many fine studies have appeared which spell out the diversified messianic expectations current at the turn of the era. E.g., W.D. Davies, The Setting of the Sermon on the Mount (Cambridge: University Press, 1966), pp. 109-190 and Shemaryahu Talmon, "Typen der Messiaserwartung um die Zeitenwende," Problems biblishcher Theologie, ed. by H.W. Wolff (Muenchen: Kaiser Verlag, 1971), pp. 571-588. It is important to note that even the canonical prophets have no uniform messianic expectation: J. Lindblom, Prophecy in Ancient Israel (Philadelphia: Fortress, 1963), esp. pp. 370-420.

26 Midrash Tehillim, Ps. 146, sec. 5; William G. Braude, tr., The Midrash on Psalms (New Haven: Yale University 1959), p. 367. In some rabbinic circles, the Messiah was identified as the one who, "in the time to come [i.e., during the Messianic Age]," would open the eyes of the blind by teaching Torah. This emphasis appears to be quite congenial to Matthew's presentation of Jesus as the Messiah. In John's Gospel, the Samaritan woman anticipates a Messiah who "will tell us everything" (John 4:25) regarding proper worship of God. For further discussion, consult: W.D. Davies, The Setting of the Sermon on the Mount (Cambridge: The University Press, 1966), pp. 156-190; Lloyd Gaston, "The Messiah of Israel as Teacher of the Gentiles," Interpretation 29 (1975) 24-40.

27 Edward Schillebeeckx, in Jesus & Christ (N.Y.: Crossroad, 1980), pp. 10-49, develops the thesis that all the Christological titles presuppose and stand upon the force of Jesus' encounter with his disciples.

28 See, for example, Robert D. Smith, Comparative Miracles (St. Louis: B. Herder Book Co., 1965).

29 Augustine De vera religione 3.3.

VI

The Transmission of Jesus' Power After His Death

No matter how supremely valid Jesus' fresh vision of God's cause might have been, if this vision was not communicated to his disciples, then it would remain exclusively his and be irretrievably lost to civilization the moment he departed. No matter how supremely powerful Jesus' redemptive divinity might have been, if this power was in no way assimilated by his disciples, then they would remain existentially unchanged and the world would slip back into the same morass that it had known prior to the advent of Jesus. As such, the career of Jesus would be remembered as a brief "Camelot" which came unexpectedly and disappeared suddenly -- leaving the kingdom of heaven just as remote from human affairs as it had previously been. Yet, this gloomy prospect did not materialize. History relates how the disciples of Jesus did assimilate the spirit/Spirit of their master and did apprentice other disciples to leaven the next generation.

Returning now to the contemporary scene, it is apparent that an apprenticeship under Jesus of Palestine is manifestly impossible. Yet, let us suppose (as history suggests) that the personal powers of the first disciples of Jesus did not die with them but were assimilated by second-generation disciples. Let us further suppose that these latter disciples did not know Jesus in the flesh but did, none the less, successfully demonstrate in their own practice that they rightly discerned and powerfully served God's cause as accredited by their masters. It then follows that the charism of Jesus might pass into a body of disciples who never knew the Palestinian master personally. By an extension of this process, it then follows that a given community, engendered and sustained by a series of reliable apprenticeships, might offer the spirit/Spirit of Jesus to persons far removed from first-century Palestine in both time and culture.

The upshot of this discussion is the realization that the personal powers of Jesus need never die. And this is true not because Jesus is in heaven but because the earthly Jesus communicated his personal vocation. "It is enough for a disciple that he should grow to be like his master" (Matt 10:25). Once communicated, the process then continues into the next generation. As a consequence, a Christian in any generation might submit him/herself to a prolonged apprenticeship under the then-living masters within the church in the expectation that his/her personal powers would be suitably informed with the spirit/Spirit of Jesus. Cultural adaptation within each generation would be taken for granted since every generation of disciples would be trained to be "salt" and "light" for their particular generation (and not for some remote bygone culture). Thus, in each age, the disciples of Jesus would be the harbingers and servants of those standards of righteousness that God was offering <u>that</u> generation. As Jesus served God's cause in his era, they would be tooled to correctly discern and promote God's cause in their own era.

The thrust of this present chapter is to give a careful look at the processes whereby discipleship continued after Jesus' death. Attention will be concentrated in the following areas:

A. How Paul received and passed on Jesus' power
B. The power of the catechumenate in the early centuries
C. The contemporary quest for spiritual power

A.   <u>How Paul Received and Passed on Jesus' Power</u>

The New Testament features Paul as the foremost Christian evangelist. His conversion experience is often celebrated as the classical instance of God's grace at work. More often that not, sermons relating Paul's conversion promote the view that Jesus zaps persons directly from heaven. Such a view imagines that Jesus put his disciples in charge of the Jesus Movement but that he entirely bypassed them in training Paul. Thus, for example, one reads accounts like the following:

> On his way to Damascus Saul was converted to the Way of Christ. . . . Saul always claimed that he had been

> instructed by Christ himself in some
> mysterious way. Thus he was a true
> disciple, although he never sat at his
> feet as the other apostles had done.[1]

Furthermore, Paul frequently is imagined to have functioned as a Billy Graham style evangelist who evokes a saving faith in the Lord but has nothing to do with systematically apprenticing converts. In sum, the transformation of Paul and his active ministry seemingly demonstrate that the strenuous and prolonged master-disciple relationship is not the mainstay of the Jesus movement.

In this initial section, I intend to show these misconceptions surrounding Paul run contrary to the Scriptures from which they are supposedly drawn. In fact, I want to use these very Scriptures to demonstrate that the apprenticeship process employed by Jesus has a decisive role (a) for the formation of Paul and (b) for providing the basis wherein Paul himself establishes Christian communities.

Turning first to Paul's life-transformation, two sources are found in the New Testament. The first is the detailed, secondhand account provided by Luke in the Acts of the Apostles. This account figures so importantly in Luke's purpose in composing Acts that he offers it three times: Acts 9:1ff, 22:5ff, and 26:10ff. The second source is the comparatively brief firsthand account in Paul's letter to the Galatians (1:11-24). Each of these sources shall be considered in its turn.

In Acts, Luke provides us with important clues concerning Paul's formation prior to his conversion. Paul, who was known as "Saul" in Jewish circles, is presented as describing himself to his fellow Jews as follows:

> I am a Jew and was born at Tarsus in
> Cilicia. I was brought up here in this
> city. I studied under [literally,
> "(sitting) at the feet of"] Gamaliel
> and was taught the exact observance of
> the Torah of our ancestors. In fact, I
> was as full of duty towards God as you
> are today. I even persecuted this Way
> [of Jesus] to the death, and sent women
> as well as men to prison in chains as
> the high priest and the whole council
> of elders [the Sanhedrin] can testify,
> since they even sent me with letters to
> their brothers in Damascus (Acts
> 22:3-5).

These are impressive credentials. Paul was apprenticed as a disciple of Gamaliel, who, in turn was one of the leading disciples of Hillel. In another place, Luke describes Gamaliel as "a master of the Torah and respected by all the people" (Acts 5:34). He was a member of the Sanhendrin and his caution prevailed over the manifest fury of the violence-prone priests (Acts 5:34-42). Paul's disregard for the pacifism of Gamaliel must indicate that either he had already completed his apprenticeship or that he had broken off his apprenticeship because he found his master too soft on defectors. In any case, Paul was undoubtedly trusted by the chief priests to conduct official house searches, to discern defectors, and to have them incarcerated (Acts 8:3, 9:14, 21). The success of Paul's "Inquisition" in Jerusalem prompted the chief priests to have him authorized to extend his (their) campaign to the large Jewish quarter in Damascus, 150 miles north of Jerusalem.

On route, everything in Paul was turned around. Luke presents him as being struck blind by "a voice" calling him into account. "For three days he was without sight and took neither food nor drink" (Acts 9:9).

To blind an enemy is a cruel punishment. Luke, in his Gospel, never presents Jesus as acting so cruelly. Such a deed, moreover, runs contrary to the Torah Jesus delivered:

> Love your enemies, do good to those who hate you, bless those who curse you, pray for those who treat you badly (Luke 6:27-28).

Luke, however, does record an instance of Paul confronting and blinding a Jew who was obstructing the conversion of his Roman superior (Acts 13:4ff). Here again, if the term "struck blind" is to be understood as an organic mutilation, then it is quite contrary to the Torah of Jesus. But this is not the case. I have previously shown in Chapter IV how "giving sight to the blind" must be correctly understood in the writings of Isaiah. In parallel fashion, Luke employs the expression "struck blind" as the appropriate metaphor for "the total disorientation that results from sharp confrontation." Careful linguistic studies confirm this usage in biblical Greek (TDNT VI: 270-293). Modern English retains the body language of "pulling the wool over someone's eyes," but this is not equivalent to Luke's expressions. Since no ready-made equivalent is available, a literal word-for-word rendering of the Greek obscures Luke's original intent.

Here again the slippage of English translations is encountered.

In response to the light, "he [Paul] fell to the ground" (Acts 9:4). Later Luke presents Paul as saying, "We all fell to the ground" (Acts 26:14). In either case, the text does not suggest that Paul was thrown to the ground, i.e., with force. Nor does the text hint that he was on a horse and fell from a height. Christian art of a later age will depict Paul having been thrown from his horse. This is artistic imagination at work and not Luke. In fact, neither Jews nor Romans in the first century had yet developed the art of horseback riding.[2] One rode on a donkey, or one harnessed a chariot to a horse. In effect, therefore, Luke's presumption was that Paul and his companions were making the journey to Damascus on foot. In response to the light, they got weak in the knees, they fell to the ground. No coercion is evident or implied (TDNT VI:163).

As for the voice that Paul heard, Luke is quite reserved in saying "he heard a voice" (Acts 9:4), without specifying that Jesus appeared or that Jesus called down from heaven. It is even possible that Luke intends to suggest to his readers that the cries of Jesus' disciples sound in Paul's ears with the force of the cry of their master. Within the Jewish horizon of understanding, it is commonplace to regard the disciple as echoing the voice of his/her master: "Anyone who listens to you listens to me" (Luke 10:16). The words heard by Paul, moreover, are entirely appropriate for a disciple complaining against Paul's cruel "Inquisition." They invite expansion to cover a specific instance:

> Paul, Paul, why are you persecuting me? [I have received you in my home and shown you respect. You have cursed me and accused me of betraying the traditions of our fathers. Yet, tell me this: is it a tradition of our fathers for a Jew to persecute his brother? Can our Father in heaven favor this? And does not the approval of the high priests seem hollow when your deeds run against Torah? Can you really believe that the ways of the high priests are more holy than the ways of Jesus whom they had crucified?] (Acts 9:4).

In response to this harrowing and accusing voice, Paul instinctively asks, "Who are you, sir?" "The voice" (again of undisclosed origin) responds, "I am Jesus and you are persecuting me" (Acts 9:5). One might expect Paul to object here that he never knew or harassed Jesus -- it was his "deceived disciples" that he persecuted. Yet, in the Jewish framework, one attacks the master when one attacks his disciple: "Anyone who rejects you, rejects me" (Luke 10:16).[3]

Luke deliberately leaves this ambiguity concerning "the voice." It could be Jesus come down from heaven. It could be a disciple echoing his master. Luke may even be creating, as a literary device, something of an ancient version of the "ghosts" which visited Scrooge and brought him to his conversion.

Luke artfully arranges panding the visual imagery of his narrative. It is midday (Acts 22:6, 26:13). Paul has the light whereby to make his journey -- to complete his designs. From heaven comes more light -- a blinding light. Luke notes that "the men travelling with Saul . . . could see no one" (Acts 9:7). As for Paul himself, Luke remarks that "even with his eyes wide open he could see nothing at all" (Acts 9:8). Paul is totally disoriented by "the voice." In an instant his whole life project comes to a halt. He is helpless. He now has to be led by others "into Damascus by the hand" (Acts 9:8). His journey is finished. His designs are meaningless. "For three days he was without his sight, and took neither food nor drink" (Acts 9:9). Even today this is appropriate body language for someone sorely distressed in spirit.

It is generally overlooked that Luke deliberately presents Paul as <u>blinded by the Jesus-voice while it is the voice of Ananias that restores his sight</u>. The sight which Paul regains, however, has an altered perception: "Jesus is the son of God" (Acts 9:20). Paul's ability to see has been irreversibly transformed. In this connection, it is interesting that later Paul has the occasion to tell of his conversion to King Agrippa (Acts 26:1-23). In this account it is the pagans who are presented as blind; and Paul, by virtue of "his vision" of Jesus, is sent "to open their eyes:"

> I [Jesus] shall deliver you from the people and from the pagans, to whom I am sending you to open their eyes, so that they may turn from darkness to light, from the dominion of Satan to God . . . (Acts 26:17-18).

In effect, this latter text presents Paul as removing the blindness of the pagans while the earlier text presents

Ananias as removing Paul's own personal blindness.[4] In terms of their metaphorical intent, both texts are quite complementary.

Ananias leans his hands upon Paul and, after he regains his sight, baptizes him (Acts 9:17, 19). The first gesture is not an "ordination" but implies that Ananias "confirms" Paul's spirit/Spirit as one with his own. Such a rite would necessarily mean that Ananias has come to know Paul quite intimately. The second rite, that of baptism by immersion, implies that Paul has been reborn as the new creature who is admonished, encouraged, and guided by Ananias into conformity with Jesus Christ. One can surmise that Ananias is a leading member of the church in Damascus. No other person would be qualified to initiate Paul into the Christian community.

Luke informs us that Paul passed "only a few days with the disciples in Damascus" (Acts 9:20). Could an apprenticeship be accomplished so quickly? For most persons, no. Paul, however, had previous training in Torah under Gamaliel and had become an expert in the way of Jesus due to his position in questioning and refuting his prisoners. His expertise, however, was that of an "outsider." Following his crisis, he undoubtedly needed many days to reorientate his spontaneous feelings and judgments as an "insider." This reorientation required little further training, however.

A second-century document of unknown authorship, the <u>Epistula Apostolorum</u> (Letter of the Apostles), endeavors to fill in some of the silences left by Luke. According to this text, it is the Twelve who are commissioned to build the Christian community at Damascus. Accordingly, it is they who will supervise the training of Paul. The text depicts Jesus as detailing, in advance, what the Twelve are to do in Paul's behalf:

> He [Paul] will hear my voice from heaven with terror, fear, and trembling; and his eyes will be darkened and by your hand be crossed with spittle. And do all to him that I have done to you. Deliver (?) (him?) to others. And this man -- immediately his eyes will be opened . . . And every word which I have spoken to you and which you have written concerning me, that I am the word of the Father and the Father is in me, so you must become also to that man, as it befits you. Teach [apprentice] and remind

> (him) what has been said in the
> [Hebrew] Scriptures and fulfilled
> concerning me, and then he will be
> [fit] for the salvation of the
> Gentiles.[5]

This text takes Luke's account for granted and then amplifies and interprets it. The voice comes "from heaven."[6] Paul's emotional response is spelled out. Spittle is introduced (perhaps due to John 9:6). The Twelve hand him over "to others" (perhaps, Ananias and the Damascus community). But then the present text takes off on its own and spells out that <u>the Twelve are to do for Paul what Jesus had originally done for them</u>. They are commissioned to apprentice Paul -- not only by spoken and written words but by "becoming" for him exactly what Jesus had become for them, namely, the word (or echo) of the Father. They must be for Paul living Torah just as Jesus was formerly living Torah for them. Furthermore, they are to break open the Hebrew Scriptures to reveal to Paul those things "fulfilled" by Jesus therein.

The <u>Epistola Apostolorum</u>, consequently, goes way beyond Luke in drawing out and highlighting the transformation of Paul at the hands of those who had originally been transformed by Jesus. There can be no doubt that the community which originated this document had a vested interest in apprenticing. Most probably the community elaborated on the text of Luke on the basis of their own understanding and practice. Instead of becoming more spectacular in accounting for Paul's transformation, they became decidedly more practical and down to earth. In so doing, they undoubtedly felt that they were specifying more clearly what Luke had originally intended.

Setting aside these secondhand accounts, I now turn my attention to what Paul himself presents of his conversion within his letters. I am surprised that Paul only explicitly treats his conversion within his Letter to the Galatians and, even there, his account is impoverished in contrast to the secondary sources just considered. In fact, it is striking that Paul himself never mentions Damascus as playing a role in his developing vocation. His sketchy, firsthand account reads as follows:

> You must have heard of my career as a
> practicing Jew, how merciless I was in
> persecuting the Church of God, how much
> damage I did to it, how I stood out
> among other Jews of my generation, and
> how enthusiastic I was for the
> traditions of my ancestors. Then God,

> who had specially chosen me while I was still in my mother's womb, called me through his grace and chose to reveal his son in me so that I might preach the Good News about him to the pagans. I did not stop to discuss this [preaching] with any human being, nor did I go up to Jerusalem to see those who were already apostles before me, but I went off to Arabia at once and later went straight back from there to Damascus (Gal 1:13-17).

The English translation above suggests that Paul's destiny was already being shaped within his mother's womb -- as other prophets had claimed (e.g., Isa 49:1, Jer 1:5). The original Greek suggests a parallel construction which might be more closely rendered as follows:

> But then the one who separated me from my mother's womb, the one who called me through his grace, was pleased to reveal his son in me . . . (Gal 1:15-16).

<u>Who</u> has called Paul? "The one" who brought him out of the womb![7] Not Jesus. <u>Why</u> has "the one" called him? "To reveal his son in [by] me!" <u>Where</u> and <u>when</u> was Paul so called? Nothing is indicated. Paul does not indicate whether his momentous transformation emerged gradually or suddenly, near Damascus or elsewhere, in solitude or in the process of interrogating Christians. <u>How</u> did Paul "hear" the calling? Again, nothing is indicated. A careful reading, however, of the remainder of Galatians does give hints in this direction: (a) negatively, that heavenly revelations are not to be trusted; (b) positively, that human persons can and do reveal the Messiah Jesus. I shall, accordingly, gather together these clues in the following paragraphs.

When Paul says that "the Good News . . . is not a human message that I was given by men [women]" (Gal 1:11-12), this does not mean that Paul received it <u>directly</u> from God any more than did the Galatians. Rather the message is always passed on person to person, yet its source is Jesus, the Messiah of God (Gal 1:7, 12). "The one having called you [the Galatians] by grace" (Gal 1:6) is precisely the same as "the one . . . having called me [Paul] through his grace" (Gal 1:15). The calling is from God; yet it is Paul who clearly preached to them (Gal 1:8,9, 11). Paul reminds the Galatians that he is the "servant of the Messiah" (Gal 1:10) who has called them out of their former existence. He reminds them that "you welcomed me as an angel of God, as if I were the Messiah Jesus himself" (Gal 4:14). The Galatians replicated him (Gal 4:12). They became mature "sons of God" (Gal 3:35, 4:7) who have put on the messianic-consciousness and breathed with the spirit/Spirit of God's son (Gal 3:27, 4:6). Should they now abandon the Way, Paul promises that he would "go through the pain of giving birth to you all over again, until Christ [i.e., the messianic-consciousness] is formed in you" (Gal 4:19).

And just as Paul reveals that Messiah Jesus to the Galatians, it follows that Paul himself might well have greeted Ananias and his community as his "revelation of the Messiah Jesus" (Gal 1:12). Unfortunately, the word "revelation" in this context conjures up images of apparitions or voices from the sky. Yet, for Paul, every disciple reveals his/her master. Paul says in another letters: "We are ambassadors for the Messiah; it is as though God were appealing through us [to the word] . . . (2 Cor 5:20). Paul never names the ambassador who brought the Good News to him.

Paul's letter to the Galatians is directed against those well-meaning Jewish Christians who are introducing circumcision and its attendant obligations to supplement the way of Jesus. Paul opposes them, not on the basis of any human authority or doctrine (Gal 1:2, 11), but solely on his familiarity with Jesus Christ. As we have already seen, Paul "did not stop to discuss" (Gal 1:16) his plan to preach to the pagans with anyone -- nor did he seek permission from Jerusalem.. Then the argument moves ahead:

> [after fourteen years] I laid before the leading men [in Jerusalem] the Good News as I proclaim it among the pagans; I did so for fear the course I was adopting or had already adopted would not be allowed. And what happened? Even though Titus who had come with me is a Greek, he was not obliged to be circumcised (Gal 2:2-3).

Here Paul is suddenly more detailed. He places great weight on the fact that Titus was not circumcised. He then goes on to sketch the discussion he had on this point with the "pillars" of the Jerusalem church, namely, James, Peter, and John. He points out that they ended up shaking hands in agreement and in confirmation of Paul's program among the Gentiles (Gal 2: 6-10). Paul then follows this up by narrating how he corrected Peter when he suddenly stopped eating with Gentiles once some friends of James arrived (Gal 2:11-14).

As if these arguments were not enough, Paul goes to great length to spell out three additional arguments against those who are pressing for circumcision. Here again, as in the former arguments, <u>he appeals to public facts</u>: (1) the fact that the Gentiles "received the Spirit" on the basis of their following of Jesus without any of the outward observances that the "troublemakers" insist upon (Gal 3:1-5); (2) the fact that Jesus was cursed and cut off from God by those who upheld the outward observances of the Torah (Gal 3:10-14); (3) the fact that God's earlier acceptance of and promises to Abraham did not embrace circumcision and that the Torah "that came four hundred and thirty years later" cannot undo what had been established for so long (Gal 3:6-9, 15-18).

After reviewing Paul's appeal to public facts, it becomes more apparent that Paul has no intention to appeal to any private religious experiences (such as visions or auditions). For one thing, Paul knows that such appeals have no standing whatsoever when it comes to determining issues of Torah.[8] On the other hand, any appeal to apparitions on Paul's part could be easily met with counter-apparitions on the part of his opponents. With this in mind, Paul may have deliberately forestalled such appeals on the part of the "troublemakers" quite early in his letter:

> Let me warn you that if anyone preaches
> a version of the Good News different
> from the one we have already preached
> to you, whether it be ourselves or an
> angel from heaven, he is to be
> condemned (Gal 1:8).

Now it would be entirely inconsistent for Paul to challenge all heaven-sent messengers and then turn around and suggest that his own version of the Good News was a message from heaven. If he were to do this, he would have to argue why a heavenly revelation made to him has precedence over a later revelation made to his opponents. But this never happens. <u>Paul claims no "revelation of Jesus Christ" in the form of voices from the sky. Furthermore, he categorically condemns anyone who appeals to such voices against him</u>.

My investigations up to this point bring me to the firm conclusion that neither firsthand nor secondhand accounts of Paul's conversion allow one to imagine that Paul becomes a Christian by bypassing the apprenticing process. Light from heaven may blind Paul, he may even hear the voice of Jesus calling him into account; none the less, the light and the voice leave him blind. It is Ananias, "who is sent by the Lord Jesus" (Acts 9:17), who gives him new sight. Or, alternatively, it is the Twelve, who are ordained by Jesus after his resurrection, to do for Paul what Jesus formerly did for them. Finally, in Paul's own firsthand accounts, he affirms the validity of the Gospel that he has received on the basis of public facts without the slightest appeal to private religious experiences. His shaking hands with the three pillars of the Jerusalem church counts more than any and every religious experience that he may or may not have had. This is not to suggest that the grace of God did not have an essential role to play in transforming Paul. On the contrary, grace is quite evident throughout Paul's life.[9] The grace of God, however, does not bypass the psychological and sociological grounds of human existence; rather, grace permeates and uplifts human events so as to make them capable of a transcendent achievement.

Having challenged popular notions of Paul's conversion, I now move on to consider misrepresentations of his ministry. All too often, Paul is imagined exclusively as an evangelical minister who evokes faith in Jesus but who has nothing to do with the systematic apprenticing which characterized Jesus in the Gospels. Here, again, the absence of any serious apprenticing in most churches renders us blind to the clues which Paul offers in his letters. So, too, misleading interpretations of Luther's doctrine "by faith alone"[10] leads us to imagine that Paul had no need to patiently nurture his converts into assimilating the patterns of thinking, feeling, and acting which characterized Jesus.

Paul's speeches in Acts are persuasive and confrontational. They are directed toward outsiders. One never gets a glimpse of how Paul addressed the small circles of disciples which he left behind in the places he visited. Even Paul's letters are generally only stop gap measures to hold things together until he can be present in person. Most of Paul's letters presuppose a previous apprenticeship and anticipate its continuation. We have no documents which directly relate the style and content of this face-to-face apprenticing when it did take place. Yet, Paul's letters do offer passing clues concerning his conduct and dispositions toward his converts when he was with them. In the next few pages, I intend to single out some of these clues. For the sake of manageability, I will limit myself to <u>Thessalonians</u>.

Initially I am struck by Paul's use of family terms. He habitually addresses the disciples as "brothers/sisters"(1 Thess 1:4; 2:1, 9, 14, 17; 3:2, 7; 4:1, 6, 10, 13; 5:1, 4, 12, 14, 25, 26, 27). Moreover, he describes his own function amoung them as <u>fathering and mothering</u>. He was "like a mother feeding and looking after her own children" (1 Thess 2:7). He writes:

> You can remember how we treated every one of you as a father treats his children, teaching you what was right, encouraging you and appealing to you to live a life worthy of God, who is calling you to share the glory of his kingdom (1 Thess 2:11-12).

Such idioms suggest that Paul's converts have entered into a new family wherein Paul takes charge of informing and nurturing drop <u>them</u> in the new spirit. It will be remembered that Jesus himself regarded his disciples as forming his family (Matt 12:49). In Paul's other letters, he also refers to his role as being "your father"(1 Cor 4:16, Gal 4:19, Phlm 10) save when he writes to the church at Rome and at Colossae, which he did not found or nurture.

Paul makes it quite clear that his whole manner of living with them constitutes part of their training:

> You observed the sort of life we lived when we were with you, which was for your instruction, and you were led to become imitators of us and of the lord . . . (1 Thess 1:5-6).

This recalls that every aspect of the life of a master constitutes a living Torah which the disciples must assimilate for themselves. Accordingly, Paul explains that the Thessalonians whom he apprenticed have become "the great example to all believers in Macedonia and Achaia"(1 Thess 1:7):

> We do not need to tell other people about it: other people tell us how we started the work among you, how you broke with idolatry when you were converted to God and became servants of the real, living God . . . (1 Thess 1:8-9).

If the Thessalonians had shared the Jewish horizon of understanding, I am quite certain Paul would have called them "the salt of the earth" and "the light of the nations."

A conversion experience may happen quickly, but the process of assimilating for oneself the holiness of another requires a long and strenuous process. It is this latter process which admits of progress and is best described in processive terms. Accordingly, Paul writes:

> May the Lord be generous in increasing your love and make you love one another and the whole human race as much as [i.e., as measured by how] we love you (1 Thess 3:12).

> We urge you and appeal to you in the Lord Jesus [i.e., <u>in his name</u>] to make more and more progress in the kind of life that you are meant to live: the life that God wants, as you learnt from us, and as you are already living it. You have not forgotten the instructions we gave you on the authority of the Lord Jesus [i.e., <u>in his name</u>] (1 Thess 4:1-2).

> We urge you, brothers, to go on making even greater progress and to make a point of living quietly, attending to your own business and earning your living, just as we told you to, so that you are seen to be respectable by those outside the Church . . . (1 Thess 4:10-11).

Each of these exhortations to progress presupposes that Paul has presented to them the standard by which they are to measure themselves. There is no question here of cultivating private "faith experiences." Paul is calling for a progressive reorientation of their lives in the way his own life is oriented.[11]

> What God wants is for you all to be holy (1 Thess 4:3, also 4:7).

In sum, Paul is much more than a Billy Graham style evangelist. In the face of outsiders, persuasive and confrontational rhetoric were entirely in order. Some of this even spills over into his letters. Surrounded by his "children," however, I cannot but imagine that Paul sat on the ground and spoke quietly and intimately. He exposed the wisdom that guided his own life. His "family" was eager to enter into his settled perceptions and habits of judgment. Paul was like a mother and father to them. Given Paul's own formation and transformation, I cannot imagine that he departed very far from the pedagogical style characteristic of the masters of his day. Like Jesus, he apprenticed disciples in addition to being a prophet.

B.   <u>The Power of the Catchumenate in the Early Centuries</u>

The practice of apprenticing disciples became systematized and ritualized with the passage of time. By the third and fourth centuries, the metropolitan churches had worked out an elaborate and awe-inspiring program of initiation. This program was designed for systematically effecting a complete change of personal identity, a rebirth, in the pagan candidate who wished to take his/her place amount the "saints." <u>The very existence of such programs is a manifest testimony to the intensive character transformation which was demanded for a would-be disciple of Jesus</u>. On the strength of these programs, Christians created an enduring subculture that went on to attract and convert major sectors of the then-existing Roman civilization. With the decline of these programs in sixth century, a veneer of Catholicism came to substitute for the depth of self-transformation necessitated by apprenticing in earlier years.

Tertullian, at the opening of the third century, coined the term <u>catechumen</u> to designate persons being apprenticed within an initiation program (the catechumenate). The program varied from church to church but each combined elements of the Jewish practice of apprenticing by a master with elements derived from the Oriental mystery religions popular throughout the Empire (e.g., the cult of Eleusis, the Osiris-Osis cult, the Adonis cult). These latter elements especially fashioned the baptismal ritual itself:

> The ceremonies took place at night, some of them in the dark, after weeks of intense preparation; they were wrapped in secrecy, and the candidate [the catechumen] knew little about them until just before, or even after, he [she] had received them. Everything was calculated to inspire religious

awe, to make these rites the occasion of a profound and lifelong conversion.[12]

Pagans who wished to be initiated into the Christian community had to be recommended in advance. The bishop, who personally supervised the admission of candidates, would inquire into the manifest conduct and motivations of potential candidates. If approved, the person's name was inscribed in a book as "chosen" (Latin: electi) or "destined for illumination" (Greek: photizomenoi). During the forty days of Lent, candidates arrived at the church at dawn each morning. There each of them was assigned an exorcist who gave them moral exhortations and stern corrections on a one-to-one basis. Such "exorcisms" were calculated to undo the patterns of living which the catechumen has assimilated within the "demonic" rites and practices of his/her former upbringing.[13] Then, the bishop arrived with his college of presbyters. While all were seated, the bishop presented an instruction calculated to open their eyes to the wisdom hidden within the Christian discipline. Periodically, the bishop tested each of the candidates to perceive to what degree they had entered into the conversion of mind and heart expected of them. Those found worthy were finally baptized before dawn on Easter after spending the entire night in prayer and fasting.

Documents relating to this apprenticing were recorded in writing, copied, distributed, and preserved until our own era. A complete set of the Lenten instructions given to catechumens by Bishop Cyril of Jerusalem (d. 386) has survived. From Bishop Gregory of Nyssa (d. 394), we also have a set of advanced lectures whereby he trained those who were assigned to supervise the apprenticing of candidates. Many lesser documents also survive.

When the words of the bishops are carefully studied, it is apparent that they have not the slightest intention to pretend that the rite of baptism offers some irresistible transforming power. Nor do they go to the opposite extreme of suggesting that the immersion in water only symbolizes the faith that has already been received. The initiation rites were to be taken seriously. Both bishops assure candidates that the intensive discipline surrounding their initiation could indeed cleanse their hearts and illumine their understanding. But, Bishop Cyril, also warns that there have been failures:

> Once upon a time there came to the font [of baptism] Simon the Sorcerer [Acts 8:13]. He was baptized, but he was not enlightened, for while his body went under the water, his heart let not in the light of the Spirit. He plunged his body and came up, but, in his soul, he was neither buried with Christ nor did he rise again with him. Now I give you sketches of failures, just so that you may not fail.[14]

Cyril also impresses upon the condidates that the apprenticeship which they are about to embrace is irrevocable and never to be repeated. Any one whose personal identity was not effectively transformed by the rites could not be admitted again. Thus, from the very beginning, Cyril charges his candidates to run a vigorous race:

> You have a long period of grace, forty days for repentance. You have plenty of time to discard and wash thoroughly your soul's apparel, and so to clothe yourself . . . . But if you just continue in your evil disposition, I have cleared myself by telling you, but you cannot expect to receive God's grace. For though the water will receive you, the Holy Spirit will not.[15]

Gregory of Nyssa speaks within this selfsame perspective. He begins by showing that those who pass through the water undergo a simulated death by drowning. "The evil mingled with our nature is destroyed by the representation of death in the water. It is not, indeed, completely destroyed; but there is a kind of break in the continuity of evil." Yet, Bishop Gregory makes his trainers aware also of the expected fruits of baptism:

> We have, I think, to consider what follows baptism. It is a point which many of those who approach its grace neglect, deluding themselves and being born in appearance only and not in reality. For the change our life undergoes through rebirth would not be a change [at all] were we to continue in our present state . . . . For it is patent to everyone that we receive the

saving birth for the purpose of renewing and changing our nature. Yet baptism produces no essential change in human nature. Neither reason nor understanding, nor capacity for knowledge, nor anything else that marks human nature, undergoes a change . . . Now it is clear that when the evil characteristics of our nature are done away, there is a change . . . . But if the washing has only affected the body, and the soul has failed to wash off the stains of passion, and the life after initiation is identical with that before, despite the boldness of my assertion I will say without shrinking that in such a case the water is only water, and the gift of the Holy Spirit is nowhere evident in the action.[16]

With sober realism, therefore, Gregory indicates that the Sacrament of Baptism can be abortive rather than lifegiving; "You will be able to tell them by their fruits" (7:20).

In this era baptism was considered such as ordeal that many persons deliberately postponed it. Tertullian, writing in the early third century, advised the church to postpone the baptism of pagans who were as yet unsettled in life (i.e., the young, the unmarried, those recently widowed).[17] In the fourth century, the pastoral seriousness surrounding baptism backfired. Christian parents were deliberately postponing having their children baptized in order to allow them to sow their wild oats before undertaking the Christian discipline in living. Thus, for instance, the pious Monica delayed the baptism of Augustine saying, "Let him alone, let him do as he pleases, for he is not yet baptized."[18] In part, such an attitude reflects the disciplined existence which followed Christian initiation; in part, also this reflects a parental permissiveness which falls back upon an exaggerated (even a superstitious) reliance upon the catechumenate.

As a consequence, the bishops of the late fourth century pressed for a return to the tradition of early baptism. Gregory of Nazianzus, in 381, advised Christian parents to submit their children at the age of three years . . .

when they can take in something of the mystery [i.e. the deep impression

> surrounding the rites] and answer [the
> baptismal inquiries], and even if they
> do not yet understand fully, can
> nevertheless retain some impression.[19]

The popularization of Augustine's doctrine of the sinful state inherited from Adam had the effect of promoting infant baptism. Thus, in the fifth century, a Christian upbringing had to replace entirely the catechumenate for children born of baptized parents. The initiation rites were reserved for outsiders.

Three factors were especially instrumental for the decline of the catechumenate in the fifth century: (1) the reinstatement of infant baptism in Christian homes, (2) the policies of imperial politics which brought masses into the church, and (3) the danger of barbarian attacks which promoted the baptism of pagans without any catechumenate.

Some explanation is needed to make sense of the second and third factors. During the second century, Christians had formed a tight subculture which both isolated them from pagan practices and served to single them out for abuse by their intolerant contemporaries. In this setting, infant baptism sufficed (without a formal catechumenate) since the enforced isolation of a protective subculture shaped the child's sensibilities. With the legalization of Christianity (313 C.E.), however, this began to change. With the favoritism of Constantine, this was even reversed. Now the pagan cults went underground and suffered abuse. With each Christian Emperor, this trend increased:

> Constantine [Emperor, 324-337 C.E.] has
> discouraged, but not forbidden, pagan
> sacrifices and ceremonies; Constans
> [Emperor in East, 337-350] forbade them
> on pain of death; Constantius [the
> Arian Emperor in West, 337-361] ordered
> all pagan temples in the Empire closed,
> and all pagan rituals to cease. Those
> who disobeyed were to forfeit their
> property and their lives; and these
> penalties were extended to provincial
> governors neglecting to enforce the
> decree.[20]

Imperial policies, therefore, swelled the numbers of those seeking admittance into the church. The political and economic advantages of being a "Christian" were now intermingled with the quest for messianic holiness. Along with this, the pressure of the barbarian advances at the borders of the Empire promoted the emergency baptism of soldiers and of endangered citizens. Such emergency measures shortened or entirely eliminated any thorough apprenticing. It was hoped that regular participation in the Christian community would suffice to provide the necessary formation after baptism. The tottering Empire never provided enough tranquility for this hope to be entirely realized.

As the barbarian hordes overran the centers of Roman government and began to settle within Roman territories, the church began a missionary movement. Baptism and admission to the Eucharist were now comparatively easy to come by. The barbarians joined a church wherein "Christianity" was only a thin veneer hastily glued over settled instincts and habits of judgment which had little in common with the Christian fiber exhibited a century or two before. The catechumenate was dead.

During the medieval period which followed, the gestures and formulae of baptism were retained but no living person remembered the dynamics of conversion which they once embraced. The efficacy of the Sacrament was no longer measured by one's visible conduct; the terms of efficacy employed by the Fathers were entirely "spiritualized." Infants were routinely baptized. Jews were scorned and sometimes even coerced into baptism. To be baptized was to enter into the mainstream of Christian society. Holiness was now only systematically cultivated in the monasteries wherein elaborate initiation rites and community discipline still flourished. It was out of this new subculture that the hope of a revolutionary Christianity was being nurtured.

Pragmatic necessity introduced changes. Formerly baptism was reserved to the bishop. Now, however, distance required that the local priest be permitted to baptize infants born among his people. The bishop later "confirmed" these baptisms by imposing his hands and anointing the child. At first, infants were confirmed a few weeks following their baptism when their parents could manage a pilgrimage to the bishop's cathedral. With time, the bishop's "confirmation" was delayed. Thus it came about that the ritualistic remains of the catechumenate of the Fathers were divided into two distinct Sacraments: Baptism and Confirmation.

Thomas Aquinas provides useful clues regarding the practice of the church in the twelfth century. He differentiates, for example, between infant baptism within Christian families and the baptism of adult converts (presumably from Judaism and Islam). In the case of infants, baptism is not to be delayed because no one who dies without spiritual regeneration can enter the kingdom of heaven. In the case of adults, however, delay is advisable:

> Baptism should not be conferred on adults as soon as they are converted, but it should be deferred until some fixed time. First, as a safeguard to the Church, lest she be deceived through baptizing those who come to her under false pretenses . . . . Secondly, this is needful as being useful for those who are baptized; for they require a certain space of time in order to be fully instructed in the faith, and to be drilled in those things which pertain to the Christian mode of life. Thirdly, a certain reverence for the sacrament demands a delay whereby men [women] are admitted to baptism at the principal festivities, viz. of Easter and Pentecost . . . (ST III, 68, 3).

In the case of adults, a certain manifest faith and Christian morals are <u>prerequisites</u> for the Sacrament. In the case of infants, Thomas explains that the church supplies what is personally wanting in the infant. As for the efficacy of the sacrament, Thomas explains that all the effects are present in the infant in a sleeping phase which gradually awakens as physical maturity blossoms (ST III, 69, 6). The adult sponsors are specifically charged with guaranteeing the efforts necessary to insure that the infant is brought up to believe and to practice Christian virtue (ST III, 71, 1, ad 3 & 4, ad 3).

Already during this period there were small movements mounted by the Petrobrussians and the Apostolic Brethren to reserve baptism for adults since it was evident that many baptized infants grew up to be scoundrels. In the Reformation period, the Anabaptist movement raised the same cry by appealing to the conversion of heart that was demanded by John the Baptizer in the New Testament. The Society of Friends, meanwhile, pressed for putting aside all the Sacraments entirely.

> The Quakers lived in a baptized society in which many persons had the external sign of baptism but showed little evidence of Christlikeness. They

> contended that the inward spirituality, of which the sacraments were intended to speak, is the constitutive thing in religious life. As long as one can have this inward reality directly, apart from the rites, what use are the rites?[21]

Each of these groups was made to suffer because of their unwillingness to accept the status quo. The Protestant churches made some reforms, but neither they nor the Catholics had enough imagination and revolutionary holiness to revivify the hollow beliefs and the nonengaging rituals that a former era had so masterfully and divinely created.

C. The Contemporary Quest for Spiritual Power

The spiritual power and the messianic holiness of Jesus can be best gauged by the historical impact of his disciples within the generations which followed him. Jesus powerfully transformed his disciples. They, in their turn, went on to powerfully transform the settled perceptions and habits of judgment of an ever-increasing number of followers. In time, the disciples of Jesus created a stable subculture which has the promise of attracting and converting the entire Roman world. The catechumenate and the disciplined patterns of holiness maintained within the church effectively insured that the Christian subculture was far removed from the standard of the prevailing society.

Once the entire Empire was nominally Christian, the task of the Christian community was to recognize true holiness among the mixture of chaff and wheat within its own walls. It could no longer be presupposed that those within the church had assimilated the personal powers of Jesus. On the other hand, there were no pagan initiation rites which offered a salvation in competition with that of the disciples of Jesus. The whole history of the medieval church is marked by periodic movements to enlarge and to enhance the depths of the holiness lived by the rank and file members of the church. Each of these movements left their mark. None of them, however, was able to produce an inner circle of saints that went on to attract and convert the larger circle of complacent Christians that surrounded them. As far as I am aware, the Ignatian renewal came as close as any other to establishing a stable subculture within Christianity. The Ignatian movement sustained its heightened standards of holiness by a totally dedicated band of followers (the Jesuits) who founded colleges throughout Europe and perfected the Ignatian Exercises as the new catechumenate for Christian renewal. But even the Ignatian movement faltered. Its supporters became tame and were assimilated by the mass of Christians without any further disturbance.

Numerous Protestant churches mark their origins within a reform movement that endeavored to revivify a lax Christianity. John Wesley was an imaginative Anglican priest who organized hundreds of persons into highly disciplined prayer-study groups which met in their private homes. Today, the style of the Methodist Church follows the forms left behind by the Wesleyan movement, but its inner dynamism is largely spent. In fact, the majority of Methodists living today no longer claim that their lives have been radically changed by the movement, and they are largely unaware of the identity change that it effected in an earlier era.

The impact of the Christian churches within American society is indeed so marginal that there is generally no manifest difference between the zealous churchgoer and the occasional churchgoer. Secular movements within the larger civic culture have almost entirely displaced the religious movements of a former era. I have met persons who credit the transformative power of Transcendental Meditation, Erhard Seminars Training, or the health-foods cult with such prophetic zeal that they put to shame the comparative inertness of the salvation offered by the conventional churches.

About a year ago, I went to the Chariot Festival held annually by the devotees of Krishna Consciousness in San Francisco. Here I was confronted with former Christians who had found nothing spiritual in their churches in contrast to "the pure, living truth" of Krishna Consciousness. Enclosed within their saffron robes, painted faces, and tufts of hair, there was little evidence that most of these people had grown up within Christian families akin to my own. When speaking to them, I was put off by their degrading references to the human body and its functions. Nothing of the material or political world mattered to them aside from their determination to attain spiritual enlightenment under the guidance of their guru. The earthly exploits of the Hindu gods had great meaning for them. One young devotee delighted in telling how Lord Krishna even today often sneaks down to earth to steal some butter or honey from a pantry of one of his followers. In his eyes this was as momentous as the miracles of Fatima.

I allude to Krishna Consciousness because it demonstrates how radical a personal transformation is possible within a systematic apprenticeship. His Divine Grace A. S. Bhaktivedanta came to the U.S. from India in 1965. Today he claims hundreds of disciples scattered throughout the large metropolitan centers of the U.S. His disciples form a veritable subculture modeled after the Hindu culture of India. Their ultimate plan is the religious salvation of those who are blinded by ambition and materialism in the United States.

The anguish and restlessness of so many of our contemporaries, ourselves included, clearly manifests that the American way of life is still far from the Kingdom of God. Everywhere I find people seeking salvation and effective societal transformation. Some have found such salvation by attaching themselves to a spiritual master from the East (e.g., Paramahasa Yogananda, Sri Chinmoy). Others have found spiritual food within one or the other world religions which embraces a higher-Christianity (e.g., The Unification Church, the Baha'i Faith). Many have joined Christian communes (e.g., The Children of God, The Church of Armageddon). And still others have found secular forms of psychological salvation to their liking (e.g., Erhard Seminars Training, Theta Seminars, Bioenergetics). In each of these modes of salvation, people have undergone momentous conversions. They emerge with an enlarged sense of life. They know clearly what their God wants of them and zealously harness their energies to the accomplishment of transcendant purposes.

I also witness this seeking within the Christian churches. Whenever an effective pastor initiates a solid program of apprenticing disciples and creates a church community, the word spreads. Persons hear this word and leave the mediocre church which they are presently attending in the hope of finding a greater portion of God's grace. Most persons, however, are content to remain where they are. They don't expect Christianity to heal the sicknesses of their society and are quite content with a periodic inspiration on a Sunday morning.

Church leaders in every denomination have energetically tried to restore the transformative power which they suspect is somehow missing in their church gatherings. At the same time, many pastors have energetically preached against many of the diseases which plague American culture: the profit motive, consumerism, isolation, racial discrimination, criminal behavior on the local and national level. But the voices of church leaders are largely nullified by the staggering grip of the status quo. People regard their pastors as idealistic. They share their hope; yet, they must live in the real world where they feel quite powerless to change things. Even when church leaders play a dynamic prophetic role within secular society, most of their admirers do not feel that they are called or equipped to follow. Church leaders, meanwhile, settle for urging and for persuading in the pulpit and have little or no notion of how to create an apprenticeship program which would enable them to communicate their charism.

Conclusion

By way of summary, I offer the following conclusions: (a) The first generation of disciples knew that they had been apprenticed to assimilate the personal powers of their master, Jesus; they accordingly diligently trained others as they themselves had been trained. (b) The mode of apprenticing was systematized and enriched by the metropolitan bishops of the second to fifth centuries such that persons coming from a pagan milieu might successfully be transformed into committed participants in the Christian subculture. (c) With the disappearance of the catechumenate in the sixth century, one's initiation into society at large was relied upon to include those publicly accredited Christian standards which were woven into secular society. (d) Now that secular society is no longer regulated or influenced to any great extent by church institutions, the prevailing culture cannot any longer be relied upon to transmit even a fraction of the Christian heritage. (e) Without the reincorporation of apprenticeships under competent masters within the churches, any saintly wisdom or prophetic holiness within Christianity will be isolated in a few graced individuals and systematically ignored by the masses who are quite pleased with their Sunday Christianity and their privatized religious experiences.

Footnotes for Chapter VI

[1] James Mohler, The School of Jesus (N.Y.: Alba House, 1973), pp. 36-37. In his book, Rev. James Mohler, S.J. takes great pains to explain how Jesus used the pedagogical practices of the rabbinic masters to train his own disciples; then, he turns around, and uncritically presents Paul as entirely bypassing that which was so necessary for every other training in discipleship.

[2] Wooden saddles have been found in Gaul dating back to the first century. It was probably the barbarians that then introduced horseback riding among the Romans.

Not until the invention of the stirrup in the eighth century, however, did the mounted rider become part of the military machine.

3 Matthew presents his parable of the final judgment in which the Son of Man says "I tell you solemnly, in so far as you did this to one of the least of these brothers of mine, you did it to me"(Matt 25:40). The upshot of this parable is to dramatize that what one does or neglects to do for a disciple, one does or neglects to do for the Master.

4 Acts 9 presents Paul's initial experience of conversion which took place a good ten years before he knows himself called to appeal to the Gentiles in the name of Jesus. Acts 26 narrates Paul's initial experience in the light of the solid ten years in which he successfully converted Gentiles to the Way of Jesus. For a complete analysis of the three variant accounts of Paul's conversion in Acts, see, e.g., Edward Schillebeeckx, Jesus (N.Y.: Seabury, 1979), pp. 360-369.

5 Epistula Apostolorum 31. English translation taken from New Testament Apocrypha, ed. by E. Hennecke and W. Schneemelcher (London: SCM Press, 1973), pp. 191-227.

6 On the one hand, the Epistola Apostolorum seems to emphasize the heavenly origin of the blinding voice; yet, in Ch. 33, the phrases "it is I who will speak (to him) through you" and "I will speak with him from heaven" are used interchangeably. This would seemingly support Norman Perrin's contention that "the early Church made no attempt to distinguish between the words the earthly Jesus had spoken and those spoken by the risen Lord through a prophet in the community" (Rediscovering the Teaching of Jesus [N.Y.: Harper & Row, 1967], p. 15).

7 Using metaphor, Paul may be intending to designate his God as having cut him off from the Pharisaic academy ("the womb") wherein he had been fashioned. At the same time, God is designated as having called him out. Why? "To reveal his/her son in [by] me." While in "the womb," Paul revealed Gamaliel. Now he has been called out of that womb to reveal the Messiah Jesus.

8 Deut 13:2-6 specifically disallows any new Torah from being delivered from heaven. The rabbis believed that there existed one Torah which existed in the beginning with God and that this Torah has been delivered to Moses. As such, there is no other Torah to be received from heaven. See esp. Deut 30:12 and b. Baba Mesi^{c}a 59b.

⁹ If Luke is to be accepted as the authoritative theologian of Paul's conversion, it must be acknowledged that the grace of God is much more integrated with life than is commonly supposed. In all fairness. Luke never isolates one or the other moment and says, "Here is where the grace of God touched Paul." It must be allowed, therefore, that grace is already knitting together Paul's destiny while he is still in the womb. Gamaliel's plea for toleration must have been felt as the lure of grace. The holiness and the impassioned complaints of Paul's captives must have nourished unseen grace. Grace triumphs when the pressure of gnawing doubts finally bursts through Paul's resistance on the Damascus road. Ananias mediates graceful acceptance and forgiveness: Paul's new spirit is "confirmed" and he is baptized into the way of Jesus. In his zeal to enrich his former colleagues, grace continues to accompany him as he "began preaching in the synagogues" (Acts 9:21).

In Acts 9, Paul is identified as the "chosen instrument to bring my [Jesus'] name before the pagans," but it is not until Acts 13 that Paul first resolves to "turn to the pagans." Luke details a whole string of events that illustrate how grace only gradually bring Paul to this determination: Barnabas brings Paul to Antioch (Acts 11:25); the prophets of Antioch discern a special vocation for Paul (Acts 13:1-3); a Roman procounsul summons Paul (Acts 13:7 parallels 10:22); finally, when Gentiles seek him out while his Jewish brothers slander him (Acts 13:44-49), Paul then knows himself "called to these Gentiles." At every new city, however, Paul again begins by appealing exclusively and directly to the Jews there (Acts 14:1, 16:13, 17:1, 10, 17; 18:4; 19:18; 28:17); it is only settled Jewish resistance that serves grace and frees Paul for a direct appeal to the Gentiles (in that place).

The upshot of this whole string of events is the realization that the personal vocation of Paul took three to six years to emerge. At no point does Luke suggest that Jesus makes some direct and immediate contact with Paul so as to send him to the Gentiles. At first Paul only wishes to share with his fellow Jews the treasure that he had found in the field. But one thing leads to another. Finally, Jewish measures directed against their mission to be "light to the nations" gives Paul the right to seek out the Gentiles. Thus Luke makes it perfectly clear that people and events are the fabric whereby God reveals his calling to Paul.

If we had examined our own lives, most of us would have concluded that our own vocation also emerges gradually with periodic key events along the way. It is only by virtue of the defective horizon of understanding that has been popularized by so many ministers of religion that we have been led to imagine that it was otherwise for Paul.

[10] The evident practice of Luther in fostering catechetical instruction and the programs of Christian nurturing that have continued in the Lutheran Church testify that justification by faith is the first impulse toward an effective sanctification. For a larger historical study, see Joerg Rothermundt, "The Meaning of Justification: A Report on Studies Conducted Within the Lutheran World Federation, 1958-63," Lutheran World, supplement to no. 1 (1965).

[11] Further discussion of Paul's apprenticing can be found in the study of Dieter Werner Kemmler, Faith and Human Reason: A Study of Paul's Method of Preaching as Illustrated by 1-2 Thess and Acts 17:2-4 (Leiden: E. J. Brill, 1975), esp. pp. 190-205.

[12] Edward Yarnold, the Awe-inspiring Rites of Initiation (Slough, England: St. Paul Pub., 1977), p. ix.

[13] When exorcism is again recognized as having a natural part in the discipline of the catechumenate, then it will be understood why the early centuries had so large a number of exorcists in every metropolitan church.

[14] Cyril of Jerusalem The Catechetical Lectures, intro., sec. 2.

[15] Ibid., sec. 4.

[16] Gregory of Nyssa Oratio catechetica magna 40.

[17] Tertullian De baptismo 18.

[18] Augustine Confessiones 1.11.

[19] Gregory of Nazianzus Oratio 40, In sanctum baptisma.

[20] Will Durant, The Story of Civilization (10 vols.; N.Y.: Simon and Schuster, 1950), IV, 8.

[21] Daniel B. Stevick, "Christian Initiation: Post-Reformation to the Present Era," Made, Not Born (Notre Dame: University Press, 1976), p. 107.

VII

The Human Dynamics Undergirding a Christian Formation

Some thirty years ago, Shinichi Suzuki made a discovery in his arena of musical training that has clear implications in the arena of religious training as well. Quite simply, Suzuki discovered that the only difference between muscially-gifted children and tone-deaf children is their respective parents. Thus, Suzuki went on to prove his point by deliberately recruiting tone-deaf children and demonstrating that, under his "parenting," such children came to share in his own musical talent.

As part of his discovery, Suzuki tells the following story to illustrate how children assimilate for themselves the practice and sensibilities of their parents:

> That I had started a new educational movement in violin teaching became known to various parents. "Will you please listen to my boy's playing? Mr. X of Nagoya City asked. He had taught his son himself. The boy was then eighteen years old and was studying the Mozart Concerto No. 5. "Gladly," I said. "Please tell him to visit me any time." About a month later the young man came alone to see me. Seeing the youth for the first time, I was surprised at how much he resembled his father -- the tone of his voice, his Nagoya dialect, his manner of speaking, even his greeting, the same habit of both hands in front of him, his laugh too -- everything just like his father. I had the illusion of speaking to Mr. X. I asked him to begin playing. He took his violin out of the case, and while tuning it handled the

bow with the same quickness and movements as his father. But that was not all. When he began to play, his posture, the movements of hands and bow, were absolutely similar to his fathers. But not only that: even the shortcomings in his performance and musical sense, sometimes linking musical intervals -- his tone, and various small details -- all resembled his father's.[1]

What Suzuki has discovered with respect to musical talent has its exact counterpart in the religious sphere. Hindu children find themselves befriended by the particular gods which their parents reverence. Moslem children instinctively regard the Prophet Mohammed as far outdistancing Jesus of Nazareth in religious importance. The children of devout Christian Scientists discover that often God heals them without the use of any medications. Each of these children have learned the "religious tune" of their parents. Even the children of atheists who routinely regard all religion as make-believe are also trained in their parents' "deafness" to God. Thus it appears that religious instincts are no more innate or a pure gift of God than musical instincts. Everything seemingly depends upon our belonging to particular parents. If this is indeed the divinely-obtained process governing one's particular religious upbringing, then it has vast ramifications for Christians who intend to pass on their own religious heritage to the next generation.

The purpose of this chapter is to explore the processes whereby parents pass on their religious experience to their children and whereby masters pass on their spiritual power to their disciples. This exploration will be divided into five sections:

- A. How one's particular upbringing fashions one's habitual religious experience
- B. How a child first learns to perceive God
- C. How adult apprenticeships enable one to transcend one's upbringing
- D. How personal faith functions throughout a Christian apprenticeship
- E. How divine initiative functions throughout a Christian apprenticeship

A. How One's Particular Upbringing Fashions One's
    Habitual Religious Experience

Each human infant who enters the world possesses certain instinctive patterns which are remarkably fitted for his/her well-being. The spontaneous sucking instinct of an infant is a case in point. More importantly, however, an infant, even when well-fed, takes an instinctive delight in observing and being with his/her parents. It is this latter dynamism which establishes interhuman contact as rewarding in itself and which forms the ground whereby the child comes to spontaneously assimilate the cultural heritage of his/her parents or guardians. Without such prolonged contact, the human infant can neither properly become "a child of these parents" nor "a child of their God."

I myself grew up in a Christian home. I can vividly remember my father making the sign of the cross and reciting the blessing before our family meals. I was taught to make the sign of the cross with him and to reverently listen to his prayer. Whenever I missed supper with the family and ate alone later, my father would invariably ask me whether I had prayed before eating. The persistent repetition of this pattern served to impress upon me that the Lord of the Universe was the unseen provider of the gifts that graced our table.

In church, every Sunday, my religious upbringing continued. As a child I was taught that God lived in the gold tabernacle upon the altar. In his presence, silence was required. It was considered a sin to speak in church unless necessity required it. In addition, I was shown how to kneel up straight. I remember, with some pride, that I would sometimes deliberately endure the pain in my knees because it seemed such a small thing in contrast to the Son of God suffering on the great cross that dominated the front of my church. The liturgy was in Latin then, so I was instructed how to use a prayer book which would allow me to follow the prayers of the priest in English. It was difficult to keep up. The communion was the most solemn moment. I felt that the same God who made the earth fertile and who died on the cross was now coming to visit me, to become my food. Now that God was within me, I felt stronger and more capable of being like Christ: obedient, hard-working, and kneeling up straight.

The concreteness of my own religious upbringing serves to immediately dispel any possibility of imagining that the Christian faith has a uniform quality which entirely originates from God. It is no divine mystery that I am a Roman Catholic and that my Catholicism bears the marks of the traditions acted out by my father, by my pastor, Fr. McMonigle, and by the religious Sisters who taught me in grade school. Had I been born of Hindu parents, I am quite certain that my settled instincts would have been attentive to the works of Vishnu and to his incarnations as Lord Rama and Lord Krishna. Even if my parents had been Quakers or Lutherans, I am quite certain that my religious experience would have been considerably different from that which resulted from my Catholic upbringing.

History has provided us with numerous instances in which children have been found who have spent prolonged periods without human interaction. In the 1930s. a priest discovered two small children who had been raised by wolves in the jungle.

> In the wolf's cave the infants crawled on all fours, their eyes seeing clearly in the dark. Their noses were extremely sensitive. They ran fast on all fours . . . . Their shoulders were wide, their legs powerful, with bent thighs that would not stretch out straight. They grasped things with their mouths, not with their hands. Food and water were taken in a doglike manner . . . .

The older girl, Kamala, was about seven years old and quite adept at living the culture proper to the wolves:

> During the day she slept, but as soon as the sun set her activity started. At night, just as she had done when she lived among wolves, she would howl three times at accurate intervals, at ten, one and three o'clock. This habit had become second nature, because for years she had been howling regularly with the wolves together in a chorus. She did not stop this howling during the nine years she was with human beings, but continued until she died, at the age of sixteen. Kamala's voice had neither human nor

animal characteristics. The sound was peculiar, indeterminate.[2]

Cases such as these dramatically demonstrate that the character of our humanity is functionally determined by our particular parents and guardians. Human infants, isolated from human contacts, go on to use their uncanny imitative powers to model themselves according to what models are available. In the case of the two girls considered above, this meant reliably assimilating the patterns proper to wolves. This and parallel cases demonstrate that, for better or worse, one's early childhood upbringing is tenacious and irreversible. Our later experiences can enhance and slowly modify our settled instincts, but they can never disregard or entirely overrule them. The plasticity of infancy and early childhood is only experienced once.

Even prior to verbal communication, infants have a stunning ability to enter into the felt meanings exhibited by their parents. Consider, for a moment, an imaginary situation in which a mother is preparing supper while her child is amusing herself on the kitchen floor next to her. The infant has become alert to something which has moved out from under the kitchen stove and is making its way across the floor. The infant moves toward this "something" anticipating the possibility of touching and tasting it. While in pursuit, the infant is bruskly pulled aside by her mother. She utters sounds of upset disapproval and frantically tries to step on "it." In this way, even before the onset of language learning, the child's perception of cockroaches is already emotionally charged with apprehension.

In sharp contrast, the kitten receives quite another set of nonverbal clues from its mother. The kitten observes its mother playing with the cockroach, alternately releasing it and pouncing upon it. In the end, this housecat will taste and eat the cockroach. Her kitten will eventually begin to do likewise.

Clearly, animals do learn successful modes of feeling and of acting from their parents. In the past, almost all animal activity was assigned to "innate instincts." Now, however, it is quite clear that even animals have a cultural inheritance which is entirely passed on by parent-infant training.[3] A striking illustration of this comes from research done with cats and mice. The research shows that kittens separated from their mother and raised with mice tend to ignore them even when they become quite hungry. When a mouse-eating cat is introduced into this setting, however, nearly all the kittens begin to trap and eat mice.

Most Christians have been raised to regard their religious experience as private and incommunicable in nature. Parents of this persuasion are convinced that they can only expose their children to the external trappings of their religion; God alone must be counted upon to shape the private experience of their children directly. This position does not bear up under close examination. The child invariably patterns him/herself within the religious modes of feeling and acting exhibited by his/her parents or guardians. This holds true even when parents are indifferent toward religion or even militantly atheistic. A Christian need not be surprised at this. A child who instinctively growns up to replicate the linguistic idiosyncracies of his/her parents will not be daunted in this feat by parents who profess that they are quite incapable of teaching a language to their child. Likewise, parents who do not have the slightest recognition that their experience of cockroaches is parochial and culturally-conditioned will not thereby be any less capable of leading their child to assimilate their particular tradition and experience of cockroaches. And the religious heritage of parents is no exception to this rule. Prolonged interpersonal contact between adult and child is all that is needed.

What has been presented up to this point can be summarized as follows: (1) When human beings are isolated from all adult contacts, they grow up being culturally deprived and only marginally removed from a completely animal existence. (2) By virtue of the fact that human infants have particular parents, sustained human interaction with them will insure that the child will grow up assimilating their modes of perceiving and of interacting with their environment. (3) Parents pass on their religious feelings and understandings in precisely the same way as they pass on other dimensions of their culture. God does not take direct and immediate charge of the religious formation of every new child born into the world. The child remains almost entirely dependent upon his/her parents for attaining the richness of the particular religious tradition to which his/her parents are attached.

B. How a Child First Learns to Perceive God

         I now want to sketch out the process by which a child first learns to perceive the particular God of his/her parents. The last section established the fact that parents do, either deliberately or unwittingly, enable their children to accomplish this feat. The human intricacies of this feat remain to be explored.

         The Christian tradition specifies that "God" is a spiritual reality. This means that our organism cannot perceive God's presence in the same way that one makes contact with tangible realities. A stone sensually manifests itself to the grasping, squeezing, pounding gestures of human hands. Even a wind storm manifests its presence sensually. This cannot be the case with God. Any "god" so available is, by definition, a deception and an idol.

         Since the human organism cannot directly perceive the presence of a spiritual reality, the Christian God must be perceived indirectly through his/her tangible effects within the cosmic/human drama. If our God were to be entirely disengaged from creation, then his/her existence would be entirely a matter of speculation. Futhermore, even if God were known to exist, the aloofness of God would make it entirely impossible to contemplate any commitments in his/her behalf. In fact, the manifest aloofness of God would seemingly indicate that the human drama was of no concern to him/her and that we were to get on, as best as we could, without taking him/her into account. Under these conditions, anyone who would establish a religious cult based on certain dreams or visions would be a fraud. Such persons would be rightly condemned for taking the figments of their own imaginings and substituting them for the aloofness of God. Not even good intentions are allowed to pass for truth -- especially in the domain of religion.

         But our God is not the kind who is disengaged from history. The Hebrew Scriptures represent the endeavors of one people to take notice of the historical initiatives of their God. Needless to say, these Scriptures do not offer an exhaustive account; YHWH's historical presence often went unnoticed and some initiatives were passed over or forgotten. In any case, the books of the Old Testament do represent the normative accounts of the concerns and the initiatives of God in the era in which they were written.

Historic events are the primary locus for discerning YHWH's insertion within human affairs. Take the events surrounding the exodus as an illustration. The cries of Abraham's children called to heaven when they were powerless and sorely abused by the Egyptians. If indeed, Pharoah and his people had continued to prosper, then it would have to be assumed that YHWH was deaf to the cries of his people and favored Pharoah. In point of fact, however, a series of disasters befell Pharoah and his court after they had introduced harsh measures against the Hebrew slaves. Moses and Aaron experience these disasters as expressing YHWH's judgment in favor of his people against the tyranny of the Pharoah. As such, therefore, Moses and Aaron act as the inspired interpreters of YHWH's judgment upon Pharoah. Seemingly some of Pharoah's advisors are also inspired to say, "This is the finger of God" (Exod 8:15a). "But Pharoah's heart was stubborn and, as YHWH had foretold, he refused to listen to Moses and Aaron"(Exod 8:15a).

When God is perceived as "present" within a given historic event, this means that those steeped in the ways of YHWH find tangible clues therein which point to God's hidden activity. There is no question of Moses hearing voices coming from the sky or from inside his head which interpret the hidden meaning of historic events. <u>The events themselves are the voice of YHWH</u>, <u>Moses hears these events rightly</u>.[4] Anyone who is sympathetic with God's ways would be expected to also "hear" YHWH's judgment in the events befalling Egypt. Only those who are strangers to YHWH are necessarily "blind and deaf" to his/her presence within events. Thus, Pharoah represents the classical figure of the person who is blind to the true nature of the events surrounding him until it is too late.

How is it that, when Moses and the Pharoah were confronted with the same series of historic events, Moses perceived the hand of YHWH therein while the Pharoah did not? Or, as a parallel instance, how is it that some contemporary Jews, when confronted with the historic events leading to the formation of the State of Israel, perceive the hand of YHWH therein while others do not (declaring the State of Israel to be a purely secular adventure)? Or, again, how is it that some Christians perceive the hand of God to be operative within particular sacramental rites while other Christians either deny or construe in an entirely different fashion God's operation therein? In each of these instances the public data is manifestly similiar for both the believer and the unbeliever alike. The believer, however, claims that the public data offers clues which allow him/her to perceive the hidden activity of God. Some naturalists would claim that the believer simply projects his/her subjective biases upon an ambiguous set of clues. Some supernaturalists, meanwhile, would suggest that divine grace assists the believer to perceive the true depth of the events while the unbeliever flounders within the limited confines of unaided reason. Following the lines of throught of Michael Polanyi, my intention here is to draw attention to the prerequisite tacit skills which allow the believer to find a given historic event transparently revealing God's initiative while the unbeliever, lacking such skills, finds the same event to be opaque. To correctly understand how tacit skills undergird the graced recognition of the believer, I intend to show, firstly, how tacit skills operate subliminally within every act of recognition and then, secondly, to explain how the appropriate tacit skills for the recognition of divine initiative are acquired and operate subliminally within the experience of believers.

By way of examining the role of tacit skills in every act of recognition, imagine, for a moment, that you are occupied in the kitchen and are distracted by some noise coming from the adjoining room. For a brief moment, the noises draw your attention away from your work. You (instinctively and/or deliberately) focus your attention upon the noises expecting that they are the clues bearing upon some known reality which is making its presence felt. Conscious straining is rewarded by a flash of recognition: "John is walking toward the outside door." Or, on another occasion, the sound discloses that someone has entered the house but does not disclose whom. In this instance, one gives a shout, "Who's there?" "It's me," comes the reply. From this you immediately know: "Linda has come home."

Such familiar experiences illustrate how decisive one's body is in every act of recognition. Initially, in the case just considered, one's body focuses upon certain clues within its field of hearing. The body can, at the same time, ignore the loud playing of the radio in the kitchen. Then the body artfully integrates the presenting clues into meaningful wholes. The straining to hear represents the body's tension in groping for a remembered pattern which matches the outline of the sound being received. The flash of recognition represents the relaxation of the search and the satisfaction which accompanies the emergence of the integrated meaning of the sound coming from the adjoining room. The "meaning" emerges within one's organism, but it is correctly projected into the source of the clues, viz., the other room. Every act of recognition, consequently, has the character of a projection.5

At any given moment, our powers of recognition are limited and defined by one's past training. In everyday living, our body makes these recognitions so rapidly and effortlessly that one can hardly recall the emotional strain that once went into their initial development. Accordingly, some people regard their particular powers of recognition as innate. Nothing could be further from the truth. One has only to follow sympathetically the torturous struggle of a child first learning to read in order to remember that one's present ease of recognition was entirely acquired through prolonged efforts. I remember my own experience with an auto mechanic who immediately recognized "loss of compression" the moment that he heard my engine run. I remember, too, how the symphony conductor could immediately spot mistakes made by his performers during the rehearsal. It is in this way that one can again remember that nothing (no thing) is ever "heard" unless one has previously developed the appropriate skill to do so.

Building upon this generalized account of human recognition, one can now understand how it is that a child first learns to detect the presence of intangibles such as "radio waves," "justice," and "God." Such intangibles do not present themselves directly to the explorations of the child. The adult, who has the sophisticated skill necessary to make such second-order recognitions, must direct the child's attention to what, as yet, the child has no power of grasping. Language is very decisive at this point. The parents' words point to a significant reality whose meaning the child has not yet grasped. By virtue of the child's active and uncanny powers to gradually enter into the "meaning" that his/her parents take into account, the first moment of recognition finally arrives. More often than not, the child uses language to indicate readiness to be stretched into the realities known to his/her parents. Thus, the child asks, "Why does the car radio stop (when passing over a steel-structured bridge)?" "Why do these people go to prison?" "Why do we pray before we eat?" The adult response in these instances directs the child's attention to the corresponding spiritual realities which each of the events exhibit: "radio waves," "justice," "God."

A child's first recognition of the presence of an intangible reality hidden within the clues offered by a particular event is always quite impoverished and selective. The child who is told that "radio waves" make the car radio work and that the steel of the bridge keeps most of the "radio waves" from getting to the car antenna has no reason to recall "radio waves" save when passing over bridges. Later, when father installs a T.V. antenna, the parent enhances the child's recognition of "radio waves" so as to cover a new historic event. The father says, "This antenna will collect the radio waves above our house, and this attached wire will bring them into our T.V. set so that we will have a better picture and a clearer sound." With time, the child becomes aware of a whole series of interrelated events which evoke the unseen presence of "radio waves." Now, with each repeated recognition of "radio waves," there is an enlarged series of past experiences which enrich and inform the present experience. The present experience, meanwhile, enhances and slightly modifies the previous experience of "radio waves."

In time, the child will spontaneously feel the presence of "radio waves" the moment that suitable clues present themselves. Furthermore, the child's powers of recognition will anticipate a whole series of extended references. Thus, for example, the child might say, "The radio waves go to sleep when ever I turn the radio off." Such extended references will invite correction or confirmation by the child's parents. This parental feedback will allow the child to enlarge and to realign his/her meaning of "radio waves" so that it corresponds to that held by his/her parents.

Everything that applies to the child's knowing of "radio waves" also applies to the child's knowing of "God." When God appears and how God appears to the child depends entirely upon those instances in which his/her parents make reference to their God. Parents refer to God from within the spontaneity of their own recognitions: "God makes the grass grow," "God will punish you if you are bad," etc. Their children gradually make these spontaneous recognitions their own.

The vulnerability of children cannot be overestimated. Every child is doomed to take into account not only the particular God but also the demonic distortions and unrecognized errors in his/her parents' religion. Some children assimilate from their parents a profound religious distrust which effectively immunizes them from ever perceiving "God." Other children are habituated to placating that "God" who is the harsh, unforgiving Judge bent upon punishing evil deeds. And still other children are marvelously enriched by a "God" who gives them an identity and a cause which enobles the whole texture of their lives. Upon each child the blessings and curses of his/her parents fall.

The principal insights of this section may be recapitulated as follows: (1) "God" belongs to the class of intangible realities that make their presence felt through the tangible effects they have in shaping particular historical events. As a consequence the presence of "God" can go unnoticed; only persons with the requisite tacit powers can competently "hear" and "see" the historic initiatives of YHWH. (2) Parents use language to alert their children to the intangible realities that they take into account. Children, by virtue of their uncanny ability to enter into the meanings held by their parents, gradually learn to sense the presence of "God" in precisely those events in which parents themselves spontaneously find him/her. With each new recognition, the child must strain so as to try to catch what his/her parents perceive. This straining allow the child to gradually enlarge his/her powers of recognition and to gradually conform them to those of his/her parents. (3) With time, the child will spontaneously sense the presence of the God of his/her parents whenever a suitable nexus of clues present themselves. With each fresh recognition of "God," there is an enlarged series of past experiences which enrich and inform the present experience. The present experience, meanwhile, enhances and slightly modifies the previous experiences of "God." When the child gives voice to his/her own spontaneous recognitions of "God," parental correction and confirmation are important for the ongoing process of enlarging and of realigning the child's innate powers of recognition. For better or for worse, a child progressively duplicates the powers of recognition exhibited by his/her parents.

C. How Adult Apprenticeships Enable One to Transcend One's Upbringing

When I was sixteen, my interests were decidedly scientific and religious. I was an active member of both the Chemistry Club and the Sodality of St. Joseph's High School. It was at this time that I met the man who was destined to entirely reshape my personal identity: Brother Mike Stimac, S.M.

Brother Mike was the energetic and imaginative moderator of the Amateur Radio Club. He had the charism for calling forth from students like myself high standards of achievement both in amateur radio and in practical Christianity. After mastering the morse code and passing a government license examination, he taught me how to plan, assemble, and operate a radio transmitter. I remember the satisfaction and growing sense of achievement as I gained more advanced licenses and constructed some very sophisticated electronic equipment. I used to arrive an hour early for school in order to work and to be with Brother Mike in the radio lab. After school this adventure would continue -- frequently prompting me to skip supper and work right up to midnight, when I would return home, do my homework, and fall exhausted into bed. With time, I became a junior executive in the Radio Club and undertook responsibilities for planning and executing educational programs for its sixty club members. It was then that I became a partner with Brother Mike in his efforts to challenge and enlarge the "boys" in the club such that they would become "men of character" -- both in the arena of amateur radio and lived Christianity. I can recall quite vividly how natural it seemed to be planning, at one moment, for outfitting student cars with two-way radios for a trip to the cyclotron lab at Ohio State University, and then, at the next moment, to be discussing remedies for "the lack of Christian gratitude" exhibited by some of the senior members of the club.

For two years, I was positively under the spell of Brother Mike. He became something of a functional father for me -- stretching and supporting me in marvelous ways that my own natural father was unable to do. At the end of this period my personal religious sensibilities and skills were greatly enlarged and transformed. I could measure how different I had become by feeling the large gap which had come to separate my religious sensibilities from those exhibited by my natural father. I now felt God was calling me to change the face of the earth in the ways which I had seen demonstrated by Brother Mike -- that hero and saint who had touched my life. This conviction dominated my life for the ten years that followed.

I again make reference to my personal history because it provides a solid point of departure for understanding the dynamics of an adult apprenticeship. Children assimilate the standards of excellence of their parents through an <u>acritical</u> imitation. Such a receptive period in which the child's instincts are plastic and uninhibited by previous habits will never again exist. It remains uncertain whether the entire future of each child will be nothing but an extension of that determination received during his/her childhood upbringing. As childhood ends, critical powers emerge which stubbornly follow the ingrained patterns of this upbringing and render it immune to any dramatic change. The character of the youth is set.

Then, in an unbidden moment, the capacity for hero worship makes itself felt. The adolescent is instinctively drawn to identify those heroes who define the sort of person that he/she aspires to become. This capacity of self-surrender to a hero represents the adolescent thirst for self-transcendence. On the one hand, the actual choice of a hero is partially determined by the character of one's past parental upbringing. On the other hand, this choice represents the providential lure for becoming much more than even one's parents ever envisioned.

The spontaneous self-surrendering of the hero-worshipper normally matures into the faith of a disciple being apprenticed by prolonged interchanges with the hero-master. In cases where no engagement is possible, hero worship remains abortive, and self-defeating imaginative encounters substitute for real ones.

Peter and Andrew were initially sons of their father before they met Jesus. Their personal religious sensibilities had already been formed within the traditions prevailing within their father's home. It would be folly to imagine that they somehow had no religious orientation prior to their meeting Jesus. Quite to the contrary, it must be imagined that it was only because of their previous religious upbringing that they were able to make sense of and be attracted to the prophet heralding the Kingdom of Heaven in their midst. The presumption, therefore, is that Jesus powerfully addressed their own religious aspirations and called forth from them the compelling desire to be like him in all things. This impulse alone can account for why these two fishermen would leave behind their families and occupations so as to remain continuallly with their self-chosen master.

Under the influence of Jesus, the disciples experienced a progressive religious transformation. They were "born again." Their former religious experience within the ways of their natural father was greatly enlarged and transformed. For this to happen, however, they had to surrender themselves wholeheartedly to be influenced, to be persuaded, to be guided by Jesus. In response to their self-giving, Jesus had to lead them through progressive feats of dicovery so that they might grasp and be grasped by those hidden realities which he knew firsthand. The expansion which a disciple experiences always seems like a marvelous work of grace that "brings the dead to life and calls into being what does not exist" (Rom 4:17).

It is sometimes supposed that a religious apprenticeship consists in a master telling, in words, the secrets of his tradition. This is manifestly impossible. The disciple before Jesus is like the child before his/her parent; neither has the requisite skills to grasp the hidden realities to which the words point. The child is bewildered when his/her father first refers to "radio waves" or "God." The disciple, on the contrary, imagines that he understands the words that his master offers. In reality, however, he projects into his master's words the simple sentiments and the systematic errors which the disciple originally learned in his parents' home. This horizon of understanding causes the disciple to initially imagine that he understands his master; whereas, in fact, he grossly misunderstands him. The disciple is thus in a worse condition than the child; he has to discover firstly that there is a momentous linguistic and experiential gap which separates him from the meanings which resonate in the master as he speaks.

The same linguistic limitations hold true in every secular apprenticeship as well. Consider, for instance, a chess apprenticeship. In the beginning, the novice finds that the chess masters have written books in which they formulate rules for chess strategy. Having received such rules, however, the novice painfully discovers that they offer no quick route to success in chess. A chess master cannot explain his strategy in words and immediately expect to create a rival. To illustrate this, consider the following rule which is offered to beginners:

> Use your opening moves so as to exert control over the four central squares of the chess board.

The chess master reads this rule and it rings true by virtue of the vastly intricate tacit skills which govern his/her playing. The novice reads this same rule, but the meaning that it carries is limited in direct proportion to the gap which separates the tacit skills of the master from his/her own. <u>Only at the end of an appropriate apprenticeship, when the novice has tacit skills which rival those of the master, does the rule become transparent to the depth of meaning that the master intends.</u>

How does the novice in chess hope to break out of his/her own limited horizon of understanding in order to rival the masters? One standard method for accomplishing this is for the novice to rehearse reverently and enter sympathetically into the performances of the masters. In chess, the performances of the masters are their tournament games which have been carefully recorded and published. Frequently a master will publish his/her best games and provide a running commentary to help disclose the intricacies of his/her strategy throughout. A novice, accordingly, has to set up a chess board and to attentively replay the recorded games of the masters. At every move, the novice has to throw him/herself into the clues offered by the position of the pieces and to endeavor to discern the hidden strategy that they conceal. To do this, the novice imagines that the game is his/her own and at each step he/she has to decide what appears to be the strongest move. In doing this, the novice stretches his/her personal powers of evaluation so as to better and better approximate the masters'. Frequently the novice becomes puzzled when a master makes a move that seemingly has no advantage. The novice strains to catch what the master must, at that moment, have perceived but which is entirely obscure to the novice. The novice racks his/her brain. Notes are consulted, if they exist. The game may then be taken forward a few moves so as to better perceive something of the consequences of the puzzling move. The novice may strain for minutes or even hours. Finally, in a moment of elation, the clues come into place and the original strategy appears. The puzzlement disappears. Everything falls into place. His/her eyes have been opened. And, more importantly, <u>his/her skills of strategy have been enlarged</u> so that the patterns of the master now grip the novice's very own.

This example from chess illustrates the basic pattern which dominates every religious apprenticeship as well. The disciple, at first, holds on to the words of his/her master without any adequate grasp of the richness of meaning that they intend. At the same time, the disciple reverently rehearses the deeds of his/her master. By puzzling over them, by imaginatively regarding them as his/her own, by exploring their consequences, the novice in religion hopes to expand his/her own powers for perceiving and for acting. The parallel can be stretched even further in so far as the deeds of Jesus have been recorded in the Gospels. It is my conviction that this written record must be used with the same modality that a novice in chess uses the recorded games of the chess masters. The Gospel narratives thus stand the chance of transforming the reader. As it is now, most Christians are thoroughly habituated to projecting their own meanings into the Gospel narratives and imagining that they thereby understand them. Nothing could be further from the truth. The same thing holds true for the sacramental rites and the credal doctrines. Without a prolonged apprenticeship, the words and the gestures convey little or nothing of what their originators once felt and intended.

D. How Personal Faith Functions Throughout a Christian Apprenticeship

Nearly every Christian would identify the attachment of a disciple to Jesus as "faith." There is little agreement, however, as to what constitutes the essential experience of this "faith in Jesus." Some want "faith" to designate a deliberate obedience to God's will. Others regard "faith" as their assent to divinely-revealed dogmas. Still others use "faith" to refer to a reoccurring experience in their lives: their wholehearted confidence in God, their overwhelming sense of absolute dependence, their conviction that their sins have been forgiven. These diverse specifications of "faith" result from the diverse denominational traditions of Christianity. I prefer not to try to sort out the strengths and limitations of these various traditions but to make a fresh start.

Within an apprenticeship model, "faith" must first of all represent the spontaneous self-surrender of a disciple to be influenced by his/her self-chosen master. The previous section of this chapter suggested that a disciple requires such a sustained self-surrender or else he/she would remain locked into his/her own settled patterns of perception and limited performance skills. <u>The "faith" of an apprentice, consequently, is the indispensable quality which makes his/her self-transformation a possibility.</u>[6] The Christian preoccupation with "faith," therefore, has ample justification.

Before I sketch the dynamics of faith, I must put aside any illusion that "faith" is a unique religious disposition which has no secular counterparts. To do this, it will suffice to make reference to the vocabulary of the New Testament. Linguistic studies show that the early church was quite content to depict the attachment of disciples to Jesus in the same secular terms by which attachment to any master would be designated.

> There is nothing very distinctive in the usage of the New Testament and early Christian writings as compared with Greek [secular and religious] usage. As in Greek <u>pisteuein</u> means "to rely on," "to trust," "to believe" (TDNT VI:203).

Consequently, even the New Testament uses <u>pisteuein</u> to designate the appropriate disposition toward the prophets (e.g., Luke 24:25, Acts 26:27), toward a message of an angel (e.g., Luke 1:20, Acts 27:25), or toward the disciples announcing the Good News about Jesus (e.g., 1 Cor 15:21, Acts 8:12).

The noun <u>pistis</u> (faith) is derived directly from the Greek verb <u>pisteuein</u> (to believe). It is a peculiarity of the English and the Latin languages that two entirely different words must be used, namely, "faith" and "to believe," <u>fides</u> and <u>credere</u>. "To believe" is derived from the middle English of our ancestors and meant "to be-leef," i.e., "to be held as dear/precious." <u>Credere</u>, meanwhile was derived from <u>cor-dare</u> which means literally "to give [one's] heart." Each of these words functions well in both secular and religious contexts.

The personal faith of a disciple exhibits three continuous phases: (1) Initially, faith is the experience of spontaneous admiration which lures toward an apprenticeship. (2) During the apprenticeship, faith is the functional disposition by which the disciple surrenders him/herself to the guidance and correction of his/her master. (3) For the competent graduate from an apprenticeship, faith is the confident expectation that his/her trained instincts will securely guide him/her into an extended series of fresh and relevant contacts with those realities which he/she serves. The first two phases will be examined immediately; the third will be left to the following chapter.

The initial phase of faith pertains to the uninitiated. Faith at this level is experienced as a spontaneous admiration which draws the uninitiated into a state of alert fascination. In the secular spheres, this is the impulse associated with the adolescent identifying his/her heroes or with the lover identifying his/her beloved. Being "spontaneous," faith at this level is not essentially reasonable or subject to rational criteria. If the fishermen at the Sea of Galilee were asked to explain their fascination for Jesus, they could only give "the reasons of the heart." Anyone who was indifferent or hostile to Jesus would have found faith in him to be blind and self-deluding.

Most segments of the Christian tradition have proposed that spontaneous admiration directed toward Jesus does not derive solely from natural operations but that the grace of God assists the believer. Scriptural texts have been cited in support of this claim. The following is illustrative:

> No one can came to me [Jesus] unless he [she] is drawn by the Father who sent me (John 6:44).

Thomas Aquinas, in his early works, did not attach any specific divine impulse to the act of faith. He presumed that faith was an inner instinct (<u>instinctus</u>) whose dynamism was naturally drawn by goodness and truth.7 In his later works, however, Thomas incorporated the arguments of Augustine against Pelagius and, accordingly, insisted that the grace of God was required to assist the human dynamism in the act of faith:

> To believe does indeed depend upon the will of the believer, but man's [woman's] will needs to be prepared by God with grace in order that he [she] may be raised to things which are above his [her] nature (ST II-II, 6, 1, ad 3).

Here, as elsewhere, Thomas implies that nature is already predisposed to grace. Divine initiative, consequently, does no violence to the human dynamism but presupposes it and strengthens it in its very operation.

As a first approximation, the latter judgment of Thomas Aquinas seems like a good point of departure, but it is hardly sufficient in terms of our present horizon of understanding. Some recognition must be made of the fact that every present impulse derives from a whole nexus of human and divine components which have ebbed and flowed within one's immediate and remote history. Thus, in particular, the fishermen who attach themselves to Jesus are necessarily predisposed by their whole prior religious formation, by their dreams, by their hopes and frustrations, by their previous encounters with the living God.

The act of faith cannot be analyzed in its operation. It operates subliminally. This means that one cannot neatly separate out the various elements that contribute to its final determination. This, in turn, explains why the disciple confesses that he/she does not know "why he [Jesus] moves me" but, none the less, "I've really changed" because of him.

It is sometimes supposed that the uninitiated can exercise their critical faculties in such a way as to judge the worthiness of any master that they would embrace. This is true -- but only within severe limits which are generally overlooked. At the onset of every specialized apprenticeship, even the adult apprentice cannot judge the true worth of his/her master's tradition because he/she cannot presume to enjoy discernment in matters over which he/she, as yet, has no adequate competence. Should an apprentice be overly critical, this resistance would largely block his/her ability to let go of settled patterns of judgment in order to be influenced by those of the master. It is impossible, therefore, to secure the appropriateness of one's faith through critical reason.[8]

The faith of the uninitiated is necessarily "blind" to the true worth if his/her master. It must even be acknowledged that some degree of emotional fascination distorts the perceptions of the admirer. As in the case of falling in love, emotional fascination operates to single out one person for one's exclusive attention. This, in itself, is a helpful function. The potential disciple is freed from the morass of trying to choose from among many contending masters. Emotional fascination, however, generally means that the master has triggered some idealized picture which the disciple projects upon the master. The blindness of faith is thus entirely akin to the blindness of love. Both one and the other, however, come up against the reality factor. A disciple goes to live with his/her master and thereby gradually the real character of the master emerges to displace the idealized picture; a man goes to live with his beloved and the same thing takes place.

When the reality factor of repeated contacts does not take place, faith can be entirely subverted and replaced by a prolonged emotion fascination that can endure for years. It can thus happen that a Christian becomes entirely intoxicated by his/her projection of Jesus which is emotionally satisfying but which has no roots in the historical Jesus and no contact with his living disciples in the church. Most pastors are afraid to disturb religious infatuation because they fear that the alternative is disillusionment. In effect, however, when a man goes to live with his beloved, three alternatives are possible: (1) he may decide that the real woman significantly disappoints his idealized image and choose to look for his dream woman elsewhere; (2) he may decide that the real woman only moderately disappoints his ideal and choose to settle down to making the most of this concrete relationship; (3) he may discover that the real woman surpasses and transforms his idealized image such that he receives from his wife much more than he ever expected according to his misshaped dreams. The reality factor in religion can thus accordingly lead to disappointment, to compromise, or to unexpected self-transformation.

Religious infatuation evades true discipleship. It is easy to conjure up an idealized image of Jesus and then to surrender imaginatively to him alone. The Jesus of dreamers never talks back, always has a consoling word. Yet, in point of fact, such a Jesus never existed and surely cannot redeem the actual structures of sin and of deception. Infatuation with Jesus, consequently, must be gradually rooted within a discipleship to the living representatives of Jesus. These representatives incarnate the charism of Jesus in our contemporary society. As such, they necessarily disturb the private delusions of dreamers just as Jesus formerly disturbed the private delusions of his followers. Settled patterns of action and of perception are overturned and transcended. This is threatening. All real growth has attendant component of mental anguish and straining. In the end, however, the disciple is redeemed from the structures of sin and of deception that were quite unnoticed as long as he/she settled for only an ethereal apprenticeship to the Jesus of his/her private fantasies.

In sum, the impulse of faith in the uninitiated can be recognized as a responsible self-giving without claiming that it is infallible. One's spontaneous admiration for a particular master is always shaped by tacit powers which defy any minute analysis. Some degree of emotional fascination even distorts the true worth of one's self-chosen master. But if one is blind in the beginning, it is in the apprenticeship itself that one regains one's sight -- not the sight of the uninitiated but the new sight of the master him/herself. It is precisely at the end of the apprenticeship, therefore, that the novice knows the full worth of the master. And this worth is nothing less than the scope and depth of the personal transformation experienced during the time of the apprenticeship.

During the time of apprenticeship, faith serves as the functional disposition which sustains the disciple in his/her day to day self-giving to the guidance and correction of his/her master. Faith in this phase implies an active engagement. The Gospels illustrate this active engagement in Jesus' own practice of apprenticing his disciples. The previous section of this present chapter explained how the disciple must endeavor again and again to enter into the inner meanings out of which the master speaks and acts. The disciples ask questions. They acknowledge and take to heart the approval or corrections of Jesus respecting their own initiatives. Finally, Jesus sends them out on their own so that their independent practice can demonstrate to him and to them how far they have come to share in his own personal powers.

Augustine defended the necessity of faith as the discipline whereby the foolish become wise and the ignorant become knowledgeable. For Augustine, faith was never an end in itself but the infallible way of participating in the wisdom and understanding of the bishops and presbyters of the church. He would say:

> All those things which to begin with we simply believed, following authority only, we come [progressively] to understand.[9]

Using secular examples, Augustine effectively dismisses those who would presume to avoid the self-surrender of an apprenticeship. He suggests that divine providence effectively determined that human wisdom regarding trading, agriculture, etc., are transmitted within apprenticeships; thus, it is all the more foolish to believe that the route to true holiness can avoid an apprenticeship.[10] If beginners seek out a guide for gaining comparatively easy skills, Augustine argues that it is all the more incumbent upon a beginner to seek a competent guide in the much more difficult religious quest. Finally, for those who spurn the Christian masters and plead that the Holy Spirit him/herself is their teacher, Augustine directs toward them the rather biting question as to why they presume to teach others rather than send them to the selfsame teacher whereby they claim to have been infallibly taught.[11] The writings of Augustine, consequently, give ample testimony that faith meant an attachment to the concrete discipline of the corporate church. Such a faith was not a sustained infatuation nor a blind servitude. True faith was expected to transform the disciple, to clothe him/her with the holiness of his/her master, and to make him/her relatively independent in the pursuit of God's cause. Such a faith implied a functioning apprenticeship model within the local church.

E. <u>How Divine Initiative Functions Throughout a Christian Apprenticeship</u>

When the religious enterprise is rightly conceived, some account must be given of both the human and divine components which shape every human experience. As an illustration of this, I find that the blessing recited before eating attains a pragmatic balance between human and divine initiative. On the one hand, the formula of the prayer recognizes the food about to be eaten as the product of divine bounty. On the other hand, this recognition of God's work does not exclude acknowledging one's gratitude toward the farmers, the millers, the butchers, the bakers, the truckers, the cook. Each of these persons has harmonized their initiative with God's initiative. God is not, by far, the only unseen benefactor present at every supper meal. In parallel fashion, one's "religious" experiences can be acknowledged as "being from God" without denying that one's parents, pastors, guardians, psyche have also been efficacious in providing for what one has received.

Given the description of the human dynamics undergirding a religious formation already spelled out in this chapter, a balanced Christian theology of grace might begin along the following lines:

1. God the Father is the one who originates and cares for all that exists. Humans reflect the character of God and cooperate with his/her supreme design when they, acting as parents, play their part in originating and caring for their children. Through this divine-human partnership, parents take the gift of their own genetic inheritance and intentionally cooperate in passing it on to their children. With even greater importance, these same parents take the spiritual powers that they have received by virtue of their religious inheritance and share this with their children. This providential plan not only enobles human initiative by giving it a necessary role in the formation of the biological and religious identity of each new human person, but it clearly indicates that, in the present order of things, God does not proceed with his/her enterprise of creation/redemption without us.

2. Human infants are providentially designed for a prolonged dependence upon their parents. In the beginning, the spontaneous sucking reflex of the child allows it to draw nourishment from his/her mother's breast. Later, this same child will exhibit a spontaneous self-giving (acritical faith) whereby he/she will progressively take on the sensibilities and performance skills exhibited by his/her parents and guardians. Without parental nourishment, the infant will die. Without prolonged parental contacts, the child will never become a child of these parents and a child of their God.

Theologically speaking, one might perceive the acritical faith of the child as the gift of God which will insure his/her progressive redemption from purely animal existence. But more than this, the strength and power of

the entire religious tradition stemming from Abraham
through Jesus up into our present day cannot create/redeem
any actual child unless the acritical faith of the infant
be met with parents or guardians who themselves incarnate
the richness of that tradition. All human infants are born
as inheritors of Adam; by virtue of a Christian upbringing,
infants are reborn as inheritors of Christ.

Every pair of actual parents both conceal and
reveal the spiritual power of Jesus Christ; the same can be
said for every church (the local community of Christians).
Most parents are conscious that their own Christian
sensibilities and performance skills are limited;
therefore, as their children advance in age, they
ordinarily enlist the assistence of trusted spiritual
masters (pastors and catechists) to augment their own
potential to train their children. By acting in this
fashion, parents insure themselves that the religious
sensibilities and performance skills assimilated by their
children are not limited by their own degree of
resourcefulness and graced existence. This same practice
normally holds true with respect to every other domain of
childhood training as well. Parents of limited musical
skills, for example, will sometimes make great sacrifices
to secure for their children masters of music who will
expand their children's musical sensibilities and
performance skills far beyond their own.

3. The practice of infant baptism has been
periodically resisted due to the fact that Christian
communities frequently applied the manifest effects of
adult baptism indiscriminately to infant baptism. Orthodox
theology, meanwhile, was careful to note that infants are
affected by the rite according to their particular
providential status (ST III, 68, 9, ad 1-3; 10, co & ad 1;
69, 8, co & ad 1). Augustine, for example, explained that
the struggles and the cries of the infant during the rite
do not indicate that the infant is resisting what the rite
intends.[12] On the contrary, it is only due to the
expressed intention of the parents and the lived faith of
the church that the lack of intention and the lack of lived
faith on the part of the infant are supplied for. Infant
baptism, consequently, was always understood as a
theological exception.

The practice of infant baptism stands on the
God-ordained interrelatedness of parents with their
children.[13] Infants exhibit an instinctive "faith"
whereby they acritically give themselves over to
assimilating the operative divine sympathies which their
parents and guardians exhibit before them. By the rite of
infant baptism, therefore, the parents and guardians

(godparents) of a particular child signify and intensify their intention and their ability to cooperate with God in transmitting to their child the religious inheritance in which they themselves abide. By so doing, the rite is understood as the <u>sacramentum</u> (Latin: "oath") whereby the child is assured of the grace and the power that God intends for this child by virtue of its progressive insertion within the fellowship of the saints and prophets, those living and those who have gone before.

It is unfortunate that those Christians who emphasize efficacious sacraments are prone to imagine that God operates wholly and entirely during the brief moments of the rite itself (e.g., as the water is being poured).[14] Thus is clearly an aberration since both the Augustinian and Thomistic theology of baptism took for granted that baptism was to be delayed for adults until such time as they would manifest not merely the grace of calling but a certain informed faith and practice as well (ST III, 68, 3, co). Even for adults, consequently, <u>baptism was envisioned as sealing and intensifying what God was already effecting prior to the rite</u> (ST III, 69, 1, ad 2; 4, ad 2; 5, ad 1). Consistency demands that infant baptism be envisioned in the same way. Both divine and human agency have been manifestly productive in creating a receptive new person; the rite itself seals and intensifies this divine-human collaboration as this new person is progressively informed with the power and wisdom of the God of his/her parents.

Existential effects take place gradually; juridical effects take place instantaneously. Thus, while it takes years to effect the transformation of a pagan or an infant into a mature disciple of Christ, the forgiveness of sins can be effected wholly and entirely during the brief moments of the baptismal rite itself. The forgiveness of sins was originally understood as the result of personal conversion. Thus the psalmist relates his/her story:

> At last I admitted to you I had sinned;
>   no longer concealing my guilt,
> I said, 'I will go to YHWH
>   and confess my fault.'
> And you [YHWH], you have forgiven the
>   wrong I did,
>   have pardoned my sin (Ps 32:5).[15]

Since baptism was used by the primitive church as the sign and seal of conversion (Acts 2:38), it was natural to associate baptism itself with the forgiveness of sins. Juridical theories of satisfaction or atonement associated with the death of Jesus, subsequently, dictated that baptism would be spoken of as washing away sins due to the merits of Jesus' death. Augustine, in his own pastoral zeal to stem the practice of delayed baptism which was prevalent in his day, emphasized that even infants suffered from the effects of original sin and needed the juridical efficacy of baptism (even when it appeared as though the existential efficacy of baptism was not yet needed). Orthodox theology thus speaks of baptism as the juridical act whereby God forgives both original sin and actual sins in the recipient.

Our present task does not necessitate that we scrutinize juridical theories of forgiveness and the various interpretations of original sin. It suffices that juridical efficacy be distinguished from existential efficacy. A church community can juridically "adopt" a son/daughter of Adam as a member of its own family -- the brothers/ sisters of Christ -- in a brief fiat. To effect this juridical transformation existentially, however, will require prolonged and strenuous efforts. In like fashion, sins can be forgiven/forgotten quite readily but even God has to labor over thousands of years before he/she can produce a people whose hearts and minds are so in sympathy with his/her own that there is no more serious sin:

> The whole creation is eagerly waiting for God to reveal his [her] sons [daughters]. . . . All of us who possess the first-fruits of the Spirit, we too groan inwardly as we wait for our bodies to be set free [from sin] (Rom 8:19, 23).

4. Young people in their teens no longer exhibit the acritical receptivity that providentially characterized their childhood. At this time, the horizon of understanding which they assimilated from their parents and their parentially chosen mentors operates tacitly and hibitually to inform their "religious experiences" (or lack thereof). It would appear as though the interiority of the young persons is thus set for life. But then another providentially designed capacity emerges: namely, the capacity for admiration and the attendant impulse for self-surrender that it implies. The identification of a religious master, and, given the right circumstances, the embarking upon a prolonged apprenticeship will continue the divine-human partnership of parenting spoken of above. In this case, however, the youth finds a "spiritual father/mother" who will enable him/her to transcend and, in some cases, even to purify or overturn his/her childhood religious upbringing.

Theologically speaking, everything that the tradition relates respecting the grace of vocation or the grace of adult conversions might be applied here. The process is not fully intentional nor deliberate. Nor is merit involved. How, for instance, can the young Augustine account for his discontent with both his mother's Christianity and his Manichean masters? How can he, at the same time, account for the peace and intellectual satisfaction that he finds at hearing the sermons of Bishop Ambrose? He does not so much choose as feel himself chosen. He does not decide so much as know himself instinctively drawn. The time and the circumstances are ripe: the grace which he has already received due to his religious quest appears to have inevitably brought him to this point. Must not the hand of God be perceived within this new burst of selfsurrender which will lead to an expanded sense of personal well-being and healing in the face of one's God?

Augustine, unlike the Thomistic school which borrowed from him, would insist that some impulse of God would be present not only within specifically Christian circumstances such as the above but within every quest for Good and Truth. How, for example, did even the pagan philosophers break away from the superstitions of the masses to discover a surer truth? How, again, did the pagan philosophers break free from habituation with lesser goods in order to attach themselves to a transcendent good? Augustine, consequently, assumed that interior grace functions universally even though external grace (Christ and his church) operates only within particular times and places.[16] Thus Augustine concludes: Many are called (via interior grace); yet, few are chosen (when exterior grace responds to the interior grace).

5. A living religious tradition is a sacrament, an efficacious sign, causing grace within its adherents. Even more marvelous, however, is the contemplation of the slow, progressive steps wherein God creates a tradition. Beginning with Abraham, continuing with Isaac, Jacob, Judah, etc., each stands on the shoulders of those who went before and each expands within his own religious quest his sympathies with the living God. Even after Jesus, we have already intimated that the religious quest never came to a stage of sheer repetition. Peter and Paul stood on the shoulders of Jesus; and, from that height, they periodically encountered fresh discoveries of the demands of God. This process continues in our own day. This entire panaroma suggests that the Spirit of God stays with his/her people in the role of "The Hidden Master" who guides and purifies the deepest intuitions of the saints and prophets who hunger and thirst for God.

An analysis of the process of discovery and its application to the Christian quest for God will be undertaken in the next chapter. In part, this analysis will specify that every religious pioneer is guided by trustworthy intuitions that eventually alter his/her knowing powers so that he/she is led to a larger and more-satisfying grasp of God's cause. Within an apprenticeship, the master leads the novice through the progressive acts of discovery that have formed the classical framework of the Christian tradition. In the end, however, the master turns the mature apprentice over to God so that God him/herself might guide his/her independent quest into a whole series of fresh encounters with him/herself. In so doing, some pioneers will end up taking a stand against their former masters in favor of the living God who has addressed them. This will unsettle the community. Factions may form. The prophet, meanwhile, will endeavor to bring his/her colleagues into the selfsame path of discovery that he/she pursued. Whatever the result, the religious tradition will have been altered by these internal convulsions. In the end, when the community discernment is true, a whole people will have advanced still another small step in their sympathetic alignment of their energies with those of their God. When the community discernment is false, a whole people will suffer from their hardness of hearts as the true prophets are excommunicated and God must wait for another day.

The initial lines of a Christian theology of grace as sketched above illustrates the following generalized principle: <u>divine initiative shows up not by displacing, diminishing, or disabling human initiative; rather, divine initiative is most apparent when it harnesses human initiative in the production of a transcendent co-achievement</u>. Grace, consequently, has been used to designate those particular "gifts" which are received, irrespective of one's merits or worthiness, through a coordination of divine and human initiative. Thus I am disposed to perceive the very organic and cultural life that I have received as grace. More especially, my religious upbringing within its particular historical circumstances is grace. This upbringing includes my initial home training, my various adult apprenticeships under self-chosen masters, and my own history of fresh encounters with the living God. Psychologically speaking, divine initiative is less apparent in the earlier processes than in the latter. This is to be expected. Routine, Augustine suggests, often blinds us from observing divine initiative.[17] Accordingly, there exists the temptation to assign only human initiative to the religious formation of a child and to assign only divine initiative to the fresh discovery of God by a prophet or saint. Closer analysis would indicate that such a temptation leads to disastrous consequences: once human and divine initiative are compartmentalized, there is little chance of later interrelating them. This is why so much of current theology suffers from schizophrenia: on the one hand, divine initiative appears only when human initiative is entirely absent or bankrupt; on the other hand, divine initiative disappears at every moment when scientific theories provide a plausible naturalistic explanation.

Roman Catholic theology, based on the Thomistic synthesis, has often been popularized in such a way as to lead Catholics to believe that they inhabit a two-layered universe. Nature, on the one hand, is fitted for natural achievements and for a natural destiny. Grace, on the other hand, is fitted for supernatural achievements and for a supernatural destiny. I am encouraged by some current Catholic theologians who have endeavored to refute this two-layered model by appealing to renewed examination of the Thomistic texts free of the prejudices introduced by later commentators. Henri de Lubac, for example, insists that the Thomistic conception of creation requires that no arena of the cosmos ought ever to be experienced as entirely "natural," i.e., unaffected by divine initiative. It follows from this, de Lubac attests, that Thomas felt an intimate harmony between redemption and creation, between grace and nature:

> Between nature and grace, he [Thomas] "admits a close parallelism and union." He is especially careful to show grace as "a perfection given to nature in the same direction towards which its own [inherent] tendencies are working." The first of the three "modes" of man's [woman's] likeness to God, he explains, consists in his [her] having "a natural aptitude for understanding and loving God . . . ."[18]

Protestant theology, meanwhile, based upon the inspiration of Augustine, has often become fixated upon the necessity of attributing every redemptive moment to God without allowing the slightest dependence upon human agency. Happily, even with such one-sided emphasis upon immediate divine initiative, these same Protestants have not neglected those diligent works (Bible study, preaching, preparing for and administering the Sacraments) which are said to be the divinely-appointed occasions for the operation of grace. Hence, their one-side fixation on sola gratia (grace alone) is generally quite effective in practice because their defective theory is supplemented by a corrective practice. The effective evangelical preachers, for instance, take pride in meticulously arranging and overseeing each of the details of a forthcoming revival meeting even though they tell the audience and themselves that <u>God alone</u> will draw the hearts of his/her listeners to him/herself. The moment that they would abandon their meticulous preparation and let mediocrity and routine set in, then it would be apparent how much God would be "absent" due to their carelessness.

Conclusion

In sum, this chapter began by spelling out the human dynamics whereby parents and guardians, initially, and self-chosen masters, subsequently, inform the settled religious sensibilities and performance skills of every new child born into the world. This chapter ended by sketching a theology of grace that endeavored to respect both the anthropology implied in the earlier part and the theological tradition stemming principally from Augustine and Thomas. Needless to say, Augustine formulated his own theology of grace so as to respect both the Neoplatonic anthropology of his former training and the biblical tradition as it was interpreted by the church of his day. Thomas, in his turn, incorporated and modified large segments of Augustine so as to fit the Aristotelian anthropology that was resurfacing within his milieu. There can be, therefore, no definitive theology of grace because there can be no definitive human self-understanding and because the impact of divine initiative on history is not yet exhausted. Even working out of the same anthropology, many complementary theologies can emerge.

The exact contribution of human and divine components that enters into each act of religion defies any exhaustive analysis. Every present "religious experience" emerges from a nexus of human and divine components which have causally ebbed and flowed within one's immediate and remote history. These components operate subliminally. This effectively means that one cannot directly examine and dissect even one's own "religious experiences." It invariably happens that much of what is due to divine causality goes entirely unnoticed and much of what appears to be due to human causality is suffused with the divine. To be human is always to perceive and to experience divine initiative on the human level and within the human arena. Christians can never leave their humanity behind even when they enter the most sacred and exalted of religious rites and experiences.[19] Even the heavenly beatific vision, according to Thomas, is a created grace -- a creaturely participation in the transcendent Other (ST I, 12, 5-7, co). Even then, God reaches us within the very fabric of our humanity -- as we are, where we are. This is the all-pervasive meaning of the Incarnation: that divinity has no need to negate, supplant, or coerce humanity since the Spirit of God has, from the beginning, been supremely intimate within the entire cosmic-human enterprise.

Footnotes for Chapter VII

¹ Shinichi Suzuki, <u>Nurtured by Love</u> (N.Y.: Exposition Press, 1977), p. 26.

² <u>Ibid.</u>, p. 21.

³ Close observations indicate that social traditions among animals are sometimes localized. For example, some troops of Japanese monkeys habitually feed on rice while others never pillage rice paddies even though they pass through them in the course of their wanderings. Along parallel lines, a troop of captive monkeys never made snowballs during the winter until a peripheral male made one during the winter of 1970-71. Since then, other males make similiar snowballs each winter. See G. Gray Easton, "The Social Order of Japanese Macaques," <u>Scientific America</u> 235, 4 (1976) 97-106. For a larger perspective on the social transmission of behavior among animals, see Stuart J. Dimond, <u>The Social Behavior of Animals</u> (N.Y.: Harper & Row, 1970) of Peter C. Reynolds, <u>On the Evolution of Human Behavior</u> (Berkeley: University of California, 1981).

⁴ I take my stand here with those theologians who are critical of the tendency to depict revelation as private, interior experiences which are cut off from public, empirical events. See, e.g., Rolf Rendtorff, "The Concept of Revelation in Ancient Israel," <u>Revelation as History</u>, ed. by Wolfhart Pannenberg (N.Y.: Macmillan, 1967), pp. 23-54. On the other hand, however, Wolfhart Pannenberg's "Dogmatic Theses on the Doctrine of Revelation" (<u>Revelation as History</u>, pp. 123-158) go too far in asserting the "fundamental givenness" of historical revelation independent of the particular tacit skills of the one receiving revelation. According to Helmut G. Harder and W. Taylor Stevenson, Pannenberg overstates his case "because he is anxious to criticize those schools of theology which have obviously neglected the facts of history" ("The Continuity of History and Faith in the Theology of Wolfhart Pannenberg," <u>The Journal of Religion</u> 51 (1971) 34-56). I agree with their analysis. Accordingly, Pannenberg might be assisted by Polanyi in recognizing that every recognition depends upon tacit skills previously acquired. This enables us to comprehend how the ancient Hebrews could find the hand of YHWH clearly evidenced in their national history while outsiders found these same events to be nonevidential.

This is not to court subjectivism (understood as pious imaginings). Consider for a moment: the garage mechanic detects "loss of compression" when listening to my car engine; the nuclear physicist detects a radiation leak in a storage area where maintenance personnel are routinely unaware of the danger. Revelation, therefore, as received revelation, presupposes the requisite tacit skills whereby particular historical events evoke the assurance of divine presence. This line of thought will be further developed in the upcoming chapter.

5 For further details on the functional dynamics of human knowing, see Michael Polanyi, The Tacit Dimension (Garden City: Doubleday, 1967), pp. 4-25.

6 Polanyi holds that this disposition of selfgiving is both appropriate and necessary for anyone hoping to assimilate any given artistic or scientific tradition. See his Science, Faith, and Society (Chicago: The University of Chicago Press, 1966), pp. 44-45; Personal Knowledge (N.Y.: Harper & Row, 1964), pp. 207-209, 265-267; The Tacit Dimension, pp.59-62.

Success and satisfaction in the business world also appear to be tied to self-surrender to an appropriate mentor. See F.J. Lunding et al., "Everyone Who Makes It Has a Mentor," Harvard Business Review 56 (1978) 89-101.

7 Edward Schillebeeckx, Revelation and Theology (N.Y.: Sheed and Ward, 1968), II, 33-35.

8 The entire program initiated by Descarte is thus illusory and self-defeating. Systematic doubting can only serve to erode those acquired tacit skills which are more vulnerable and leave a smug aura of certainty around those which are more tenaciously ingrained within the knowing powers. More importantly, however, systematic doubting renders one immune to any further learning from another. Accordingly, one can be cut off from the streams of culture that have been legitimately and laboriously acquired over many generations. Pushed to extremes, one ends up within a paralyzing solipsism and/or skepticism. Michael Polanyi provides an elaborate refutation of the heuristic claims made on behalf of systematic doubting in Personal Knowledge, pp. 269-298.

9 Augustine De vera religione 8.14.

10 Augustine De utilitate credendi 12.27.

11 Augustine De doctrina Christiana prologue, 8.

12 Augustine Epistola 187; ST III, 69, 6, ad 2.

13 Thomas Aquinas strongly implies this understanding when he rules that the children of Jews

should not be baptized since "according to the natural law they are under the care of their parents as long as they cannot look after themselves" (ST III, 67, 8, co).

In the final report of the dialogue between the Secretariat for Promoting Christian Unity of the Roman Catholic Church and the leaders of various Pentecostal Churches, the interrelatedness of parents with their children was especially highlighted:

> Where paedobaptism is practiced it is fully meaningful only in the context of the faith of the parents and the community. The parents must undertake to nurture the child in the Christian life, in the expectation that, when he or she grows up, the child will personally live and affirm faith in Christ (Kilian McDonnel, ed., Presence, Power, Praise [Collegeville: The Liturgical Press, 1980] III, 391).

Nearly all the recent literature justifying infant baptism is intent upon recognizing the actual lack of faith and/or conversion in the case of infants and the necessary role of Christian parenting if the rite is to attain its intended purposes.

[14] For a historical exposition of how Sacraments came to be regarded "the means of grace" in isolation from the rest of life, see Joseph Martos, Doors to the Sacred (Garden City: Doubleday & Co., 1981), pp. 29-158. For a dogmatic critique of this view, see Karl Rahner, "Considerations on the Active Role of the Person in the Sacramental Event," Theological Investigations (N.Y.: Seabury, 1967) XIII, 161-184.

[15] "Forgiveness," Encyclopedia Judaica (1971) VI, 1434: "This doctrine [of repentance] implies that man [woman] has been endowed by God with the power of 'turning.' He [she] can turn from evil to good, and the very act of turning will activate God's concern and lead to forgiveness."

[16] Today it is fashionable for Christians to assert that the human dynamics within Christianity are shot through with divine initiative while the human dynamics within the artistic and scientific enterprises are considered as "secular", i.e., cut off from divine initiative. This was not always the case, however. The Fathers of the Church and the medieval Franciscan School of theology asserted that divine intervention must figure into every artistic or scientific production. Thus, it is not

strange to find Augustine arguing that even mathematical formulations require some divine assistance if their "truth" is to be humanly experienced:

> Listen while I teach you something concerning God from the analogy of sensible things .... The earth cannot be seen unless it is illumined. Anyone who knows the mathematical symbols admits that they are true without the shadow of a doubt. But he must also believe that they cannot be known unless they are illumined by something else corresponding to the sun. About this corporeal sun notice three things. It exists. It shines. It illumines. So in knowing the hidden God you must observe three things. He exists. He is known. He causes other things to be known. (Soliloquiae 2.8.15).

God's activity was thus acknowledged as secretly directing even pagan philophers and mathematicians.

Within the medieval synthesis of the Thomistic School, however, the operations of the innate human power of reason were so defined as to insure their successful operation <u>without any divine assistance</u>. The eventual triumph of the Thomistic School over the contending Augustinian-Franciscan tradition has led modern Christians (a) to envision divine assistance as solely occupied with religious understanding and, (b) to deliberately downplay the human dynamics implicated in religious knowing.

[17] Familiar events, such as seeds sprouting or human infants awakening rationally and sexually, often operate with such regularity that Augustine found them to conceal their divine initiative (<u>De Genesi ad litteram opus imperfectum</u> 6.13.25; <u>De Trinitate</u> 3.6.11; <u>Tractatus in Joannis evangelium</u> 8.1 & 9.1). Miracles, consequently, far from exhausting divine initiative, are seen by Augustine as only those brief moments when humans are startled into perceiving divine initiative which is already silently attested and overlooked due to routine (<u>Sermones</u> 241.1; <u>Epistola</u> 102. q. 1.5-6).

[18] Henri de Lubac, <u>The Mystery of the Supernatural</u> (N.Y.: Herder and Herder, 1967), pp. 31-32. De Lubac's appeal to the authentic mind of Thomas relative to the intimate harmony between nature and grace was severely ridiculed and penalized prior to its acceptance among Catholic theologians in the late 60s. Karl Rahner,

in his writings, has also strongly advocated the interpenetration of the natural and the supernatural orders so that there is one and only one actual destiny for all humans.

[19] Karl Rahner, "The Body in the Order of Salvation," *Theological Investigations* (N.Y.: Crossroad, 1981), esp. pp. 80-82.

VIII

How Fresh Discoveries of God Transform Mature Commitments

The last chapter emphasized the human dynamics by which a religious heritage is passed from one generation to the next. All in all, the focus was upon those elements which insure the conservation of the past. When the religious enterprise is so conceived, it sometimes falls under the suspicion of existing as a form of indoctrination which enforces duplication and extols an exaggerated orthodoxy. This overlooks the fact, however, that the mature religious adherent has been trained to perceive <u>a living reality which will manifest itself in an indeterminate set of future manifestations</u>. Thus, Isaac hears the voice of YHWH afresh. New historic events serve to disclose to Isaac an enlarged and transformed vision of God's cause. By no means is Isaac condemned merely to the banal repetition of his father's religious experience. The same is true for Peter many years after the death of Jesus. Peter is moved by events toward a fresh vision of God's cause -- a vision, which, it would seem, partially overturns the commitments which Peter had undertaken due to his apprenticeship under Jesus. By focusing upon such examples, this present chapter will examine how the prophet's fresh visions of God go on to disrupt the <u>status quo</u> and to serve as a point of departure for the creative renewal of religion. On a smaller scale, the extended experiences of God during the whole of a mature Christian's life can be understood as periodically reshaping the permanent commitments of each Christian's past. In the end, therefore, true religion will be understood as sustaining a continual thirst for the living God: "If only you would listen to him [YHWH] today; do not harden your hearts" (Heb 3:7, 15; 4:7; Ps 95:7).

The last chapter explored the dynamics whereby a person replicates the religious experience of his/her parents and self-chosen masters. This chapter will now go on to examine how mature religious adherents are open to fresh prophetic experiences which modify and reform the very tradition which gave them birth. Our inquiry will be divided into three sections:

- A. The importance of making fresh discoveries of God
- B. Examining classical instances of prophetic discovery
- C. How fresh discoveries of God are to be authenticated

A.   The Importance of Making Fresh Discoveries of God

Traditionally, Christians have been taught to regard prophetic experience as reserved for certain elite persons, all of whom are long dead. This is a tragic misunderstanding. In fact, without prophetic experience there would be no experiential evidence (a) that one's God was a living reality or (b) that one's religious commitments were authentic. Both of these areas are so important that I want to consider them prior to the main body of material in this chapter.

Many persons find that their God is "absent" from the real world. This means that they had been trained to perceive God within certain historic events that are all in the past. There is no doubt that God did appear within these events; but there is also no doubt that this "God" now no longer appears anywhere. As such, this "God" is much like Santa Claus -- as long as the surprise on Christmas morning lasted, he was quite "alive"; as soon as the surprise faded, he became quite "absent" from the real world.

The assertion that one's God is "alive" implies that he/she continues to show up in unexpected ways.

A stone is real, but it is not alive. This is because the range of its manifestations to the human organism are quite repetitive and fall within a narrow, predictable range. The same thing can be said for radio waves or cosmic rays, both of which are intangibles. Living things, such as plants and animals have a much wider range of novel self-manifestations. Stones and cosmic rays do sometimes exhibit a novel self-manifestation, but it may take years of patient and trained observation to detect it. This explains why geologists and physicists are so excited when they finally do find that some "dead" reality has finally appeared in a novel manner. This also explains why plants and animals are so intrinsically interesting in the variety of novel manifestations that they so readily exhibit. But even the most clever animals have a range of novel self-manifestations which is narrower than that exhibited by human persons. This is why human friends can literally spend hours and years together and still find that they are fascinated with each other.

Applying this to one's God, it is apparent that those who encounter "God" within a limited and highly predictable range of self-manifestations may be entirely justified in calling their God "the Cosmic Force" or "the Energy of Love." For those, however, who find that their God often shows up in novel ways, they would be justified in calling their God a "living reality." If, in addition, one's God is the kind that has fascinated his/her people by a prodigious range of novel manifestations extending over many generations, then one would designate such a God as a "personal reality" or, simply, as "a person." When the Christian tradition designates its God as both living and personal, it thereby points to the enormous range of prophetic experiences of this God. If and when the selfmanifestations of this God should become frozen and repetitive, then this God might well be called "dead" even though he/she remains quite real.

Many Christians are taught that their God is "unchanging and unchangeable" and conclude from this that God's insertion within the dynamics of history is eternally fixed and unchanging. Fortunately, the Scriptures provide a ready correction for such views. Any attempt to freeze God within some abstract characterization is immediately confronted with the evidence of YHWH's changing historical dress. Occasionally, God was perceived as creating. At other times, however, historical events disclosed him/her as the Destroyer. This happened, for instance, when Abraham perceived YHWH as raining fire and brimstone on Sodom and Gomorrah (Gen 19:28) and when Moses perceived YHWH as opening the earth and swallowing Korah and his family alive (Num 16). It is mistaken, therefore, to honor God as the Creator without recognizing that our God is occasionally the Destroyer. The same thing applies to all other abstract characterizations of God. YHWH, for instance, is occasionally a redeeming God. In the days of King Zedekiah, however, the prophet Jeremiah opposed the optimistic court prophets and announced that YHWH would not redeem his people from the threat of King Nebuchadnezzar (Jer 14:13-16, 23:9-40, 28:1-17). History confirmed Jeremiah in his recognition that YHWH had already abandoned his/her people to their self-destructive follies. It is dangerous, consequently, to select one or more abstract characterizations of God and to imagine that YHWH is somehow eternally fixed for all time into some static, defined relationship to human history.

The sacred task of the adherents of every vital religious tradition consists in discerning the initiatives of their God and in harmonizing their own personal energies with those of their God. In this task, the record and the remembrance of the past is important, but it cannot substitute for the present discernment of God's cause in one's personal history. The Christian, consequently, must use the biblical record in asking how God today is disposed toward the modern proliferation of arms, the Women's Movement, the limitation and uneven distribution of the world's resources. The Christian who is indeed sympathetic with the pathos of his/her God will then be constrained to act in harmony with his/her God in the concrete engagements of daily life -- in the home, in the shop, in the city, in the world.

The decisive importance of prophetic experience can also be viewed from the perspective that it dispels the suspicion that one's personal religious upbringing was merely an empty indoctrination. Thus, the impressionable child is trained to perceive spontaneously God's initiative within particular historic events and not in others. The resulting conditioned response of the child operates habitually and stubbornly. By virtue of one's childhood training, therefore, each of us enters into a situation which is functionally circular: one perceives what one has been trained to perceive, and one accredits these perceptions as "reality." The same holds true for our freely chosen adult apprenticeships: one accredits and esteems that which one has freely learned to accredit and to esteem. Each of us, consequently, operates out of a closed system of tacit skills which selectively perceives the God of one's mentors and stubbornly militates against the experience of any novel god or any novel experience of God. Given such an immunity, it is indeed a refreshing sign of authentic religion that dedicated adherents are occasionally grasped and transformed by novel experiences of their God.

When such prophetic experiences are wanting, indoctrination and authoritative constraints can effectively sanction demonic errors and prop up meaningless rituals without the Spirit of God being able to enter in. This is why any historic religion which ignores or stifles prophetic experience inevitably generates an idolatry, no matter how divinely authentic its origins may have been.

How Fresh Discoveries Transform Mature Commitments

The task of every authentic religious tradition is to follow in the steps of the living God which gave it birth.

What I have just said about the importance of prophetic experience does not mean that novelty is necessarily the mark of authentic religion. Far from it. Novelty can easily result when persons who are superficially apprenticed within their religious tradition surrender to their religious fantasies. Every mature religious tradition must know how to equip its adherents to discern authentic prophetic experience and to neutralize those deceiving claims made by subversive charlatans and pious quacks within the community. Needless to say, discernment of truth can never be merely reduced to opinion polls or dogmatic appeals to past traditions.

Prophetic experience presupposes that an authentically novel human contact has been made with the very divine realities which the tradition serves. Thus, every prophetic experience challenges the existing tradition and calls it into becoming more of what it ought to be. The prophets are vulnerable, however, and the upholders of the reigning orthodoxy are fallible. It is by no means inevitable, consequently, that the divinely inspired truth win out in every case. Truth often suffers.

Abraham Heshel is fond of characterizing the whole religious enterprise as being directed toward bringing a person into sympathy with his/her God. Heshel identifies this sympathy as the root of every valid religious and prophetic experience:

> The prophet is stirred by an intimate concern for the divine concern. Sympathy, then, is the essential mode in which he [she] responds to the divine situation . . . .[1]

It is this active sympathy with God that enables the prophet to faithfully "hear" the divine pathos within the unfolding historical drama. Having heard the divine pathos, the prophet's sympathy then goes on actively to transform the prophet's priorities into an intimate harmony with divine initiative.

> The unique feature of prophetic sympathy is not self-conquest, but self-dedication; not the suppression of emotion, but its redirection; not silent subordination, but active co-operation with God; not love which aspires to the Being of God in

Him[/Her]self, but harmony of the soul with the concern of God. To be a prophet means to identify one's concern with the concern of God.²

Most Christians are eager to claim that Jesus of Nazareth achieved the most intimate sympathy attainable with God's cause. Mistakenly, however, many of these same Christians imagine that they do not have to cultivate any active sympathy with the living God since Jesus has achieved this in their stead. They imagine themselves as mere "repeaters" who rigorously conform themselves to the ethical and doctrinal norms which Jesus set down for his disciples. This conception of Christianity is tacitly enforced by the Protestant insistence that the New Testament is the final and exhaustive norm for the belief and practice of the contemporary church. Some segments of the Catholic tradition, meanwhile, have sought to elevate the religious sympathies of the Pope as infallibly normative, so that Catholics need only conform to the beliefs and the practices of the Pope to be assured of divine conformity.

I would contend that a reverent submission to biblical norms and to authorized teachers necessarily characterizes every Christian apprenticeship. The end of such an apprenticeship, however, is never a banal repetition of a set of papal or biblical beliefs and practices. The end, rather, is a manifest personal competence in sympathetically hearing and responding to divine initiative within the modern world.

If the earliest churches had defined themselves as mere "repeaters," the disciples of Jesus would have rigorously locked the Jesus Movement into the first-century Palestinian culture and condemned it to be fossilized there as that historical milieu passed away. The very fact that Christianity is not a quaint museum piece testifies that each past age has had its saints and prophets who did courageously innovate and revivify the generative commitments which were handed down to them. Even the New Testament documents themselves retain something of the rich diversity of beliefs and practices present within the various early church communities. No movement dedicated to a lockstep conformity could have embraced such diversity within its official canon of inspired writings.

A lockstep conformity, even to a divine master, would invariably go on to embarrass and discredit the master himself. It would be as though Jesus were the Divine Physician who trained his understudies in all the intricacies of medicine and stifled their creative powers at the same time. The graduates of such a training would initially be hailed as the saviors of the world because they would marvelously cure all those diseases which their master trained them to diagnose. With time, however, the disciples would encounter unfamiliar diseases. These they would categorically deem as incurable since their all-knowing master had prescribed no cure for such diseases while he lived. In the end, such a school of medicine would expand in time and in place and be faced with a growing number of "incurable diseases." What had begun as a blessing to society would thus end up as a conservative and authority-bound tradition which artificially stifled the growth of medicine for the sake of preserving the genius of one master.

I, for one, cannot believe that Jesus, the Divine Physician, was of this kind. On the contrary, I firmly believe that the Divine Physician trained his disciples not only to diagnose and treat the specific diseases of his own era but that he equipped them with the art to extend and to innovate upon his practice. By so doing, the Divine Physician wisely determined that future disciples would bring a saving health to peoples and cultures which were far removed from his own in terms of the diseases that stifled their humanity. The disciples of such a Divine Physician would have no cause to discredit their master. Their false counterparts might feel more security as mere "repeaters" of their master; yet, in the end, their very security would become an inhibiting curse. If Jesus is the kind of master who modified and transformed the religious traditions of his own day in the name of God; then it appears inescapable that true disciples of this master must often do this very same thing in their own day.

Up to this point I have argued for the necessity of prophetic experiences. On theological grounds, a God who is said to be "living" and "personal" must present a range of self-manifestations that exceeds that of fixed cosmic forces. On historical grounds, a religious movement that went on to attract and redeem the variety of Western cultures must have embraced leaders who were much more than mindless repeaters of their Jewish Master. It now remains to consider some specific instances of prophetic innovations within the Christian experience and to analyze the human dynamics undergirding such experiences.

B.   Examining Classical Instances of Prophetic Discovery

I now want to examine two classical instances of prophetic discoveries within the Christian tradition. For the first instance, I have decided to examine the details of Peter's conversion which Luke narrates in the Acts of the Apostles (Acts 10:1-48, 11:1-18). I have chosen this instance because it clearly presents Peter as exhibiting a sympathy with the divine pathos which requires him to reverse his settled instincts respecting "kosher" foods and "kosher" persons. As a second instance, I will briefly consider factors involved in the early Christian antislavery movement. This instance I have chosen because it represents a case in which Christians have had to reinterpret numerous scriptural texts in order to follow the divine pathos.

Peter's discovery experience is initiated by a trance conditioned by hunger pangs. In this trance, Peter witnesses various kosher and unkosher animals being offered to him with the mandate, "Now, Peter, kill and eat . . . . What God has made clean [kosher], you have no right to profane [i.e., to treat as unkosher]" (Acts 10:15-16). Peter vigorously protests the import of this suggestion: "I have never yet eaten anything profane or unclean"(Acts 10:14). Luke mentions that this exchange is repeated three times.

From this secondhand account, I find that Luke makes it evident that Peter is struggling within himself. There is no crass suggestion that Peter is receiving direct instructions from heaven. If this were the case, Peter would have had to dismiss the whole thing as demonic forgery since the evident impact of the mandate is to oppose the training that Peter had received from Jesus. But Peter does not dismiss his vision -- he is profoundly troubled by it (Acts 10:17). This suggests that Peter is struggling with a possible innovation of the practice of Jesus which cannot be dismissed out of hand.

In the Greek text, Luke uses ekstasis to designate the kind of experience that Peter is having. In this instance, ekstasis has been rendered into English as "trance." As it stands, ekstasis could signify a trance, but it might just as well signify a daydream. Ekstasis literally refers to "the experience of being carried outside of oneself." In the particular case here, Luke deliberately mentions Peter's hunger pangs (Acts 10:10) as occasioning the ekstasis. I would prefer to think that Luke has in mind "a daydream," therefore, and not some abnormal trance.

In the next moment, Luke presents Peter as receiving an invitation to eat at the house of Cornelius (Acts 10:18). Since Cornelius is a Gentile, his table is unkosher. The inner struggle of Peter is thus put to the test by a concrete invitation. To stretch the case even more, the host, Cornelius, is described as "an upright and God-fearing man, highly regarded by the Jewish people"(Acts 10:22). Peter, meanwhile, is still hungry. His daydream of a moment ago heightened the struggle within him. He is tempted to say again, "I have never yet eaten anything profane or unclean." None the less, in this instance, Peter agrees to the invitation.

Luke assures his readers that "the spirit/Spirit" (Acts 10:19) prompts Peter to hear the request made by the servants of Cornelius in his behalf. However, Luke does not say that it is the Spirit that alters Peter's settled instincts. The struggle of the daydream speaks for itself; Peter is already half-suspecting that his God has made all animals kosher; yet, his apprenticeship with Jesus demonstrated exactly the contrary. When Peter finally arrives at Cornelius' house, Luke presents Peter as accounting for his "irregular" conduct:

> You know that it is forbidden for Jews to mix with people of another race and visit them [i.e., eat with them], but God has made it clear to me that I must not call anyone profane or unclean. That is why I made no objection to coming when I was sent for (Acts 10:28-29).

The impact of Peter's prophetic experience is now expanded: not only are all animals to be declared kosher but all persons as well. Here again, Peter makes no appeal to the training he received from Jesus. He does, however, affirm the God of Jesus who has overturned his prejudice.

Luke presents Cornelius and his household as ready to hear the "message God has given you" (Acts 10:33). Thus Peter presumes to introduce the household of Cornelius to his master, Jesus of Nazareth. Then, to the astonishment of Peter and his six companions, "while Peter was still speaking the Holy Spirit came down on all the listeners" (Acts 10:44). Luke undoubtedly implies here that the household of Cornelius is profoundly changed in their religious orientation so that Peter recognizes they now have the same spirit/Spirit, the same sympathy with the divine pathos, as he himself has. Luke describes the visible signs shown by Cornelius as the selfsame signs shown by the disciples on the first Pentecost (Acts 10:46, 2:4). On the basis of this discernment, Peter feels authorized to baptize them "in the name of Jesus the Messiah" (Acts 10:48). And so they are baptized (and apprenticed) by the "six brothers" who accompanied Peter.

After remaining a period of time with Cornelius, Peter and his companions return to Jerusalem. The scandal of their conduct has gone before them. They are immediately challenged: "So you have been visiting the uncircumcised and eating with them, have you?" (Acts 11:3). The presumption here is that not even the chief of Jesus' disciples is free to change the very Torah that he previously delivered over to the community. Jesus has set the standard, and not even Peter is free to disregard that. But Peter does not apologize or rationalize his conduct. He knows that it was no whimsical spirit that altered his own perception of things. Thus he sets out to explain his prophetic experience in its concrete details (Acts 11:4-18). By so doing, Peter must hope to engage their sympathies so that they too will share his prophetic experience. To do this they must enter into the same struggle that formerly gripped Peter. They must allow their settled instincts to be transformed just as Peter's were transformed earlier. If anyone with less stature in the community had made such an irregular move, one could be sure that such a one would be severely corrected and perhaps excluded from the community. Peter, however, is the recognized master who has apprenticed many of those in the audience that he is now addressing. They listen. And they are converted. "God," they said, "can evidently grant even the pagans the repentance that leads to life" (Acts 11:18).

The annals of science are filled with accounts of the controversy and resistance which greets new discoveries. As in this case, the discoverer has made a breakthrough. If his/her prophetic experience is to have a future, he/she must lead his/her colleagues into the same altered state of consciousness to which he/she was formerly drawn.

> To the extent to which a discoverer has committed him[/her]self to a new vision of reality, he[she] has separated him[/her]self from others who think on the old lines .... Proponents of a new system can convince their audience

> only by first winning their intellectual sympathy for a doctrine they have not yet grasped. Those who listen synpathetically will discover for themselves what they would otherwise never have understood. Such an acceptance is a heuristic process, a self-modifying act, and to this extent a conversion.[3]

Everything said here applies with an equal force to describe Peter's task in overcoming the resistance of the Jerusalem community which he left behind and to which he now returns.

From our own vantage point, it is indeed difficult to estimate how "absurd" and "irresponsible" Peter's departure from Jesus' practice must have been. We are accustomed to find clearly delineated passages in the Gospels which caution us not to regard "what goes into the mouth" as capable of making a person unkosher (Matt 15:11 and parallels). Undoubtedly such passages were generated by the prophetic experience of Peter and <u>were not delivered by Jesus himself</u>. Otherwise, how are we to explain Peter's resistance prior to his crisis, and how is it that Peter can make no appeal against his critics by pointing to the teaching/practice of Jesus? It must be recognized, then, that Jesus was quite kosher and that his practice was unquestionably shared by Peter. After Peter's conversion, however, Peter himself must be convinced that <u>Jesus himself would have altered his own practice if he had encountered the selfsame crisis that Peter underwent</u>. Peter, therefore, would be entirely legitimate in supposing that his present practice was indeed his master's. And any disciple would presume to equate the actual living Torah of Peter with the lived Torah of Jesus before him. It is entirely natural, consequently, that the prophetic discoveries of Peter were read back into the life of Jesus and portrayed as Jesus' instructions to his disciples.[4]

The history of Christianity is shot through with periodic revelatory discoveries which dramatically altered the face of Christian commitments. Think, for instance, of the hundreds of years in which Christians instinctively felt that slavery was a natural institution sanctioned by divine purposes. In the Hebrew Scriptures, it was a routine matter for YHWH to instruct Israel to destroy towns and to seize persons who would become slaves. The Torah of Moses specified a limitation upon the duration of slavery and even defined certain rights that slaves held in the face of their masters; yet, slavery itself was taken for granted. Jesus mentions nothing regarding slavery. Again, it is taken for granted. Paul treats of specific cases but his emphasis is rather to insure that Christian slaves remain loyal to their masters and that Christian masters do not abuse their slaves.

On the American soil, it was not until 1688 that we have the first evidence that a group of Christians (Dutch and German Friends) was moved to regard slavery as an abomination before God. In the reverent silence of Quaker worship, this sentiment grew. In 1776, the Yearly Meeting of Friends in Philadelphia was unanimously moved to desist from holding slaves and to expel any member among them who persisted in remaining a slaveowner. This issue later went on to divide the nation and to divide the Christian churches as well. It is a sobering experience today to read the tracts written by Christians who cited the authority of Paul and of numerous Fathers of the Church in support of the divine approbation of slavery. The antislavery movement was cursed as contrary to God and to nature. On the other side of the issue, Lincoln made public in his Second Inaugural Address his own prophetic judgment ot the effect that God permitted the war to continue so as to further purge from the Nation its cumulative crimes of slavery:

> If we shall suppose . . . that He [the Almighty] gives to both North and South this terrible war as the woe due to those by whom the offense [of slavery] came, shall we discern therein any departure from those divine attributes which believers in a living God always ascribe to Him? Fondly do we hope, fervently do we pray, that this mighty scourge of war may speedily pass away. Yet, if God wills that it continue until all the wealth piled by the bondsman's two hundred and fifty years of unrequited toil shall be sunk, and until every drop of blood drawn by the lash shall be paid by another drawn with the sword, as was said three thousand years ago, so still it must be said, "The judgments of the Lord are true and righteous altogether."

Such words clearly express how Lincoln saw the justice of God being worked out through the scourge of war that then marked the beginning of his second term. It must be expected that Lincoln's listeners were moved to share his prophetic insight respecting the future magnitude and duration of the war then being fought.

Nor is this an isolated instance. One has only to read the documents from this era to know that most Christians were habituated to perceive the hand of God within the historic events that marked their private and social existence.[5] If anything, the remembrance of this era magnifies our own present inability to interpret our own times as woven with the threads of the Lord of History.

The Quaker experience in the new world indicates that the Scriptures and the tradition of the church are not supreme. The early Quakers were well aware that the explicit texts of the Holy Bible spoke out in favor of slavery as a divinely-sanctioned reality. They were also aware that the unbroken tradition of the church had taken the stance of moderating slavery but never of condemning it. None the less, they were constrained by the Spirit of God to put aside the Christian tradition as it had been and to take courageously their stand for the tradition as it ought to be. They suffered on behalf of their altered commitments, but they could not do otherwise than to acknowledge the living God as he/she had freshly revealed him/herself to them.

This instance also ably illustrates how prophetic experience profoundly transforms the standards of holiness present among the living disciples of Jesus. In an earlier chapter, I have already pointed out how Jesus took his stand in the Torah of YHWH and apprenticed his disciples to "be perfect just as your heavenly Father is perfect" (Matt 5:48). Jesus' style of living Torah was heavily criticized by his generation. This means that Jesus had already been guided by his own prophetic experience to innovate upon the standards of holiness proposed in his own day. He tested that holiness with his life and taught his disciples to do likewise. The efficacy of their holiness was demonstrated by the healing that it brought to those who sympathetically entered into contact with them.

Those Quakers who were moved by their sympathy with God to take their stand against religion as it had been were thereby doing precisely what Jesus and Peter had done in their own day. The healing that Quakers brought to the lives of slaves and slaveowners alike was a measure of the truth-power in the measures that they had undertaken. One has only to read Harriet Beecher Stowe's <u>Uncle Tom's Cabin</u> or Alex Haley's <u>Roots</u> to perceive how the slaveowners themselves were in need of liberation from their demonic self-deception and mastery over other human beings. These issues still move us today. This is a sign that the prophetic experience of the seventeenth-century Quakers has not yet entirely penetrated our personal spirits. Our own generation will continue what has already begun.

C.   How Fresh Discoveries of God Are To Be Authenticated

I accept the fact that my particular calling was fashioned by virtue of my having had particular parents and particular apprenticeships. I accept my personal identity as it was fashioned by the particular traditions which I assimilated as a result of my particular belonging. I accept the realities that I have been trained to perceive sympathetically and acknowledge them as the source of lifelong obligations and blessings. At the same time, I hold that I am personally responsible to remain open and attentive to future manifestations of those realities to which I am committed. I hold that the prophetic discoveries which come my way (whether first or secondhand) present the occasions to purify and to enhance my personal functioning within the traditions in which I stand. I commit myself to embrace graciously the prophetic discoveries that come my way and to take personal responsibility for making such discoveries available to others.

It remains to consider by what power a solitary pioneer can make his/her way clear of his/her cumulative past so as to make authentically a fresh contact with the realities he/she serves: "God," "justice," "cosmic rays," or whatever. It also remains to be considered by what power persons can accredit fresh discoveries which others have made. The material here will be divided into five areas: (1) rational appeals, (2) pragmatic appeals, (3) supernatural appeals, (4) authoritarian appeals, and (5) personal appeals.

(1) Rational Appeals

The science of geometry ably illustrates how one can begin with certain established definitions and assumptions and go on from there to demonstrate logically a large number of sophisticated conclusions. Many persons suppose, therefore, that every prophetic discovery can be formulated as the logical deduction of definitions and assumptions held prior to the discovery. Thus, in the case of the early Quakers who took their stand against slavery, one would suppose that they believed that "all person were created equal in the sight of God." Their stance against slavery, therefore, can be made to appear as the logically compelling moment in which they first recognized that "slaves are persons." The consequences follow.

In point of fact, however, rational appeals did not suffice to establish the Quaker experience. Within a given horizon of understanding, one can make rational deductions which serve to make explicit those applications of the system of thought which were formerly implicit. A discovery experience, however, changes one's horizon of understanding. The fabric of one's rationality is altered irreversibly. Thus, initially, even the Quakers in question felt that the slaves were "black savages." They were created by God, to be sure, but they were created "less" than their masters. Only after being converted did the Quakers first perceive that the slaves were persons like themselves. There is, consequently, a momentous alteration of one's settled instincts which accompanies the discovery experience. Such an alteration cannot be induced by rational appeals made from inside the former horizon of understanding. If this were the case, one would then expect all rational persons to be converted immediately the moment that Quakers set forth their logical premises for abolishing slavery.

(2) Pragmatic Appeals

Every system of beliefs recommends itself to the believer on the basis of its workability. At the moment of any innovative conversion, however, the full weight of tested success stories lies with the old system. Thus, pragmatic appeals do not and cannot sustain the validity of prophetic experience.

When Peter was faced with the invitation of Cornelius, the dietary laws of his religious tradition were part and parcel of his daily routine. They were manifestly workable. No purely pragmatic appeals would have sufficed to convince Peter to lay aside his divinely ordained tradition of kosher. Only after Peter has been moved to abandon his trained instincts of kosher on other grounds can he begin to experience what may be the pragmatic advantages and disadvantages of his new position. In fact, one might well suppose that Peter may have become sick to his stomach after eating Gentile cooking on the first few occasions. If such were the case, one can see that prophetic innovations can even be entirely unpragmatic. The Quaker determination to free their own slaves was a clear case of prophetic experience standing in opposition to pragmatism.

(3) Supernatural Appeals

Within religious circles, both Christian and pagan, it is quite common to find that prophetic experience is accounted for in terms of pointing to the direct agency of God/a god. As an illustration of this, consider the analysis of the prophetic experience supplied by Philo (d. 50 C.E.):

> A [male] prophet (being a spokesman) has no utterance of his own, but all his utterance comes from elsewhere . . . , he is the vocal instrument of God . . . . The mind is evicted at the arrival of the divine Spirit, but when that departs the mind returns to its tenancy. Mortal and immortal may not share the same home; And therefore the setting of reason and the darkness which surrounds it produces ecstasy and inspired frenzy . . . .[6]

Philo's description of Abraham's prophetic discovery of YHWH makes it akin to a divinely-induced madness. The reliability of his creative act is preserved by imagining that his human operations are entirely displaced by the divine Spirit. Such notions as these have been almost universally upheld by Christian theologians in the past (e.g., ST II-II, 172).[7]

The problem with supernatural appeals is that they create more difficulties than they repond to. How, for example, can the prophet discern that the "spirit" that has overtaken him/her is indeed from YHWH and not from some demonic source? In so far as the "spirit" displaces his human powers, one must presume that the prophet can only know him/herself possessed, but, by what manner of spirit, he/she knows not. The task of discernment, accordingly, falls to those who listen to the prophet. How are they to discern a true from a deceiving spirit? The medieval rules of discernment dismissed giving any critical weight to the prophet's austerity, virtue, or passionate sincerity (ST II-II, 172, 3-4, co). Even miracles could not be decisive since the demons knew how to dazzle the crowds with their supernatural powers also (ST II-II, 178, 2, co). In the end, therefore, the final appeal had to rest with the very content of the prophet's disclosure; one had to decide whether it contained traces of falsehood:

> The prophecy of the demons can be distinguished from Divine prophecy by certain, and even outward, signs. Hence, Chrysostom says that <u>some prophesy by the spirit of the devil, such as diviners, but they may be discerned by the fact that the devil sometimes utters what is false, the Holy Spirit never</u>. Wherefore it is written (Deut 18:21-22): . . . <u>Thou shalt have this sign; Whatsoever that same prophet foretelleth in the name of the Lord, and it come not to pass, that thing the Lord hath not spoken</u> (ST II-II, 172, 5, ad 3).

The final appeal is decidely enigmatic. I have already shown the difficulties surrounding pragmatic appeals. They serve well from the vantage point of examining the distant past but they are quite useless for deciding which prophets to honor in the present. Consider Peter's new stance regarding kosher. Today our very practice of Christianity decides in his favor. But how about the colleagues of Peter in Jerusalem who find out that he has trampled their lifelong practice of eating only those foods and associating only with those people who are kosher to the Lord? For them, pragmatic testing was unthinkable! The truth of Peter's deviation had to be decided upon quite other grounds.

(4) Authoritarian Appeals

In any given community, authoritarian appeals naturally have their place, The beginners in any profession must entrust themselves to the authority of the leading representative of the community. Even when conflicts break out between the mature members of the community, certain persons are always recognized as having more experience and more competence than others. Within the existing churches, therefore, one finds an appropriate hierarchy of authorities and of processes whereby sound teachers and sound doctrine are communicated to the faithful. Any tradition which could not distinguish its foremost spokespersons and its norms of belief and practice would soon flounder under the weight of a disintegrating confusion or an arbitrarily imposed authoritarianism. A clerical hierarchy, therefore, is just as necessary for safeguarding the proper training of religious adherents as is the scientific hierarchy (established within the foremost centers of learning and research) necessary for the proper training of adherents/practitioners of the various scientific traditions.

The novice in the community cannot hope to decide an issue upon which the masters themselves cannot reach agreement. Should the novice easily decide the issue, his/her opinion would not weigh heavily since it necessarily lacks the trained instincts and the depth of understanding necessary for grasping adequately both sides of the issue. The novice generally appeals to the authority of those masters whom he/she respects more highly. But this is only to recognize that the novice is being influenced by some more than others. The novice cannot deny that he/she has less faith in those authorities who oppose the stand that he/she prefers. In the end, when a profession is split on a particular issue, any appeal to authority must appear arbitrary. Appeals to authority only serve their proper function when the leading proponents of a tradition are unanimously agreed on a particular issue.

It is evident that an innovator cannot appeal effectively to any authority. The authority of the tradition as it has been is against his/her prophetic breakthrough. Any appeal to the authority of other segments of the culture are generally abortive because it cannot be presumed that outsiders are competent to judge internal issues. Thus, when Peter returns to face his critics in his own community after leaving Cornelius, he cannot appeal to his own authority as chief of the apostles. Such an appeal would be self-contradictory. Was he not chief of the apostles when he formerly trained the disciples of Jesus to keep kosher as did the Master? Assuredly. Consequently, if Peter were simply to appeal to his authority, authority itself would appear arbitrary. If this is Peter's only appeal, the community would have to declare Peter heretical by virtue of his own orthodoxy which he was now irresponsibly violating. Meanwhile, it would have been ludicrous for Peter to appeal to the authority of the Gentile tradition which has no particular competence to discern the ways of YHWH. In sum, Peter's conversion provides a classical instance in which authoritarian appeals fail to justify prophetic innovations even when such innovations are upheld by the leading member of the community.

(5) Personal Appeals

The experience of the solitary prophet pushing back the horizons of his/her tradition can never be fully specified nor fully defended. How can any person account for why, at any given moment, some things appear self-evident and other things appear problematic? How is it that Peter can spend the greater part of his life in the routine experience of kosher and then, in an unbidden moment, find such traditions troublesome? Furthermore, how can any discoverer lay out before another, or even before him/ herself, those personal intimations of growing coherence which guided him/her to a satisfying final alteration of his/her personal commitments. Assuredly, Peter can point to some of the critical events which guided him; yet, to be quite honest, even Peter could only properly perceive the hidden intent of these events from the perspective of the self-transformation of which they were leading. Anyone who does not sympathetically enter into Peter's new horizon of understanding would have to chide Peter for being confused by demonic daydreams and then enforcing his will by arbitrary authoritarianism. After all, tradition has it that even the Master found Peter to be sadly deficient in judgment on numerous occasions (e.g., Matt 14:32, 16:23, 26:34, 52).

Yet, in the face of these indeterminacies, I still maintain that the solitary prophet knows him/herself to be acting responsibly and conscientiously through the entire act of discovery. The discoverer gives him/herself over to trusted intuitions which must be credited with reliably (but not infallibly) as they guide the seeker in his/her thirst for God. I wish to sketch out, therefore, the general character of those trained intuitions which figure in every prophetic experience.[8]

The first moment that a person is troubled with a problem, he/she must rely upon trusted intuitions so as to decide whether the importance of a possible discovery would warrant the investment of the human energies and resources needed for its pursuit. Without this initial discernment a person is doomed to waste his/her energies pursuing trivialities or problems which exceed his/her powers. This very thing takes place each time one tackles a crossword puzzle or a chess teaser. Initially, one must survey the puzzle and rely upon one's trained intuitions to gauge whether one's personal powers are sufficient to master it. Alternately, one must decide whether the puzzle is so simplistic that its routine solution would carry no personal satisfaction. A creative genius is similiarly situated whenever he/she examines a problem or difficulty for which there is no known solution.

The moment that one says "yes" to a source of puzzlement, one's energies are released toward its solution. One deliberately pours oneself into the problem so as to intensify the strain that the problem evokes. This deliberate intensification allows unseen and unnoticed intuitive powers to sense out an appropriate route toward the solution. In the banal case of a crossword puzzle, one turns one's attention to the offered clues: "A six-letter word for a furry mammal." Peter, in his situation, begins to rehearse in his mind those specific historical events which have a bearing upon kosher.

Intellectual straining has its counterpart in sensory straining, e.g., as when one is straining to detect the meaning of the sounds coming from an adjoining room. When one is learning a foreign language, it is apparent that the straining to hear every syllable gradually subsides into a routine and seemingly effortless recognition. Straining, consequently, clearly enlarges one's powers of hearing such that they are responsive to the particular patterns which are being heard. The same thing holds true for Peter who is straining to come to grips with kosher. His daydream perfectly exemplifies the impasse that separates him from the solution. By returning again and again to the impasse he hopes that he will eventually enlarge his ability to "hear" what he, for the moment at least, is entirely deaf to.

Deliberate straining over a problem also allows the imagination to sally forth toward a solution to which the guiding intuitions are leading. When the imagination comes up with something that is promising, the discoverer has the sensation of feeling the greater coherence that appears within the open-ended clues which are involved in his/her search. The anticipation of the solution serves to accredit promising leads in advance by the satisfaction of the heuristic craving which was deliberately intensified so as to evoke its arrival.

In simpler cases, the final solution may pop up quickly (as in those instances when one is searching for some "gem" of learning that one has momentarily forgotten). In the more complex cases, however, the final solution may only come after months of sustained efforts, after abandoning many preliminary solutions and overturning many obstacles, after tossing and turning during many restless nights. Sometimes the solution can arrive only after it has become an obsession which intrudes into every idle moment and interrupts even the normal rhythms of life -- one is literally "hounded" by the problem. Chance conversations, browsing through the Scriptures or research papers, musing over dreams upon waking up -- any of these moments might trigger a sudden recognition that has a bearing upon the preoccupying problem. A subliminal preoccupation allows the body to be alert even when the inquirer has no conscious effort directed toward the problem. Both scientists and saints, consequently, often report that their final prophetic breakthrough came in the most unexpected moment: e.g., just before going to sleep at night or when being awakened in the middle of the night after an unaccountable restlessness.

When the final solution finally does appear, it releases an avalanche of intellectual satisfaction. This satisfaction is felt as the deep sign and/or excitement that come when all the puzzling clues fall into a coherent whole. This satisfaction partly results from the relief of the strain set up during the time of puzzlement. Here again, trusted intuitions signal whether the imagined solution suffices to respond to the intricacies of the puzzlement it hopes to resolve. If some hesitation remains, one can initiate the strains of puzzlement again and perhaps come up with an alternative solution which carries with it an increased satisfaction. Now trusted intuitions are required to sense the comparative worth of alternative solutions. In the end, one knows that one has come up with a final solution when one reenters the problem and the preferred solution automatically flows in to resolve the strain. Now one cannot hear the problem without spontaneously being carried away toward its resolution. One's tacit powers have been irreversibly altered.

One's personal judgment of rightness, therefore, is entirely bound up with the sensed intellectual satisfaction which accompanies various solutions. To accredit one is to accredit the other. This accreditation is reliable and free of self-indulgence even though it cannot claim infallibility.

In the case of a crossword puzzle the clues are nicely specified and the final solution can be neatly arranged. In the case of a fresh inquiry to which a given tradition has no solution, the clues are often difficult to specify. In fact, only after the end of such an inquiry can the pioneer finally distinguish what clues he/she should have isolated from the very beginning in order to successfully arrive at the final solution. It is from this vantage point that a scientist will report his discovery as a smooth process from beginning to end; his/her daily scientific log, on the other hand, tells quite another story. Here one finds promising leads which, when pursued, seemed to be going nowhere and were abandoned. At this point, the tacit intuitions of the scientist were relied upon for sensing that certain leads may have been the source of some intellectual satisfaction at first but that this satisfaction dried up before they offered a final solution. Thus, the discoverer had to free him/herself again and again from dead ends and to deliberately renew the inquiry of some former stage which still held some promise. Trained intuitions are here called into play and trustingly followed.

When Luke reports how Peter first came to have Gentiles apprenticed to Jesus, he also writes his report from the vantage point of the final solution. As such, Luke writes as though it was one clean and smooth process from beginning to end. In fact, however, when one consults the particulars of one's own religious conversions following times of turmoil, one knows that no human quest is ever fully recorded in its actual messiness: the starts and the stops, the dead ends and the reverses, the frustrations and the minor satisfactions along the way.

Once the act of discovery has been completed, the discoverer uses the same passionate intuitions which brought him/her securely to his/her solution as the guide whereby he/she will guide others toward being enriched by what he/she has found. The discoverer always knows that he/she was once exactly where his/her colleagues still are. The discoverer thus sympathetically knows who he/she once was and how he/she came to be different. If the discoverer did not know this, he/she could not help those who have been left behind. As it is, however, the discoverer endeavors to guide his/her colleagues to retrace the route by which the pioneer him/herself was converted.

> Proponents of a new system can convince their audience only by first winning their intellectual sympathy for a doctrine they have not yet grasped. Those who listen sympathetically will discover for themselves what they would otherwise never have understood. Such an acceptance is a heuristic process, a self-modifying act, and to this extent a conversion.[9]

Sympathy, meanwhile, is strongest among those persons sharing the same tacit powers and pouring themselves into common issues and problems. The experience of that pioneer convinces him/her that these are the very persons that are most "ripe" and most interested in the truth that has gripped their colleague.

In the end, the discoverer can honestly say that he/she has been led along paths that were not of his/her own making. It is with real validity, therefore, that the Fathers of the Church felt that the Spirit of God often met and led them in their deliberations.[10] The very presence of prophetic experience implies that there is a living God who persistently lures us forward and towards which guiding and competent intuitions grope. Each Christian can sincerely say, "God is not finished with me yet." And, for those who do indeed believe this, God lures them ahead in their quest to enlarge themselves so as to embrace the entire holiness and the manifest pathos of their God.

The last chapter emphasized the faith of the apprentice as the necessary disposition whereby the novice is enabled to assimilate progressively the informed dispositions of his/her master. At the end of an apprenticeship, faith does not cease but it takes on a new orientation. In fact, the competent master already prepares for this new orientation from the first day of the novice's calling. In the religious apprenticeship, the novice is reverently attentive to the master, but the master is already drawing the novice's attention to God. In the end, consequently, God spontaneously appears and is sympathetically known to the disciple just as he/she exists for the master. The mature disciple is thus ready to leave his/her master and to follow God, the Supreme Master. Faith, accordingly, means a reverent submission directly to God. It is by this faith that a new master allows him/herself to let go of cherished elements in his/her settled dispositions in order to yield to the deep intuitions that lead to fresh revelations of God's cause. Before, the human master did the disciplining and the converting. In the end, the new master waits upon God to discipline and purify the very tradition which he/she incarnates.

When gifted by prophetic experiences, the new master knows that he/she must go against some part of the torah of his/her former master(s). He/she knows that this will cause them some pain. Yet, the new master also knows that his/her old master encouraged dissent and even now awaits his/her disciples to return to teach what God has revealed and the old master was not yet ready to hear. But, I am perhaps speaking of perfect masters. One's actual masters may become embittered and disappointed at one's deviation from the doctrines and practices which he/she so passionately upheld. The prophets are thus often persecuted by those who formerly brought them up and gave them everything that they are, save the prophetic discovery which came from sources that the opponents recognize not.

The scientific apprenticeship is similarly oriented. In fact, an apprentice in the physical sciences cannot be granted a doctor's degree prior to having demonstrated his/her ability to select and to design some novel scientific inquiry. At times such doctoral research is merely an extension of research being conducted by the candidate's advisor. At other times, however, a doctoral candidate will show such originality in his/her doctoral dissertation that even the candidate's professors will have a difficult time estimating its true worth. In any case, the new doctor of physics knows that he/she has to pursue courageously self-chosen lines of investigation that may partially overthrow the current consensus which is enshrined in textbooks and routinely upheld by all the leading adherents. In the pursuit of a discovery, the discoverer has faith in the ability of his/her trained intuitions to make a fesh contact with the reality under investigation. Once this prophetic contact has been made, the discoverer knows that his/her strenuous groping was justified.

> There can be no explicit justification of a [novel] scientific truth. But as we can know a problem, and feel sure that it is pointing to something hidden behind it, we can be aware also of the hidden implications of a scientific discovery, and feel confident that they [the researchers] will prove right . . . . The pursuit of discovery is conducted from the start in these terms; all the time we are guided by sensing the presence of a hidden reality toward which our clues are pointing; and the discovery which terminates and satisfies this pursuit is still sustained by the same vision. It claims to have made contact with reality: a reality which, being real, may yet reveal itself to future eyes in an indefinite range of unexpected manifestations.[11]

Such words on the lips of a productive scientist could easily be shared by the Christian who has been transformed by a prophetic encounter with his/her God. The human dynamics are the same while the realities involved are quite distinct.

Conclusion

I began this chapter with the conviction that every apprenticeship is functionally circular. Prior to an apprenticeship, one cannot adequately judge the worth of a tradition which one is entering. Following upon an adequate apprenticeship, however, one cannot escape noticing and taking into account those realities which have become the source of one's well-being. In the end therefore, one's apprenticeship has fashioned one's settled commitments, and one's settled commitments uphold the worth of one's apprenticeship.

If each of us is caught red-handed in upholding what one has been trained to uphold, how then is one to validate one's most cherished commitments? I have already shown that pragmatic appeals are always caught in the circularity of one's particular commitments: every belief has some degree of pragmatic advantage in the experience of the believer. As for authoritative appeals, one must always acknowledge that one's training embraces a selective adherence to some authorities and a systematic overlooking of alternative authorities. In religious controversies, sacred texts are commonly appealed to by both sides of the argument. In scientific controversies, selected experiments are commonly appealed to by both sides. It is always a case of "my facts" against "your facts" -- "my prophetic visions" against "your prophetic visions."

By virtue of being fixed within a particular body, there can be no strictly neutral stand. One can uphold a responsible perspective, but an impersonal and impartial perspective can nowhere exist. Anyone who insists that his/her judgment is "strictly impersonal" is victim of a gross self-deception:[12] he/she disguises from him/herself the very sources by which any and every mature and informed judgment is possible.

In the end, therefore, there is no hiding place. Appeals to one's austerity, or one's virtue, or one's passionate sincerity cannot override the necessary circularity of one's commitments. Each of us must accept his/her particular calling according to the historically-conditioned apprenticeships that one has undertaken. Each of us must abide within those realities which he/she habitually perceives and acknowledge them as the source of lifelong obligations and blessings. In sum, each must take his/her stand on the personal grounds to which one adheres.

But within the circularity of one's commitments, one can acknowledge that prophetic discoveries also appear. Such discoveries are normally preceded by a period of conscious straining which is rewarded by a critical realignment of the discoverer's trained instincts. Thus it happened that Peter dedicated himself to the way of Jesus, and this very dedication brought him to a personal crises which overturned his settled instincts relative to kosher. Similiarly, Copernicus gave himself entirely over to perfecting the Ptolemaic system, and this led him into a crises that entirely overturned his conception of the cosmos. And, in our own day, many women have dedicated themselves to the Victorian model of womanhood only to find that their very dedication thereto brought on a crisis situation that ushered in what is now known as the Women's Movement. Examples could be drawn from every other existing domain of culture as well.

While the mechanism of prophetic discoveries cannot be exhaustively detailed, those who yield to their deepest intuitions know that they are reliably (but not infallibly) guided and divinely inspired in their quest. Historically, one can observe that the historic transformation of every cultural domain rides on the energy of the prophetic discoveries that have purified and enhanced the tradition in question. On the personal level, the increased intellectual satisfaction of the discoverer is the mark of a closer approach to the truth that was being sought. On the relational level, the very phenomenon of discovery illustrates that the human powers of the discoverer were responsive to existing realities which unaccountably made their presence felt despite the immunity of existing indoctrination.

In the end, consequently, the religious prophet is compelled by higher obligations to give voice to that aspect of God which the religious populace is as yet deaf to hear. The scientific prophet, moved by a comparable compulsion, is constrained to humbly submit before the scientific community those fresh perceptions of scientific realities which have erupted in his/her inquiries. Religious discoveries may be rarer and more passionate because of the depth of the personal transformation that they entail. Every scientific discovery, however, implies some comparable degree of personal transformation and a reliance upon passionate instincts. Scientist have been known to risk their reputations and sometimes even their lives in the defense of what they believed.

Once the myth of objectivity is exploded, then both science and Christianity will again be acknowledged in parallel terms: demanding faith, guided by an authoritative tradition, transmitted through apprenticeships, responsive to prophetic discoveries.[13] Beyond this, no method is open to mortal, embodied creatures. Yet, I do believe that this is enough!

Footnotes for Chapter VIII

[1] Abraham J. Heschel, <u>The Prophets</u> (N.Y.: Harper & Row, 1962) II, 88.

[2] <u>Ibid</u>. II, 89.

[3] Michael Polanyi, <u>Personal Knowledge</u> (N.Y.: Harper & Row, 1964), p. 151.

[4] Mark's Gospel has Jesus teaching that "nothing that goes into a man [woman] from outside can make him [her] unclean" (Mark 7:15). Luke drops this from the material that he takes over from Mark's Gospel because he is aware that this ruling will emerge only due to Peter's conversion many years after the death of Jesus (Acts 10). Matthew retains Mark's material and knowingly places it late in the life of Jesus (Matt 15:10-20) just prior to his excursion into the region of Tyre and Sidon where he will encounter Gentiles. Thus, while Matthew reads back into the life of Jesus a decision which was reached later (in the name of Jesus), he clearly does not want to place it with the material he collects as the Sermon on the Mount (i.e., the summary statements of what Jesus taught his disciples in Galilee).

[5] Robert N. Bellah provides a provocative interpretation of how prophetic discernment has fashioned American experience: <u>The Broken Covenant: American Civil Religion in Time of Trial</u> (N.Y.: The Seabury Press, 1975).

[6] Philo <u>Quis rerum divinarum heres sit</u> 259-264.

[7] In recent times, theologians have recognized that divine initiative need not displace the proper human operations of the prophet. Paul Synave and Pierre Benoit explain that this was indeed the original intent of Thomas Aquinas but that commentators obscured his original intent: <u>Prophecy and Inspiration</u> (N.Y.: Desclee Co., 1961), esp. pp. 78-83. For a historic study and critique of prophetic ecstasy/madness, see Heschel, <u>The Prophets</u> II, 115-253.

[8] Michael Polanyi spells out the place of guiding intuitions in scientific inquiry in "The Creative Imagination," <u>Chemical and Engineering News</u> 44 (April 25, 1966) 85-92, and in "Logic and Psychology," <u>The American Psychologist</u> 12 (January, 1968) 27-43. I have not yet found a theologian who assigns a heuristic efficacy to intuition in the act of prophetic experience.

[9] Polanyi, Personal Knowledge, p. 151.

[10] Joseph A. Labarge, "The Assistance of the Holy Spirit and the Issue of Infallibility," Eglise et theologie 5 (1974) 43-74.

[11] Polanyi, The Tacit Dimension (Garden City: Doubleday & Co., Inc., 1966), pp. 23-24.

[12] Polanyi, Personal Knowledge, esp. pp. 160-174, 253-257.

[13] Polanyi, "Science and Religion: Separate Dimensions or Common Ground?" Philosophy Today 7 (1963) 4-14. See also Charles A. Coulson, "The Similarity of Science and Religion," Science and Religion, ed. by Ian G. Bargour (N.Y.: Harper & Row, 1968), pp. 64-100; Karl Rahner, "Science as a 'Confession'?" Theological Investigations (Baltimore: Helicon Press, 1967) III, 385-400; Harold K. Schilling, "On Relating Science and Religion," The Christian Scholar 41 (1958) 423-430.

IX

Recovering the Power of the Scriptures in Today's Church

      My intention in this chapter is to take the framework developed in the last two chapters and to apply it to the use of the sacred texts within the church. I intend to show that the Gospels originated out of the practice of apprenticing and that the power of the Gospels is negligible unless they are used within the context of an apprenticeship. I also need to consider how the text of the New Testament serves not only to sanction the status quo but that it serves as a point of departure for prophetic experience that goes on to alter the belief and practice of the church. Finally, I wish to offer a tentative program by which the Gospels might again be used for evoking and transmitting spiritual power within a traditional church structure. The material will be grouped within the following subheadings:

    A. The origin of the Gospels in the practice of apprenticing
    B. Authority and free initiative in the interpretation of the Scriptures
    C. The use of the Scriptures as the Christian classics which both conserve the past and evoke prophetic experience
    D. The limitations of scholarly exegesis and of fundamentalism
    E. A tentative program for renewing the church using the Scriptures

A.   The Origin of the Gospels in the Practice of Apprenticing

        I once spent an entire sabbath with the Jewish Hassidic community in San Francisco known as the House of Love and Prayer. Just prior to sundown on Friday evening, the members of the community welcomed guests and made last minute preparations for the celebration of the sabbath. As a precaution, light switches were taped in their "on" or "off" position so as to prevent any accidental violation of the sabbath injunction against kindling a fire. The oven was set at the desired temperature for the heating of meals for the forthcoming day. When all the preparations were complete, the thirty of us gathered in the front room. Various women were invited to welcome the "bride of the sabbath" by kindling the sabbath candles which had been placed in appropriate settings throughout the room. Then the joy of the sabbath rest settled upon the group as all linked arms, closed eyes, and swayed back and forth to the rhythm of Hebrew rounds. A round would be repeated nearly twenty times, then it would die out, and someone would begin another. By the end of an hour, the swaying had moved into rhythmic dance shuffles which were both reverential and joyous. After a final burst of animated dancing, everyone grew still and sat down on the floor. One of the leaders of the community then proceeded to give "his torah." He was a stocky, young fellow in shirt sleeves. He told three stories about the adventures of the Baal Shem Tov, the eighteenth-century founder of the Hassidic Movement. Everyone present listened very reverentially to the narrations. There followed the blessing and the cutting of the sabbath bread and the blessing of the sabbath cup. The sabbath meal, the holy meal which anticipates the kingdom of heaven, had begun.

        I was powerfully intrigued by the stories that had been told. In a free moment on the following day, I asked the storyteller of the night before about the source of his narratives. He responded:

> There was no particular source. All in all, I know the way of the Baal Shem Tov. He himself was a storyteller. His disciples told stories about him. All of these stories are told and retold so as to keep alive the holiness of the past. Yet, each storyteller must also know how to give torah which

is relevant to the current needs facing the community. It is by reflecting upon these needs that I come gradually to recognize what torah must be given. So I create the story so as to present how the Baal Shem Tov acted or would act would he find himself in circumstances parallel to our own. Those who have ears to hear know how to receive my torah and to bring it to bear upon their current lives.

I was dumbfounded. Here, for the first time, I sensed how it must have been in the primitive sabbaths when Jesus' disciples gathered following his death. The sabbath candles were lit and the accredited leaders of the community were called upon to give their torah. This torah consisted, by and large, of the telling of the adventures from Jesus' life. These narratives were by no means just information sessions for those interested in the past. The narrators were intent upon imaginatively carrying their listeners away into allowing the way of Jesus to address their present circumstances. The various stories carried guidance, consolation, rebuke. Those who were being apprenticed into messianic holiness were obliged to reverentially enter into the stories and to reverentially assimilate for themselves the dispositions which Jesus exemplifies. They were assisted in this by their personal interactions with the Twelve who were the normative personal embodiments of Jesus' spirit/Spirit.

With time, a given community would have developed a repertoire of favorite and oft-repeated narratives about Jesus. Finally, a gifted writer would set these short narrative segments down in an orderly fashion and the Gospels, as we now know them, would have been created. The written narratives served as an aid to the memory and as a source of the collected torah of the community. On the sabbath evenings, however, the leaders of the community continued to give their <u>oral</u> torah. At times, they employed the traditional stories recorded in the Gospels; at other times, they created their own narratives so as to better respond to the needs of their community.

With the passage of time, it would appear as though the art of apprenticing through creative storytelling was lost. In its place, the Christian community developed the practice of having someone read one of the recorded narratives of the now-dead storytellers and the community leaders would artfully draw out the meaning and implications of the canonical text for the present needs of their listeners. Apprenticing through storytelling was thus replaced by apprenticing through homilies based upon the Scriptures.

Initially no Gospel had universal recognition.[1] Each rose out of the particular needs and the normative practices of local communities. In practice, therefore, each community had the ability and the right to edit an existing Gospel or to produce one of its own. We now have evidence that over twenty different Gospels were produced in the first five generations following Jesus' death. Both Matthew and Luke edited Mark's Gospel. Matthew's Gospel was, in its turn, edited and published as the Gospel of the Armenians and the Gospel of Peter. Luke's Gospel was edited by Marcion. Entirely new Gospels appeared: The Gospel of Perfection, the Gospel of Thomas, the Gospel of the Seventy [Disciples], the Gospel of John. Some of these Gospels claimed apostolic authorship; others claimed to have been given through heavenly visions; still others spoke of very modest origins (e.g., Luke 1:1-4).

When the metropolitan churches of the third century were drawing up their canons of the Scriptures, it is impossible to suppose that "divine inspiration" was somehow overtly evident in some writings and totally absent in others. Thus, it seems necessary to suppose that the churches had an additional inspiration whereby they might correctly discern writings faithful to the Spirit of Jesus from those which distort his Spirit.[2]

I would judge that both the initial inspiration of the scriptural authors as well as the additional inspiration which recognizes the worth of the true Scriptures are rooted within a competent apprenticeship under approved masters. The authors of the canonical texts did not invent what they wrote. They merely wrote what they knew to be true as a result of their training under a disciple of Jesus. Once a Gospel was so written, its repeated and reliable usage in the hands of successive, authentic disciples continued to recommend it as divinely inspired to produce the holiness recognized by the community as its own. Heretical Gospels gave rise to heretical holiness just as heretical practices gave rise to heretical Gospels. "You will be able to tell them by their fruits" (Matt 7:20). Accordingly, <u>it was the normative apprenticing of the leading masters of the third century that decided what texts were to be deemed as authentically inspired</u>. Meanwhile, the various heretical sects succeeded for a while but finally dwindled to nothing. The heretical Gospels which they had used found no place in the orthodox churches and thus fell into oblivion.

B. <u>Authority and Free Initiative in the Interpretation of the Scriptures</u>

The Reformation period produced two opposing theories as to how the Scriptures were to be correctly used in the church. The Protestant reformers insisted that the Holy Spirit provided individual Christians with the sovereign inner experience by which they were infallibly led to a progressive conformity with God's cause through their reverent contemplation of the texts. Roman Catholics, in contrast, insisted that the Holy Spirit and pious delusions were functionally indistinguishable in the private experience of the faithful. In the Roman Church, therefore, Catholics were instructed to regard the bishops (and, more especially, the bishop of Rome) as so much under the influence of the Holy Spirit that they could infallibly guide the faithful into perceiving the truth and avoiding the self-delusions which sometimes accompanied the private contemplation of the Scriptures.

The Protestant scholar, Adolph von Harnack, well represented the persuasion of his tradition when he wrote that . . .

> Protestantism reckons . . . upon the Gospel being something so simple, so divine, and therefore so truly human, as to be most certain of being understood when it is left entirely free, and also as to produce essentially the same experience and convictions in individual souls.[3]

In sharp contrast, John Henry Newman reckoned the Scriptures to be utterly complex:

> It is in point to notice that also the structure and style of Scripture, a structure so unsystematic and various, and a style so figurative and indirect, that no one could presume at first sight to say what is in it and what is not . . . . Of no doctrine whatever, which does not actually contradict what has been delivered, can it be preemptorily asserted that it is not in Scripture; of no reader, whatever be his study of it, can it be said that he

[she] has mastered every doctrine which it contains.[4]

On the basis of this perception, Newman argued that the Scriptures would be entirely useless and the source of conflictual experiences and interpretations unless some divinely authorized interpreter were established to discern the intended meaning of the text. Faced with this need, Newman judged that the Catholic hierarchy provided the necessary and divinely authorized court of appeals for resolving conflictual interpretations of the Sacred Scriptures.

I believe that these two seemingly incompatible assessments of the Scriptures can be reconciled. In effect, I find that there are valuable truths on both sides of the Protestant-Catholic impasse that need to be brought together if ever the Scriptures are going to be rightly used within the churches.

In order to integrate "the divine simplicity" of Harnack and "the utterly unsystematic" of Newman, I want to draw attention to a purely secular phenomenon. Consider, for a moment, the initial experience of a student of physics who is paging through his/her newly purchased text book at the beginning of the academic term. He/she may come across something like the following:

> With an electron removed from an inner shell, the ion will be surrounded by a field, due to the nucleus and the remaining electrons, approximating that of a hydrogen nucleus, and in this field there will exist a discrete set of quantum states. An electron removed from the K shell, for example, may stop in one of these states.[5]

At first sight, even though the text is printed in English, the student cannot say what it is that he/she has read. At the end of the academic term, however, he/she will reckon this text to be something so simple that its full intent will be immediately and effortlessly apparent.

This secular example illustrates how a guiding text undergoes a <u>phenomenal transformation</u> during the period of one's apprenticeship. When applied to the Sacred Scriptures, Newman is quite correct in discerning how unsystematic and figurative the New Testament appears to the uninitiated. Harnack, for his part, correctly discerns the divine simplicity which appears when a community of

Christians have been apprenticed by the same masters standing in the same tradition.

Prior to any systematic training, it is not uncommon to find Christians identifying Herman Hesse's <u>Siddhartha</u> as having more evocative power than Matthew's Gospel. During a Christian apprenticeship, all of this is changed. What was formerly obscure and inconsequential now appears to have the power to inspire and to guide. What was formerly of mere historical interest now becomes the two-edged sword which cuts through the confusion and murkiness of life and gives the power to do the things of God. Following upon an apprenticeship based upon the Scriptures, the Christian for the first time discovers the depth and the power of Matthew's Gospel and it is <u>Siddhartha</u> that now appears shallow and superficial in contrast.

When properly understood, the Scriptures present only a set of coded symbols. As such, the Scriptures are entirely mute. They are like the scores of Mozart's violin concertos: a living master is required to bring the score alive and to thrill us with the depth of aesthetic feeling that it contains. In parallel fashion, it requires a Christian master to break open the text of Scripture and to correctly nourish the messianic holiness proper to our own time.

Harnack may insist on the divine simplicity of the Scriptures, but it is manifestly impossible to expect that free interpretation alone can "produce essentially the same experience and convictions in individual souls." If such were indeed the case, how can one account for the inability of Christians from different denominational traditions to agree upon the meaning of certain key texts? Catholics and Lutherans, for example, have for many generations disputed over the meaning of Matt 16:18: "You are Peter and on this rock I will build my church . . . ." Neither Catholics nor Lutherans, however, would support Rev. Liston Pack in his contention that Mark 16:18 ("In my name . . . they shall take up serpents . . . .") authorizes members of his parish in Newport, Tennessee, to handle poisonous snakes as the divinely commissioned testimony to their personal faith. Moreover, hardly a week passes when I don't stumble upon some self-appointed minister of religion or some self-instructed devotee of the Bible who sincerely and passionately authorizes his/her personal judgments by artfully clothing them with selected texts from Sacred Scriptures. In effect, therefore, <u>behind every Protestant assertion of biblical supremacy lies an unnoticed system of effective biblical training which follows and perpetuates</u>

the beliefs and practices of the particular denominational tradition involved.⁶

When the masters of a tradition are indeed competent and dedicated to the advancement of their tradition, then authority and free initiative are quite compatible. Masters in such a tradition know how to discipline the efforts of their understudies while at the same time fostering their creative ingenuity. In practice, however, every viable tradition has its share of insecure and pedantic masters. Such masters systematically communicate to their disciples their authoritatian propensities. In extreme cases, they stifle the initiative of their disciples so that the master-disciple relationship serves to disguise a dehumanizing tyranny. With time, such abusive masters are eventually censured by their peers and their influence upon future adherents in the profession is checked.

Augustine, in his own day, ably exemplified how his authoritative teaching as bishop was entirely compatible with the independence of action of his charges. In offering rules for the interpretation of Scripture, Augustine assured his readers that he intended to enhance their personal powers so that they would indeed be free of any further need to rely upon him. Thus he states that . . .

> The man who lays down rules for interpretation is like one who teaches reading, that is, shows others how to read for themselves. Just as he [she] who knows how to read is not dependent on someone else, when he [she] finds a book, to tell him [her] what is written in it, so the man [woman] who is in possession of the rules which I here attempt to lay down, if he [she] meet with an obscure passage in the books which he [she] reads will not need an interpreter to lay open the secret to him [her], but, holding fast by certain rules and following certain indications, will arrive at the hidden sense without any error, or at least without falling into any gross absurdity.⁷

C. The Use of the Scriptures as the Christian Classics Which Both Conserve the Past and Evoke Prophetic Experience

The Gospels and letters of the early church offer clues to the sacred obligations and the divine vocation which characterized Jesus and his disciples. Throughout the centuries, Christians have used these texts as the normative guide in Christian formation. Within the catechumenate, the Gospels were upheld as exemplifying the messianic holiness toward which the catechumen was being conformed by the discipline of the church. Within the Sunday liturgy, the Gospels were carefully broken open by the bishops of the urban churches for the expressed purpose of continually nourishing the hunger for truth and blessedness which animated the elect.

The Sacred Scriptures functioned within the church much in the same way as the classics in art, music, and science function to evoke and to impose correct modes of feeling and perception upon a widely dispersed (in place and in time) body of adherents to their respective traditions. Every apprentice is required to contemplate reverentially and to reproduce painstakingly the classics for him/herself. In so doing, the novice's tacit powers are informed with correct sensitivities and standards of performance. At the end of an apprenticeship, the novice knows that he/she has arrived by the fact that the classics evoke the same depth of feeling and the same powers of performance that exemplify the masters of the tradition who supervised the training of the novice.

The classics represent the inexhaustible sources which evoke and sustain a living tradition. Thus, the violinist returns again and again to Mozart's concertoes and the artist reproduces the sketches and paintings of the great masters fully convinced that he/she will never exhaust the depth, beauty, and power of meaning that they invoke. Augustine, in his own day, was firmly convinced that the Christian was similarly situated with respect to the New Testament:

> Such is the profundity of the Christian Scriptures, that if I were to attempt to study them and nothing else from early childhood to decrepit old age, with the utmost leisure, the more unwearying zeal, and greater talents

than I have, I should still daily find something new in them.[8]

The Scriptures paradoxically serve both to conserve and to innovate. They function to conserve when they are used as the basis of a Christian initiation into the standards of holiness which dominate the status quo of the existing church community. They function to innovate when they provoke and disturb the mature inquirer and usher in prophetic experiences which are calculated to disrupt the status quo. Those prophetic experiences that are finally accepted by the community become part of the new status quo and the Scriptures are habitually read so as to evoke and foster the particular prophetic experience that has been assimilated. The stage is now set for yet other texts of Scripture to become troublesome or to evoke fresh discoveries of God. At any given time, the established meaning of Scriptures is dominant; yet, even the most familiar texts are pregnant with and subservient to an unpredictable chain of innovative encounters with the living God.

Consider the Scriptures relative to the slavery issue. At one point, the New Testament seemingly advocated a benign forebearance on the part of slaves:

> Slaves must be respectful and obedient to their master, not only when they are kind and gentle but also when they are unfair. You see, there is some merit in putting up with the pains of unearned punishment if it is done for the sake of God . . . (1 Pet 2:18-19).

Yet, in these same Scriptures, one finds the narrative of how YHWH was moved by "the sons of Israel, groaning in their slavery" (Exod 2:23) and how YHWH raised up Moses as the great liberator of the slaves. In effect, therefore, the Scriptures bear the marks of their culturally conditioned origins at every point. Moses could no more follow the advice of 1 Peter than could Peter feel the call to be the liberator of slavery in his own day.

In parallel fashion, the religious controversies surrounding the slavery issue in the United States found ample biblical backing on both sides. Only after the end of the Civil War and the effective liberation of the slaves could Frederick Douglass deliver his famous oration in which he meticulously paralleled the vocation of Abraham Lincoln with that of Moses. Today, in a climate in which the passion for liberty and justice are high, one can hardly envision a Christian minister using the text of 1 Peter as evoking the demands of God for his/her people. in effect, therefore, <u>while the words of Scripture remain the same, they undergo a phenomenal transformation from epoch to epoch in accordance with the enacted church traditions of the day. By so doing, the Scriptures remain fresh and demanding in each generation even though they were written for persons far removed from us in time and in culture.</u>

During a Christian apprenticeship, a novice learns to discover within the Scriptures the religious experiences which characterize his/her mentors. Progressively, however, a novice is taught to open him/herself up to the experience of God which the contemplation of Scriptures may freshly evoke. As such, the dynamics for prophetic discovery are thus set into play.

In the typical instance the reader of the Bible brings him/herself into a contemplative frame of mind and reads over a self-chosen text or texts. Meanwhile, the reader is subliminally guided by the whole array of successes and failures, joys and anxieties, hopes and fears which fabricate the texture of his/her subconscious existence. So, too, the reader feels the lure of God which has some marginal influence on each of us at every moment. The divine lure is never coercive or clearly separable from the nexus of subconscious drives; yet, it is quietly present. And it is the quiet meditation of the reader which tries to intuitively discern the sympathies of God. The reader passes over much of the text without being noticeably affected. A familiar text might trigger a group of associated meanings coming from past encounters. The reader may sense again that he/she is being warned, judged, comforted, guided, blessed. Events of the past filter into the mind of the reader. Some of them fade quickly. Others are mulled over and their relationship to the text is again enforced and further digested. The mind wanders. Occasionally it reaches an impasse. A once-familiar text might become suddenly puzzling. Or, an unfamiliar text might become the source of a deep anxiety or fascination. The wise and experienced meditator will stay with these moods and even endeavor to intensify them. In the more dramatic cases, the reader/meditator will feel him/herself unsettled or captivated by impulses which are not yet clearly defined. He/she will be impelled to come back to them again and again -- even in those brief moments throughout the day when the mind wanders and daydreaming sets in. After weeks or months, the inquirer senses that he/she is being led by trusted intuitions into a truer perception of God's cause or into a closer sympathy with God's way. Then, in a moment of sudden and overwhelming emotion or, gradually, over a prolonged period, the truth overwhelms the seeker. The inquirer knows that he/she has arrived in so far as the contemplation of the discovery has an inherent satisfaction which relieves the former straining of the quest.

The discovery brings with it an enlargement of life. Maybe the discovery will entail changing one's career in order to seek the accomplishment of a task which is urgent for God. At other times, the discovery will entail a calming reconciliation with someone who marred one's past life and who has been quietly hated for countless years. At still other times, one will be led to reassess the priorities which make one's life so strenuous and achievement-oriented. Whatever the nature of the discovery, however, the expansion of life which it entails will be greeted as a sign that one has been touched and blessed by God.

Discoveries based upon the meditative use of Scriptures can never be fully specified nor fully defended. How is it that any person can account for why some texts appear self-evident while others appear problematic? And how is it that one can go for years reading and hearing a text from the Gospel with a quiet acquiescence until, in one unbidden moment, this same text creates a disruptive challenge? Furthermore, how can any person lay out before another, or even before oneself, those intuitions of a growing coherence which guide one toward a final resolution? Assuredly, one can point to critical clues and critical events along the way; yet, it is only after one's settled commitments have been irreversibly altered that one correctly perceives the clues themselves in terms of where they were leading. While biblical inquiry cannot be fully specified nor fully defended, the process is, none the less, reliable, without claiming infallibility. The inquirer senses that demands are being made upon him/her that are entirely different from a self-serving emotionalism. At times, one may even make a profoundly moving discovery which will subsequently show itself to be false and deceptive. In effect, one's very ability to catch and correct one's own errors gives one an even larger sense of confidence in the inquiry process itself. Meanwhile, however, one never forgets that some of the greatest heretics in the Christian tradition were fashioned by the discoveries that they made while pondering the same classics that had fashioned the great Saints.

Recovering the Power of the Scriptures   253

D.   The Limitations of Scholarly Exegesis and of
              Fundamentalism

         Within recent years, there has been a tendency for
Christians to overestimate the impact of scholarly studies
bent upon recovering the original meaning of the biblical
texts.[9] Some Christians have mistakenly believed that
once scholars have come to a consensus as to what the
primitive church believed and practiced, then there will no
longer be any doubt as to how God wants us to believe and
to act today.

         Nothing could be more misleading. In the first
place, there is no single set of beliefs and practices
represented in the New Testament. The separate sources
grouped into the New Testament canon present the
diversified beliefs and the varied practices which were
suited to different communities in the first century.[10]
It would be arbitrary to accept one set of beliefs and
practices and to quietly imagine that there are no others.
In the second place, the original beliefs and practices of
the New Testament communities presented authentic patterns
of messianic holiness suited to their particular historical
and cultural milieux. No Christian today is living in a
setting exactly comparable to any of those represented by
the first-century communities. In effect, therefore, there
is not a single belief or practice in the New Testament
which ought to be reproduced within the twentieth century
without making a careful inquiry as to whether such a
belief or such conduct is indeed harmonious with God's
sympathies today.

         Biblical fundamentalism endeavors to take one
interpretative period of biblical theology and to canonize
it as the definitive rule for all past and all future
generations. At first sight, fundamentalism appears to
insure a stable adherence to a set of truths already
experientially tested and lived. Upon closer examination,
however, fundamentalism codifies a mechanism which is
calculated to destroy the very thing which it was designed
to protect.

         In order to appreciate the hazards and the
deceptiveness of biblical fundamentalism, one has only to
analyze the comparable movement within the musical
enterprise. Thus, for example, among the devotees of
Mozart one finds "fundamentalists" who insist that all
personal, subjective interpretations are to be excluded

from the performance of Mozart's works; rather, the greatest efforts must be made to reconstruct his original scores and to perform them with absolute rigor (i.e., "literally"). One must grant that the program of musical fundamentalism presents difficulties but that it does not appear impossible. One can, for example, collect the oldest existant copies of Mozart's scores and make an accurate study of the minor variations found among them. Then, as in the parallel New Testament studies, one can devise rules whereby one can decide which of the variations is most likely to be the original and, thus, to reconstruct the "original score" for all of Mozart's works.

Mozart used a notational system which was peculiar to his day and which has no exact counterpart within modern notational systems. As a consequence, musical fundamentalists must either require that all musicians learn "Greek" (i.e., the archaic notational system of Mozart) or produce translations into our modern notational system. Fundamentalists have chosen the latter course of action. Here again, however, some degree of personal judgment must enter into every "scientific" interpretation of Mozart's notations, and every translation of an "original score" must betray the inevitable slippage that mars even the best of translations.

Let's assume that musical fundamentalism did arrive at agreement in preparing a common translation for all the reconstructed scores of Mozart. The next task would be to insure that listeners hear the score of Mozart performed "literally." This not only requires that conductor and musicians execute only what is written but that they play as in the days of Mozart. This demands, among other things, that one uses the instruments of Mozart's period in a hall with acoustical conditions comparable to his rococo halls. In point of fact, Mozart composed at a time when the pianoforte was a very recent invention and he himself was its first great virtuoso. Since Mozart's time, a steel frame has been introduced, three strings have replaced Mozart's single string, three additional octaves have been added to the keyboard, felt hammers have replaced the leather-covered hammers, the tuning of all the notes had gradually risen about a semitone. Yet, even supposing that a sufficient supply of old instruments could be found or reconstructed . . . ,

> There is a further problem in using historic instruments: we are no longer able to play them as they used to be played. Not only has our performance technique altered, but our perception of sound is attuned to modern

> conditions, and complete re-education would be necessary in order to learn how to play old instruments approximately as they used to be played in Mozart's time. If some particular musician, after years of contact with old instruments, succeeds in reconditioning himself in this way, a public accustomed to the sound of modern insturments will probably find his reconstruction of an older ideal of beauty peculiar or downright unpleasant.[11]

In the end, therefore, the more effectively that fundamentalists achieved their goal, the more completely would they succeed in freezing Mozart in the past and dooming him to a museum-like sterility. Fortunately for classic music, fundamentalism did not exist at an earlier epoch. As such, the instruments changed, the notation changed, the halls changed, tonality changed, the romantic period of music was born; yet, despite all these changes, Mozart continued to be, for each generation, a living classic to be produced and enjoyed. In fact, one should not say "despite all these changes" but "in accordance with all these changes." Sensitive persons in each generation changed Mozart so as to allow him to better fit the emerging world of music which he had originally helped to create. Thus, by losing something of the original, Mozart's work gained in an influence and life-giving spirit that has enhanced the aesthetic development of untold generations. Most living musicians oppose the fundamentalist movement in music, not because they are opposed to the past or only loosely tied to its standards of excellence but because they have a greater respect for what the works of Mozart have become and have little interest in trying to arrest and turn back this development in favor of a misguided reverence of the past.

All of this applies precisely to the Christian classics. By allowing their original meanings to shift, the same texts gathered to themselves the fresh prophetic discoveries which presented the cause of God in each successive generation. Far from regretting the loss of the original intent of the past, the Scriptures were enabled to become the vehicle for a living tradition. Unless this "unscholarly" use of Scriptures continues -- unless Christians continue to expand and refine God's call by making reference to biblical texts -- the Scriptures will cease to be living classics and become dead artifacts of a bygone set of commitments which have no relevance to the issues faced by modern persons.

A strict fundamentalism would require that Christians abandon their modernity in order to cultivate the historical sensibilities of a bygone era. Presumably, all the advances which prophetic movements have brought to the Christian tradition would have to be reversed. Slavery would be reintroduced. Medicine and psychiatry would be abandoned so that numerous human disorders would again be spontaneously viewed as possessions by unclean spirits. Women would be again admonished to remain silent in the churches with their heads covered (Cor 14:34-35, 11:2-16). Or, following Matthew, maybe the churches would be empty and all prayer would be reserved for one's "private room" (Matt 6:6). Taken to an extreme, the case for fundamentalism in Christianity is just as disastrous as the comparable movement relative to the works of Mozart.

The greatest immediate benefit of modern biblical exegesis is to demonstrate once and for all that the faith and the practices of our forebears in religion were culturally and socially situated in an epoch different from our own. No existing church tradition (even those which advocate the fundamentalist ideal) can remotely hope to produce the cultural and social milieu in which those Scriptures were created and life-giving. Should such a church be found in some isolated pocket of the world, one can be sure that its ironclad rule of mindless conformity would be condemned on the basis of the Gospels themselves.

Jesus himself was bent upon transforming society. As that redeeming transformation was felt, the Christian way of life was bound to change in both thought and deed. Just as Mozart set afoot an innovative movement in music, so, too, it was to be expected that his very works would be altered by virtue of the very maturing of that which he himself had released. With Jesus it could be no different. His spirit/Spirit continued to spread its lifegiving energies to different times and cultures only by virtue of changing its shape and definition. As John Henry Newman so amply testified, there was no alternative:

> Whatever be the risk of corruption from intercourse with the world around it [a developing idea], such a risk must be undergone, if it is duly to be understood, and much more if it is to be fully exhibited. It is elicited by trial, and struggles into perfection . . . . It is indeed sometimes said that the stream is clearest near the spring. Whatever use may fairly be made of this image, it does not apply to the history of a philosophy or

> [religious] sect, which, on the
> contrary, is more equable, and purer,
> and stronger, when its bed has become
> deep, and broad, and full. It neces-
> sarily rises out of an existing state
> of things, and, for a time, savours of
> the soil. Its vital element needs dis-
> engaging from what is foreign and tem-
> porary . . . . At first, no one knows
> what it is, or what it is worth. . . .
> From time to time, it makes essays
> which fail, and are in consequence
> abandoned. It seems in suspense which
> way to go; it waivers, and at length
> strikes out in one definite direction.
> In time it enters upon strange
> territory; points of controversy alter
> their bearing . . . . In a higher
> world it is otherwise; but here below
> to live is to change, and to be perfect
> is to have changed often.[12]

E. <u>A Tentative Program for Renewing the Church Using the Scriptures</u>

By way of envisioning how the above discussion might function in practice, I would like to offer a tentative scenario whereby the Scriptures might be used as the source of renewal and nourishment in a traditional church structure. My particular scenario will assume that I am dealing with a given hierarchy of bishop, priests, deacons as currently operative within the Catholic, Episcopalian, and Lutheran traditions. Methodists would naturally think of bishop, elders, deacons. The scenario need not be taken as a whole but might be made to operate within any local church wherein the Scriptures are taken seriously as a source for Christian renewal and orientation.[13]

It is Friday evening in the living room of the bishop's home. Here the bishop, or someone whom he/she appoints, has prepared to celebrate the Liturgy of the Word with the ten to twelve local priests who have pledged to form a living-community together each Friday evening. The format varies from week to week, but in each case the Liturgy of the Word is celebrated using the rubrics that would be appropriate at a home church. Care is taken that each is reconciled with all those present. In this intimate setting, forgiveness is sometimes openly requested, and grievances (even if imagined) are aired and resolved. The kiss of peace is shared. Then all listen attentively to the biblical readings which each has been prayerfully meditating on during the week. The bishop then takes these readings and offers, in a familiar homily, the joys and the pains, the correction and the guidance that the Holy Scriptures read provoke in his/her life. In the silence/prayer which follows, all freely give voice to the various sentiments that the Liturgy of the Word arouses in their hearts.

A simple meal follows. Using the Jewish traditions which go back to the time of Jesus, the bishop blesses and distributes the bread and the wine at his own table.

After the meal, the extended group reflection begins. The purpose of this exchange is to allow the time and the space for the Spirit present within the group to guide them to a shared understanding and sympathy with the biblical texts used during the Liturgy of the Word. Using the bishop's reflections as a point of departure, each one present endeavors to expand and to enrich the breaking open of the Word of God. The exchange should continue until all present are of one mind and one heart relative to what "the Spirit of God is saying to us today." Personal experience, the documents of church councils, the findings of biblical scholars, and current events all have their place in fashioning the group consensus.

At the end, time might be alotted in which each person gives voice to the message and the mood that he/she intends to carry from the "bishop's church" into their own parishes. Perhaps, on some occasions, a joint written statement might also be prepared. After a time of prayer, the bishop gives his personal blessing to each of the members of his church. Then all depart.

The bishop's church represents the forum in which the Sacred Scriptures are brought to bear upon the lives of the participating pastors. Bonded together by mutual esteem and charity, the bishop's church should be expected to develop a rich base of shared holiness and shared pastoral commitments.

Care would be taken that each bishop's church would embrace persons competent in biblical exegesis, in group processes and facilitation, and in social/political action on the local and national levels. Perhaps one person would be specifically designated as heading up and focusing the group energies relative to each of the three areas. Such persons would not operate as mere consultants in their area of competence but would be charged with deliberately sharing their skills so that others might enlarge their own competencies. Thus, the biblical exegete would enable the church to become aware of how the original New Testament authors (and the Fathers of the Church) either support or diverge from the shared felt-meanings which the church is adapting as its own. The facilitator would assure that each member of the church is accurately heard and fairly responded to. More especially, the facilitator would model how dominant personalities can exercise their charisms without intimidating those who are more reserved. He/she must also model how honest disagreements can be resolved and healed. Finally, the social organizer would clarify with the group how "the voice of the Spirit speaking to us today" cannot ignore the necessity of deciding upon personal and collective forms of social action directed toward implementing the Word of God within society at large.

The scenario that I am proposing would continue the following evening (Saturday) as each of the members of the bishop's church gathered together their own respective "churches." Within each pastor's church would be gathered together eight to twelve deacons who have pledged themselves to form a pastoral community with their parish priest. Any assistant priests in the parish would also be present. Within the pastor's church, everything would proceed according to the pattern and the spirit/Spirit of the bishop's liturgy of the night before. Reconciliation. Hymns. Readings. Then, the pastor would break open the Scriptures with the full recognition that he/she was largely influenced by his/her participation in the bishop's church. The nourishment presented, therefore, would be welcomed as embracing the collective inspiration of the bishop's church. Meanwhile, the individuality of the pastor would not be lost or overlooked.

A simple meal would follow. The pastor would bless and distribute the bread and the wine in his own home. The procedure after the meal would follow the same format that was used in the bishop's church the evening before. Now, however, each deacon would endeavor to allow the Liturgy of the Word to penetrate into his/her own heart. Together the deacons would wrestle with the sentiments and the demands that have emerged from the bishop's church. Great care would be given to bringing the Word to bear upon their own particular circumstances and the actual needs of their own parish. In this reverent and caring atmosphere, each deacon would prayerfully discern how he/she is going to present "the voice of the Spirit speaking to the church today" within his/her deacon church the following morning.

After this is shared, the pastor gives each deacon a parting blessing and sends them out to their respective "churches."

Sunday morning, each of the deacons would find him/herself surrounded by the members of five to ten families who form the "deacon's church." The deacon brings to this gathering the weight and the presence, not only of the bishop's church, but of the pastor's church in which he/she participated the evening before. The Liturgy of the Word would be celebrated in this setting with a format and a spirit/Spirit that followed that of the pastor's church. Reconciliation. Hymns. Readings. The deacon's homily.

Immediately following the homily, each of those present would endeavor to bring the wisdom of the Word to bear upon their personal and social lives. In such a family and familiar setting, great care is taken to apply the Gospel to the small routines as well as the traumatic moments of one's daily life. In the end, each person present explains and pledges to those present what commitments they will undertake during the forthcoming week so as to bring "the voice of the Spirit speaking to the church today" to bear upon their practical lives. Prayer and silence will seal these commitments. The deacon would then gather together the hopes and the fears, the consolations and the anxieties, of those present into a simple communion service (or a homestyle Liturgy of the Eucharist). The deacon blesses each one personally at the conclusion of the liturgy.

The deacon endeavors to become a model of worldly holiness and of pastoral caring outside of the Sunday-morning gatherings. In this task he would be stimulated and guided by the other members within his/her pastor's church. The local priest, in his/her turn, would be stimulated and guided in his/her pastoral outreach by the other members of the bishop's church.

Church members who do not participate in a deacon's church might continue to have their Sunday worship as usual. The parish priest and one or two deacons would strive to aesthetically and spiritually nourish those gathered with "the voice of the Spirit speaking to the church today" that was formulated during the pastor's church the evening before. Once a month all the deacon churches would meet with the rest of the parish so as to proclaim and to celebrate their larger unity and their united commitments as a parish.

With a bishop's church of ten members and with pastors' churches of ten members each, a hundred persons would be directly committed and pastorally engaged in sharing the Gospel ministry of the bishop. With an average of fifteen persons in each deacon's church, 1280 persons in each diocese would be immediately and personally nourished by the bishop's shared pastoral office. From among these persons, one would expect to find a ferment for renewing and healing all manner of modern personal and social infirmities. Special attention would be given to allowing this scenario to serve as a practical format whereby over a thousand Christians might be personally apprenticed in the sympathies and commitments which dominate the bishop's church. Within such systematic apprenticing, I believe the Scriptures could again function to create living disciples from the dry bones which are now scattered and dejected (Ezek 37).

As grace is made visible in the lives of those within the deacon churches, more and more persons will ask to become participants. Great care should be taken to insure that new members were suitably initiated and that the church would wisely be divided into two churches whenever a sufficient size is attained. With each division, a new deacon would be trained and admitted into the local pastor's church. As the number of deacons grows, one among them would prepare for priestly ordination by way of anticipating the splitting of the pastor's church. Nothing would be done in haste. Great care would be taken that suitable training and nurturing were maintained at each level without overextending the demands made on any individual person. Procedures would have to be developed to correct internal abuses and even to dismiss those who prove unworthy of their calling.

Within such a structure, a bishop might again, as in a former era, become the chief healer, sanctifier, and model of holiness for his/her people. Then bishops will again bring to realization the role descriptions that they have already designated for themselves but have been unable to implement:

> Among the principal duties of bishops, the preaching of the gospel occupies an eminent place. For bishops are preachers of the faith who lead new disciples to Christ. They are authentic teachers [masters], that is, teachers [masters] endowed with the authority [i.e., the messianic charisms] of Christ, who preach to the people committed to them the faith that they must believe and put into practice. By the light of the Holy

Spirit they make that faith clear, bringing forth from the treasure of revelation new things and old (cf. Matt 13:52), making faith bear fruit and vigilantly warding off any errors which threaten their flock (cf. 2 Tim 4:1-4).[14]

In a diocese where such a dream was approaching reality through sustained human channels (as in my scenario), it would not be uncommon for a bishop who senses him/herself inadequate for the new demands of his/her office to voluntarily step down in favor of that person who does indeed express ths charism for spiritual leadership within the bishop's church. Those who stepped down would be admired for their courage and their service to Christ's church. Origen, in the second century, explained that the bishop should be that foremost in spiritual advancement in his own church. If this were not the case, Origen asserted that one must look to either a failure of nerve on the part of the bishop or an inadequate process for selecting bishops.[15] The same observation could be applied to defective leadership at every level of the above scenario.

Conclusion

By way of summary, I would like to again recall that the Sacred Scriptures are like the written scores of Mozart's classical performances. As such, the Scriptures require a great master of messianic holiness to bring them alive and to thrill us with the many nuanced sympathies of God which they rightly evoke. The Gospels were written by those who were inspired and filled by the original messianic holiness of Jesus and his "bishop's church" of the Twelve. Throughout the centuries, these Gospels were carefully preserved and faithfully broken open by the bishops, priests, and catechists who were the master performers of their sacred tradition. Meanwhile, apprentices were attracted by the living holiness of these masters and confidently submitted to their direction. Using the Scriptures under the guidance of these masters, novices were led through progressive feats of discovery so as to touch and to taste for themselves the sublime sympathy with God that their masters already exercised. That which they only blindly admired in the beginning, they came by faith to share. The foremost masters in the church again and again gave themselves over to the reverent contemplation of the Scriptures fully expectant that they held an unexpected wealth of progressively unfolding manifestations of the living Spirit of the Father of Jesus and his Saints. They were not disappointed in this

Recovering the Power of the Scriptures

expectation. The history of the use of the Scriptures shows them to be not only the continual source for assimilating the charism of messianic holiness but also the provocative source for prophetic discoveries which stretched and transformed the messianic holiness already achieved. It was not unusual, therefore, to find that the bishop who led his people to himself be led by the living God whom the bishop met during his struggling with the Scriptures.

In the light of this experience, the Sacred Scriptures showed themselves to possess a depth dimension which was comparable to that of the living God. This being so, the Sacred Scriptures were often called the inscripturalized Word of God in the same sense as Jesus was called the incarnate Word of God. And just as many persons knew Jesus of Nazareth yet never profited from any depth relationship with him; so, too, many persons have known the Bible but have never profited from a correct relationship with it. These latter are like the young boy in John's account of the feeding with loaves. The boy carries the five loaves (which are the five books of the written Torah in Augustine's eyes) and perishes from hunger since his loaves are no more than an additional burden to him.[16] In the hands of Jesus and his disciples, however, the burden of Israel is blessed and broken open so that those who hunger for God are fed, those who are blind are made to see, those who are crippled are made strong, those with unclean spirits are liberated and filled with the Spirit of the living God. The right use of the Scriptures thus insures that the affairs of God on earth are promoted just as they are already accomplished in heaven.

Footnotes for Chapter IX

[1] For a careful study of the origin of the New Testament canon, see Hans F. von Campenhausen, The Formation of the Chrisitan Bible (Philadelphia: Fortress, 1972) and W. Schneemelcher, "The History of the New Testament Canon," New Testament Apocrypha, ed. by W. Schneemelcher (Great Britian: SCM Press, 1973), pp. 28-59.

[2] John L. McKenzie, "The Social Character of Inspiration," Cross Currents 12 (1962) 423-431.

[3] Adolph von Harnack, What is Christianity? (N.Y.: G.P. Putman's Sons, 1902), p. 295.

[4] John Henry Newman, An Essay on the Development of Christian Doctrine (Harmondsworth: Penguin Books Ltd., 1974, orig. pub. in 1845), p. 162.

[5] F.K. Richtmyer, et al., Introduction to Modern Physics (N.Y.: McGraw-Hill Book Co., Inc., 1955), p. 400.

[6] C.H. Dodd, The Authority of the Bible (N.Y.: Harper Torchbooks, 1960), pp. 17, 20-22; John Henry Newman, An Essay on the Development of Christian Doctrine, pp. 149-165.

[7] Augustine De doctrina Christiana prologue, 9.

[8] Augustine Epistolae 137.3.

[9] Walter Wink, in The Bible in Human Transformation (Philadelphia: Fortress, 1973), makes a passionate plea for recognizing the alienation and false consciousness that biblical scholarship has introduced in the seminaries of liberal Protestants. Peter Stuhlmacher, in Historical Criticism and Theological Interpretatin of Scripture (Philadelphia: Fortress, 1977), endeavors to legitimate modern biblical criticism in the face of many conservative churches that have dismissed the new exegesis as the work of the devil. Such representative studies indicate that many Protestant theologians have become severely disenchanted with scholarly exegesis. Catholics, meanwhile, are slowly and optimistically giving great scope to exegesis within their theological and pastoral endeavors. See Raymond E. Brown, "Difficulties in Using the New Testament in American Catholic Discussions," Catholic Mind 1314 (June, 1977) 10-23.

[10] With the development of form criticism in the 40s, there has been, for the first time, a studied attention to accounting for the differences within the New Testament sources. Differences were always recognized but formerly they were reduced to inconsequential alternatives in emphasis. Cf. John Charlot, New Testament Disunity (N.Y.: E.P. Dutton and Co., 1970) and Ernest F. Scott, The Varieties of New Testament Religion (N.Y.: Charles Scribner's Sons, 1943).

[11] Eva and Paul Badura-Skoda, Interpreting Mozart on the Keyboard (N.Y.: St. Martin, 1965), pp. 6-7.

[12] John Henry Newman, An Essay on the Development of Christian Doctrine, p. 100.

[13] Many fine programs of Scripture study have been developed, especially within the various Protestant churches. Most programs, however, do not systematically develop small cohesive groups which demand a mutual accountability for living out what one discovers in the Gospel. An exception to this is the RENEW program developed by the Archdiocese of Newark, N.J. This program, which began in October of 1978, endeavors to renew the entire diocese by training selected lay persons and clergy from each parish to create little "home churches" somewhat similar to those about to be described.
Meanwhile, the ferment within Latin America has largely come about due to pastoral teams organizing poor farming families into comunidades de base wherein economic sharing and conscience raising are based upon the Gospel message. Groups such as this are using the Gospels not only for personal edification but for establishing shared commitments to the implementation of the way of Jesus in today's society.

[14] Catholic Bishops of Vatican II, Dogmatic Constitution on the Church, sec. 25, tr. from The Documents of Vatican II, ed. by Walter M. Abbott (N.Y.: Guild Press, 1966).

[15] Origen held that the bishop needs be the one who is most advanced in perfection or else he cannot suppose to be the true spiritual leader of his community. Cf. Hans von Campenhausen, "Church Office and Authority in the Time of Origen," Ecclesiastical Authority and Spiritual Power (Stanford, University Press, 1969), esp. pp. 254-59.

[16] Augustine Tractatus in Joannis evangelium 24.5.

X

Prayer, Sacraments, and the Messianic Hope in Today's World

In this chapter, I intend to explore how a Christian apprenticeship is intimately involved in praying rightly, in receiving the Sacraments efficaciously, and in working within a divinely inspired messianic hope for today's world. Without an adequate apprenticeship, personal prayer is either impossible or it is plagued with self-delusions and superstitions which fail to embrace the sympathies of the living God. In parallel fashion, without an adequate apprenticeship, the sacramental rites can produce a deadening boredom or carry the participants into a deceiving idolatry. Messianic hope, in its turn, can be mere wishful thinking. In God's world, not everything is possible; meanwhile, those who correctly harness their energies to God's cause will see the Kingdom of Heaven coming to fulfull their wildest dreams.

The material in this chapter will be divided as follows:

- A. The thrust of private prayer: sympathy with God
- B. The thrust of public rites: acting with God
- C. The thrust of messianic hope: thy Kingdom come

A. <u>The Thrust of Private Prayer: Sympathy With God</u>

Prayer functions within a religious tradition by way of leading its adherents to actively cultivate an emotional and intellectual sympathy with their God/god(s).

Perfect prayer results in perfect unity. Christianity is no exception to this rule.

The Christian traditions have artfully designed and painstakingly cultivated various forms of private prayer. Within even the same tradition, the postures and the rituals have been altered from time to time. As a result, there exists today a vast diversity of actual practice. Some Christians pray at specified times and places; others pray only when and where they are instinctively drawn to do so. Some Christians speak of prayer as meaning those quiet moments in which they sense that their God comes close and wordlessly fills their silences. For them, prayer requires a no-thinking and a no-doing such that a hollow stillness is created in the expectation that God comes by to fill it. Other Christians consider private prayer to refer to their time of "night prayer" when they pass in review the dominant events of the day. Jesus or the Father are imagined to be present during this review -- affirming, correcting, guiding. Resolutions are taken and carefully recorded in a journal for periodic review. Still other Christians associate prayer with reciting for themselves the printed prayers that have been composed by others: the psalms, the Eucharistic prayers, Malcolm Boyd's <u>Are You Running With Me Jesus</u>? They reverently read or recite aloud the prayers they have chosen until they find one or the other which particularly addresses their personal condition. They come back to such prayers again and again until they make them entirely their own. This latter form of prayer has a kinship to the reverent reflection upon the Scriptures as discussed in the previous chapter.

Not only is the style of one's praying an acquired art, but even the content of one's prayer is shaped by one's cumulative training and past history. Each time a religious person closes his/her eyes and places him/herself in the presence of god/God, it invariably happens that the familiar god/God of one's particular belonging appears. Christians should not doubt that the Moslem senses the approach of his beloved Allah during the moments of his/her prayer just as every Christian meets the God of his/her denominational Christianity. The character of one's religious experience is invariably stamped by one's particular, culturally conditioned upbringing.

The pervasive influence of one's particular religious upbringing in determining the content of one's prayer can be illustrated by a recent cross-cultural study of near-death experiences. Karlis Osis and Erlunder Haraldsson interviewed doctors and nurses in America and India.1 In so doing, they collected information regarding five hundred instances in which persons who were near death reported unusual out-of-the-body experiences in which they met with deceased love ones or with religious personages. There was not a single instance in which a Christian reported meeting a Hindu god, just as there was not a single instance in which a Hindu reported meeting Jesus. Every religious person invariably met his/her familiar deity; there were no surprises. I conclude from this that even when persons are in a nonvolitional "coma" condition, their religious experience is still mediated by their previously acquired powers of knowing. To recognize this is not to discredit the efficacy and reliability of such experiences; rather, it is to recognize that the presence of God exerts only a marginal influence, which contributes to the resulting experience but does not overwhelmingly or exclusively determine it. The same sort of thing can be said relative to the religious experience of the one who is sensing the presence of God in prayer.

The experience of God in prayer is always influenced by human elements which escape voluntary control and defy exact accountability. That this is so is clear from the following reasons: (1) In the first place, the <u>act of prayer requires that the Christian relax his/her sense of control so that he/she might be carried away by the impulse of God</u>. Anyone who is excessively preoccupied cannot properly pray; such persons are constantly distracted from God by the pressure of their own preoccupations. (2) In the second place, <u>every experience of God requires subconscious skills which cannot be directly inspected nor evaluated</u>. Such skills are shaped by one's cumulative past training and experience. Without these skills, the present impulse of God would be as meaningless as when a child or an atheist are confronted with the clues which have a direct bearing upon God's initiative. Given appropriate skills, however, the Christian always recognizes the present impulse of God as an extension of and as informed by his/her cumulative past experience. While these skills are enabling, they always contain partially twisted and deformed elements which contribute to the present meaning. (3) In the last place, <u>one cannot neatly dissect and catalog the clues which enter into any specific prayer experience</u>. With even greater force, one cannot separate out divine elements from human elements. Both are indeterminably intermingled in the present and historically interpenetrating in the past. The indeterminacy regarding the clues, however, does not imply that the final recognition is indeterminate. A lover can securely read the gestures of his/her beloved without being able to exactly specify which clues led to the recognition which emerged. The same holds for the Christian who is carried away by the sympathies of God during prayer.

Private prayer, in isolation from an apprenticeship within an established community, is open to unchecked self-deceptions. Cut off from a tested religious tradition, "God" will most probably be met as a private idolatry fabricated from a nexus of voices from the subconscious that are projected into the skies. Such idolatries can embrace a fascination and a terror that enables them to be self-sustaining and immune to most experiential or scriptural correctives. At their worst, such voices from the subconscious can erupt into a demonic fracturing of the human personality.

Great caution should be taken when initiating Christians in prayer. The uninitiated are often misled when prayer is characterized as "a conversation with God" or when it is suggested that "God answers our prayers." The still, small voices that speak within one's heart are by no means always from God. Our hearts are indeed sensitive to God's lure, but they are also prey to the parental tapes and compulsive messages of one's particular upbringing. When the novice in prayer is first taught to silence the mental chatter and to create an interior stillness attentive to God, the "voices" which emerge might well be suppressed parental tapes and archetypal images that have been lurking in the subconscious and patiently awaiting the present moment of stillness for their release. It is unfortunate when novices take these "voices" to be of divine origin. Beginners, therefore, are in need of wise guidance (spiritual direction) if they are to securely sort out their inner "voices" so as to discover among them the lure of the living God.

The Synoptic Gospels retain the sketches of Jesus apprenticing his disciples in the art of prayer. In particular, Jesus cautioned his disciples against praying in public as a show of piety (Matt 6:5-6). He also cautioned them against imagining that God can be goaded into playing favorites for those who multiply their prayers (Matt 6:7-8). Jesus even introduced his disciples to the habitual content of his prayer: how YHWH was to be approached familiarly as "Father/Dad," how his sympathies were aligned to the coming of the kingdom on earth, how asking the Father's forgiveness requires that one enlarge the measure of one's own forgiveness (Matt 6:9-15). It is doubtful that Jesus indicated fixed times and formulae for praying since the Gospels testify that he himself allowed prayer to arise out of the life situations which he faced (Matt 11:25-27, 16:39-45, 27:46). In like fashion, we also know that John the Baptizer trained his disciples in the art of prayer (Luke 11:2).

The fathers of the desert gave themselves to prayer and asceticism. The deceiving voices which St. Anthony heard in the desert have become an inspiration for art and drama. Even the great saints had to fight their way to God through the distorted yearnings and alluring fantasies which broke into the silent places that they had created for God. Novices in the desert were strictly warned to submit the contents of their prayer to the wise discernment of their spiritual guide who had the maturity and the experience to safeguard them from self-delusion. The following narrative was circulated as affirming this principle even when (and especially when) heavenly voices and miracles seemingly confirmed the contents of one's prayers.

> Saint Friard and his companion, the Deacon Secondel, remained perfectly stable in their anchoretic vocation upon an island, each having his own cell . . . . As they were laboring in strenuous prayer, the Tempter appeared at night to the Deacon Secondel in the likeness of the Lord, saying: "I am Christ to whom you continually pray. And now you are a Saint, and I have written your name in the Book of Life with the rest of my Saints. Depart now from this island, and go among the people healing the sick."
>
> Deceived by this illusion, he departed from the island <u>without telling his companion</u>: and when he placed his hands upon the sick in the name of Christ they were moreover healed [by demonic power].
>
> After a long time he returned to the island and came with great glory to his companion . . . . The other was appalled and asked what he meant; and he told him simply all that he had done. But the old man was amazed and said with sighs and tears: "Woe to us! How terrible do I hear that you have been deceived by the Tempter! Come now and do penance, lest his [her] wiles prevail over you."
>
> Secondel, understanding his error, fell weeping at his feet and begged him to intercede for him with God 2

This narrative clearly suggests that the novice "laboring in strenuous prayer" cannot correctly discern the "voices" that he/she encounters in prayer. <u>By virtue of the fact that the novice is expecting Christ, "the Tempter" easily takes his place.</u> Later, however his mentor immediately discerns the deception upon hearing of the novice's account. It would appear that Saint Friard knew that his novice was quite far from any effective holiness and that the "voices" which he heard bore the marks of a deluding wish-fulfillment. In the end, however, the novice was saved and converted by hearing the truth of his mentor.

In our own day, many adults habitually think of prayer as asking God to do for them what they cannot or are unwilling to do for themselves. Such prayers indicate how many well-meaning and sincere Christians have never enlarged the form and the mood of their prayer since the time when they were children. A popular song sung by Janis Joplin strongly spoofs such religious infatalism:

> Oh Lord, won't you buy me a Mercedes Benz? All my friends drive Porsches, and I must make amends.[3]

When we were children in our parent's home, we habitually petitioned our parents for favors, and they responded with their seemingly infinite powers to do our bidding or, at other times, they refused our requests for inscrutable reasons. As children, we were necessarily constrained to approach our Father/Mother in heaven with the same childish simplicity. As we matured, however, our parents gradually informed us with their torah so that we knew, in advance, what was included and what was excluded in their program for rendering us assistance. So, too, we were often pressed to supply our own efforts in realizing those blessings which our parents showered upon us. Thus, for example, the infant is given its daily food without any exertion on its own part. A child, however, might be required to wash his/her hands and to help set the table. The adolescent may go so far as to be expected to participate in the very preparation (in the fields or in the kitchen) of the food which he/she requests from his/her parents. In parallel fashion, the growing maturity of a child of God requires that he/she be led to take progressively more responsibility for realizing those blessings which the Father in heaven is disposed to give. A Christian adolescent ought to be taught to discriminate in prayer in accord with the sense of God's Torah that he/she possesses. The childish prayer of requesting indiscriminate and immediate gratifications should give way to an informed compassion for God's cause and a growing willingness to harmonize one's personal powers with the divine initiative that blesses and heals one's life and the lives of those whom one loves.

Mature pastors know how to gently discourage childish modes of prayer while at the same time nurturing progressively adult relations with God. Other pastors, meanwhile, are regrettably content to paternalistically sanction and artificially protect religious infantilism among adults.

For the mature Christian, the prayer of petition is always a demanding adventure. It must be undertaken with caution and responsibility. Thus, for example, if I become concerned with peace in the Middle East or with peace among the conflicting factions in my own family and come to find out in prayer that God, too, is indeed invested in bringing peace to these areas, then I cannot continue to pray for "peace" without committing my own energies to be with my God in this enterprise of creating peace. If I wish to remain uninvolved and merely be a spectator of the Lord of History, then I must give up any serious praying. Prayer is thus an engaging and a risking affair -- not to be lightly undertaken.

The person who develops the discipline to quiet his/her own preoccupations in order to be attentive to the sympathies of his/her God must necessarily anticipate being changed in his/her encounter with the living God. There is nothing especially complicated or magic in prayer. Whenever someone in love quietly rehearses in his/her imagination the deeds and the standards of excellence of his/her beloved, this very "reverent reflection" operates to align the lovers within shared sympathies and instincts for action. For those who contemplate the deeds and standards of excellence of their God, the selfsame transformation takes place. Prayer, therefore, brings a Christian to share the sympathies and mainsprings of action that animate the Lord of History. Sustained and regular prayer is calculated to enlarge one's narrow and selfish interests and to give one the selfsame spirit/Spirit as those who act as God's representatives: Jesus and his saints. It is for this reason that prayer always has a major role to play in the tradition of messianic holiness proposed by the Christian tradition.

The living God has created the world without our help but its ongoing redemption and divinization cannot take place without human cooperation. Through prayer, a Christian opens him/herself to being nudged and proded into an active sympathy with God's cause. This sort of prayer is hard work and needs competent direction; the petitions of a child are easy and of little consequence for a God who already knows that we are needful. Of this, Jesus was quite clear:

> Set your hearts on his [the Father's] kingdom first and on his righteousness, and all these other things will be given you as well (Matt 6:33).

B. The Thrust of Public Rites: Acting With God

Public prayer has always been extremely important for the ongoing training of Christians engaged in private prayer. Accordingly, during the second and third centuries when the prayer in the Christian assemblies was largely extemporaneous, it is not surprising that the most competent members of the community, namely the bishop and presbyters, were specifically charged to lead the public worship. Lay persons were required to be entirely silent at these public gatherings unless they were specifically trained for an office or a ministry in the church. During the public liturgy, those present surrendered themselves to the ritual being enacted. As such they were securely carried away into perceiving the character of God as this character was competently evoked within the ritual itself.

It would be irresponsible to imagine that any prayer suffices in the public assemblies of the church. Many prayers so entirely distort God's cause and God's standards of excellence that they evoke nothing but the idols of the imagination. <u>Prayer under the guidance of foreign or heretical spirits calls up foreign and heretical gods.</u> Persons who have been recently converted from pagan cults require a long period of training before they can clearly distinguish between the Spirit of the Father from the spirit of that god which they have abandoned. If public prayer is to shape and correct the religious imaginations of the participants, the liturgy must indeed be competently designed and artfully executed.

Within a worthy ritual, the participants are deeply moved. The pain and the joys of their lives are addressed. Some are consoled; others are distressed. All are guided and stretched. Human ambition is redirected and purified so as to harmonize with the interests of the Holy One invoked. The participants go away distressed by the brokenness of their former lives and strengthened in their

Prayer, Sacraments, and the Messianic Hope 275

determination to rectify their social and private relations. At the same time, the participants come away with a sober trust in the gentle persuasion of God who draws all persons and all events into a harmony of becoming and of mutual helpfulness that creates the Kingdom of God on earth. The public prayer of the saints and the prophets in one's church echoes in the minds of the participants as the prayer that they wish to come back to in their own private moments with God. The novice thereby enlarges his/her sensibilities so as to embrace the Spirit that was visibly enacted within the sacred prayers of the public rite. In this fashion, the deceiving spirits and the false hopes which plague the novice are gradually displaced by the true Spirit and real hope of the saints.

Today's Christian denominations exemplify significant variations within their public rites. Consider, for example, the marked contrast between the Roman Catholic Mass and the Sunday meeting of a Quaker congregation. The Catholic Mass is largely composed of prayers and gestures that date back for more than a thousand years in the Catholic tradition. The parts of the liturgy are ordered and predictable: invocation, penentential rite, the three readings designated for the Sunday in question, homily, prayer of the faithful, offertory, a Eucharistic canon, communion, final exploration and blessing. The Mass has been most at home in lofty-arched cathedrals. This selfsame liturgy, however, has been scaled down and simplified for use in a home setting.

In contrast, Quakers have no prearranged prayers or liturgical ministers. At the appointed hour, Quakers silently enter the room that they have set aside for their Sunday prayer meeting. Each one sits in reverent silence and disposes him/herself to be attentive to the divine presence. From time to time, individual members stand and share in words the movements of the Spirit that they have felt penetrating their silences. There is no expected continuity among the movements of the Spirit that are voiced. At the end of an hour, the prayer meeting is closed with the same silence that initiated it. For our purposes here, it is evident the Quaker tradition is as much informed with time-honored rituals as is the Catholic even though their rituals vastly differ.

I have often remarked that a significant liturgy has the power to carry me away in the way that significant plays and movies have been able to do. I can remember for example, the afternoon that I was present at the off-Broadway production of "Man from La Mancha." During the production I was entirely carried away and stunned by a vivid recognition of who-I-was and who-I-was-meant-to-be. This recognition overwhelmed me with tears. After the production, I wanted to be still. I didn't want to talk to anyone -- not just yet. My deep intuitions told me that I had been powerfully addressed by the drama in a way that I myself did not yet entirely grasp. I had to go apart and mull over the outstanding words and gestures in order to progressively assimilate their full intent. In the weeks that followed, I made it a point to listen to the profound spell that this one production had cast over my life. Tears came again and again. Slowly the spirit/Spirit that had addressed me altered my own self-understanding and habitual sympathies so that I became one with the revelation that had overwhelmed me. From time to time I have been similiarly affected during the production of a Sunday liturgy. With equal vividness, I can still recall those moments when my deepest self was addressed and the God-who-Is lured me one step toward becoming that person that he/she intended me to be.

Some Christians might object that no comparison is possible between the efficacy of Christian liturgy and the efficacy of secular drama. Traditionally, many Christians have regarded their liturgical rites as divinely instituted and thus entirely removed from drama originating from human inspiration. Moreover, the evocative power of worship is commonly assigned to God while the evocative power of drama lies in the artistry of human agents. Such hard and fast distinctions cannot be encouraged here. The next few pages shall explain why.

The guidelines established in the last chapter relative to the interpenetration of human and divine initiative in the production of the Bible can be equally applied here. Thus, it would be just as heretical to exaggerate the divine institution of the Sacraments as it would be to exaggerate their human institution. To make the humanity of the Sacraments incompatible with their divinity would be to make the full humanity of Jesus incompatible with his full divinity. An orthodox Christology, therefore, prompts an orthodox sacramentology.

Historical research demonstrates that every sacramental ritual has specific culturally conditioned origins which were modified in accord with changing pastoral requirements in the course of time.[4] Even Quakers have seen a birth and development in their Sunday rituals since the time of George Fox. In fact, there is nothing to prevent Quakers from eventually affirming that their silent worship was divinely instituted since Quaker experience overwhelmingly attests that their hallowed silences form the arena in which they are authentically

Prayer, Sacraments, and the Messianic Hope   277

grasped by their living God. Quakers originally rejected Anglican Sacraments and an ordained priesthood because they recognized a huge gap between what the Sacraments claimed to accomplish and the meager actual fruits that they bore in their lives. The pregnant silence of Quaker worship, therefore, was specifically inspired and designed by the God-given thirst for establishing a rite where the religious claims and the actual fruits were again in close harmony.

What makes a particular ritual "sacred" is that it adequately serves to express and to impress upon the worshippers the particular character of their god/God. The ancient rites of Dionysius were "sacred" to his devotees while they presented an abomination to those outsiders who had neither the training nor the sensibilities to properly enter into the rites. The dances and the meals of contemporary initiates of Krishna consciousness are likewise "sacred" to those who have been apprenticed within this particular Hindu tradition. The various Christian liturgies can be no exception to this rule. The following conclusions can thus be drawn: (1) Liturgical rites within any given religious tradition presuppose an adequate apprenticeship within that tradition. With this in mind, the early centuries of Christianity never admitted candidates to the Eucharist until after they had successfully passed through the initiation rites of the church. (2) Liturgical rites which have been inspired by and produced within the spirit/Spirit of one religious tradition cannot be used correctly by outsiders. An outsider will either be uninspired by the unfamiliar rite or be led into discovering a heretical divine presence which is the product of his/her own training and has little to do with the intended result received by the properly initiated devotees. In sum, liturgical rites reveal to the insider what is concealed before the outsider.

In the light of these conclusions, it makes little sense to imagine that a particular ritual produces its intended results simply because a traditional rite is duly performed by an authorized minister/priest. Juridical efficacy must not be confused with pastoral efficacy.[5] Thus, to take a purely secular instance, it is evident that the classical, dramatic dance of northern India (Kathak) can be performed before Western audiences. It is equally evident, however, that Western sensibilities do not prepare the audience to be suitably carried away by the rhythms of the feet, by the complex hand gestures, by the movements of the eyes of the dancers. In contrast, a Hindu audience with refined sensibilities trained to appreciate Kathak dance, are powerfully moved by the religious drama that is unfolding. The table would be reversed should a symphonic orchestra give a performance of Mozart and Bach before an Indian audience. It can sometimes happen that a particular liturgical form can die because there is no longer an audience capable of appreciating the depth of nuanced feeling that the rite formerly evoked.

The liturgical minister/priest has a critical role in the production of a liturgical rite. In the first place, the liturgical minister must be thoroughly inbued with the spirit/Spirit of holiness representing his/her particular tradition. The Christian minister/priest normally undergoes a long seminary training designed to insure that the candidate assimilates for him/herself the very Spirit of Jesus as represented (i.e., as re-presented) by the leading masters of the denominational tradition to which the candidate belongs. But, over and beyond this, the liturgical minister must be professionally trained to enact the sacred rituals of his/her tradition with the utmost aesthetic competence. Even before an appreciative audience, the musical classics can be performed routinely and lifelessly. Boredom sets in and attention wanders. The approval of a bishop and the sincerity of a minister/priest can never redeem a hollow and incompetent production of the classical rites of the Christian community.

In performing the classical liturgies, the minister/priest must strike a balance between fidelity to the original and fidelity to the particular group of God's people who are gathered. The competent minister/priest knows how to wear the classical prayers and gestures as his/her very own. This competence has been gained by a painstaking and repeated entrance into the original such that the spirit/Spirit that animates it comes through as the celebrant's very own. But beyond this, the competent minister/priest has been sympathetically informed by the particular hopes and disappointments, the particular joys and sorrows, of his/her congregation. Accordingly, such a minister/priest knows how to artfully modify the classical rite so that the genius of the past picks up and embraces the moods of the present moment. In this fashion, a classical rite can mediate and influence the present just as the present contributes and enlarges the classical rite. It is only the purist who would insist that Mozart be performed today using the instrumentation and performance technique of the seventeenth century. Such rigor would find little appeal among contemporary audiences. Mozart continues to have a wide appeal precisely because adept performers have judiciously adapted and enhanced Mozart's classics according to the aesthetic standards of their own day. The same ought to be said for the rites of the church.

Within the Christian traditions, the Sunday rituals have the effect of promoting an ongoing apprenticeship among the participants. To appreciate how this takes place, it helps little to make any appeal to the dramatic or musical traditions. Drama and music bind together the actual performers into a community of shared sensibilities and performance skills; the spectators, however, are by no means bound into a community as are the participants in a religious tradition. I would like to appeal, therefore, to est (Erhard Seminars Training) as providing a fitting secular model for how liturgical rites promote and direct personal and communal transformation.

Werner Erhard, the founder of est, was first and foremost a very influential and successful personnel manager. As part of his middle-age crisis, Werner sought to find increased life-satisfaction in hypnosis, yoga, mind science, Scientology, drugs. Then in 1971, while driving south on California's highway 101, Werner was overwhelmed with an experience which entirely resolved the gnawing discontent within his life.

> I didn't find out another new thing -- I didn't add to my store of fact and information. This experience transformed the quality of everything I knew -- of my whole store of facts, memories, etc. Even the way I felt in my little finger was transformed. I didn't add any new facts -- everything I knew, I knew now in a new way.[6]

Unlike most people, Werner did not rest content with his personal revelatory discovery. Rather, he set out to design a series of rituals whereby he might lead others to come to the same experience that he had discovered. In so doing, est was born.

The initiation rites for est occupy two consecutive weekends. During these weekends, approximately forty persons are assembled in a rented hotel meeting room, and Werner (or one of his approved disciples) leads the participants through a systematic set of "exorcisms" and rites calculated to induce "what may be the most important experience of their lives." At the end of each weekend, each participant solemnly mounts the podium and gives "witness" to any signs to the new birth that have shown up due to the seminar program. Among those who "found it" (most do), the following testimonies are typical:

> An elderly man who had experienced tremendous withholding through most of

the training and then cried his eyes out on the final day . . . shared that he had been in this world for over seventy years and had only just now begun to live. Because he was living with his full being, he told us, he no longer feared death . . . .

A woman in her mid-thirties who had looked mousy and frightened when she began the training now looked beautiful and radiant. "I want to share that my asthma, which I've had since I was ten years old, has simply disappeared." Others shared remissions, sounding like Lourdes cures, including two migraine headaches, bladder weakness, and a chronic lower-back pain.

"I want to share that my husband and I have stopped arguing for the first time in three years," a stunning young woman told us . . . .[7]

During these testimonies, Werner, or one of his disciples, acknowledges and, occasionally, challenges these manifest life-changes. Those who graduate from this initiation rite are now permitted to go on to advanced training in special seminars which cover some of the more specialized skills in implementing their new life. Initiates feel a great sense of being bonded to those who passed through the same rituals: they arrange reunions and make great sacrifices to attend the advanced seminars.

The *est* program gives an accurate idea of how an efficacious ritual is designed and implemented. Initially, the impulse for creating a ritual grew out of Werner Erhard's revelatory discovery that he passionately wanted to share. Then, in an interim period, Werner brought together small groups and guided them through his self-designed rites. By giving close attention to what hindered and to what facilitated the movement of his participants, Werner gradually modified and improved his rituals. During this period of experimentation, only Werner could judge whether participants were faithfully reproducing the experiential patterns whereby he himself was reborn. Within these trial sessions, some of Werner's first disciples emerged. Once his program was systematized and marketed, these persons and only these persons would be authorized to assist him in running his seminars and, at a later stage, run them by themselves. In 1975, Werner recognized only fourteen such disciples. At that time, well over 50,000 persons had received his training.

Est offers only one illustration of how purely secular rites can be designed to effectively communicate a given charism -- that of Werner Erhard. The rapid growth of the charismatic movement within the mainline denominations also points to the organizational genius and enthusiasm which knows how to transmit another particular charism.

Since religious, as well as secular charisms, can be systematically communicated, it seems foolish for the Christian churches to imagine that they want to leave everything up to God and not to take their legitimate responsibility in promoting Christian charisms. I can appreciate the great dangers of pride and self-delusion should Christians realize that their rites are the tools for enhancing and for communicating their own personal charisms. On the other hand, a systematic apprenticeship within one's denominational tradition provides a great assurance that one's personal charism is an authentic expression of the Spirit of Jesus. As things stand, the strong denial of human agency in the charismatic movement serves to perpetuate an acritical pietism which forms another mode of self-delusion. Ignorance may be blissful, but awareness provides a more responsible grasp of human responsibility for promoting God's cause.

The liturgical renewal presently taking place within the Roman Catholic Church provides a good illustration of how the people of God can be apprenticed into a new charism through liturgical change. In the early 60s, there was a movement afoot to have every Catholic silently pray the Mass in English while the priest whispered his Latin liturgy at the altar. Then the people were asked to respond to the priest in Latin as the altar boys had once done for them. English hymns were next introduced. Within a period of four years, momentous changes were introduced. The entire spirit and mood of the liturgy was changed. Formerly, the Mass was meditative and solemn and private. Now the Mass is decisively centered on reconciliation, breaking open the Word of God, and collectively sharing the Eucharistic prayers. Some Catholics were shocked and scandalized by the secular and communitarian intrusions into their private meditation. Some of these Catholics have even banded together into small groups around dissatisfied priests who continue to honor only the old rites in Latin. A large percentage of priests have obediently taken up the new rites, but they celebrate them with much of the old spirit. An even larger percentage, however, have discovered for themselves the spirit/spirit of in the new rites and have marvelously brought their parishoners to enjoy the new demands and responsibilities of their Catholic commitments. I would personally judge that the Catholic bishops are profoundly inspired by God in instituting their liturgical changes and that they are courageously promoting a truer following of Jesus Christ and a closer sympathy with the Spirit of the living God.

As Catholics and other Christians continue to take increased responsibility for implementing effective liturgies, will it any longer be possible to honestly acknowledge the Spirit of God as the author and the effector of every liturgy? Yes. The persons who design new liturgies do so because they are impelled thereto by the Spirit that grasped them in the old rites. The instincts which guide their choices as to what to modify and how to modify are also derived from their deepest sympathies which they rightly believe are informed by the living God. Even the execution of liturgy evokes in the very designer experiences which could not have been entirely foreseen in advance. An effective liturgy has power over its creator, therefore, that surpasses all intentional planning. This unanticipated power will always have to be carefully discerned in order to avoid calling "God" those demonic/foreign spirits that sometimes break into holy rites. More often, however, the unanticipated power of a rite will be discovered to be the Spirit of God whose subsidiary influence accumulates within every rite.[8] In the end, consequently, a new rite can gather momentum. The fragile experiences surrounding the rite grow. Each new addition is enriched and intensified by one's past experiences. Meanwhile, such experiences all have their transformative effect upon the devotee; the rite progressively carries them away in the same way as repeated contacts with Jesus carried the disciples away as they were assimilating his messianic holiness. As a result, the hope of Ezekiel might well be fulfilled by the faithful self-surrender to appropriate rites celebrated by competent ministers/priests:

> I [YHWH] shall give you a new heart, and put a new spirit in you; I shall remove the heart of stone from your bodies and give you a heart of flesh instead. I shall put my spirit in you, and make you keep my Torah . . . (Ezek 36:26-27).

C. **The Thrust of Messianic Hope: Thy Kingdom Come**

In the first section of this chapter, private prayer was shown to be a learned skill. Without a competent spiritual guide and without being informed by public prayer, private prayer has no guarantee of discovering God but only the phantoms of one's subconscious. With proper direction, however, prayer can become a powerful instrument for that profound self-transformation which imbues a Christian with the sympathies of God. In the second section, the sacred rituals of the church were shown to be the responsible creations of the masters of the Christian tradition. Christians, with a proper initiation, could be assured of being carried away by these rituals so as to intensify and expand the particular messianic charism that they were designed to communicate. Habitual encounters with the rites of the church could thus effect what the habitual encounters with Jesus formerly effected for his disciples. Now, in this third and final section, I wish to indicate that the charism of Jesus was not an end in itself but that it was entirely oriented toward serving the messianic hope of the prophets: "Thy kingdom come, thy will be done on earth" (Matt 6:10). Such is the fruit of every true Christian tradition and the unimpeachable test of its vitality.

The Synoptic Gospels make it abundantly clear that Jesus did not regard himself as important in and for himself. In effect, therefore, Jesus did not attempt to have people honor him with sacred titles. He did not want even his disciples to separate him from themselves, to put him on a "pedestal," and to worship him at a distance. In Chapter V, I indicated how the Synoptics present Jesus as habitually intent upon having his disciples live up to their exalted calling as "salt of the earth" and "light of the world." In Chapter VII, I clarified the meaning of faith by divorcing it from blind fascination and the instinct to leave everything up to God. Faith was shown to be the spontaneous attachment and the prolonged efforts whereby a disciple assimilates the spiritual power of his/her master.

The prophets of old brought God's judgment to bear upon the prevailing order and announced their God-inspired hope for the future reign of God. By and large, however, the prophets never felt the power to correct and heal the present order or to usher in a new and better order. They passionately proclaimed God's sympathies and waited to see how their listeners would respond.

Jesus was born out of this prophetic tradition. He was also born out of the Pharisaic movement that had perfected the practices whereby a saintly master could systematically transmit his/her charism to chosen disciples. By uniquely integrating these two, Jesus was both a prophetic voice and a pragmatic implementer.

Jesus gave his best energies to implementing the messianic holiness which he knew within his small circle of disciples. I would conjecture that Jesus <u>purposely</u> chose his disciples from among the common folk and not from among the elite or the dregs of society. If Jesus had proved unable to share his charism with the common person, he himself would have conceded that the time was not ripe -- that the Spirit of God had not yet prepared the masses for the new order that he himself had tasted and lived. Jesus then would have been reduced to a prophetic voice and revolutionary critic without being able to bring the Kingdom any closer. But such was not the case.

Jesus did not have to pretend that he could redeem the world single-handed. He needed disciples. The evil rooted within the settled sensibilities and habitual judgments of Israel could not be uprooted in a day. The efforts of a single individual were insufficient, no matter how exceptional he/she might have been. The God-ordained parameters undergirding the human condition dictate gradualism. God can drown his/her adversaries or extinguish them in fire, but not even God can instantaneously alter the instincts of his/her enemies without entirely destroying their humanity at the same time. God is the patient Persuader. Those who sympathize with God must be patient also. The juridic salvation associated with the cross is quite far removed from the pastoral salvation which embraces the concrete people of God. Jesus suffered on the cross alone but, in God's world, he cannot by any means effect the pastoral redemption of the world alone. Disciples are a necessity.

History has already established the redemptive impact of the Jesus movement within the Roman Empire of the early centuries of this era. This can never be denied or reversed. History has also confirmed the strengths and the weaknesses of the medieval church in maintaining the new feudal order which was gradually created out of the chaos of the barbarian invasions. In this Christian society, the threat of hell fire loomed large as the effective restraint that pious Christians held out before those who believed "might is right." The hope of heaven, meanwhile, brought a necessary restraint and patience to those who suffered unjustly at the hands of sinners. With the dawn of the Enlightenment, purely secular movements emerged which sought to ameliorate the social order on the basis of humanitarian instincts alone. Some of these movements (notably the French Revolution and Marxism) took an anti-Christian stance because the Christians of the day opposed these prophetic innovations in the name of God. I would judge, however, that the humanitarian instincts undergirding such godless innovations were partially imbued with the secularization of Christianity during the middle ages. Following the Enlightenment, therefore, it is quite possible that secular movements have, in some instances, done more to promote the Kingdom of God than those who called out, "Lord, Lord," and failed to bear the fruit of God's Spirit.

The Christian churches must be careful not to rely upon false guarantees. Just because Jesus is honored as Lord or because members of the church have worked "miracles" does not mean that the Spirit of the living God imbues its members. Claims to possess the Spirit of God or to have infallible leaders is a small consolation when the fruits of messianic holiness are not empirically evident. Nor does the evident fruit of one historic moment automatically spell out fidelity to grace in every subsequent moment. As far as humans are concerned, an invisible and unnoticed sanctity is no sanctity at all.

> A field that has been well watered by frequent rain, and gives the crops that are wanted by the owners who grew them, is given God's blessing; but one that grows brambles and thistles is abandoned, and practically cursed. It will end up by being burnt (Heb 6:7-8).

Either the Christian church (or churches) will become an acknowledged source of light and of truth for all people seeking the Kingdom of God or it will be passed over and left to die in the obscurity of history.

No authentic church can imagine itself as a community of saints without effectively presenting in practice God's sympathy for the universal human plight. Schemes of salvation which are the private reserve of church members are illusory unless such schemes offer the blessings of God upon the broken human condition. Christians need to be acknowledged as "the light of the world" by outsiders. The mutual congratulations of a private club of salvation is suspect.

In the end, therefore, the Christian today has no escape. Either the Christian has found the power of God moving within his/her contemporary history and has harnessed his/her own personal powers with God's or the Christian is a stumbling block. No amount of personal orthodoxy, good works, or mystical experiences can shield a Christian from taking his/her place as a herald for God's Future. Hanging on to the past and burying oneself within it, for whatever pious motive, is to court the judgment of the steward who buries his talent in the field.

The Christian community is that group which is empowered to rightly discern God's Cause within their contemporary world and to heal the demonic hindrances which obstruct individuals and societies from attaining the blessedness that God's Future holds for them. This discernment and the power to heal do not arrive as the innate gifts of Christians -- they must work for them through the strenuous efforts of sustained apprenticeships under masters who are the living saints/prophets of the church assembly to which one belongs. In the secular spheres, one can sometimes be condemned to mediocrity because one never has the opportunity for an adequate apprenticeship in art, music, carpentry, gardening, automechanics, parenting, finances. In the religious sphere, the same principle applies with even a greater urgency.

Conclusion

I have selected the foregoing considerations so as to illustrate how I would apply the general framework of Chapters VII and VIII to concrete usage within the church. My readers will undoubtedly envision further applications which are peculiar to their own experiences and special concerns. This is as it should be.

All in all, the apprenticeship mentality endeavors to close the gap between the rhetoric of redemption and its concrete implementation. All too often one hears claims being made of the efficacy of private prayer or of religious rites that appear, even to committed Christians, as entirely inflated and out of touch with actual practice. Baptism, for instance, is frequently spoken of as effecting a spiritual rebirth -- the broken, sinful existence of the candidate is said to die and the faith and holiness of Jesus Christ takes its place. In part, this rhetoric surrounding baptism is legitimately derived from biblical tradition. On the other hand, however, the early centuries of Christianity spoke as they did because of the abundant experiential confirmations of their claims. Each

Easter, adults were brought forward who were recognized as former pagans whose lives once initiated the gods whom they served. Now, however, their habitual conduct demonstrated that their personal identities were modeled after Jesus Christ. In this atmosphere, there was little gap between the efficacy of the baptismal rites and their concrete implementation. In a later era, when infant baptism became the common practice, the entire rhetoric of a former era was maintained even though the baptized infants gave no immediate signs of the sacrament's efficacy. As a result, Christians have been seduced into imagining that the traditional claims surrounding baptism are largely invisible, spiritual, and due to God's initiative alone. It is not surprising, accordingly, that committed Christians have periodically attempted either to reduce the inflated claims attached to infant baptism or to suppress infant baptism entirely so that adult conversion would again become the normative experience manifest within the rites of baptism.

The entire future of Western civilization rests upon the ability of Christians to be able to distinguish the placebo from the effective remedy -- to distinguish what God does without us from what God will do only with our cooperation. When Christians are muddled and confused on these points, they cannot competently guide their own spiritual growth nor contribute to the renewal of their religious tradition. For the undiscerning, everything seems equally important and the redemption of the world lies in an indiscriminate call for "more religion." It is my fond hope that the readers of this book will have acquired a clarification of their own powers of discernment so that they will know what to discard, what to change, and what to introduce. Far from calling for "more religion," they will insist upon "better religion."

God sent his/her only Son into the world so as to show us the pattern of divine redemption. Unlike the godmother of the Cinderella fable, Jesus did not offer us any magic wand or magic words whereby we might effortlessly and instantaneously become what God intends us to be. Rather, Jesus demonstrated in his practice that his disciples could become healers and transformers of persons through the longer, surer mode of apprenticing. There is less glamor here. There is pain and sweat and occasional failure. But this is the stuff out of which God's redemption takes place. This is the ground of our profoundest hopes. A small messianic band goes on to transform the character and instincts of Western culture. For those who have eyes to see, this is the ongoing miracle of redemption. God's future among his people is secure.

Our task is to courageously and wisely continue what our forebears have so rightly begun.

May God, the great Dreamer and Doer, be praised for raising us up as dreamers and doers in the footsteps of his/her beloved Son.

Footnotes for Chapter X

¹ A summary of the research of Karlis Osis and Erlunder Haraldsson was provided by Daniel Goleman, "Back From the Brink," Psychology Today 10 (1977) 58.

² Brother Francesco Maria Guazzi, Compendium Maleficarum (Secaucus, N.J.: University Books, 1974; orig. pub. in 1608) II, 16 (p. 146).

³ Janis Joplin, "Mercedes Benz."

⁴ The Fathers of the Church did not hesitate to compare and contrast their sacred rites with those of "the ancient church" (Israel). Furthermore, the Fathers were aware that they had borrowed many sane and efficacious practices from the then-existing religions of their day. This served both to enhance the efficacy of the Christian rites and to provide an experiential bridge for pagans who were being transformed within the Christian rites of adult initiation. The medieval theologians continued to speak of the sacraments of the Old Law as prefiguring the Sacraments of the New Law. The age of exploration and colonization called a halt to this practice. Missionaries condemned foreign rites as "pagan" and completely replaced them by Catholic rites. Only in the last half-century have Christians again taken an active interest in non-Christian religious rites as a point of departure for a wiser evangelization and for a better appreciating their own rites. Studies in cultural anthropology, consequently, are frequently cited and upheld. A noteworthy example of this is Joseph Martos' Doors to the Sacred: A Historical Introduction to Sacraments in the Catholic Church (Garden City: Doubleday, 1981).

⁵ George S. Worgul, in From Magic to Metaphor (N.Y.: Paulist, 1980), provides an excellent historical and theological analysis of the modes of efficacy rightly and wrongly attributed to the Christian Sacraments. See also Karl Rahner, "Considerations on the Active Role of the Person in the Sacramental Event," Theological Investigations (N.Y.: Seabury, 1976) XIII, 161-184. Within this article Rahner refers to the sacramental efficacy of the world as well as the secular efficacy of the Sacraments. In so doing, Rahner takes a position which partially harmonizes with my own.

⁶Adelaide Bry, est (N.Y.: Harper & Row, 1976), p. 115. For a description and analysis of est, see Mark

Brewer, "We're Gonna Tear You Down and Put You Back Together," Psychology Today 9,3 (August, 1975) 35-40, 82-89.

[7] Ibid., p. 64.

[8] The subsidiary influence of the Spirit within a given rite is both (a) remote and (b) immediate. The Eucharistic liturgy, for instance, is the product of a long historical development. Each age was divinely inspired to modify and enhance what had been passed down so that the ritual would more capably express and impress upon the worshippers the Spirit of their God. Every Eucharistic liturgy, consequently, represents the cumulative presence of God historically fashioning the rite. The same cumulative factor can be noted within the interiority of each person who habitually submits to the repeated rite. Just as every new celebration of Christmas brings with it the subliminal presence of every past Christmas experience, so, too, every new celebration of the Eucharist is charged with the cumulative richness of the person's past Eucharistic experiences.

From this vantage point, it can now be noted that the immediate influence of the Spirit of God during the Eucharist may be quite small compared to the cumulative remote causality that is artfully and uncontrollably released during the rite. This remote activity of the Spirit is exhibited not only in the long, historical presence of the Spirit in the formation of the rite but in the series of past immediate experiences of Eucharist which are subliminally operative in contributing to the worshippers present experience.

In particular cases, it must accordingly be acknowledged that the Eucharist might evoke unpleasant and/or destructive influence. For example, consider the case of the boy of ten who is repeatedly regimented by his father into "correct postures" during the entire span of the Eucharist. Such a child develops a cumulative distaste for the Eucharist. Time and grace will have to soften this cumulative experience before anything of the true character of the Eucharist will be available to this young boy.

The historical development of the Eucharistic liturgy can likewise, in particular cases, be partially influenced by destructive influences which are masquerading as divine influences. Every age, therefore, must be discerning and take the necessary steps to purify its rites so that they express and impress upon the worshippers the true Spirit of messianic holiness. Such discernment is principally the responsibility of the hierarchical and charismatic leaders of the community.

XI

Jesus as the One Fashioned and Apprenticed by God

Within the foregoing chapters, I used the Gospel of Matthew in order to examine Jesus' relationship to his disciples. It became clear that Jesus himself was passionately consumed with the forthcoming Kingdom of God and its standards of righteousness. Jesus did not perceive his calling as exclusively his own; he undertook to train disciples who would share his mission received from the Father. To effect this, Jesus had to rectify and enhance the religious sensibilities of his disciples. The Gospel of Matthew never suggests that this process is effortless or instantaneous. On the contrary, Matthew offers clues which indicate that Jesus must painstakingly and progressively enlarge the personal powers of his disciples such that, in the end, they can accomplish on their own those feats which Jesus exemplified in his own ministry.

Against this background, the question naturally arises as to how Jesus himself was empowered by God. Are we to presume that this empowering is instantaneous and effortless? Or, on the contrary, are we to presume that Jesus is subject to the selfsame divine-human dynamics whereby every human person first learns to perceive God and then, at a later phase, goes on to make fresh discoveries of the living God?

The medieval orthodox tradition has overwhelmingly favored the first response. In so far as Jesus was the incarnation of the Son of God, it seemed fitting to presume that his divinity instantaneously and effortlessly empowered him with his mature powers from the first moment of his conception. The classical rule was that "an agent of infinite power can dispose matter instantaneously to its due form" (ST III, 33, 1, co). Of late, however, even advocates of the classical medieval tradition have been wondering whether such an emphasis on Jesus' divinity does not either erode or bypass a correct honoring of Jesus' human dynamics.[1] After all, the orthodox Fathers of the church described the historical Jesus as "of one substance with the Father (homoousion to patri) as regards his Godhead" and "at the same time of one substance with us (homoousion hemin) as regards his manhood; like us in all respects apart from sin" (DS 148).

In recognition of Jesus' substantial unity with us, the medieval theologians occasionally demonstrated restraint in painting Jesus as the paragon of perfection. Consider, for instance, how Thomas Aquinas respected the texts of the New Testament and the incarnational theology of the Fathers in arguing that the Son of God deliberately assumed a body subject to human infirmities and defects:

> It was fitting for the body assumed by the Son of God to be subject to human infirmities and defects for three reasons:
>
> (1) because it was in order to satisfy for the sin of the human race that the Son of God, having taken flesh, came into the world. Now one satisfies for another's sin by taking on himself the punishment due to the sin of the other . . . .
>
> (2) in order to cause belief in the Incarnation. For since human nature is known to men [women] only as it is subject to these defects, if the Son of God had assumed human nature without these defects, he would not have seemed to be a true [hu]man . . . .
>
> (3) in order to show us an example of patience by valiantly bearing up against human passibility and defects (ST III, 14, 1, co).

At another point, Thomas puts forward a principle of limitations which applies even to the miracles of Christ:

> What the divine power achieved in Christ was in proportion to the needs of the salvation of [hu]mankind, the achievement of which was the purpose of his [the Logos's] taking flesh. Consequently he so worked miracles by the divine power as not to prejudice

our belief in the reality of his flesh
(ST III, 43, 3, ad 2).²

Encouraged by this classical restraint, I am prompted to explore how I might imagine Jesus as being empowered by the Father if he indeed was subject to the selfsame human dynamics within which all of us are constrained. In so doing, I would not only hope to offset the current tendency to submerge Jesus' human powers within his divinity as the Logos, but I would hope to show that Jesus himself exemplifies the way to salvation to which we too are called. Furthermore, I would hope to establish that the human dynamics of apprenticeship and of discovery are so divinely established and so supremely reliable that they in themselves suffice to account for Jesus' place as "the eldest of many brothers [sisters]" (Rom 8:29) and as "the pioneer (archegos) of salvation" (Heb 2:10). Thus, rather than presenting Jesus as the supreme exception to the divine-human dynamics which undergird our salvation, Jesus himself would be perceived as the guarantee that the Logos reaches us within the selfsame patterns in which Jesus himself was met and transformed as the "compassionate and trustworthy high priest of God's religion" (Heb 2:17).

The aim of this chapter must be quite modest. I cannot hope to address all the issues surrounding a full blown Christology.³ I shall content myself with examining two issues:

A. How the Logos fashioned the organic identity of the Messiah
B. How the Logos apprenticed the spiritual identity of the Messiah

In examining both of these issues, I will begin with the classical Logos doctrine of the Fathers of the Church. I will modify and enlarge their perspective at those points where modern biblical research and our contemporary anthropology/cosmology require us to speak and to think differently so as to retain our modernity and respect their original intent.

A.   How the Logos Fashioned the Organic Identity of the Messiah

         Before going on to specify the "how" of the Incarnation, I have to briefly clarify the identity of the Logos among the Fathers of the Church. Ontologically speaking, the Logos is "the only-begotten Son of God, born of the Father before all time" (DS 86). Functionally speaking, the Logos is the Grand Master of the cosmic unfolding: "through him/her all things were made" (DS 86).[4] Creation, consequently, is from the Father through the Son. What amazed the Fathers of the Church was not so much the past origins of the cosmos as the present unity and harmony that was so evident among the diverse elements of creation. Consider, for instance, how the Logos changes the seasons in an orderly pattern.[5] As fall turns into winter, the Logos sends strong winds and frosty rains over the land to scatter the mature seeds and bury them, there to abide in their long sleep before being awakened by the gentle, warm rains of spring. Meanwhile, the pond, covered by seeds, allows the fish to gorge themselves prior to the time when the Logos guides them to nestle deep into the mud which blankets the pond floor. The Logos keeps them safe there as winter ices over the surface of the pond. Meanwhile, the Logos instructs various animals to gather food and to store it in the earth; others the Logos instructs to gorge themselves as do the fish in order to prepare for their Logos-induced hibernation.[6] Birds are so fashioned that they can flee south. The gentle persuasion of the Logos prompts them as to when, in what direction, and how far to conduct their annual migration. All in all, it can be said that the Fathers clearly perceived the Logos as the dynamic and ever-present reality that guided all the individual elements of the cosmos into a unity and harmony of becoming. St. Athanasius (d. 373) liked to compare the cosmic harmony to that of a symphonic choir under the direction of the Logos:

> The chorus is composed of different men, children, women, old people and youths. There is one leader [the Logos], and when he [she] conducts each one sings according to his own nature and ability, the man as a man, the child as a child, the old man as an old man, and the youth as a youth, but they all produce a single harmony.[7]

Now it is this Logos, the Master Conductor of the cosmic symphony, who, "in the days of King Herod of Judea" (Luke 1:5, Matt 2:1), "was made flesh and pitched his tent among us" (John 1:14 literally translated).

How did the Logos take on human nature? Some Christians in the early church imagined that the Logos seized the man Jesus by a kind of holy "possession." Just as demonic spirits were represented as entering in and dominating humans, so, too, the Holy Spirit could accomplish the same thing for the work of God. The orthodox Fathers of the church flinched at this representation for it presents the Logos as functioning coercively in a flesh that is supposedly resistant to the influence of Logos. Quite to the contrary, the Fathers perceived that the Logos is the hidden designer and the constant companion to everything and every person that has come to be. The Logos, consequently, has no need to seize upon Jesus as though he existed in a foreign realm -- the Logos already possesses all creation in the palm of his/her hand, Jesus included.

Still other Christians imagined that the Logos took on flesh in the way that the heavenly angels took on human form when they appeared to Abraham at the Oak of Mamre (Gen 18). This presentation had a strong appeal to Hellenized Christians in the second century for it allowed the Lord of Creation to enter into human affairs without actually being burdened with the "crudities" of the flesh (defecating, sex, passion). The orthodox Fathers of the church, however, objected to this presentation on the grounds that the very Lord of Creation made our bodies "good" and had every intention to redeem both body and soul together. Irenaeus, for example, argued that the Eucharist nourishes and sanctifies our bodies even before it purifies our souls.[8] Furthermore, the Sacred Scriptures assured the Fathers that Jesus entered into life and exited therefrom in the normative human mode. Hence, just as we are conceived in our mother's womb and born into the world, so, too, the earliest creed spoke of Jesus being "<u>conceived</u> by the Holy Spirit and <u>born</u> of the virgin Mary" (DS 6). And just as we will depart from this world when our bodies can no longer sustain our spirits; so, too, Jesus was spoken of as the kind that "<u>suffered</u> under Pontious Pilate, was crucified, <u>died</u>, and was buried" (DS 6).

Following this cue, Irenaeus (d. 202) was fond of explaining the Incarnation as employing the selfsame mode that had originally been employed by the Logos in the formation of Adam:

> From where does the substance of the first man come? From God's Will and Wisdom [Logos], and from the virgin earth. Scripture says, "God had not sent rain on the earth, nor was there any man to till the soil" (Gen 2:5). From this earth, then, while it was still virgin, God took dust and fashioned Adam, the beginning of humanity. So the Lord [Logos], summing up afresh [the formation of] this man, reproduced the scheme of his incarnation, being born of a virgin by God's Will and Wisdom that he might copy the incarnation of Adam, and man might be made, as was written in the beginning, "according to the image and likeness of God" (Gen 1:26).[9]

Irenaeus is instructive in so far as he parallels two incarnations: that of the first Adam and that of the second/final Adam. Virginity, in this scheme, does not have anything to do with anti-sexuality but specifies a fresh start. The anthropology throughout is consistent. Irenaeus has no fear that he detracts from Jesus by explaining how both he and Adam have common origins; rather, those who mistakingly taught that the Logos was too spiritual, too exalted, too divine to enter into the realm of the flesh -- these were the ones who falsified the Good News of God.

How the Logos Fashions Each Human Organism

As anthropology changes, so too must our theological explanations change.[10] Today, in particular, modern Christians cannot instinctively feel that God fashioned Adam immediately and from scratch out of the soil of the earth. Our evolutionary horizon of understanding prompts us to assume that the first humans emerged gradually from the higher primates that preceded them. These primates, in their turn, emerged from roughly two billion years of a tortuous evolutionary assent. "Adam" and "Eve," consequently, participate in a causal pre-existence which stretches backward in time and place to the first microscopic forms of life that first emerged in sea water on our planet.

While many of our contemporaries regard the biological emergence of the human organism as the product of trial and error combined with an extraordinary amount of "good luck" in Nature, Christians acknowledge the Logos as "the hidden mechanism" responsible for the creative advance.[11]

> In the beginning was the Logos: the Logos was with God and the Logos was God. He was with God in the beginning. Through him all things came to be, not one thing had its being but through him. All that came to be had life in him . . . . (John 1:1-3).

Many Christians have even come to prefer the image of the Logos patiently guiding and transforming genetic mutations as a superior sign of the creative fidelity of God over the older image of a God who makes Adam immediately and from scratch.

Similar observations can be made relative to cosmology. Genesis, for example, depicts Elohim as directing the formation of a cosmos in which a flat earth is established under a huge protective astrodome ("vault/ firmament" Gen 1:6) which prevents the primal waters from invading the air space beneath it. We can allow our ancient forebears their own proper modes of understanding. We can even teach ourselves that they make sense: the sky does appear to meet the horizon on all sides and the rain which falls might be imagined to come from tiny holes in the astrodome. In the final analysis, however, our contemporary instincts inform us that the actual cosmos is quite otherwise. We can only hold Genesis as moving us to assent when we read into the text our contemporary image of the Logos creating from chaos our vast array of stars and planets moving within a magnificent gravitational nexus. The ancient perceptions are interesting as historic relics; our living faith, however, grips us within the anthropology and cosmology which is peculiarly our own. Accordingly, when I hear that God fashioned Adam out of the dust of the earth (Gen 2:7), this brings to mind the tortuous journey of two billion years of evolutionary development in which the Logos prepared the human organism.

Just as "Adam" had a long genetic pre-existence that traces itself back to the first specks of living matter, so, too, every human person born into the world has a genetic pre-existence that traces itself back to "Adam." Each new human being, therefore, is not created ex nihilo, an unmediated production of the divine Logos. Quite to the contrary, once the Logos had perfected the human organism within the two billion year drama of human creation, the Logos expected and depended upon sexual reproduction to pass on the cumulative achievement of the past. There is no embarrassment in acknowledging the DNA code as the master engineer which artfully guides the embryonic development of each new human person. Undoubtedly the Logos is subsidiarily present in this process also.[12] Most directly, however, it is the master engineer that is in charge. No Christian forgets, meanwhile, that it was the Logos who taught the master engineer everything that it knows. As such, the Logos is the Grand Master. The evolutionary journey is the long apprenticeship process whereby the DNA molecule progressively assimilated the divine wisdom of this Grand Master. It is only when we forget this that we have to again make believe that the Logos has to engineer each new person from scratch.

Now, if this is the program whereby the Logos creates every human person, this must necessarily be taken into account when it comes to understanding the Incarnation. For Jesus Christ to be "of one substance with us" must accordingly be translated as being completely and genuinely a product of the evolutionary process like everyone else.[13] This means, of course, that Jesus participates in a causal pre-existence that traces itself all the way back through David, through Abraham, through "Adam". It also means that Jesus passes through the same stages of embryonic development that are the hallmark of the DNA code in question. Even after birth, the Jesus-organism would be baffled and intrigued by the panorama of sights and tastes that were previously unknown in the womb. As in the case of other children, Jesus would take fright at the "disappearance" of his mother. His conceptuality and his sexuality, meanwhile, would take five to twelve years of further development before they emerged as effective powers. If these processes are the hallmarks of our humanity, then, following the thrust of the Church Fathers, it must be supposed that these selfsame processes characterized the Incarnation.

The Dogmatic Tradition

The moment that I begin to think this way, I am seemingly blocked by the doctrine of the virginal conception. How can Jesus take part in the genetic pool if one has to suppose that Jesus has no human father? Let us consider this for a moment.

Some contemporary Christians undoubtedly imagine that Jesus is divine in so far as he has a divine Father and Jesus is human in so far as he has a human mother. The orthodox Fathers would have cringed at this because it smacks of the old pagan myths whereby a god comes down from heaven to impregnate some human virgin on earth.[14]

Even aside from this erroneous conception, many contemporary Christians believe that Jesus received a genetic inheritance from Mary's ovum (given the absence of male seed). I recall having read an article which speculated that spontaneous fertilization (parthenogenesis) does sometimes occur. Meanwhile, scientists are currently persuaded that cloning is technically possible. The only problem with such speculation is that neither process would result in a female offspring (given the absence of the Y-chromosome). More fundamentally, however, the doctrine of the virginal conception was formulated against the background of the agricultural model of sexuality. According to this model, the male sows his seed (<u>sperma</u> in Greek, <u>semen</u> in Latin) in the female womb, which nourishes the seed as does a fertile field. In this case, a woman's "fertility" implied no genetic contribution to the offspring; the male seed alone carried the entire genetic inheritance. This model of sexuality was dominant until the late nineteenth century when the ovum was discovered. It would be absurd to image that the Fathers had "an advanced model of sexuality" in mind when they formulated the dogma of the virginal conception.

Knowing this, it would appear that the virginal conception requires us to suppose that the Logos bypassed both the sexual contribution of Joseph and Mary in favor of creating, from scratch, the fertilized ovum which was to become his/her humanity.[15] One might further suppose that this fertilized ovum was originated in Mary's womb at that time within her menstrual cycle when her womb was prepared for such an implantation. Otherwise, we should have to suppose that the Logos had to coerce or to modify Mary's organic integrity so as to prevent a spontaneous abortion.

At first sight, the miraculous implantation of a fertilized ovum seems attractive. Upon further reflection, however, it appears scandalous. The scandal is threefold: first, that the Grand Master should have patiently "apprenticed" the DNA code over two billion years of awe-inspiring genetic advancement and then, in the last moment, entirely set this aside in favor of implanting an extraterrestrial set of genes; second, that the Designer of human sexuality should have side-stepped his own gift of fertility to Mary and Joseph in the production of their Messiah; and, thirdly, that the Logos should have faked the genetic inheritance so as to make it appear as though he was son of Joseph, son of David, son of Abraham; whereas, in fact, he has no terrestrial pre-existence whatsoever.

The first two sources of scandal might be dismissed on the grounds that the Lord of Creation can do what he/she well pleases. Even so, a modern person might ask how the Logos can hope to produce, in the twinkling of an eye, a genetic endowment for Jesus that can even favorably compare to the product of two billion years of sustained attention by the selfsame Grand Master of creation. Sensitive persons might inquire whether the Logos does not mean to downgrade human sexuality and to meddle in the sex lives of others through his arranged implantation. The third scandal, however, would have been especially painful to anyone with Jewish instincts. "Did not YHWH betray his solemn promises to Abraham and to David?" they would inquire. YHWH said to Abraham, "All the nations of the earth shall bless themselves by your descendents, as a reward for your obedience" (Gen 22:18). Yet, YHWH bypassed the "seed of Abraham" in producing his Messiah. And, in parallel fashion, YHWH said to David, "I will preserve your offspring after you, a son of your own, and make his sovereignty secure . . . . His throne shall be established for ever" (1 Chr 17:11, 14). Yet YHWH bypassed the "seed of David" in producing his Messiah.

The medieval theologians endeavored to console Jewish disappointment by asserting that Jesus is a son of David and Abraham "through adoption". First-century Jewish Christians would not have been consoled by this strategem, however. There are no provisions in biblical or Talmudic law for adoption with the right of inheritance.[16] Even in the case where a child is raised by foster parents, the child always retained the rights of his/her father's tribe. Joseph's custody of Jesus can not suffice, therefore, to provide Jesus the rights of Davidic descent. In Jewish tradition, however, when paternity cannot be accurately established (as in the instances of rape), the husband may acknowledge the child as his own flesh. It is in this sense only, that Joseph takes Mary into his home and claims Jesus as his own flesh and blood (Matt 1:25). This solution resolves the third scandal, but, given the terms of the solution, it creates another. It can only be "strange" and "uncompassionate" to have the Logos violate Joseph's rights and to endanger the life of Mary all by way of introducing the Messiah into the world in a sexless manner.

The New Testament Evidence

Faced with these difficulties, we must ask whether the New Testament does indeed affirm that Jesus' origins are extraterrestrial? . . . whether Jesus has no earthly father? If it does, then I should find it necessary to live with that fact as an expression of God's incomprehensible ways and adjust my theologizing accordingly. An examination of the New Testament data, even by careful, orthodox scholars, however, convinces me that no conclusive "yes" or "no" can be given to these questions. Raymond Brown, for instance, who has discussed this question in his two books on the subject, comes to the following conclusion:

> In my book on the virginal conception, written before I did this commentary, I came to the conclusion that the <u>scientifically controllable</u> biblical evidence leaves the question of the historicity of the virginal conception unresolved. The resurvey of the evidence necessitated by the commentary leaves me even more convinced of that.[17]

This judgment is based, in part, upon the following difficulties: (1) There is no explicit reference to a virginal conception outside of the infancy narratives of Matthew and Luke.[18] (2) Matthew's infancy narratives have little similarity and even open contradictions with those of Luke.[19] (3) Finally, it cannot be certain which elements in the infancy narratives are theological dramatizations and which are historical testimonies.[20] This final difficulty applies to every other segment of the Gospels as well. At times this separation is relatively easy. Consider, for instance, a text of Matthew's Gospel that was examined in an earlier chapter: Jesus' "yielding up his spirit" (Matt 27:50) on the cross is undoubtedly historical testimony; the rending of the Temple veil which immediately follows (Matt 27:51), however, is undoubtedly theological dramatization -- Matthew presents the acute grief of the Father who rends his garment from top to bottom at the death of his innocent Son.

My own personal persuasion is that the narratives of the virginal conception are preminently theological dramatizations.[21] Consider Matthew's Gospel, for instance. In his first chapter, Matthew appears to present two antithetical accounts of Jesus' origins. On the one hand, Jesus is genetically and spiritually linked to a chain of ancestors tracing itself back to David and to Abraham (Matt 1:1-17). On the other hand, Jesus is entirely "begotten by the Holy Spirit" independent of all human fatherhood (Matt 1:18-25). The first account envisions Jesus as having "many fathers"; the second account presents Jesus as entirely "fatherless." The first account (taken by itself) presumes that Joseph is the actual father of Jesus; the second account (taken by itself) excludes human paternity without embracing the slightest suggestion that the Holy Spirit is to be considered as "father" of Jesus.22 The first account sexually and culturally links Jesus to the "inherited blessings" associated with the "seed of Abraham" (Gen 12:2-3, 18:18-19, 22:17-18, 26:4 as acknowledged by Gal 3:16) and with the "seed of David" (2 Sam 7:12-17; Ps 89:3-45; 1 Chr 17:12-13, 22:9-10 as acknowledged by Acts 2:30). The second account determines that what Jesus will in fact become is due to the creative Spirit that fashions him as a new creation with a unique identity that sets him off from all the other sons of David. What appears to me as most decisive is that Matthew needs to affirm <u>both</u> accounts of Jesus' origins. On the one hand, God has pledged to produce the Messiah from the seed of David (and so it is accomplished). On the other hand, flesh and blood are incapable of producing the Messiah -- God's Spirit alone can create such a marvel.

John A.T. Robinson summarizes his own studies relative to the dual origins of the Messiah in the following terms:

> To us these two stories -- the geneology traced through Joseph and the virgin birth supposing no human father -- seem contradictory, just as Genesis and Darwin did a hundred years ago. But here as there we can now see that they are making statements at very different levels -- statements that can supplement each other rather than cancel each other out. The purpose of the virgin birth story is not to make a negative statement about the flesh (thus making nonsense of the geneologies) but to make a positive statement about the spirit. It is not concerned with gynecology any more then Genesis is concerned with geology.23

This conclusion does not represent the current scholarly consensus. The research and exchange continue. If the studies of Raymond Brown are an indicator, it appears as though the issue cannot be decided solely on the basis of the New Testament texts. Broader theological and pastoral considerations will dictate the final choice. I will content myself here to merely note that assertion of the virginal conception as a biological fact has served both to safeguard and to undercut a correct estimation of who Jesus is. Those who insist upon the historicity of the virginal conception must also take into account its pastoral difficulties (some of which have already been mentioned above). Those who favor the virginal conception as a theological dramatization are likewise obliged to safeguard a correct estimation of Jesus. On the pastoral level for instance, many persons wrongly believe that a sexual generation for Jesus would cancel out his divinity and negate the holiness of both Jesus and his parents.[24] In sum, therefore, both sides of this thorny issue have pastoral repercussions that must be taken into account.

John's Gospel repeatedly makes reference to Jesus as the one "who comes from heaven/God/above" (John 3:2, 13, 17, 19, 31; 4:34; 5:23, 24, 37, 38, 44; etc.). Many may be tempted to take this metaphorical language of John as attesting to the extraterrestrial origins of Jesus. Here the theologians of the church are of one accord in denying that the humanity of Jesus was ever "in heaven" before it emerged in the womb of the Virgin. Thomas Aquinas summarizes the tradition thusly:

> Christ is said to have come down from heaven in two ways: (1) as regards his divine nature, not indeed that the divine nature ceased to be in heaven, but inasmuch as he [as Logos] began to be here below in a new way . . . ; (2) as regards his body, not indeed that the very substance of the body of Christ descended from heaven, but that his body was formed by a heavenly power . . . . (ST III, 5, 3, ad 1).

A Tentative Resolution

Even if one imagines that the genetic inheritance of Jesus was created from scratch by the Logos, this still allows one to affirm an embryonic development that is quite like our own. The fact that the church calandar allows a full nine months from the Annunciation/conception to Christmas attests to the belief that the vital parts of Jesus emerged progressively.[25] This means, of course, that for some time there was no heartbeat, no limbs, no consciousness. The Fathers of the church favored this understanding; they allowed that the flesh of the Logos would be initially unformed and unknowing. This was all part of what it meant to reach us as we are and where we are. Deficiencies, consequently, were taken for granted.

Did Jesus ever have the mentality of a child? Did he hear strange sounds that frightened him? Did the very speech of his parents ever strike his ears as just a string of noises? Did he have to learn to focus his eyes? . . . to recognize the face of his mother? Did he have to learn to count? . . . to wash his face? Did he take time and years before he was able to think conceptually? . . . to add numbers? . . . to know that YHWH was real even though he/she could never be seen? Did Jesus learn by making mistakes: touching a hot poker, cutting a board too short, hurting a playmate in a game? Did Jesus feel sleepy at times? Lazy? Angry? Was Jesus ever confused? Unsure of himself? Overconfident?

Questions such as these test one to see what degree of reality one allows the organism of the Messiah. Hebrews puts it this way:

> For it was not the angels that he took to himself; he took to himself descent from Abraham [literally, "the seed of Abraham"]. It was essential that he should in this way become completely like his brothers [sisters] so that he could be a compassionate and trustworthy high priest . . . (Heb 2:16-17).

Irenaeus, whom we have already cited as insisting upon a parallel formation for the first and second Adam, taught that Jesus had to pass through the various developmental stages by way of demonstrating that deification/sanctification is appropriate to every period of life:

> Thus he [the incarnate Logos] passes through every age: having become an infant among the infants, he sanctifies the infants; as a little child among little children, he sanctifies those who are of that age . . . ; as a youth among youths, he becomes an example to youth, and sanctifies them in the Lord . . . .[26]

Athanasius (d. 373), in his day, found it natural to put forward the general principle: "The Logos bore the infirmities of the flesh as his own."[27] This meant, among other things, that the Lord of All had to accustom him/herself to the modes of human thought expressed in human language:

> Because of our need, the Logos, though being Creator, endured words which are used by creatures and which are not proper to him [her], as being the Logos . . . . Thus, when for our needs he became [hu]man, he consistently used language as we ourselves do.[28]

This theme, "because of our need," meant that the Logos embraced the human condition as it was -- broken by sin and ignorance. Thus, unlike the medieval theologians, Athanasius had no inclination to imagine that Jesus had somehow embraced a presanctified or idealized flesh:[29]

> Ignorance is proper to humans . . . . Since he [the Logos] was made human, he is not ashamed, because of the flesh which is ignorant, to say, "I know not," that he may show, although knowing [everything] as God, he is but ignorant according to the flesh.
>
> By receiving our infirmities, he is said to be infirm . . . . He became sin for us and a curse, not as though he sinned himself, but because he himself bore our sins and our curse.[30]

This is precisely what Paul had in mind when he said quite flatly:

> God dealt with sin by sending his own Son in a body as physical as any sinful body (Rom 8:3).

Already in the second century, certain oral and written traditions were in circulation which attempted to honor Jesus by lifting him out of the human situation. For instance, there is the story of how the boy-Jesus made twelve sparrows out of clay on the sabbath.[31] Later, in order to escape the correction of "his father Joseph," he clapped his hands and sent the twelve sparrows away in flight. On another occasion, the boy-Jesus changes his playmates into goats and back again.[32] The boy-Jesus, in another story, is a clairvoyant who informs his mother that her cousin, Elizabeth, has just died. Mary wishes to visit her for the last time. Jesus calls down a luminous cloud which serves as a magic carpet and takes them there within an hour.[33] All in all, about eighty such stories have come down to us. There may have been many more had not the orthodox Fathers condemned such narratives as either dogmatically false or as exhibiting bad taste. In any case, such narratives are indicators of the direction that the free religious imagination is inclined to take. Our own contemporary fascination for the lone hero/heroine (as in "Walking Tall," "Raiders of the Lost Ark," "My Brilliant Career," Clint Eastwood's Westerns) demonstrates that, even today, we are instinctively tempted to include our Jesus-fantasies in the same pattern. We, too, are hungry for a Jesus who dazzles us, who does it all for us. It is quite threatening to imagine Jesus as the one who reaches down and draws us to our feet and sets about empowering us to do everything that he does -- and more.

Some theologians have tried to use an evolutionary perspective by way of demonstrating the innate superiority of Jesus. In doing this, however, they have mistakenly made Jesus into a "Superman." Consider, for instance, the line of argumentation put forward by Fr. A. Hulsbosch of the University of Nijmegen:

> The fact that Jesus speaks of God in a higher and different way than other men [women] has its basis in the fact that he is [hu]man in a higher and different way . . . .
>
> When I say that Jesus, in his human consciousness, has an experience of God which is different from other men [women], I am saying at the same time that he differs essentially from other men [women]. In him a new creation takes place: his appearance is as new and different with respect to humanity as the appearance of the first man [woman] was new with respect to the animals who preceded him.[34]

Hulsbosch insists that Jesus emerges from the genetic pool; yet, he likewise insists that he constitutes an evolutionary advance which transcends our humanity. Thus, I find that he effectively undercuts the essential ground whereby Jesus is presented as apprenticing his disciples. The comic book character, Superman, can awe us and deliver us from evil, but he cannot hope to apprentice earthlings to share in his ministry to humankind. Thus, it seems futile to try to imagine that Jesus' uniqueness stands upon his being organically superior: more intelligent, more sympathetic, more creative, stronger, faster.[35] The New Testament writers give not the slightest hint to support this; rather, his uniqueness is centered in his relationship to the Father. It is accordingly to this "religious superiority" that we must now turn our attention.

B. How the Logos Apprenticed the Spiritual Identity of the Messiah

How does the Christian discover God's cause and harness his/her power thereto? Here the response of our tradition is uniform and clear: follow Jesus and his Saints.[36] This following of Jesus, however, is legitimated only in so far as Jesus himself follows God. Accordingly, the task of this section is to explore in what sense and how the humanity of the Logos discovers God's cause and harnesses his powers thereto.

In the Synoptic Gospels, Jesus is recommended to us by the heavenly Father saying, "This is my Son, the Beloved; he enjoys my favor. Listen to him" (Matt 16:5 and parallels). The stunning image here is that of a father who assures us that his son is so much like himself that he can reliably speak for him on every occasion. Not all sons turn out to be so recommended by their fathers. Jesus, however, is a spitting "image" of his father -- a divine chip off the eternal block. Jesus, accordingly, does not hesitate to use this selfsame paradigm by way of legitimating his disciples' confidence in him:

> Everything has been entrusted to me by my Father; and no one knows a son except a father, just as no one knows a father except a son and those to whom a son chooses to reveal him (Matt 11:27, an alternate translation).

Like father, like son. Thus it appears as though Jesus' metaphysical sonship is, in the first instance, exemplified through the expectation that a son of Israel would grow up to be like his Father and that Jesus fulfilled this expectation profoundly.[37]

> If anyone wants to boast, let him boast in this: of understanding and knowing me [YHWH] (Jer 9:23).

In the Gospel according to St. John, the Father is repeatedly spoken of as being inaccessible and unknowable unless he reveals himself through the one "who comes from God/heaven/above" (John 3:2, 13, 17, 19, 27, 31; 4:34; 5:23, 24, 37, 38, 44; etc.):[38]

> No one has ever seen God; it is the
> only Son, who is nearest to the
> Father's heart, who has made him known
> (John 1:18).

At one point, John depicts Jesus as surrounded by inquiring Jews in the Temple and declaring, "The Father and I are one" (John 10:30). The Jews are scandalized: "You are only a man and you claim to be god" (John 10:33). Then Jesus explains that the Torah itself calls those who have received the knowledge of YHWH "gods" and that he is thereby entitled to be called "Son of God" by virtue of the fact that he is "doing my Father's work" (John 10:37, 38). The unity between Father and Son, consequently, is again and again being exemplified as sharing the selfsame dispositions, concerns, and activities. In this unity, Jesus is presented functionally as having become everything that he is by virtue of his training received from his Father:

> The Son can do nothing by himself; he
> can only do what he sees the Father
> doing: and whatever the Father does
> the Son does too. For the Father loves
> the Son and shows him everything he
> does himself . . . (John 5:19-20).

> I can do nothing by myself; I can only
> judge as I am told to judge (John 5:30).

> It is my Father who gives you the bread
> from heaven, the true bread [=Torah];
> for the bread of God is that which
> comes down from heaven and gives life
> to the world . . . . I am the bread of
> life . . . . To hear the teaching of
> the Father, and learn from it, is to
> come to me [and eat my flesh] (John
> 6:32, 33, 35, 45).

The imagery of bread and feeding is very strongly associated with the training that YHWH gave his children in the desert (Deut 8:3-6). Matthew and Luke use this same theme by way of asserting that, when Jesus is tempted to create his own bread/torah, he stops cold and insists that God's Torah should alone be his food (Matt 4:1-4, Luke 4:1-4).

> As I, who am sent by the living Father,
> myself draw life from the Father, so
> whoever eats me will draw life from me

> [just as I have eaten and drawn life from the Father] (John 6:57).
>
> The one who sent me is truthful, and what I have learnt from him I declare to the world . . . . What the Father has taught me is what I preach . . . . (John 8:26, 28).
>
> What I, for my part, speak of is what I have seen with my Father; but you [unbelieving Jews], you put into action the lessons learnt from your father [the devil] (John 8:38).

In this last citation, the theme "like father, like son" is applied to the case wherein the devil is one's father. All in all, John's Gospel makes it abundantly clear that Jesus' reliability for our imitation is based entirely on Jesus' own prior apprenticeship to God. Clement of Alexandria caught this exactly and succinctly when he wrote to the Greeks:

> The Logos of God has become human so that you might learn from a human how a human may become god/God.[39]

What all this establishes is that Jesus' superiority does not reside in his ability to leap tall buildings or to have fewer cavities. His superiority lies primordially in his ability to reveal to his disciples the divine pathos and to transform their own sensibilities such that they too can be one with their Father. Thus, near the end of Jesus' training of his disciples, John can have him say, "I have given them the glory you [Father] gave to me, that they may be one as we are one" (John 17:22).

The question naturally occurs as to how Jesus himself was apprenticed by his Father in heaven. The previous chapters of this book have already spelled out the processes whereby Jesus corrects and enlarges the innate sensibilities of his disciples such that they harmonize with his own. It remains to be told how Jesus himself is trained by God. The previous section of this chapter spelled out how it is that the Logos fashioned the organism of the Messiah. It remains to consider how the Logos fashioned the interiority (the "soul") of the Messiah. To this we must now turn our attention. In order to do so effectively, however, I must first consider in what sense the Logos fashions the interiority of every human being that enters the world.

How the Logos Apprentices Each Human Interiority

Our genetic inheritance makes us potentially human; it is our cultural inheritance which specifically fashions the humanity of our interiority (our "spirit" or "soul").[40] Organically our primitive ancestors were constituted much like ourselves; their cultural inheritance, however, was severely impoverished. Within the last thousand generations of human development, genetic advances have leveled off; yet, in this same period, cultural mutations and evolutionary development have been rampant. Cultural evolution presupposes a linguistic code which is the metaphorical counterpart of the genetic code. Animals do learn from their experience and are taught successful modes of acting and feeling by their parents. This cultural tradition, however, scarcely shows any cumulative gain from generation to generation. In contrast, language learning allows humans to transmit rapidly and easily an enormously sophisticated cultural tradition. Every creative thought and action in each human's life is a veritable mutation. Even after the event, the human easily remembers, repeats, and communicates his/her successful mutation to those in his/her tribe or clan. One's cultural inheritance can be advanced, consequently, without waiting for the sexual transmission of inherited characteristics. Language also breaks the animal dependency upon immediacy. Human imagination allows one to create possible futures. Such possibilities enter into the social sphere when personal dreams are shared and formally adapted by the family or the tribe. In this way not only the past of successful innovations but the future of relevant possibilities go on to transform and enlarge both the private and the collective spirit of a tribe or nation. Through such like processes, one's cultural inheritance is transformed. Genetic evolution appears to be static and uninteresting in comparison with cultural evolution.

Being born of human parents provides us with a human organism; our "interiority," however, has a long way to go before it is distinctly "human." The feats performed by a human infant are only marginally different from those performed by an infant monkey of the same age. A Mr. and Mrs. Kellogg tested this proposition by adopting an infant monkey to become a companion to their child, Donald.

> During the following nine months the two infants were brought up exactly the same way and their development was recorded by identical texts. A graph comparing the number of successful

> intelligence tests passed by them showed a striking parallelism in the development of the two . . . . At the age of 15 to 18 months the mental development of the chimpanzee is nearing completion; that of the child is only about to start. By responding to people who talk to it, the child soon begins to understand speech and to speak itself. By this one single trick in which it surpasses the animal, the child acquires the capacity for sustained thought and enters on the whole cultural heritage of its ancestors.[41]

This being the case, it is no wonder that human infants who are deprived of human contact for prolonged periods turn out to be brutish and animal-like in their behavior even though they have human form and human capabilities. In sum, therefore, one does not become human simply in virtue of one's birth; the qualities of spirit which characterize humans are only gradually assimilated through prolonged human contacts with one's parents and guardians.

Having recognized this, it hardly suffices to affirm that the Logos fashions the human organism and then to presume that cultural evolution is purely a matter of chance innovations followed by free consensus. Quite to the contrary, Christians will naturally want to affirm that the Logos exerts a persuasive influence guiding cultural mutations[42] as the fitting counterpart to the causal determination which the Logos exerts relative to genetic mutations. The Fathers identified the Logos as the Grand Master who "apprenticed" the prophets and seers of each generation.[43] Some divine illumination was required for every discovery of truth -- be it secular or religious.[44] With sober universality: "The Logos was the true light that enlightens all men [women]" (John 1:9).

Now, if this is the program whereby the Logos creates the interiority of every human person, this must necessarily be taken into account when it comes to understanding the Incarnation. For Jesus Christ to be "of one substance with us" must accordingly suggest that he was completely and genuinely dependent upon human interactions with his parents for obtaining his initial religious training. In effect, this means, that Jesus' initial religious sensibilities were acquired by virtue of his belonging to particular parents within a particularly rich cultural heritage -- that of the children of Abraham. As such, therefore, the Logos can be supposed to apprentice his/her humanity in the ways of the Father indirectly, i.e., by imparting to him the cumulative training that Israel has received from God through the patriarchs, the kings, the prophets, down to Mary and Joseph. It may be supposed that Jesus' subsequent adult apprenticeships and his later fresh discoveries of God purified and enlarged this initial childhood acquisition; but it should not be supposed that such future experiences were either possible or desirable for Jesus without having first learned of God's ways on his mother's knee. Furthermore, whatever Jesus may mean by his "having been trained by his Father" need not be asserted in such a way as to undercut this human ground by which each and every human person is "apprenticed to the Logos."

The Dogmatic Tradition

The moment that I began to think this way, I am seemingly blocked by the long church tradition, stemming from medieval theology, whereby it was presumed that Jesus never had a human teacher -- he was in all things directly taught by God. To support this, Thomas Aquinas could identify no text of Scripture, but his keen mind detected a strong rational argument for his doctrine:

> That which is the first mover is not moved [by another] . . . . Now Christ is established by God as the Head of the church . . . that all might receive the doctrine of truth from him . . . and thus it did not benefit his dignity that he should be taught by any person (ST III, 12, 4, co).

Following from this, Thomas argued that the human intellect of Jesus received, from the first moment of his conception, an immediate, infused theoretical understanding of all things (ST III, 9, 3, co). It would follow from this that Jesus knew physics, astronomy, medicine, art without any human apprenticeships; he was taught by the Logos as are the angels. In going to such extremes, however, Thomas Aquinas never forgot that Jesus knew things in the human measure.[45] In other words, he did not wish to undercut the human limitations inherent within Jesus by virtue of his status as creature:

> The infinite is not comprehended by the finite . . . . Although the knowledge of the soul of Christ which he has in the Word [Logos] is equal to the knowledge of [the beatific] vision as

Jesus as the One Fashioned and Apprenticed by God   313

> regards the number of things known; nevertheless, the knowledge of God infinitely exceeds the knowledge of the soul of Christ in clearness of cognition . . . (ST III, 10, 1, co and 10, 2, ad 4).

Following through on this, Thomas also asserted that Jesus must also have some acquired knowledge:

> Although I wrote differently [in the past], it must be said that in Christ there was acquired knowledge, which is properly knowledge in the human fashion (ST III, 9, 4, co).

At first glance, this is puzzling, for Thomas does not indicate a single thing which Jesus learned. It appears that he is asserting this on principle: any operation which, in fact, is not used by Jesus must remain dormant and unperfected (ST III, 9, 1, & 12, 1). Thomas carefully notes that Jesus' active knowing powers allowed him to increase his knowledge exclusively by personal discovery -- never was he taught anything by anyone else but the Logos (ST III, 9, 4, ad 1).

Many current theologians find extreme difficulties with the Thomistic imagination. By way of insuring the reliability of the knowledge of Jesus, Jesus' participation within the nexus of life is severely endangered. How can Jesus, for instance, really experience what all of us remember as "growing up" if he knew everything in advance? Moreover, how can Jesus have entered into the day to day elements of surprise and of risk if he lived each day as though he were walking through a movie that he had seen a hundred times before. And, finally, how are we to suppose that Jesus consistently came across as an insignificant carpenter for thirty years? In this case, the real marvel is not that Jesus knew so much but that he managed to reveal so little. He supposedly had an exhaustive knowledge of carpentry (including the ability to produce pieces of furniture rivaling those of the court of Louis XIV); yet, he bracketed all this and, following the crudities of his day, remained an undistinguished carpenter. He supposedly had an exhaustive knowledge of the world's languages, both past and present and future; yet, here again we must suppose that he bracketed all this in favor of limiting himself to the Galilean dialect of Aramaic and the biblical Hebrew peculiar to his day. Jesus supposedly had a detailed knowledge of the Jewish patriarchs (e.g., what led Abraham to his initial conversion); yet, in point of fact, Jesus never distinguished himself either as a popular story teller or a biblical historian.

What is amazing in all this is how Jesus could live a normalized existence when, at every moment, he had to carefully suppress 99.44% of all he knew. The more straightforward explanation as to why Jesus habitually employed the peculiarities of language, of diet, of craftmanship, of politeness, and of religious understanding familiar to his contemporaries was that he indeed was <u>only</u> their contemporary. And one becomes a contemporary by having assimilated from one's parents their complete range of culturally and historically conditioned sensibilities and practices.

One could bypass the problems associated in intellectual overkill by assuming that the Logos directly imparted to Jesus only a historically and culturally conditioned religious understanding that would be sufficiently advanced but also relevant to Jews of his day. This miraculous implantation of religious experiences and judgments may seem attractive at first, but it also appears scandalous on the same grounds that our earlier consideration of a miraculous implantation appears scandalous. The scandal here is threefold: first, that the Grand Master should have patiently "apprenticed" the children of Abraham during two thousand years of progressive religious awakening and then, in the last moment, entirely set this aside in favor of fitting Jesus with a faked replica of the cumulative Jewish heritage; second, that the Designer of parent-child training should have side-stepped the prepared receptivity of the infant-Jesus and the parental competence of Joseph and Mary in producing the interiority of their Messiah; and, thirdly, that it would be expected that a Messiah so miraculously outfitted for his mission should be a Master in the art of apprenticing disciples by virtue of the fact that he had never participated in that art himself.

The first two sources of scandal might be dismissed on the grounds that the Lord of Creation can do what he/she well pleases. Mary and Joseph might even be able to get used to the idea that they have nothing to offer Jesus since he appears to know everthing they want to teach him (esp. in the religious domain) in advance. The third scandal, however, seems especially apt to subvert the deepest purposes of the Incarnation. No matter how elevated and expansive Jesus' sense of divine pathos may be, if he is not able to relate this artfully and relavantly to the situation of his disciples, it will remain exclusively his. Imagine, for instance, what would

Jesus as the One Fashioned and Apprenticed by God   315

happen should the Logos try to advance science at the time of the patriarchs by infusing into some willing lad of the day the scientific insights of a Pasteur or an Isaac Newton. Such a lad might be greeted as a divine marvel, but he would be hopelessly incapable of making intelligible to even a single individual his miraculously gained wisdom. Thus, he would pass away leaving the scientific heritage of the patriarchs precisely where he had found it. The same thing applies to Jesus. Any supreme advantage which betrays his mission as a Master of Torah calling the Lost Sheep of the House of Israel back to their Father must be ruthlessly curtailed. Not to do so is to render the would-be Messiah either as a Super-saint or as an incomprehensible freak -- in either case, his passing leaves the religious heritage of the children of Abraham precisely where he found it. Thus it is that again and again a Christian must be reminded that the Messiah is for us and for our salvation. We can indeed exalt Jesus, as did the medieval theologians, by exempting Jesus from this or that dimension of the human condition. We can elevate him above all humans by awarding him miraculously gained wisdom and a superabundance of (unearned) grace. In so doing, however, we must face the risk that we are undermining the very common ground whereby he can meet and heal our broken condition of religious delusions and estrangement from God.

The New Testament Evidence

Before advancing any further, I must ask whether the New Testament does affirm extraterrestrial knowledge for Jesus? . . . whether Jesus has no earthly teachers? If it does, then I would find it necessary to live with that fact as an expression of God's incomprehensible ways and adjust my theologizing accordingly. An examination of the New Testament data seems to favor two diametrically opposed traditions. The first tradition is represented by Luke 2:41-52. Herein the Evangelist finds no embarrassment at presenting the boy-Jesus as "sitting among the masters [of Torah], listening to them, and asking them questions" (Luke 2:46). There is no hint here that Jesus is teaching them; rather, he is being taught and the masters of Torah are "astonished at his intelligence and his replies" (Luke 2:47) since he is only twelve.[46] Luke is casting this story so as to emphasize the punch line: "I must be busy with my Father's affairs" (Luke 2:49) -- a superb summary of Jesus' orientation during his entire life. Luke's narrative closes with the following generalized account:

> He [Jesus] then went down with them [his parents] and came to Nazareth and

> lived under their authority . . . . And
> Jesus increased in wisdom, in stature,
> and in favor with God and men [women]
> (Luke 2:41-42 also 2:40 and 1:80).

A diametrically opposed tradition is represented by John's Gospel. John presents Jesus as clairvoyant: "Before Philip came to call you, I say you under the fig tree" (John 1:48). When John takes over the feeding narratives from the Synoptic tradition, he carefully suppressed the intent of Jesus' question to his disciples by adding parenthetically: "he himself knew exactly what he was going to do" (John 6:7). According to John, Jesus appears to know from the very beginning that Judas Iscariot would betray him (John 6:71, 13:11). At another point, John seems to imply that the Father in heaven taught Jesus both to read and to interpret the Scriptures:

> Jesus went to the Temple and began to
> teach [i.e., to give religious guidance
> beginning with a text of the Scrip-
> tures]. The Jews were astonished and
> said, "How did he learn to read? He
> has not been taught [by any human
> teacher]" (John 7:14-15).

Synoptic Gospels are more apt to retain the historical features of Jesus than John's Gospel, wherein a glorified Christ addresses the community. In all four Gospels, however, Jesus is clearly making use of the historically and culturally-conditioned theological framework of his day. In Raymond Brown's investigation of the religious understanding of Jesus, he arrives at the following conclusion:

> In the three areas of demonology, the
> afterlife, and apocalyptic, Jesus seems
> to draw on the imperfect religious
> concepts of his time without indication
> of superior knowledge and without
> substantially correcting the con-
> cepts.[47]

In some religious details, Jesus even appears to error. He does, for example, name "Abiathar" (Mark 2:26) as high priest when David took the loaves from the Temple. In fact, the Hebrew Scriptures name "Ahimelech" (1 Sam 21:1-6) as high priest. These errors in detail, do not hamper Jesus' mission. Neither does his frequent use of the faulty exegesis of his day. For example:

We find another hermeneutic problem in Jesus' insistence that Ps 110 refers to the Messiah. He presumes that in "The Lord [=God] said to my Lord" the "my Lord" is the Messiah. Few modern scholars, Catholics included, would think that there was an expectation of "the Messiah" when Ps 110 was composed. The Pharisees were not able [so it seems] to refute Jesus' argument since, seemingly, they too thought that the psalm referred to the Messiah; but if taken <u>literally</u>, Ps 110 would not establish Jesus' point.[48]

If Jesus is perceived as a man with extra-terrestrial sources of knowing, these evident limitations of Jesus' religious knowledge might prove embarrassing. One can, for example, always assume that Jesus just pretended ignorance. The more natural response, however, is to assume that Jesus grew up sharing the religious horizon of understanding that he had received from his parents and guardians.

Great weight should not be placed on the silence of the Gospels regarding Jesus' own formation in Torah. If one finds Jesus at home in the synagogues of Galilee during his active ministry, the presumption is that he himself profited from the synagogue of Nazareth as a house of prayer and of learning. In any case, Jesus would have distinguished himself if he did not attend the synagogue while living thirty years in Nazareth. For a Jew the synagogue was as normal a part of life as washing and eating. The fact that the Gospels are silent regarding Jesus' bathing, for example, cannot be regarded as casting the least doubt upon the supposition that he did. More to the point, the enemies of Jesus never seek to discredit him by claiming that he never studied Torah or that he never names anyone as his principle master. And it must be made perfectly clear that, not even in the rabbinic sources, does one get the impression that a would-be master is accepted the moment that he can name his distinguished mentor. To illustrate this, the rabbinic sources reveal that Hillel the Elder was apprenticed in Babylon and came as an obscure immigrant into Jerusalem (c. 20 B.C.E.). Initially he antagonized the Jerusalem masters. By and by, however, he came to be recognized as the wisest among them. It was, more especially, his ability to unravel the guidance of Torah which established his acceptance as a great master and not any appeal to his mentors. The Gospel shows clear signs of Jesus striving to establish before the Pharisees the legitimacy of his own unraveling of Torah (e.g., Matt 12:1-14). If he fails in this, it is not because he has no accredited diploma. The Pharisees distrust the freedom that Jesus allows for interpreting the provisions of Torah in favor of human welfare. The Pharisees too knew how to make exceptions for humanitarian reasons; these exceptions, however, were carefully restricted by historical precedents and teaching. Jesus, on the contrary, trains his disciples to sense the very pathos of God and to act accordingly -- even when it means setting aside the stubborn religious expectations of his day.

A Tentative Resolution

The Incarnation might thus be cast along the following lines. The Logos, the Eternal One forever at the Father's side, hovers over the cosmos for eons upon eons until, in the course of time, the human organism appears. Then, over thousands of years, the Logos creates a people of his own -- a people with the interiority of children of God. It is this interiority which looms and grows, which rises and falls, which sets the stage for Jesus. One might even say that the Logos had impregnated the whole nation such that it was getting ready to give birth to the awaited Son. Or, following Irenaeus, one might say that the Logos was progressively fashioning a people attuned to the divine pathos:

> God simply out of his [her] own generosity, formed humanity from the beginning: for the sake of salvation, he [she] chose the patriarchs; he [she] shaped his [her] people in advance, teaching the unteachable to follow God; he [she] established his [her] prophets on the earth, accustoming men [women] to bear his Spirit within them and to have communion with God.[49]

When the awaited One appears, the eons upon eons of genetic wisdom that had been accumulated are unfolded as the Master's design in the formation of this organism. Then, the infant is born and cared for by Joseph and Mary -- these two bear the spirit of Israel within them. Their settled instincts and patterns of judgment are attuned to God through a cultural pre-existence that stretches backward in time through Isaiah, through David, through Abraham, back to the Adam and Eve who present the first blossomings of primitive human culture. By virtue of Jesus' belong to these parents and by virtue of his organism's uncanny ability to enter into the hidden meanings of his parent's psyche, Jesus emerges, in his adolescence, as a child with the interiority of Joseph and Mary. And, in so far as these parents are themselves interiorly fashioned by the Logos, so too their son is apprenticed by the Logos in and through their training.

Assuming this to be the case, we must not only honor Mary and Joseph for their virtuous lives and heroic sacrifices in sustaining and protecting their child, Jesus, but we must likewise honor them for so artfully harmonizing their energies with divine initiative in the organic and religious formation of the Messiah. The image of Joseph as entrusting himself to the designs of God as revealed in his dreaming intuitions now takes on a new importance for it would be such like intimations that would lead his son to also put aside the prescriptions of the written Torah. Mary's own sympathy with and anticipation of God's Reign as seen in her Magnificat or in her meditation on the Hebrew Scriptures[50] also provides an intimation of how Jesus turned out to be so zealous for the Kingdom and the Word of God. It is not only her passive acceptance, her "let it be done unto me," that accounts for her greatness; full account must be given to her graced performance as a bearer of the rich heritage of Israel to and for her Son.[51]

Having successfully completed his home training, the adolescent-Jesus was undoubtedly drawn to admire and learn from his self-chosen heroes and models. Who were the heroes of Jesus? Their names are not known. Nor do we know exactly how they contributed to the ongoing formation of Jesus by the Logos. One can only speculate that John the Baptizer played a critical role in this regard. Whatever happened in Jesus' interactions with John, the Gospels are clear that Jesus was torn away from his carpentry and provoked to imitate in Galilee the heralding zeal of John: "Repent, for the kingdom of God is close at hand" (Matt 4:17 = 3:2). The Gospels retain the highest praises in the mouth of Jesus for John:

> I tell you solemnly, of all the children born of women, a greater than John the Baptist has never been seen . . . .
> It was towards John that all the prophesies of the prophets and of the Torah were leading . . . (Matt 1:11, 13).

It is precisely these praises that Jesus' disciples will later direct toward Jesus as first-born in the kingdom of heaven (Matt 11:11b). Thus it is that we might honor John, especially, as well as the unnamed or unknown mentors who played their part in facilitating the route whereby Jesus progressively enlarged his encounters with the living God.

Over and beyond this, however, it must be remembered that Jesus emerged as the Master who excelled his own teachers and mentors by virtue of his own pioneering discoveries of the pathos of YHWH.[52] Exemplary parenting and assiduous apprenticing do not dictate nor necessitate a further chain of fresh personal discoveries of God; they do, however, make the independent quest for God possible and fruitful. Following the completion of prolonged training, the mature disciple enters into an uncharted quest:

> The mature disciple is . . . ready to leave his/her master and to follow God, the Supreme Master. Faith, accordingly, means a reverent submission directly to God. It is by this faith that a new master allows him/herself to let go of cherished elements in his/her settled dispositions in order to yield to the deep intuitions that lead to fresh revelations of God's cause. Before the human master did the disciplining and the converting. In the end, the new master waits upon God to discipline and purify the very tradition which he/she incarnates.[53]

The Synoptics present Jesus as compelled by the Spirit to go off alone and remain forty days in the wilderness (Matt 4:1 and parallels). These forty days call to mind the forty days that Moses spent on the mountain being apprenticed by YHWH. What happened to Jesus during those forty days? Here the Gospels are silent -- and with a purpose. The quest of genius to break new ground is a solitary one. Advances in medicine, in art, in science, in religion, all follow the same general lines. It runs like this. For thirty years Jesus has been passionately preoccupied with Torah; he has sought to align himself with the divine pathos that he had assimilated through extended apprenticeships. He is now at the cutting edge. He has exhausted the given resources of his day and, yet, he is still "unsettled," "perplexed," "hungry for more." He pours himself into a pursuit that needs time and space to hear God. Meanwhile, the imagination and guiding intuitions are at work subliminally. He racks his brain; he cries out to his Father; he deliberately intensifies the unsettled/perplexed/hungry intuition that drives him on. He is actively pouring himself into the search for God; yet, at the same time he senses that God too is drawing close to reveal something to him that he cannot yet "grasp" or "say." In this quest, the settled instincts and habits of judgment which Jesus assimilated in his training are being progressively stretched and transformed along lines that are not of his own making. Every religious tradition both enlarges and cripples its adherents. Jesus is no stranger to this. The crippling pains are relived; dissonance is enlarged. Then, there are progressive waves of peace that overtake Jesus. They arrive as a visitation from God. Jesus feels that the Logos which is his ground and source has healed him, has realigned him, has recreated him. His interiority has passed through the fire and emerged purified and strong. He has sought God and found him. He can now laugh at much of the stupidity and blindness that characterized his previous existence. He is unafraid. He can never fall back there. Discovery is irreversable; the settled instincts and habits of judgment are manifestly transformed.[54]

After the forty days, Jesus is forced to think through the rest of his life by way of implementing the fresh discoveries of God that he has made. Temptations assail him.[55] He might make believe that it is his own efforts or his own merits that allowed him to turn stones to bread; no -- he was fed by God. He might make his way to the Temple and climb up the established religious hierarchy so as to throw himself into "religion"; no -- so much of the Temple religion is an affront to God. He might enter into politics, even revolutionary politics, so as to have a platform to implement his new vision; no -- political compromises would only lead him to worship the devil rather than God.

Jesus may have left the wilderness having eliminated some poor choices but without having formulated any clear plan of what his own religious transformation meant for him to be and do. Then, as Matthew recounts, John the Baptizer was arrested. Jesus prudently leaves the Jordan and returns to Nazareth to pack his bags and settle in Capernaum (Matt 4:13). The absence of John's heralding of the Kingdom must have moved him, for now he too commences to undertake the same prophetic heralding along the shores of the Sea of Galilee (Matt 4:17). Finally it comes to him. The "revival-meeting" type of ministry has its distinct limitations: some people are moved but they receive no profound reorientation towards God and life. He himself, as the Logos enfleshed, knows the profound reorientation that he has experienced. With time and effort, he could bring many of his contemporaries along the same paths that he has travelled. He knows the way. He was formerly where they are now, i.e., as both enlarged and crippled by conventional religion. He thus resolves to serve them by making available his pioneering discoveries to others -- to disciples. Accordingly, he discerns and selects four fishermen, men who already admire him, men who might be willing to abandon their homes and occupations for a time so as to become like unto him in all things. From there on in, Jesus continues his prophetic mission to all the towns of Galilee but he gives his best time and energy to the disciples who will soon share and enlarge his zeal for the Kingdom of God. One day they too will go out and do by themselves just precisely what Jesus had been enabled to do by virtue of his own religious transformation:

> These twelve Jesus sent out, instructing them as follows: "Do not turn your steps to pagan territory, and do not enter any Samaritan town; go rather to the lost sheep of the House of Israel. And as you go, proclaim that the kingdom of God is close at hand. Cure the sick, raise the dead, cleanse the lepers, cast out devils. You received [what I offered you] without charge, give without charge . . . (Matt 10:5-8).

The circle is thus complete. Just as Jesus had been transformed and empowered through his fresh encounters with God; so too now, through a strenuous apprenticeship, the Twelve demonstrate themselves to be likewise transformed and empowered. They share the interiority of Jesus and reach out to others so that many new circles can begin. We are thus left with this stunning realization: The actual nature of Jesus' own fresh discoveries of God cannot be specified, but it can be entirely assimilated by the disciple. In the end, the Fathers were quite right: Everything that he is by nature, we become by grace.

Conclusion

What I have done in the above Christology is to retrain myself to talk about Jesus in such a way that I acknowledge the actual processes whereby the Logos enters into the cosmic-human drama. This Christology has the advantage of situating Jesus as the supreme exemplification of those divine-human dynamics that determine our own personal and collective well-being. So often Jesus Christ is presented as the supreme exception of those very processes that we judge and feel are the parameters of our own lives. This is a serious error and it has the consequence of cutting us off from Jesus and of misconstruing the processes which contribute to our growth and sanctification.

In very simple terms, therefore, I have personally decided to talk about Jesus in such a way that I give guidance about ourselves. Like ourselves Jesus enters into the world by belonging to particular parents who themselves belong to a particular time and culture. By virtue of this belonging, he receives, through his parents, the rich genetic inheritance that the Logos had been fashioning during two billion years. Again, by virtue of his belonging, he receives the rich cultural and religious heritage that the Logos had been fashioning among his/her people. Yet, just as in our own day, the religious tradition that Jesus assimilated both revealed and distorted the divine pathos. Thus Jesus naturally emerges from his childhood training both enlarged and crippled by religion. But the work of the Logos is not yet done. Jesus is hungry and thirsty for the wisdom of God, and, for the moment, this is enough. Later, Jesus will be unaccountably drawn to John the Baptizer. He and other unnamed and unknown persons will advance and purify "traditional religion" in the hearts of those who know how to hear and to follow them. Then, something is unleashed in Jesus. He himself is driven to pursue deep intuitions that slowly and painfully draw him into further enlarging and enhancing his sense of the divine pathos. Jesus thus testifies in his own existence that the Logos is leading, drawing, seducing his human spirit. In the end Jesus emerged transformed. The passion of his own self-transformation was poured out in attracting and converting others to his own graced existence. Those who apprenticed themselves to him knew him as the one who purified and healed their own religious identity. In the end, they felt that Jesus' wisdom was aligned with the divine wisdom, Jesus' human sensibilities were aligned with the divine sensibilities, Jesus' standards of excellence were aligned with the divine standards of excellence. In philosophical terms, this is precisely the truth that the later Greek Fathers tried to respect in speaking of the hypostatic unity.

Many contemporary theologians are speaking of the hypostatic unity in terms that again take note of the spirit of the Fathers. For my purposes here, I wish to illustrate this by summarizing, with unfair brevity, some of the considerations that have guided Edward Schillebeeckx in his own attempts to make sense of the hypostatic unity. To begin with, Schillebeeckx takes note that "humanity" and "divinity" are the essential categories within which every person can be correctly envisioned. Thus, every person is "humanly self-sufficient" at the same time that he/she is "entirely dependent upon God." Likewise, every person is "self-actualizing" at the same time that he/she is "actualized by God." Furthermore, every person "reveals and conceals him/herself" and also, at the same time, "reveals and conceals his/her Maker." Hence, an appropriate "duality" characterizes what, against the background of divine creation, we know about ourselves. Furthermore . . .

> Their being-themselves and their being-creatures are not two partial aspects, two components, but two views of the totality: they are themselves precisely in that they are from and for God.[56]

Against this background, Schillebeeckx considers the intent of the hypostatic unity as mirroring a deep truth about the created reality of Jesus:

> Just as every creature, and especially every man [woman], "represents" and renders God present by what it is, so also Jesus, by what he is as a [hu]man, renders God present. Thus the unique character of this presence will have to appear out of the unique manner of Jesus' very being [hu]man.[57]

When the Logos fashions for him/herself the humanity which we identify as Jesus of Nazareth, it must be remarked that this is the most intimate mode that the Unbounded One can achieve with the finite stuff of the earth.[58] Jesus, after all, is and remains a creature. It would be mistaken, therefore, to imagine that somehow there exists an independent human person whom the Logos later overpowers or adopts as united to God. No: everything that Jesus is, from the first moment of his existence, is due to the Logos. It would be equally absurd to imagine that Jesus demonstrates an unquenchable thirst for God and an admirable progress in holiness, for which, the Logos rewards him. No: everything that Jesus becomes (including his thirst for God and his progress in holiness) is due to the Logos. This and this alone is what the various formulations of the hypostatic unity are designed to protect.

However I end up honoring Jesus, I must be quite careful to remember that I can never honor him correctly if I make him in the least way inaccessible as the Guarantor and Paridigm of our salvation. This is expressed admirably in the Athanasian prayer which forms part of the Roman liturgy:

Jesus as the One Fashioned and Apprenticed by God   325

> By the mingling of this water and wine,
> may we become one with his divinity
> just as he became one with our humanity.

In our contemporary ears, this prayer sounds like a blasphemy in so far as our contemporary spirituality has largely forgotten the rule of the Fathers: Everything that Jesus Christ is by nature, we become by grace. This is the selfsame rule which is already hinted at in various parts of the New Testament:

> Whoever keeps his [Jesus'] commandments [torah] lives in God and God lives in him [her] (1 John 3:24).

> Everyone moved by the Spirit is a son of God . . . . They are the ones he chose specially long ago and intended to become true images of his Son, so that his Son might be the eldest of many brothers [sisters] (Rom 8:14, 29).

> By his [Jesus'] divine power, he has given us all the things that we need for life and for true devotion, bringing us to know God himself. . . . Through them [his gifts] you will be able to share the divine nature and to escape corruption in this world (2 Pet 1:3-4).

Hundreds of citations along these selfsame lines can be found among the Fathers: Typical expressions of Athanasius and Augustine are the following:

> He[she] has taken to him[/her]self flesh and, being in the flesh, deifies the flesh.

> Every man [woman], from the commencement of his [her] faith, becomes a Christian by the same grace by which that man, from his formation, became Christ.[59]

The formulations respecting the hypostatic unity were consequently neither esoteric doctrines nor pious riddles; they gave expression to the plan of God that was being experienced by the then-living disciples of Jesus.

The revolution that Jesus provoked proved to be healing and power for those who shared in it. And thus it created the next generation. This generation was also under the sustained influence of the Logos. It modified and enlarged the legacy of Jesus such that the spirit of these disciples continued to be healing and power for those contemporaries who shared it. This and only this can account for how the Messiah of Jews could become the Truth and Wisdom which the Hellenists sought. The Greek Fathers of the Church grew up with their interior life formed by the philosophers of the Platonic school; they found in Christianity the new Platonism that <u>enabled them to effect what had only been theorizing</u> within Platonic circles. The statement of Augustine, to this effect, shows how the soul of the Jesus movement had been so marvelously transformed through the first four centuries:

> If Plato and the rest of them in whose names men [women] glory were to come to life again and find the churches full and the temples empty, and that the human race was being called away from desire for temporal and transient goods to spiritual and intelligible goods . . . , they would perhaps say: "That is what we did not dare to preach to the people. We preferred to yield to popular custom rather than to bring the people over to our way of thinking and living."[60]

Jesus altered the identities of his followers. His spirit transformed their spirits. They, in their turn, went on to attract and to convert the then-known world. As such, this is the irreversible and irrefutable datum of history. Every epoch has had its frenzied zealots for God's cause and those who claim to be "god." In many cases their disciples heralded them as divinely-ordained Saviors and as divinely-approved miracle workers. The historians of religion find their texts and their relics in the dead museum pieces left behind. Jesus, in contradistinction to all these, left behind a body of saints which transformed and elevated Western civilization.

But what of the churches today? Jesus and the early generations of disciples were shown reliable; they healed the infirmities of their age and infused a new life into the personal and collective spirit. Can the same be said of the contemporary churches? The recent historical record is oftentimes pessimistic. Many within the mainline churches do not distinguish themselves markedly from those who have entirely abandoned religious practices. Meanwhile, the heavy weight of tradition and of routine quickly wear down any fresh, prophetic energy within such mainline churches. People already assume that they know what it is to be "Christian" and naturally resist anyone who would presume to change their personal or institutional identities. Many Christians who have discovered God in a fresh mode are thus worn down or entirely unrecognized within the church of their upbringing and are forced to make disciples at the fringes or entirely outside the existing structures.

But I am not disheartened. The Logos continues to abide among us. Meanwhile, our past continues to prod and disturb us: "This may be a wicked age, but your lives should redeem it" (Eph 5:16). In effect, therefore, our world is like that boat rocked on the stormy sea. There is a sleeping "giant" in the prow. We will some day awaken him. The original awakening took place because of the frantic cries of the disciples: The Lord sternly rebuked them for their "lack of faith" (Matt 8:26) for so acting. The second awakening will take place because the disciples have recovered the way of acting that he had originally taught them. This recovery will be a long and painful process. Throughout this recovery process, however, we are subliminally guided by the selfsame Logos that apprenticed the original Craftsman (Jesus). Those who have spiritual power in the church will learn to discern the real processes from the placebos; they will again learn to empower disciples. Meanwhile, those who are crippled, blinded, or dead will again be healed by finding and adhering to their spiritual masters who know how to "produce good fruit" (Matt 7:17). In the end, Christ's body (i.e., "his church" [Col 1:18, Eph 1:23]) will awaken and again breathe deeply with the Spirit of Jesus. The storm will then be silenced. Toward this day, we work and dream through him/her, with him/her, and in him/her [the Logos]. "The whole creation is eagerly awaiting for God to reveal his/her sons [daughters]" (Rom 8:19).

Footnotes for Chapter XI

¹ See, for example, Jean Galot, Who is Christ? (Chicago: Franciscan Herald Press, 1981), esp. pp. 346ff.

² Even in the Thomistic synthesis, each of the outward cures of Jesus is interpreted as the visible manifestation of the invisible "healing of the soul" (ST III, 44, 3, ad 3). In this light, all of the "miracles" of Jesus are inherently designed to reveal and implement the spiritual ministry of the Son of God enfleshed. Furthermore, Thomas asserts that "the grace of mighty works" is given to Jesus "not only that he might work miracles, but also that he might communicate this grace to others [viz., his disciples]" (ST III, 13, 2, ad 3).

³ Chapter III dealt with the efficacy of the death of Jesus, but here the positions of Matthew and Paul were sketched out by way of counteracting the excesses of the Anselmian atonement theory. Chapters IV and V dealt with the Christological titles of "kyrios" and "christos," but here again my treatment was by way of making room for the Master of Torah who apprentices disciples. Within this book I have neither the space nor the necessity to fashion a complete Christology. The complexities of even the New Testament Christologies is staggering, as shown by the recent research of James D. G. Dunn, Christology in the Making (Philadelphia: Westminister, 1980) and Edward Schillebeeckx, Christ (N.Y.: Seabury, 1980).

⁴ The eternal Logos has no inherent sexual identity, hence I have elected to use dual pronouns when the noun referred to is the Logos. The incarnate Logos was embodied as a male (Jesus of Nazareth), hence, exclusively masculine pronouns are utilized when the incarnate Logos is referred to.

⁵ These instances provided here are modern adaptations of the functions of the Logos as described by Athanasius in Contra Gentes 44.

⁶ What we now refer to as "instinct" in animals still remains a mystery which puzzles contemporary scientists. The Fathers regarded the "instincts" of animals and the "natures" of minerals as visible tokens of the all-pervasive guidance of the Logos.

⁷ Athanasius Contra Gentes 43:1-5; my emphasis added.

⁸ Irenaeus *Aversus haereses* 5.2.2.

⁹ Irenaeus *Demonstratio apostolicae praedicationis* 32.

¹⁰ Modern historical theology is persuaded that the formulations of belief must change in different sociocultural situations so that the truths passed down continue to retain their hold upon those who are instructed/guided by them. See, for example, Avery Dulles, *The Survival of Dogma*, esp. pp. 17-31, or Karl Rahner, "Theology and Anthropology," *The Word in History*, ed. by T. Patrick Burke (N.Y.: Sheed & Ward, 1966), pp. 1-23.

¹¹ Michael Polanyi, in *Personal Knowledge* (N.Y.: Harper & Row, 1964), pp. 381-405, convincingly argues that no accumulation of accidental advantages can add up to the evolution of a new set of operational principles. Accordingly, Polanyi criticizes the present theories of evolution as philosophically defective. In their place, Polanyi specifies that there must be "a phylogenetic field" that functions as an ordering principle whenever random processes effect creative genetic mutations. I would equate this phylogenetic field as one of the functions of the Logos within cosmogenesis.

¹² This subsidiary presence of the Logos in each new production of a human organism is of two kinds: (a) remote and (b) immediate. The remote presence of the Logos is due to the sustained historical presence of the Logos shaping the DNA code down to the present moment. The DNA code which is the master engineer of embryonic development is thus nothing less than the faithful apprentice of the Grand Master of cosmogenesis. In addition to this, however, one must surmise that the Logos also exerts some immediate causal efficacy in the production of each new organism. The Grand Master who has "apprenticed" the DNA code during the long years of advance from amoeba to human surely does not abandon his/her brood at this late date. Yet, since the creative novelty exemplified by each new human being is indistinguishable from the novelty produced from the genetic recombining of the distinctive male and female genes, one cannot specify the contribution of the Logos in each instance. How each new human being is being modified by the Logos toward the future shape of the human organism, we are not yet able to say -- only time will tell.

¹³ Karl Rahner, in "Christology Within an Evolutionary View of the World," *Theological Investigations* (Baltimore: Helicon Press, 1966) V, 157-192, argues for this same position. Rahner makes it clear that his task is not to somehow use the evolutionary theory to legitimate

the Incarnation. The task, rather, is to demonstrate to those who are already believers that there are no formal logical contradictions when the Incarnation is described as "truly a moment in the biological evolution of this world." It is unfortunate that Rahner conducts his investigation without any reference to the doctrine of the virginal conception.

[14] Raymond E. Brown, The Birth of the Messiah (Garden City: Doubleday, 1977), pp. 124-125, 522-523; also see ST III, 32, 3, co.

[15] ST III, 31, 8; 32, 4; 33, 4 would support this conclusion in so far as the entire active principle in Christ's conception is supplied by the Holy Spirit.

[16] "Adoption," Encyclopedia Judaica (1971) II, 298-302.

[17] Brown, The Birth of the Messiah, p. 527.

[18] Paul, for example speaks of the Messiah as "the seed" (sperma) awaited to fulfill the promises made to Abraham (Gal 3:16-19 interpreting Gen 12:2-3, 18:18-19, 22:17-18, 26:4). Luke, the Evangelist who narrates the Annunciation, later does not scruple to pen a sermon by Peter in which the Messiah is presented as "the fruit of [David's] loins" (Acts 2:30) whom God has raised up due to the oath sworn to him (2 Sam 7:12-17; Ps 89:3-45; 1 Chr 17:12-13, 22:9-10).

[19] Compare Matt 2:14 with Luke 2:39. For further details, see Raymond E. Brown, The Virginal Conception & Bodily Resurrection of Jesus (N.Y.: Paulist, 1973), pp. 53-56.

[20] Brown, The Birth of the Messiah, pp. 37-38, 505-556, esp. 517-518.

[21] My thesis here is further developed in my article, "Matthew's Integration of Sexual and Divine Begetting," Biblical Theological Bulletin 8 (1978) 108-116.

[22] Bruce Vawter, in This Man Jesus (Garden City: Doubleday, 1973), p. 206, argues that "the genealogies of Matthew 1:1-17 and Luke 3:23-37, which trace Jesus' ancestry through Joseph, must have originally had in mind a natural procreation . . . ." Raymond E. Brown, in The Virginal Conception & Bodily Resurrection of Jesus (N.Y.: Paulist, 1973), p. 45, n. 63, further concludes that "since the same evangelists who tell us about the virginal conception also give us genealogies of Jesus, they did not

think that the conception ruptured the chain of human descent." See also the excellent studies of Joseph A. Fitzmyer, "The Virginal Conception of Jesus in the New Testament," Theological Studies 3 (1973) 541-575, and Herman C. Waetjen, "The Genealogy as the Key to the Gospel According to Matthew," Journal of Biblical Literature 95 (1976) 295-230. Relative to the absence of any suggestion that the Holy Spirit is the "father" of Jesus, see Brown, The Birh of the Messiah, pp. 124-25.

[23] John A.T. Robinson, "Our Image of God Must Change," The Christian Century 90 (1973) 340.

[24] Brown, in The Virginal Conception & Bodily Resurrection, concludes that "both Protestant and Catholic theologians have stated clearly that the bodily fatherhood of Joseph would not have excluded the fatherhood of God" (p. 42). Earlier, in this same study, Brown also concluded that "it is difficult to argue that in order to be free from original sin Jesus had to be conceived of a virgin" (p. 41). See also John A.T. Robinson, The Human Face of God (Philadelphia: Westminister, 1973), pp. 47-56.
Robert Glenn Gromacki, in The Virgin Birth: Doctrine of Deity (Nashville: Thomas Nelson, 1974), goes to great lengths to argue just the contrary: "If he [Jesus] was born apart from male parentage, then he must be God manifest in the flesh. If he were not virgin born, then he was not God" (p. 15). Gromacki's logic may be defective, but it demonstrates the passionate bond which many Christians make between the virginal conception and Jesus' divinity.

[25] Thomas Aquinas argues that it was only fitting that the body of Jesus be instantaneously and perfectly formed from the first moment of his miraculous conception such that a rational soul would animate it from the beginning, instead of having it inform the fetus after the sixth month (ST III, 33, 2 & 3). This instantaneous formation implies only a miniaturized Jesus, since Thomas allows that nine months was required for its growth in size.

[26] Irenaeus Adversus haereses 2.22.4.

[27] Athanasius Orationes contra Arianos 3.26.31.

[29] Chalcedon affirmed that the body of Christ was "homoousios with us," but it did not specify whether his body was (a) like Adam's before the fall, (b) like our own in the present fallen state, or (c) like those sanctified bodies of the Saints. The post-Chalcedonian controversies tended to read back the transcendent properties of Jesus' glorified body back into his earthly existence. The route

was thus paved to minimize the tears, hunger, and temptations of Jesus by considering these states as voluntarily undertaken <u>for our instruction</u>. The medieval theologians codified and standardized these tendencies within Christian thought. It was not until the advent of modern biblical studies that a fresh look at the historical Jesus emerged along side that of dogmatic theology.

[30] Athanasius <u>Orationes contra Arianos</u> 3.28.43 & 2.20.55.

[31] <u>Gospel of Thomas</u> 2.

[32] <u>Arabic Infancy Gospel</u> 40. Printed in E. Hennecke, <u>New Testament Apocrypha</u> (London: SCM, 1973), p. 409.

[33] <u>The Life of John [the Baptizer] According to Serapion</u>. Printed in E. Hennecke, op. cit., pp. 414-416.

[34] A. Hulsbosch, "Jezus Christus, gekend als mens, beleden als Zoon Gods," <u>Tijdschrift voor Theologie</u> 6 (1966) 261 & 271. I am grateful to the translation prepared by my former professor, Rev. Joseph Powers, S.J.

[35] History itself offer instances of persons who have made great contributions to our religious, artistic, scientific development and yet suffered from a comparatively inferior organic health and vitality.

[36] Irenaeus, in a classical definition, declared that "to follow the Savior is to participate in salvation" (<u>Adversus haereses</u> 4.14.1). For a historical and pastoral treatment of this thesis, see "Imitation du Christ," <u>Dictionnaire de Spiritualite</u> (Paris: Beauchesne, 1971) VII, 1536-1601: English translation under the title of <u>Imitating Christ</u> (St. Meinrad: Abbey Press, 1974).

[37] This functional identity between Jesus and the Father is the sufficient, necessary foundation for what the tradition will later define in ontological terms. For a critical exposition of the priority of this functional identity, see Wolfhart Pannenberg, <u>Jesus -- God and Man</u> (Philadelphia: Westminister, 1968), esp. pp. 332f, 334-349, and Edward Schillebeeckx, <u>Christ</u> (N.Y.: Seabury, 1980), esp. pp. 427-432.

[38] C. H. Dodd, in <u>The Interpretation of the Fourth Gospel</u> (Cambridge: University Press, 1968), pp. 151-169, presents a fuller development of how "knowing God" is central to the soteriology of John's Gospel.

39 Clement of Alexandria *Protrepticus* 1.8.4.

40 Karl Rahner has repeatedly endeavored to show the indivisible unity of each human person as an "incarnate spirit." Rahner specifies the soul as referring to our "inwardness." Contrary to those evolutionists who posit a direct creation of the human spirit (outside of and independent of the developing organism), Rahner insists that the soul is the forma corporis (DS 902) and has no proper "existence" apart from the body (VI, 173f; XVII, 85f). "The loftiest spiritual thought, the most sublime moral decision, the most radical act of a responsible liberty is still a bodily perception or a bodily decision" (XVII, 92). See Karl Rahner, "The Unity of Spirit and Matter in the Christian Understanding of Faith," Theological Investigations VI, 153-177, and "The Body in the Order of Salvation." Theological Investigations XVII, 71-89.
In the last section, I described the organic formation of Jesus. This embraces the body-soul unity in the terms of Rahner's treatment. The "interiority" of Jesus, however, is informed through historical experiences following its formation. This is what I am treating here.

41 Polanyi, Personal Knowledge, p. 69.

42 Polanyi, in Personal Knowledge, pp. 402-405, theorizes that "a heuristic field" may be assumed to guide the innovating mind in its quest for a truer, richer grasp upon those realities which one's culture honors and takes into account. This heuristic field guides innovations in the noosphere just as does its counterpart, the phylogenetic field (n. 11 above), guide innovations in the biosphere. Accordingly, I would equate the heuristic field as an additional function of the Logos within cosmogenesis.

43 Irenaeus (d. 110), in his Proof of the Apostolic Teaching, proposes that all the visions, auditions, and dreams throughout the Hebrew Scriptures are ancient manifestations of the Logos. Clement of Alexandria (d. 215), in his day, proposed that "just as the kerygma has now come at its proper time [with Jesus], so in their proper times the Torah and the Prophets were given to the barbarians, and Philosophy to the Greeks, attuning their hearing to the kerygma" (Stromata 6.6.44.1). Augustine (d. 430), for his part, suggested that the leading intuitions that bring a searcher to discover and to adhere to the truth are due to the Logos "who is said to dwell in the inner person -- he [she] it is who teaches" (De magistro 38).

44 See n. 16 in Chapter VII.

⁴⁵ In the fourth century, Bishop Apollinarius endeavored to account for the unity between the humanity and the divinity of Jesus by suggesting that the flesh of Jesus was united to the Logos in the same fashion that our flesh is united to our soul. With the Logos replacing the human soul, it consequently followed that Jesus knew all things with the divine mind exclusively. The orthodox Fathers rejected this proposal on the grounds that the Scriptures convinced them that Jesus exhibited a normal human psychology (i.e., he suffered human ignorance, anxiety with respect the future, etc.). Following this, orthodox theology has subsequently spoken of how "each nature performs the functions proper to itself, yet in conjunction with the other nature" (DS 144). Thomas incorporated this tradition into his own synthesis (ST III, 16-19).

⁴⁶ I am interpreting Luke's narrative at its face value. One could always suggest, as did the medieval theologians, that Jesus was pretending ignorance by way of drawing them out and teaching them a thing or two through his artful questioning.

⁴⁷ Raymond E. Brown, Jesus God and Man (Milwaukee: Bruce, 1967), p. 59.

⁴⁸ Ibid., pp. 53-54.

⁴⁹ Irenaeus Adversus Haereses 4.14.2. In his own way, Irenaeus envisions the Hebraic tradition as a prolonged apprenticeship preparing the chosen people to become accustomed to the Logos. Meanwhile, the Logos is accustoming him/herself to the ways of humanity. For a fuller exposition, see Jean Danielou, Gospel Message and Hellenistic Culture (Philadelphia: Westminister, 1961), pp. 167-176. Thomas embraces this perspective partially in ST II-II, 1, 7, ad 2.

⁵⁰ Religious art has frequently presented Mary as receiving the word of the angel at the time she was meditating upon the Word of God (i.e., the Hebrew Scriptures). Here a mental "conceiving" of the Logos/Word parallels the physical conceiving of the enfleshed Logos in her womb.

⁵¹ The personal religious development of Mary and Joseph is quite unknown to us. The Protevangelium of James endeavors to flesh out the religious development of these two extraordinary people. The parents of Mary, Joachim and Anne, also figure as the aged and pious grandparents of Jesus who win God's favor and hand Mary over to the priests of the Temple when she is six such that she might be

prepared therein to receive the "supreme and unsurpassable blessing" -- that of becoming a living "Temple" for her Lord.

⁵² Supra, p. 217f.

⁵³ Supra, p. 235.

⁵⁴ Thomas Aquinas proposed that even though it was unfitting for the Teacher of All to himself be taught by another "it was more fitting for Christ to possess knowledge acquired by discovery" (ST III, 9, 4, ad 1). Karl Rahner, in his "Dogmatic Reflections on the Knowledge and Self-consciousness of Christ," Theological Investigations V, 193-218, proposed that, by grace of the hypostatic union, Jesus began with only an unreflective and unobjectified awareness of God and of his divine sonship. "Only gradually during his spiritual history" does Jesus come to a self-conscious, reflective interpretation and articulation of this originally subliminal awareness. Relative to this spiritual history . . . .

> It is absolutely legitimate to desire to see which of the notions prescribed by his religious environment Jesus actually used in order to express slowly what he had already known about himself in the very depth of his being. In principle, at least, such a history of his self-declaration has in no way to be interpreted merely as a history of his pedagogical accommodation, but can quite legitimately be seen also as the history of his own personal self-interpretation of himself to himself. For this does not mean that Jesus 'discovered something' which he did not know in any way up until then, but it means rather that he grasped more and more what he already always is and basically [i.e. unreflectively] also already knows (p. 212).

I welcome this theologizing of Rahner as arriving quite close to my own position. Rahner does not have a psychology and epistemology of discovery spelled out as in Polanyi; none the less, he does root Jesus' interiority in a historically conditioned series of discoveries. Furthermore, Rahner supposes that Jesus' own direct presence of God "shares in the characteristics of the spiritual, basic condition of a [hu]man" in so far as every human is ontologically grounded in the Creator:

> This direct and conscious presence to God must not be understood [for Jesus] in the sense of the vision of an object . . . . A direct presence to God belongs to the nature of a [i.e., every] spiritual person, in the sense of an unsystematic attunement and an unreflected horizon which determines everything else and within which the whole spiritual life of this spirit is lived (p. 209).

From this vantage point, it would appear that a revelation of the divine pathos always takes place as an enlargement and purification of the discoverer's human pathos as he/she assiduously seeks God. Knowing God and interior conversion are thus existentially and epistemologically correlated. In this case, "the new self" that emerges is in resonance to "the divine creativity" which is the ground and guide of every creaturely development. As established above, it is the Logos who permeates our lives and subsidiarily draws us into feats approaching the image and likeness of God. In sum, therefore, I find a close parallelism between what Rahner and I intend relative to the role of discovery in fashioning the interiority of Jesus, the incarnate Logos.

55 All three Synoptic Gospels make reference to temptations at the end of forty days precisely because they knew that Jesus <u>could have failed but did not</u>. Jesus had been empowered by his fresh discoveries of God; it now remained to be seen whether he had the wisdom to implement his new-found power and insight. Outside of this context, the temptations become a hoax in which Jesus merely plays games with the gullible demons. Maybe, as moderns, the temptations only become real when we understand that the "demons" that attempt to subvert and disorientate Jesus are the untamed "voices" of his own subconscious which come to the surface in the silence of the desert. Jesus is thus forced to wrestle with his own "dark side" in just the same way as did the later Fathers of the desert. In any case, Hebrews situates the reality of the temptations as part of the necessary training program for "a compassionate and trustworthy high priest of God's religion" (Heb 2:17):

> Because he [Jesus] has himself been through temptation, he is able to help others who are tempted (Heb 2:19).

56 Edward Schillebeeckx, "Persoonlijke Openbaringegestalte van de Vader," *Tijdschrift voor Theologie* 6 (1966) 276. Here again I am grateful for the translation prepared by my former professor, Rev. Joseph Powers, S.J.

57 *Ibid*.

58 Jaroslav Pelikan, in *The Emergence of the Catholic Tradition* (Chicago: University Press, 1971), p. 254, rightly remarks that "the human and the divine had to be united closely enough to achieve the salvation, but not so closely as to render it irrelevant to man as man [i.e., to us as humans] -- or [so closely as] to involve the divine in the suffering of the cross."

59 Athanasius *Orationes contra Arianos* 3.26.38 & Augustine *De praedestinatione sanctorum* 1.15.

60 Augustine *De vera religione* 4.6. See also 2.2.

Index

Abbreviations:
@ = according to
n12 = footnote 12
w/r = with respect to

Abraham
* seed of, 302
* training Isaac, 5, 203

accrediting
* @ Polanyi, 230-238
* faith in Jesus, 141-44, 196f
* Peter's discovery, 223f, 227, 229, 231, 237
* prophetic discoveries, 226-238, 252
* through empowering, 149f, 252, 285f
* through miracles, 136f, 140, 141, 157-160, 171, 211n17, 228f, 271f, 285, 305, 328n2
* through papal infallibility, 230, 245f
* through scriptural testimony, 247f, 253

Anselm
* atonement theory of, 41f, 43-46, 64f, 72

Anslem cont.
* corrected by Thomas Aquinas, 64-71
* lacking biblical support, 47-64

apprenticing, in general
* in art of praying, 268f, 272f
* comparing religious and secular, 5, 9, 11, 26, 84, 128, 171f, 181f, 186-88, 191f, 209n6, 210n16, 235f, 246f, 254-57, 279-81, 286
* necessity of, 149, 163f, 178, 179f, 198
* of children, 7f, 179-188

apprenticing in Torah
* nature of, 84f, 132f, 162, 190f
* place of, 93, 120f
* posture during, 94, 121-24

apprenticing in early church
* as "mothering/fathering," 161
* catechumenate program, 163- 170, 286f, 289n4
* chain of, 142, 149f, 170
* Paul's practice, 159-163

Athanasius, 294, 304f, 324f

atheism, 11, 178

atonement theory of Anselm
* corrected by Thomas Aquinas, 64-71
* not in Matthew, 47-63
* not in Paul, 57-64
* origins of, 43-46

Augustine
* necessity of training, 5f, 198
* sources of his theology, 64, 206
* theology of, 65f, 103n8, 142-44, 198, 203, 204, 206, 210n16, 211n17, 248, 249, 263, 326

authority
* function of, 198, 216f, 229f
* w/r interpreting Scripture, 245-48
* w/r accrediting innovations, 229f

Baltimore Catechism, 24f, 30f, 38, 45f, 56

baptism, 16, 155, 164-170, 200-202, 209n13, 286f

Brown, Raymond E., 99, 301f, 316f

children
* acritical imitation by, 181f, 189
* assimilate religion of parents, 7-9, 178, 179-183, 272, 310f
* learn to perceive God, 9, 11, 178, 179-188, 199f
* raised without humans, 180f, 311

church(es)
* Jesus' presence in, 133, 142, 149f, 162, 170, 283
* mission of, 126f, 130-33, 216, 285f, 286-88, 326f
* malfunctioning, 1f, 132, 170f, 172f, 196, 272f, 285, 287, 326f
* use of Scriptures in, 249f, 257-263

Cinderella mentality
* defective character of, 21, 23, 27, 37, 287
* described, 16f
* used for explaining, 16f, 21, 27

conversion of sinners, 126f

demons/devils, 20-23, 32

disciples
* act "in his name," 133, 162
* as re-presenting his Master, 67f, 94, 153f, 156, 158
* becomes like his Master, 67f, 132, 141f, 149
* calling of, 107-112, 283
* critical powers of, 195f, 209n8, 236f

Index   341

disciples cont.
* emotional fascination of, 142, 190, 194
* faith of, 21f, 190, 193-198
* financing of, 114-120
* feed the multitudes, 95, 103n8, 263
* identity change of, 125f, 326
* marriage of, 111
* mission of, 18f, 23, 67f, 87, 155f, 218f, 284
* not spectators or puppets, 15, 21, 67, 129, 133, 149

discovery, process of
* @ Polanyi, 22f, 231-36, 333n42
* accreditation of, 226-238
* biblical instances of, 150-160, 220-224, 320-324
* discription of, 204, 231-238, 251f, 320-22
* through use of Scriptures, 251-52

doctrine, development of, 72-74, 105-107, 145nn3-5, 223, 239n4, 297

evolution
* biological, 296-98, 329n12
* cultural, 310f
* divine initiative in, 296-98, 310-12

exegesis, 105-107, 145nn3-5, 245-48, 253-57, 296-98, 301f

eyesight
* blinding, 152
* healing, 50, 137f, 154f, 219

experience, religious
* communicating, 182, 222, 234, 281
* denominational differences in, 11, 178, 247f, 268, 275

faith
* as emotional fascination, 190, 194
* as gift of God, 199f
* as surrender, 34, 194, 202
* grace and, 194f
* moving mountains, 22
* nature of, 193-98, 235
* <u>sola fidei</u>, 160, 176n10

forgiveness of sins, 44f, 54f, 59f, 201f, 210n15

fundamentalism, 253-57

Gospels
* production of, 146n8, 242f
* use in apprenticing, 243f, 249, 262f

glossolalia, 17, 31-37

God
* anger of, 51
* as landowner, 50f
* as Master, 203, 235
* depends upon our skills, 6f, 11, 178, 180f, 199
* evoked by prayer, 268, 274
* grief of, 56f
* intangible nature of, 183
* learning to perceive, 9, 11, 179-188
* patience of, 50f

342   Index

grace
* @ Thomas Aquinas, 205f
* nature of, 204-207
* sola gratia, 205f
* throughout religious formation, 26, 175n9, 198-206
* within discovery process, 185, 210n16, 234f, 239n7, 311
* within rites, 276f, 282, 290n8
* w/r natural processes, 25f, 37f, 199-206, 211n18, 269

hero worship, 188-190, 194, 196

Holy Spirit
* w/r scriptural interpretation, 245, 251-52
* w/r Jesus, 295, 301f
* w/r priestly ordination, 30
* w/r speaking in tongues, 31f, 35f

indoctrination, 216

infatuation, 196f

intellectual satisfaction, 223f, 238, 251f

intuitions, guiding, 231-34, 239n8

Jesus
* apprenticing disciples, 6, 84f, 132f, 149f, 270, 314
* as apprenticed by God, 218, 291-94, 307-309, 311-13, 320-22
* as kyrios, 96-101, 140f

Jesus cont.
* as Master of Torah/Truth, 66-68, 83f, 90f, 91-96, 101f, 133f, 141-43, 320
* as prophet, 91-96
* as Logos incarnate, 207, 263, 294f
* as Second Adam, 295f, 304
* as "sent from heaven," 300, 303
* as "Superman," 306, 309
* as sin offering, 54, 59, 76n10
* childhood of, 303-305, 315f, 318f
* choosing disciples, 108, 110, 113f
* content of his torah, 124-133
* death of, 44f, 48, 50-57, 60-63, 68f, 71f, 73f, 75n5, 76n8
* healing & exorcisms of, 16, 21f, 94
* human infirmities of, 292f, 303-306, 313-318, 334nn45-46
* John the Baptizer and, 93, 136, 319
* mission of, 49-52, 66-68, 86f, 149f, 321f
* preexistence of, 298
* resurrection of, 61f, 77n13, 101
* self-awareness of, 139f, 315-18, 335n54
* teaching in synagogue or Temple, 121, 123f
* temptations of, 320f, 336n55
* trained in Torah, 317f, 318f
* transmitting power to disciples, 15, 18-23, 190
* trial of, 55f
* uniqueness of, 98f, 113f, 134f, 141-43

Index   343

Jesus cont.
* unity with the Father (hypostatic unity), 308f, 323f, 325, 332n37, 337n58
* virginal conception of, 295, 298-304, 330nn18-25

language, function of
* limitations within an apprenticeship, 190-92
* projection of meaning, 79-82

Logos, 294f, 296f, 310-12, 315, 324, 333n43

Lord (<u>kyrios</u>), 96-101, 104n11

Messiah = Christ
* diverse expectations of, 136f, 148n25f
* Jesus identified as, 135f, 138f
* secret identity of, 139
* self-awareness of, 139f, 315-318, 335n54

miracles, claims based upon, 136f, 140, 141, 157-160, 171, 211n17, 228f, 271f, 285, 305, 328n2

Moses, 29, 88f, 103n6, 184

mission
* of disciples, 15f, 18f, 67f, 87f, 155f, 218f, 284
* of Jesus, 49-52, 66-68, 86f, 149f, 321f
* of Israel, 86

Newman, John Henry, 245f, 256f

ordination rite
* in NT, 27f, 29f, 155
* in OT, 28f
* nature of, 25-30
* used by Jesus? 28

parental upbringing
* transmits tone deafness, 10f
* transmits religious experience, 7-9, 11, 178, 179-88, 199f

Paul
* accrediting his message, 156-160
* apprenticing by, 159-163
* apprenticing of, 155-160
* conversion of, 150-160, 174nn4-7

perfection, nature of religious, 126-130

Peter, prophetic discovery of, 220-23

Pharisees
* challenge Jesus, 130f
* compared and contrasted with Jesus, 108f, 111-14, 115f, 121-24, 130-35
* origin of, 108

power, spiritual
* nature of, 136-38
* transmission of, 18-23, 24-26, 67f, 155f, 321f

prayer
* as acquired skill, 178, 268f
* as a demanding enterprise, 23, 270, 273f
* developmental aspect of, 272f
* nature of, 23, 267f, 272-74
* public leadership of, 274, 278
* varieties of, 268f, 275

Protestant
* fundamentalism, 205f, 253-57
* sola fidei, 160, 176n10
* sola gratia, 205f
* sola scriptura, 245-48

preaching, 16f, 258-261

prophetic experiences
* accrediting of, 157f, 226-238, 251f
* as sympathy with the divine pathos, 217f
* instances of, 220-225
* necessity of, 214, 216

Quakers, 169f, 224f, 227, 275-77

ransom, 49-53

redemption
* @ Anselm, 43-46
* @ Matthew, 47-53, 73
* @ Paul, 61-63, 73, 87f, 102n4
* @ Thomas Aquinas, 66-71
* as effected by Jesus alone? 41f

religion, sacred task of, 216

renting of Temple veil, 56f

resurrection interpreted, 61f, 77n13, 101

revelation of God
* through personal experience, 150-160, 214-217, 220-224, 231-35, 251f, 320-24
* through historic events, 184, 208n4, 215f

sacraments/public rites
* as sacred encounters, 163-65, 274-78
* baptism, 16, 155, 164-170, 200-202, 209n13, 286f
* can fail, 165f, 169, 277f
* efficacy of, 163-65, 169, 200-202, 276f, 283, 289nn4f
* grace and, 28-31, 200-202, 210n14, 276f, 290n8
* purpose of, 163-65, 274-78, 283
* religious tradition as sacrament, 203
* renewal of, 281f, 286-88
* role of minister in, 274, 277f
* w/r secular rites, 26, 275f, 278-81

Scriptures (Bible)
* as a classic, 249f, 254f, 262
* function to conserve and to innovate, 250-52
* fundamentalism and, 253-57
* transmutation of textual meaning, 72-74, 105-107, 145nn3-5, 223, 239n4, 297

Scriptures cont.
* interpretation of, 105-107, 145nn3-5, 245-48, 253-57, 296-98, 301f, 329n10
* modern criticism and, 253-57, 264n9, 329n10
* origins of Gospels, 146n8, 242f
* phenomenal transformation of, 246f
* translating of, 80-83, 84, 92, 97-101, 102, 107f, 147n10, 220f
* use for renewing church, 257-263
* use in apprenticing, 243f, 249, 262f

speaking in tongues, 17, 31-37

sex and divine initiative, 299-302

Suzuki, Shinichi, 9-11, 177f

Torah
* @ Hassidic tradition, 242f
* @ Jesus, 86f, 140f
* @ Paul, 87f
* living, 114, 129
* nature of, 77n12, 85-89, 129-133, 174n8

virginal conception
* in N.T.? 300-303
* nature of, 295f, 296-300, 301-303
* scandal of, 299f

Yohanan ben Zakkai, 112f, 115, 121f

TORONTO STUDIES IN THEOLOGY
  I. Robert R.N. Ross, **The Non-Existence of God: Linguistic Paradox in Tillich's Thought**
  II. Gustaf Wingren, **Creation and Gospel: The New Situation in European Theology**
  III. John C. Meagher, **Clumsy Construction in Mark's Gospel: A Critique of *Form and Redaktionsgeschichte***
  IV. Patrick Primeaux, **Richard R. Niebuhr on Christ and Religion: The Four Stage Development of His Theology**
  V. Bernard Lonergan, **Understanding and Being: An Introduction and Companion to *Insight***
  Edited by: Elizabeth A Morelli and Mark D. Morelli
  VI. John D. Godsey and Geffrey B. Kelly, ed., **Ethical Responsibility: Bonhoeffer's Legacy to the Churches**
  VII. Darrell J. Fasching, **The Thought of Jacques Ellul: A Systematic Exposition**
  VIII. Joseph T. Culliton, C.S.B., ed., **Non-violence — Central to Christian Spirituality: Perspectives from Scripture to the Present**
  IX. Aaron Milavec, **To Empower as Jesus Did: Acquiring Spiritual Power Through Apprenticeship**

FOR A COMPLETE LIST OF TITLES
AND PRICES PLEASE WRITE:

The Edwin Mellen Press
P.O. Box 450
Lewiston, New York 14092